Psychology A2

The Exam Companion

THIRD EDITION

Mike Cardwell • Cara Flanagan

OXFORD
UNIVERSITY PRESS

OXFORD
UNIVERSITY PRESS

Great Clarendon Street, Oxford OX2 6DP

Oxford University Press is a department of the University of Oxford. It furthers the University's objective of excellence in research, scholarship, and education by publishing worldwide in

Oxford New York

Auckland Cape Town Dar es Salaam Hong Kong Karachi Kuala Lumpur Madrid Melbourne Mexico City Nairobi New Delhi Shanghai Taipei Toronto

With offices in

Argentina Austria Brazil Chile Czech Republic France Greece Guatemala Hungary Italy Japan Poland Portugal Singapore South Korea Switzerland Thailand Turkey Ukraine Vietnam

First published 2012

British Library Cataloguing in Publication Data

Data available

ISBN 978 019 912985 0

10 9 8 7 6 5

Printed in Great Britain by Bell & Bain Ltd, Glasgow

Paper used in the production of this book is a natural, recyclable product made from wood grown in sustainable forests. The manufacturing process conforms to the environmental regulations of the country of origin.

Acknowledgements

Project development: Rick Jackman (Jackman Publishing Solutions Ltd)
Editorial & project management: GreenGate Publishing Services, Tonbridge
Design & layout: Nigel Harriss
Cover design: Patricia Briggs
Cover photography: Chris Cardwell

AQA examination questions are reproduced by permission of the Assessment and Qualifications Alliance.

Image credits

Chris Cardwell: p.3; **Fotolia:** p.6 © Christos Georghiou

Contents

Don't just read the chapters you are studying, all the chapters have useful advice so dip into some other topic areas.

How to write Grade A answers using this book

1. Sample questions

We have provided is a collection of past and possible exam questions. All questions are based on the wording of the specification, so make sure you are familiar with its requirements.

There are several question types:

- *The blockbuster* – One question worth 8 marks + 16 marks.
- *Parted* – All AO1 in part (a) and all AO2 in part (b) OR a mixture of AO1 and AO2 in each part.
- *Quotation* – There is a short piece of stimulus material to help you think about the question.

2. Answer plans

Our rule has been that an ideal answer should be 600–720 words in length. This is based on counting the number of words in students' exam answers. This is what students can write in 30 minutes. An answer that is 600 words long (and focused on the question) can gain full marks.

On that basis we recommend writing 25–30 words for every mark. Therefore, in a 24-mark essay:

- 200–240 words of AO1 (8 marks)
- 400–480 words of AO2 (16 marks)

The 12 paragraph plan – An easy way to achieve the right length essay and right AO1:AO2 division is to write an answer with 12 paragraphs.

- Each paragraph should be about 50–60 words.
- Four paragraphs should be description.
- Eight paragraphs should be evaluation.

Common building blocks – One thing you will notice is that the plans in this book often share identical elements. You may have felt that the list of sample exam questions is quite daunting but, in reality, it's just a matter of re-arranging similar building blocks.

3. Model answers

We have used our answer plans to write model answers.

These model answers are not the 'perfect' answer but just our attempt to show you how to build a good enough answer using the essay plans.

In particular notice how we have used paragraphs to make the essay readable and also ensure that we have written the right amount of description (AO1) and evaluation (AO2).

4. Student answers for you to mark

We believe that one of the best ways to improve your own performance is to understand how exam answers are marked, i.e. to get inside the head of an examiner.

In order for you to mark the answers at the end of each chapter we have provided training in how to mark on the following three spreads.

On pages 170–176 we have provided examiner comments and marks for these answers.

The A2 exam

Unit 3 (PSYA3) Topics in Psychology

50% of A2 Level marks 1½ hours

The exam paper contains eight questions, one question drawn from each of the eight topics in the specification. You must answer three questions. Each question may be divided into sub-parts.

- Biological rhythms and sleep
- Perception
- Relationships
- Aggression
- Eating behaviour
- Gender
- Intelligence and learning
- Cognition and development

Unit 4 (PSYA4) Topics in Psychology

50% of A2 Level marks 2 hours

The exam paper is divided into three sections. You must answer one question from each section.

Section A – Psychopathology

- Schizophrenia
- Depression
- Phobias
- Obsessive compulsive disorder

Section B – Psychology in action

- Media psychology
- The psychology of addictive behaviour
- Anomalistic psychology

Section C – Psychological Research and Scientific Method

One compulsory structured question worth 35 marks.

The questions on 'Psychology in action' are slightly different from the rest. They are still worth 24 marks in total and are still split into 8 AO1 marks and 16 AO2 marks, but they are divided into at least four parts and quite a lot of stimulus material is used so you have to apply your knowledge to a novel situation (a bit like some of your AS questions).

THE KEY TO SUCCESSFUL EXAM PERFORMANCE

Look at what is in the specification → generate questions that would be permissible → prepare answers for these questions from your textbooks → in your answers use common building blocks and follow the advice below.

All exam questions are worth a total of 24 marks: 8 marks description (AO1) and 16 marks evaluation (AO2). Questions may be parted. In each question part you need to know how many AO1 marks are available and how many AO2 marks are available. This is indicated by the use of injunctions (see right) and by the marks at the end of the question.

Injunctions

AO1: outline, describe, identify, explain

AO2: evaluate, consider, explain (note that 'explain' is used for both AO1 and AO2)

AO1 + AO2: discuss

BEST AO1 advice

Don't try to do too much! Description is generally easier and often students know a lot about the theories/studies. However, you should remember the marks are restricted for AO1. Be brutal in sticking to a 10-minute limit.

BEST AO2 advice

Top and tail your paragraphs.

Top = Start every AO2 paragraph (including IDA paragraphs – issues, debates, approaches) with a lead-in sentence, such as 'One study that supported this …' or 'There are limitations to this approach, for example …'. Make it clear to the examiner that this is an AO2 paragraph. There are many useful lead-in phrases, such as 'However', 'An alternative approach is …', 'The implications of this theory are …'.

Tail = Finish every AO2 paragraph by answering the 'so what' question, e.g. 'This suggests that …'. Link the critical point back to the AO1 point you are criticising.

Changes to the AQA A specification from 2012

From January 2012 there were some changes to the specification. This means that past exam papers contain questions that would no longer be set.
We have produced new material to match the new content, which can be downloaded free from www.oup.com/oxed/secondary/psychology/aqapsych/
The contents of this book match the new specification.

Make your answers fit the mark allocation

Examiners mark your answers using mark allocation tables. These are shown on the following pages. The mark allocation tables have various criteria, such as 'depth and breadth' and 'focus'. It makes sense that, if the examiner is assessing you on these criteria, you need to (a) know what they mean and (b) you need to be able to demonstrate them in your answers.

AO1

Knowledge and understanding – The AO1 content of your answer should display what you know and also display your understanding of a topic. Using examples is a good way to show understanding but often understanding comes across just in the way you express yourself. So if you don't understand a theory or study, don't just try to wing it in the hope it won't be apparent. You must develop your understanding.

Detail – In order to gain high AO1 marks your answer should be detailed. This can be achieved by using specific information, such as psychological terms and researchers' names and dates. It is not necessarily about writing lots, it is about ensuring that what you write is very focused.

Range of material refers to how many things are covered in your answer – this might be the number of studies or the number of different aspects of a theory.

Depth and breadth – Depth refers to detail and breadth refers to the range of material. There is inevitably a **depth/ breadth trade off**. If you try to provide too much detail for any one study/aspect you won't have time to cover a range of studies. Equally if you cover lots of studies you won't have time for the details. So there is a compromise that has evidence of both depth and breadth.

Organisation and structure – A well-organised answer does not need an introduction or a conclusion. The main feature is that the reader can see that each point is clearly made. One way to do this is to use lots of paragraphs. In each paragraph, make your point and provide a detailed explanation of that point – that way you will have depth and also breadth because you have presented a number of different points.

AO2

Analysis and understanding – The analysis bit is your attempt to work out what features of the topic can be criticised/discussed. For example 'Explain some of the difficulties in conducting research on topic X' – you would need to think of possible difficulties and apply these to topic X.

Focus – You won't receive credit for information that isn't directly relevant to the question, in fact you will lose marks if your answer is not focused on the specific requirements of the question set.

Elaboration – There is very limited credit for presenting comments, such as 'The study by Jones (1990) supported the theory'. Such comments lack effectiveness. You need to provide evidence to support your claim (for example, you should provide key details of findings and conclusions of the study). You should also provide an explanation of why this point matters. We have called this the **three-point rule**: identify, provide evidence, justify.

Line of argument concerns how you logically unfold your material in response to the question. It should read a bit like a story so that each paragraph makes sense coming after the previous one.

Issues, debates and approaches (IDA) refers to ethical issues, gender or cultural or historical bias, real-world applications, determinism, reductionism, nature–nurture and any of the approaches (cognitive, social, biological, and so on). A good essay will include *one or two* IDA points. That is the maximum you should cover (and the easiest ones are ethical issues, real-world applications and approaches). But most importantly these points must be *elaborated* (using the three-point rule) and *contextualised*. The way to check whether you have achieved this is to imagine moving the IDA point you have written and drop it into another essay (called the **drop in**) – does it still seem appropriate? If so, then you have failed to contextualise it and will get NO credit for a generic point.

Quality of written communication assesses the fluency of your writing and the extent to which you have used psychological terms effectively as well as your grammar, punctuation and spelling.

AO3

In fact AO2 is called AO2/AO3 but this is a bit misleading because there are no criteria in the mark allocation tables that mention 'how science works' (AO3). Therefore, you can still receive full marks without any mention of methodological problems in the research.

Of course, if you do make any AO3 criticisms (e.g. of methodology used) these could demonstrate the skill of analysis and would be credited.

HOWEVER, you must contextualise any such comments and you also must state the implications of the criticism. It is not sufficient to say 'One of the issues with this study is that all the participants were university students'. You then need to add 'This means that the findings may not apply to older people as well, *which suggests that the theory is restricted to a certain age group*'.

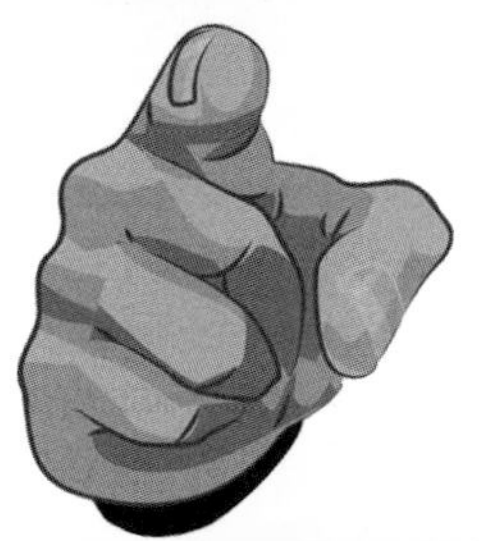

Training yourself to be an examiner

At the end of each chapter in this book there is a student essay for you to mark. No one likes marking so you might decide not to bother – but these student answers are there for a reason. They give you precious insight into what you have to do to improve your own performance. We know this is true and have always given our own students the benefit of a marking experience. On this spread and the following two spreads we have provided training for you.

Step 1

The first answer we are going to mark is below and on the facing page. Don't worry if this is not a section of the specification you have studied – what matters is whether you can read the descriptions/evaluations and understand them. If you can (even though it is all new to you) then it must be well-detailed, coherent and sound. If you are confused it is probably best described as 'muddled'.

This answer is parted so all the AO1 marks are in part (a) and all the AO2 marks are in part (b).

Your first task is to read through part (a) below.

TRAINING TASK 1

Part (a) Describe Kohlberg's theory of gender development.

(8 marks)

Kohlberg's theory of gender development is based on the principle that a child's thinking matures as the child gets older. He proposed that there are three stages in gender development. The first stage is Gender Identity, around the age of 2–3 years. At this stage a child is able to identify that some people are boys and some are girls. This identification is based on external features. The second stage goes from 3 to 7 years and is called Gender Stability. This is when a child comes to realise that their gender is fixed and will not change as they get older. This has been shown in research when children are asked questions, such as 'When you get older, will you be a Mummy or Daddy?' The third and final stage is Gender Consistency. This is where a child realises that not only is their gender fixed over time but it is also fixed across different situations, such as wearing different clothes. This stage matches up to Piaget's idea of conservation. This is the understanding that even if things appear to change externally (such as the amount of water in different shaped glasses) there are certain aspects that can't change like volume. In the case of gender children over the age of 7 apply this same cognitive development to gender. The importance of this stage is that when a child recognises that their gender is not going to change and this means they start paying attention to same-sex models so they know how to behave. Kohlberg called this gender constancy. Slaby and Frey (1975) showed this in a study where children gave more attention to same sex models as their sense of constancy increased.

(285 words)

Why do students resist separating the text into paragraphs? It makes it much more difficult to mark their answer.

Step 2

Next you need to consider the quality of the AO1 points.

←**Basic** introduction identifying a key principle.

←First stage described **accurately. Reasonable detail**.

←Second stage of the theory, tending towards **well-detailed** (given that this is written under timed conditions). The reference to research could be seen as evaluation but in the context of this part of the question adds a small amount to understanding the second stage.

←The third stage is certainly **well-detailed** with extra information on the link to the concept of conservation.

Comments and marks for AO1

Mark	Knowledge and understanding	Range of material	Depth and breadth	Organisation and structure
8–7	Accurate and well-detailed	Good range	Substantial evidence of depth and breadth	Coherent
6–5	Generally accurate and reasonably detailed	Range	Depth and/or breadth	Reasonably coherent
4–3	Basic, relatively superficial	Restricted	Generally accurate	Basic
2–1	Rudimentary and may be muddled and/or inaccurate	Very brief or largely irrelevant		Lacking
0	No creditworthy material			

The **AO1** mark I would give is ☐

Step 3

We now must consider each of the criteria in the mark allocation table:

Knowledge and understanding is accurate and well-detailed, though perhaps we are tempted by the band below (reasonably detailed). On the other hand, in the time available, this is about how detailed you can get.

Range of material is good.

Depth and breadth – there is depth (lots of detail) and also breadth (good coverage of different aspects of the theory).

Organisation and structure is clear, though paragraphs would have helped.

Decide on a mark for AO1. *See page 170 for our decision.*

Step 4

Now read through part (b) and consider the quality of the AO2 points.

The magnet effect

The mark allocation tables below are called 'banded' mark allocation tables. An examiner doesn't just decide on a numerical mark for an answer. He or she considers the criteria in the mark allocation table and then probably feels that two or even three of the bands describe the essay. In order to determine the final, numerical mark the examiner selects the best fit. For example, the examiner might decide on the basic band (8–5 marks). Then the examiner fine tunes the final mark by considering whether they were tempted more by the band above (and would award 8 marks) or below (and would award 5 marks). If there was actually very little temptation to other bands, then the mark should be 6 or 7.

Part (b) Evaluate Kohlberg's theory of gender development.

(16 marks)

This theory has been very influential in psychology and understanding gender. We will now look at a number of research studies that demonstrate the value of the theory.

Thomson (1975) conducted a study that supported the gender identity stage. He found that children age 2 could identify different genders but weren't always sure of their own gender. Older children were able to do this.

One criticism of this research is that the young children may simply be unaware how you judge gender. If it is based on clothing then it isn't really surprising that young children decide that someone is a girl if they are dressed in girls' clothing. In a study by Bem (1989) she showed that many very young children couldn't correctly identify a naked child when asked what the child's gender was.

Slaby and Frey (1975) investigated the gender stability and gender consistency stages. They asked children various questions, such as 'Were you a little girl or a little boy when you were a baby?' and 'When you grow up will you be a mummy or a daddy?'. These questions concern gender stability. They also asked questions about consistency, for example asking boys 'If you wore this dress would you be boy or a girl?' Slaby and Frey found that children didn't reach stability until they were about 3 or 4 years old and gender consistency didn't come until later.

Slaby and Frey also found, as Kohlberg predicted, that when children reached the consistency stage they then were more likely to pay attention to same-sex models. The validity of this study was improved by using a double blind design where the observers didn't know the gender of the model when rating the child's level of attention. This increases the validity.

This theory is an example of the cognitive developmental approach. There are other approaches to explaining gender, such as biological or social learning.

(317 words)

Step 5

←Introductory paragraph, scene setting but not really creditworthy.

←Supporting evidence, **some evidence of elaboration**. The point would be more effective if linked to Kohlberg's theory. **Basic analysis and understanding**.

←A criticism of the study above, **reasonable elaboration**. The point again could be linked to the implications for Kohlberg's theory.

←Further research evidence that supports Kohlberg's theory. This paragraph contains quite a bit of description of the study itself but a certain amount of detail is necessary in order to understand the critical point. **Reasonable analysis and understanding**.

←Further research evidence, **basic/ superficial**.

←Comment on methodology but not linked back to Kohlberg's theory, so little credit.

←**Superficial IDA** point.

Comments and marks for AO2

Mark	Analysis and understanding	Focus	Elaboration	Line of argument	Issues/ debates/ approaches	Quality of written communication
16–13	Sound	Well-focused	Coherent	Clear	Used effectively	Fluent, effective use of terms
12–9	Reasonable	Generally focused	Reasonable	Evident	Reasonably effective	Clear, appropriate
8–5	Basic, superficial	Sometimes focused	Some evidence		Superficial reference	Lacks clarity, limited use of terms
4–1	Rudimentary, limited understanding	Weak, muddled and incomplete	Not effective	May be mainly irrelevant	Absent or muddled/ inaccurate	Often unconnected assertions, errors
0	No creditworthy material					

The **AO2** mark I would give is ☐

Step 6

We now must consider each of the criteria in the mark allocation table:

Analysis and understanding lies between '**reasonable**' and '**basic**'.

Answer is **well-focused**.

Elaboration – Some **reasonable** but on balance just '**some evidence**'.

Line of argument is **clear**.

IDA is **superficial**.

Quality of written communication is **fluent**.

Now decide on a mark for AO2. *See page 170 for our decision.*

Step 1

This answer is slightly different from Task 1 for two reasons:

- Part (a) is marked using an adjusted AO1 mark allocation table as it is worth 4 not 8 marks.
- Part (b) includes both AO1 and AO2 marks so the examiner now has to identify where AO1 and AO2 occurs in the text, and then determine the marks for each.

Your first task is to read through the answer below.

Step 2

TRAINING TASK 2

Part (a) Outline **one** example of a circadian rhythm. (4 marks)

The best known example of a circadian rhythm is the sleep–wake cycle. This cycle governs when we go to sleep and wake up each day. The cycle is, to some extent, controlled by the body's endogendous pacemaker which is the suprachiasmatic nucleus (SCN, internal biological clock). The SCN has been demonstrated in research with hamsters which showed that when it is transplanted from one mutant hamster to a normal one, the result was that the normal hamster had the same abnormal rhythms as the mutant one. However, research with Michel Siffre showed that there are other factors involved as well because, if you are shut away in a cave, the sleep–wake cycle changes from 24 hours. In his case it sometimes was as long as 48 hours.

(129 words)

When reading part (b) we have left a space at the end of every sentence for you to note whether the sentence was description (AO1) or evaluation (AO2). In some cases you may think the point is an issue/debate or approach, so mark it as IDA. If you think the point is poor add a cross.

Separating AO1 and AO2

You might consider whether this answer would read much more clearly if all the AO1 was at the beginning of the essay and all the AO2 afterwards. It certainly might have helped this student to see more clearly that there was too much AO1 and not enough AO2.

Part (b) Outline and evaluate explanations for insomnia. (4 marks + 16 marks)

Insomnia is a condition where people can't sleep enough ( ). It is not defined in terms of number of hours of sleep a person has because there are large individual differences in the amount of sleep that is 'normal' for each person ( ). Some people are fine even though they have had very little sleep so they would not be classed as insomniacs ( ).

It is possible to explain insomnia in terms of the risk factors that are associated with it ( ). One such risk factor is sleep apnoea ( ). This is when a person stops breathing during sleep ( ). There is research support for this because it can explain why older people are more likely to suffer from insomnia than younger people ( ). Research has found that sleep apnoea is more likely to occur in older people ( ). There is also research that shows that there is a link between insomnia and sleep apnoea ( ). It showed that people who have sleep apnoea are also more likely to suffer from insomnia ( ).

Another risk factor is personality ( ). Research has found that people who score highly on anxiety tests and score low on self-esteem tests are more likely to be suffer from insomnia ( ). However, the problem with this kind of research is you can't tell which causes which ( ). It could be that insomnia causes anxiety and low self-esteem rather than the other way round ( ).

Age and gender are also risk factors for insomnia ( ). We have already seen that age may be linked to insomnia because of sleep apnoea increasing in old age ( ). It is also likely that older people will have other physical problems, such as arthritis or other things which cause them pain, which makes sleep difficult for them ( ). Although it may be rather surprising that teenagers often suffer from insomnia too, so insomnia can't just be explained in terms of age ( ). Women may be more likely to get insomnia because their hormones go up and down a lot over the month and this may affect their sleep problems ( ).

There is primary insomnia which is insomnia on its own and there is secondary insomnia when it is caused by something else ( ). It is only the secondary insomnia that is related to risk factors because primary insomnia is a disease in itself ( ). Primary insomnia may be related to anxiety or bad sleep habits ( ). Sometimes it is not possible to identify a cause ( ).

It is important to conduct research on insomnia because so many people suffer from it ( ). In order to do this it is important to distinguish between the different kinds of insomnia ( ). In the case of secondary insomnia you should treat the actual cause rather than the insomnia so you need to know whether it is primary or secondary insomnia ( ).

This approach to insomnia might be considered to be reductionist because it reduces insomnia to a small set of factors and this may mean that other important factors are ignored ( ).

(481 words)

Next you need to consider the quality of the AO1 and AO2 points.

Part (a)

- ←The sleep–wake cycle is a good example but there is no mention that this is a 24-hour cycle.
- ←A bit too much information about the SCN which is not directly relevant to this topic.
- ←The text hints at exogenous zeitgebers when talking about Siffre's experiences in the cave but they are not specified.

Part (b)

- ←Definitions are only creditworthy if you are explaining a term you have used. 'Insomnia' is in the essay title and therefore requires no definition.
- ←First explanation = sleep apnoea. The first three sentences are **AO1**, a **limited** outline of sleep apnoea as an explanation.
- ←The remainder of the paragraph is **AO2**, showing **basic analysis**. There is **some evidence of elaboration**. The details of the research studies are vague.
- ←Second explanation = personality. Some examples of personality are identified, **limited AO1**.
- ←The two sentences are **AO2**, with **some elaboration**.
- ←Third explanation = age. The first part of this paragraph contains a **reasonably thorough** explanation of how age may be linked to insomnia.
- ←The sentence beginning with 'Although it may be …' can be counted as **AO2.**
- ←Fourth explanation = gender, **weak AO1**.
- ←Fifth explanation = primary insomnia/secondary insomnia. The explanation of primary insomnia is **limited AO1**.
- ←Consideration of a real world application counts because **IDA**, though this is **superficial** because no actual applications are mentioned.
- ←Reductionism is potentially **IDA** but there is no contextualisation so not creditworthy.

Step 3

We now must consider each of the criteria in the mark allocation tables:

Part (a)

Knowledge and understanding – An appropriate example has been selected but the details of the sleep–wake cycle are limited.

Accuracy is fine.

Organisation and structure – Not all of the content is relevant, so 'reasonably structured'.

Step 4

Decide on a mark for AO1. See page 170 for our decision.

Comments and marks for part (a) AO1

Mark	Knowledge and understanding	Accuracy	Organisation and structure
4	Reasonably thorough	Accurate	Coherent
3–2	Limited	Generally accurate	Reasonably coherent
1	Weak and muddled		
0	No creditworthy material		

The **AO1** mark I would give for part (a) is ☐

Part (b) AO1

Knowledge and understanding – Five explanations have been presented but only one was reasonably thorough in terms of detail. The breadth of explanations can count towards 'reasonably thorough'.

Accuracy is fine.

Organisation and structure – Coherent.

Part (b) AO2

Analysis and understanding is clearly **basic**.

Focus – The first and last paragraphs are not relevant, therefore only **generally focused**.

Elaboration – **Some evidence** but more often **not effective**.

Line of argument is **clear**.

IDA is **superficial**.

Quality of written communication is fluent.

Step 5

Decide on a mark for AO1 and AO2. See page 170 for our decision.

Comments and marks for part (b) AO1 and AO2

Mark	Analysis and understanding	Focus	Elaboration	Line of argument	Issues/ debates/ approaches	Quality of written communication
16–13	Sound	Well focused	Coherent	Clear	Used effectively	Fluent, effective use of terms
12–9	Reasonable	Generally focused	Reasonable	Evident	Reasonably effective	Clear, appropriate
8–5	Basic, superficial	Sometimes focused	Some evidence		Superficial reference	Lacks clarity, limited use of terms
4–1	Rudimentary, limited understanding	Weak, muddled and incomplete	Not effective	May be mainly irrelevant	Absent or muddled/ inaccurate	Often unconnected assertions, errors
0	No creditworthy material					

The **AO1** mark I would give for part (b) is (use grid at top of page) ☐

The **AO2** mark I would give for part (b) is ☐

Training yourself to be an examiner

Step 1

On this spread we are looking at questions from the 'Psychology in action' section of Unit 4. The questions in this section are different to other parts of the exam because:

- They are usually in three or four parts. The question is still worth 24 marks, consisting of 8 AO1 marks and 16 AO2 marks but these are distributed across the parts of the question.
- Some of the parts are likely to be all AO2 which has implications for marking.
- Some of the parts require you to *apply* your knowledge to a novel situation (similar to some of the questions on the AS exam).

TRAINING TASK 3

We have selected one question from each of the three areas of 'Psychology in action'. You will get valuable insights from looking at all three of these even though two of them are areas you have not studied.

MEDIA PSYCHOLOGY

Question (a) A psychology class decide to prepare a leaflet for other students about the positive and negative effects of computers and video games on behaviour. Use your knowledge of psychological research in this area to justify your advice. (10 marks)

The students would certainly want to include information about both positive and negative effects in the leaflet. Greitmeyer and Osswald found that people who played a prosocial video game called 'Lemmings' later showed more prosocial behaviour than people who played and aggressive game or a neutral game. Kahne found that people who played the life simulation game The Sims learned about society and explored social issues. Using Facebook also encourages social insights and Gonzalez found that using Facebook increased people's self-esteem.

In terms of negative effects, Gentile and Anderson conducted a lab experiment and found short-term increases of physiological arousal, hostile feelings and aggressive behaviour from violent game play compared with non-violent game play. Anderson also conducted a longitudinal study following primary school children and found that children who played violent video games became verbally and physically aggressive and less prosocial. The bi-directional model has proposed that it may not just be a case of violent games causing people to be more violent, but it is also likely to be the case that people with aggressive tendencies are more likely to play such games, which means it just appears that playing violent games makes people more aggressive. An interesting negative effect has emerged from the use of Facebook with children reporting increased levels of anxiety linked to the use of such social networking sites (Charles et al.). The stresses come from the pressures to be entertaining, dealing with unwanted contacts and worrying about being nice to friends.

(247 words)

THE PSYCHOLOGY OF ADDICTIVE BEHAVIOUR

Question (b) Use your knowledge of research into media influence on addictive behaviour to explain why films might encourage young people to start smoking. (4 marks)

The media plays an important role in portraying addiction, which affects the likelihood that young people might take up smoking. Gunaskera et al. found that films tended to portray the use of drugs and smoking positively and did not show the negative consequences. This means that young people are more likely to imitate this behaviour according to social learning theory because they are probably vicariously reinforced.

Research has also found that the media has an effect on willingness to change addictive behaviour, such as Kramer et al. who found people reduced their drinking after watching a TV series.

(98 words)

ANOMALISTIC PSYCHOLOGY

Question (c) Consider how explanations for anomalous experience could be used to explain belief in psychic healing. (8 marks)

Psychic healing refers to any method used to deal with health problems using mental rather than physical means. There is research evidence that has supported psychic healing but much of it is methodologically unsound. Most of the research evidence suggests that any success of psychic healers is due to belief rather than the fact that it is real. An Australian study found that people who believed in psychic healing were later found to rate the success of a psychic healer more positively.

Personality factors are important in explaining why some people are more likely to believe in psychic healing. For example, people who have a more active imagination are more likely to believe in psychic healing. They may be more fantasy prone and also more suggestible. Hergovich found a positive correlation between suggestibility and belief in the paranormal. It is possible that such people are just more likely to believe the deceptions by psychic healers.

Another explanation might be coincidence. In psychic healing people get better but their recovery might actually have nothing to do with the healer, they may just have spontaneously recovered. Coincidence is when two things happen at the same time and a person believes one caused the other.

Magical thinking might also be related to psychic healing because a person thinks that the objects used by a psychic healer have some magical properties.

(227 words)

Step 2

Next you need to consider the quality of the AO2 points.

←First sentence refers to the leaflet but this is the only mention of the leaflet.

←Detailed and relevant research evidence based on three sources. A number of suggestions could have been made as to what to include in the leaflet.

←The same applies to this paragraph on negative effects. Detailed and plentiful research evidence which has not been applied to the novel situation.

←The candidate should have listed the contents of the proposed leaflet, e.g. 'Playing violent games leads to more aggressive behaviour' and then linked this to relevant research evidence.

←Research evidence linked to an explanation (social learning theory). Deals appropriately with smoking behaviour and does what the question asks.

←Not creditworthy because not relevant to *initiation* of addiction and not made relevant to smoking.

←The definition is not creditworthy but the discussion of the importance of belief is peripherally relevant to the question, so some credit.

←An explanation for belief is identified and linked to research. There is an attempt to apply this knowledge to psychic healing. The paragraph could equally apply to any kind of paranormal belief.

←Again an explanation is identified and there is a more effective link made to psychic healing.

←A final explanation, weak application of knowledge.

Step 3

We now must consider each of the criteria in the mark allocation table:

Question (a)

Analysis and understanding – Despite the plentiful research evidence and some evaluation (the bidirectional model) there is only a **rudimentary** level of analysis.

Application of knowledge on the question is **basic**, appropriate evidence not used effectively.

Elaboration is not appropriate as the question hasn't been answered.

Quality of written communication is **fluent**.

Question (b)

Analysis and understanding – The first paragraph is sound.

Application of knowledge is effective, but only one point covered.

Elaboration – Some evidence.

Quality of written communication – Good use of terms.

Question (c)

Analysis and understanding – **Reasonable**, lacks firm basis in research.

Application of knowledge – Reasonably effective.

Elaboration – **Coherent** in parts.

Quality of written communication – **Clear, appropriate use of terms.**

Step 4

Decide on a mark for AO2 for questions (a), (b) and (c). *See page 170 for our decision.*

On Unit 4 there is no requirement for issues, debates and approaches (IDA). If such material is included it would gain AO2 credit – if suitably contextualised.

In questions on application of knowledge you will only score about 50% of the marks if you simply describe research OR just give appropriate suggestions without any justification.

In questions on application of knowledge a slightly different AO2 mark allocation table has come into use, as shown below.

Comments and marks for AO2

Mark (a)	Mark (b)	Mark (c)	Analysis and understanding	Application of knowledge	Elaboration	Quality of written communication
10–9	4	8–7	Sound	Effective	Coherent	Fluent, effective use of terms
8–6	3	6–5	Reasonable	Reasonably effective	Some elaboration	Clear, appropriate
5–3	4	4–3	Basic, superficial	Basic		Lacks clarity, limited use of terms
2–1	1	2–1	Rudimentary, limited understanding	Weak, muddled and mainly irrelevant		Often unconnected assertions, errors
0		0	No creditworthy material			

The **AO2** mark I would give question (a) is ☐

The **AO2** mark I would give question (b) is ☐

The **AO2** mark I would give question (c) is ☐

Chapter 1 Biological rhythms and sleep

There have been changes to the specification from September 2011 – therefore the updated specification details here are slightly different to those in some editions of the *A2 Complete Companion*.

Division 1 Biological rhythms	**• Circadian, infradian and ultradian rhythms, including the role of endogenous pacemakers and of exogenous zeitgebers in the control of circadian rhythms**
	• Disruption of biological rhythms, for example shift work, jet lag

Possible exam questions for this division

Discuss research into circadian rhythms. (8 marks + 16 marks)	It is legitimate to ask about research (which means theories or studies) in any area of the specification, even though it is not mentioned in the specification extract.
Discuss research into infradian **and/or** ultradian rhythms. (8 marks + 16 marks)	Notice this question offers a choice. Given that AO1 only requires 8 marks worth of material, you might do better to just write about research into infradian *or* ultradian rhythms rather than try to stuff both into your answer and end up writing too much AO1.
Discuss research into biological rhythms. (8 marks + 16 marks)	This question gives you a free choice about what rhythms to cover, but again don't fall into the trap of trying to do it all. Select what you know best. As 'rhythms' is in the plural it means you must cover at least two rhythms, though one account could be briefer than the other. See model answer on page 15.
Discuss the role of exogenous zeitgebers in the control of **one or more** biological rhythms. (8 marks + 16 marks)	'One or more' means exactly what it says – if you only discuss one biological rhythm you can get full marks. You do not have to do two rhythms for full marks. Note that the question focus is on exogenous zeitgebers – this means that material on endogenous pacemakers is not creditworthy unless used solely as contrast for AO2 marks.
Discuss the role of endogenous pacemakers in the control of circadian rhythms. (8 marks + 16 marks)	This time you have to write about circadian rhythms – but not just any research on circadian rhythms. The focus of your answer must be on endogenous pacemakers but you could contrast this with the effects of exogenous zeitgebers as part of your AO2.
(a) Outline **one** example of a circadian rhythm. (4 marks) (b) Discuss the role of endogenous pacemakers in the control of circadian rhythms. (4 marks + 16 marks)	In part (a) there is no credit for either IDA as it is all AO1 (IDA is only creditworthy in sections with AO2 marks). In part (b) you need to ensure you write very little AO1 and focus on evaluation. The AO1 content should be about 100–120 words whereas the AO2 should be about 400–480 words.
'Shift work and jet lag are two examples of how biological rhythms may be disrupted.' Discuss the disruption of biological rhythms. (8 marks + 16 marks)	Quotations are included for 'inspiration'. In this case the quotation is there to remind you that you could write about shift work and/or jet lag. The most important thing is to focus on the question itself – don't answer the quotation, answer the question.

Division 2 Sleep	**• The nature of sleep including stages of sleep and lifespan changes in sleep**
	• Functions of sleep, including evolutionary and restoration explanations

Possible exam questions for this division

Discuss the nature of sleep. (8 marks + 16 marks)	A 'blockbuster' question on the nature of sleep is possible – although less likely because you could really include anything about sleep in your answer. This means that such a question would not discriminate well between candidates because everyone should do well.
Discuss lifespan changes in sleep. (8 marks + 16 marks)	It is also unlikely that a full 24-mark question will be set solely on lifespan changes, but it could be – so be prepared.
Outline and evaluate stages of sleep. (8 marks + 16 marks)	The AO1 component of this question is straightforward (as long as you have revised enough to write for 8 marks), but how would you evaluate it? You might consider the value of the different kinds of sleep (SWS for growth hormone and REM for dreams). You could also consider the effects of SWS and REM deprivation and age-related differences in sleep stages. You should be particularly careful to make any evaluation effective (i.e. use those AO2 'lead-in phrases' described on page 4).

Question	Guidance
(a) Outline lifespan changes in sleep. (4 marks) (b) Discuss **one** explanation for the functions of sleep. (4 marks + 16 marks)	In this parted question be careful to write just a short outline of lifespan changes (probably about 100–120 words). In part (b) you must be careful about writing too much AO1 – again about 100–120 words would be sufficient for full marks. You also must be careful to restrict your answer to one explanation (evolutionary or restoration). See model answer on page 17.
Describe and evaluate the restoration explanation of the function of sleep. (8 marks + 16 marks)	In the question above the choice is yours as to what explanation you select. Questions may be set that ask about one particular type of explanation – in this case it is the restoration explanation. In such a question you might use your evolutionary explanation as a form of evaluation – but take care to make it evaluation and not description. In order to do this you should focus on the relative strengths and/or weaknesses of the two different explanations.
(a) Describe the stages of sleep. (4 marks) (b) Outline and evaluate the evolutionary explanation of the function of sleep. (4 marks + 16 marks)	Combination questions are popular, as in this example where the topic of the stages of sleep is combined with one explanation of sleep (the evolutionary approach). In part (b) you need to be mindful that there are only 4 marks (maximum about 120 words) for describing the explanation. You main focus should be on evaluation (worth the remaining 16 marks for this part).
(a) Outline research into biological rhythms. (8 marks). (b) Evaluate **one or more** explanations of the function of sleep. (16 marks)	Remember that questions can span divisions, as in this question. In this split question the AO1 and AO2 components are separated. This means that there is no credit for IDA in part (a) – just a description of research. In part (b) you will gain no credit for any description of your explanations, but you can evaluate either restoration or evolutionary explanations, or both. It might be a good idea to consider the relative strengths and/or weaknesses of the two different explanations.

Division 3 Disorders of sleep

- **Explanations for sleep disorders, including insomnia, sleep walking and narcolepsy**

Possible exam questions for this division

Question	Guidance
Discuss explanations for **one or more** sleep disorders. (8 marks + 16 marks)	Questions from this part of the specification may be set on the specific sleep disorders included in the specification (as in some of the exam questions that follow) or may be set on sleep disorders generally, allowing you to choose. In a question such as this the danger is that you will have lots to write on sleep disorders and will feel tempted to describe all three of the ones you are familiar with. However, the maximum descriptive mark is 8 – so you probably would do better to limit yourself to describing just one or possibly two explanations of sleep disorders. You can then evaluate all of them if you wish – just don't overdo the AO1. **In all of these questions you must focus on explanations – there are no marks for definitions of the disorders.**
(a) Outline **one** explanation for insomnia. (4 marks) (b) Outline **one** explanation for sleep walking. (4 marks) (c) Evaluate explanations for sleep disorders. (16 marks)	This question is a variation of the one above, this time you are directed to produce two short explanations of specific disorders and then evaluate at least two explanations of sleep disorders. Essentially the answer to this question would be an appropriate answer to the question above.
Discuss explanations of narcolepsy. (8 marks + 16 marks)	A full 24-mark blockbuster question could be set on any one of the three disorders named in the specification, so be prepared. In the evaluation you could use the other explanations as evaluation – but only if you focus on similarities and/or differences rather than just describing the alternatives. See model answer on page 19.
'There are both biological and psychological explanations for sleep disorders.' (a) Outline explanations of sleep disorders. (8 marks) (b) Evaluate explanations of sleep disorders. (16 marks)	The quotation at the start serves to remind you about the range of potential explanations – if you do cover both biological and psychological explanations this contributes to the IDA content of your answer. But remember that IDA is only creditworthy for the AO2 component of your answer. There would be no penalty if you did not cover both psychological and biological explanations. This question is actually no different to the first one given in this division – except you have to cover two rather than just one disorder (and could cover three).
(a) Outline **one** example of a circadian rhythm. (4 marks) (b) Outline explanations for sleep disorders. (4 marks) (c) Evaluate explanations for sleep disorders. (16 marks)	This question illustrates how topics across the division may be combined in one exam question. In such cases you should be careful to limit how much you write for each section as appropriate for the marks available, and be careful to provide evaluation only in part (c). In parts (b) and (c) at least two explanations must be covered. See student answer on page 20.

Division 1 Biological rhythms

Answer plans

Answer plan 1
Discuss research into biological rhythms.
(8 marks + 16 marks)

Rhythm 1: Circadian rhythms, e.g. sleep–wake cycle	
AO1	Temporal isolation studies, e.g. Siffre (1975) in a cave
AO1	E.g. Aschoff and Wever (1976) WWII bunker
AO2	Exposure to artificial light sufficient to shift rhythms (Czeisler *et al.*, 1999)
AO2	Individual differences in cycle length (Czeisler *et al.*, 1999)
AO2	Case studies lack validity but have strengths
IDA	Real-world application – chronotherapeutics, heart attacks and aspirin; time of day and work
Rhythm 2: Ultradian rhythms	
AO1	E.g. sleep stages (stages 1 and 2, 3, 4, SWS and REM)
AO1	E.g. basic rest–activity cycle, Friedman and Fisher (1967) psychiatric patients eating/drinking
AO2	Age differences, e.g. babies quiet/active sleep, older people less SWS (van Cauter *et al.*, 2000)
AO2	REM sleep may not be equivalent to dreams, mistaken assumption of neurobiological theories of dreaming
AO2	Value of 90-minute rhythm, orchestrates metabolic processes in the body
AO2	Endogenous and exogenous control, advantages with this blended system, e.g. copes with changing day lengths in Arctic circle communities

DIY
Work out your own plan for this question and then write your answer.
Discuss research into circadian rhythms.
(8 marks + 16 marks)

Example 1: Sleep–wake cycle	
AO1	
AO1	
AO2	
AO2	
AO2	
AO2 or IDA	
Example 2: Core body temperature	
AO1	
AO2	
AO2 or IDA	
Example 3: Hormones	
AO1	
AO2	
AO2 or IDA	

Answer plan 2
(a) Describe **one** circadian rhythm. (4 marks)
(b) Discuss the role of endogenous pacemakers in the control of circadian rhythms. (4 marks + 16 marks)

Part (a) Sleep–wake cycle	
AO1	Rhythm 1 – circadian rhythms = 24 hours, e.g. sleep–wake cycle
AO1	Temporal isolation studies, e.g. Aschoff and Wever (1976)
Part (b) Role of endogenous pacemakers	
AO1	SCN – controlled by light, ventral and dorsal SCN have different functions
AO1	Negative feedback loop (CLK+BLMAL1, PER+CRY)
AO2	Mutant hamsters (Morgan, 1995) demonstrated SCN
AO2	Ventral/dorsal SCN can explain jet and shift lag
IDA	Use of non-human animals, e.g. permanent harm from transplanting mutant SCN
IDA	Evolutionary approach, endogenous rhythms have adaptive function, e.g. chipmunks (deCoursey *et al.*, 2000)
AO2	Light entrains the free running endogenous rhythm, e.g. Campbell and Murphy (1998)
AO2	Artificial lighting may be enough to reset rhythms, e.g. Boivin *et al.* (1996)
AO2	Problems when the biological system fails, e.g. FASPS
AO2	There are advantages with this blended system, e.g. copes with changing day lengths in Arctic circle communities

Answer plan 3
Discuss the disruption of biological rhythms.
(8 marks + 16 marks)

Example 1: Shift work and shift lag	
AO1	Circadian trough – alertness and core body temperature lowest at night
AO1	Effects on health, e.g. heart disease (Knutssen *et al.*, 1986)
IDA	Real-world application, reduce major disasters through help with shift lag
IDA	Real-world application, non-fluctuating, forward-rotating shifts (Gold *et al.*, 1992, Bambra *et al.*, 2008)
AO2	Lab experiments should be verified by natural experiments e.g. nurses at work (Boivin and James, 2002)
AO2	Alternative explanation, effects due to family disruption, e.g. 60% divorce rate (Solomon, 1993)
Example 2: Jet travel and jet lag	
AO1	Ventral and dorsal part of SCN desynchronise
AO1	Phase delay (travel east to west, stay up late), phase advance, e.g. US Baseball teams (Recht *et al.*, 1995)
AO2	An alternative explanation, effects due to tiredness, etc.
IDA	Real-world application, use melatonin to deal with jet lag (Herxheimer and Petrie, 2001)
IDA	Real-world application, use eating times to deal with jet lag (Fuller *et al.*, 2008)
AO2	Individual differences, some people's rhythms adjust more slowly; may find shift/jet lag easier (Reinberg *et al.*, 1984)

Model answer

Discuss research into biological rhythms. (8 marks + 16 marks)

The most well-researched biological rhythms are circadian rhythms, such as the sleep–wake cycle. One of the ways to investigate the free-running circadian sleep cycle is to isolate people from their usual cues about time of day (temporal isolation studies). Siffre (1975) reported his own experiences underground over a period of about 2 months. He had no daylight, radio, etc. and found that his sleep–wake cycle generally adjusted to a 24-hour cycle, though it sometimes changed dramatically to as much as 48 hours.

Aschoff and Wever (1976) placed participants in an underground WWII bunker with no environmental and social time cues. They also found that the free-running cycle persisted – participants had a sleep–wake cycle of 24–25 hours, which sometimes increased up to 29 hours.

One of the criticisms of this research concerns the question of artificial light. In the early studies described above participants were cut off from temporal cues but they were exposed to artificial light. People thought that artificial light would not reset the endogenous rhythm but research has shown this may not be true. For example Czeisler *et al.* (1999) altered participants' circadian rhythms down to 22 hours and up to 28 hours using just dim lighting.

It is always important to consider individual differences because research has shown that people vary in their cycle length. Czeisler *et al.* (1999) found circadian rhythms as low as 13 hours in some people to as much as 65 hours in others. This may explain some of the differences found in the studies.

Siffre's research has been criticised because it was a case study and there may be unique characteristics of Siffre that mean the findings cannot be generalised (such as his willingness to be isolated for so long). However, the fact that other research has produced similar findings supports Siffre's data and his study (as a case study) has the advantage of providing rich data which can enhance our understanding of the experiences of temporal isolation.

This research has real-world applications. Chronotherapeutics is the application of biological rhythms to the treatment of disorders, for example it is advantageous to take medication or activities at certain times of day, such as taking aspirin at 11pm to treat heart attacks. Aspirin levels then peak in the bloodstream at the time when heart attacks commonly occur (about 3am). Another application is knowing when is the best time to work – people are most alert in the morning and early evening, so those are the best times to work.

The ultradian rhythm has a cycle of less than 24 hours, such as the stages of sleep. Sleep starts with stages 1 and 2, when the brain starts to produce alpha and theta waves. Stages 3 and 4 are deep sleep (slow wave sleep, SWS) when it is hard to wake someone. Finally is REM sleep (rapid eye movement), associated with dreaming. The brain and eyes are active but the body is paralysed. One cycle takes about 90 minutes and repeats several times during the night.

During the daytime we also have 90-minute cycles, such as the basic rest-activity cycle (BRAC). Friedman and Fisher (1967) observed psychiatric patients over a 6-hour period, and noted a clear pattern of 90 minutes between eating and drinking 'episodes'.

There are important age differences in sleep stages. Babies don't have the same stages, they display quiet and active sleep which are immature versions of SWS and REM sleep. Older people experience reduced SWS and an associated reduction in the production of growth hormones. This may explain some of the symptoms associated with old age, e.g. lower bone density (van Cauter *et al.*, 2000).

It is assumed that people are dreaming during REM sleep but this may not be true. For example, neurobiological theories of dreaming make the assumption that REM sleep = dreams and explain the function of dreaming in terms of the function of REM sleep. In fact people dream during deep sleep but simply may not remember their dreams as easily.

There are advantages to having a 90-minute rhythm. It ensures that biological processes in the body work in unison. Complex metabolic processes are active in many different parts of the body at any time and some coordination between these is advantageous.

Both circadian and ultradian rhythms are controlled jointly by exogenous and endogenous mechanisms. There are advantages with this blended system, for example people living in the Arctic circle have winter days with little daylight. If their circadian rhythms were solely controlled by sunlight they would sleep most of the day.

Note how each paragraph in this essay mirrors the original answer plan.

Using paragraphs like this helps you keep a track of how much AO1 and AO2 you have covered, and also helps the examiner to read your answer because each separate point is clear.

It is important that each AO2 point is elaborated in order to end up with twice as much AO2 material as AO1 – though they don't all have to be elaborated equally! Overall each AO2 point should be an average of 50–60 words.

Each AO2 and IDA point begins with a lead-in phrase that makes it clear that this is AO2 or IDA.

Some students write too much on stages of sleep because it is easy to remember such details – the danger is that you end up with less time for the important AO2.

This essay plan has two separate sections, a kind of 4+8+4+8 plan. Make sure you have an overall plan so you get the AO1:AO2 proportions right.

In this essay there is a total of about 750 words, about 250 AO1 and 500 AO2 – just the right ratio of AO1:AO2 (twice as much AO2).

Division 2 Sleep

Answer plans

Answer plan 1

Discuss the nature of sleep. (8 marks + 16 marks)

What happens during sleep

AO1	Reduced light increases melatonin levels which inhibits areas of brain that promote wakefulness
AO1	Sleep stages (stages 1 and 2, 3, 4, SWS and REM)
IDA	Real-world application, melatonin levels affected by artificial light, link to cancer
AO2	Age differences in stages, e.g. babies (quiet/active sleep)
AO2	Cultural differences, e.g. adolescence (Tynjälä *et al.*, 1993)
AO2	REM sleep may not be equivalent to dreams

Functions of sleep

AO1	Restoration, e.g. growth hormone, neurotransmitters
AO1	Adaptive, e.g. conserve energy, balanced against foraging needs and predator risk
AO2	Sleep deprivation negative effects, e.g. Tripp not Gardner
AO2	Methodological issues, e.g. case studies, microsleep
AO2	Phylogenetic signal shows sleep patterns evolved (Capallini *et al.*, 2008)
IDA	Combined approach is best, e.g. core and optional sleep (Horne, 1988), sleep as waste of time (Meddis, 1975)

Work out your own plan for these questions and then write your answers.

(a) Describe the stages of sleep. (4 marks)

(b) Outline and evaluate the evolutionary explanation of the function of sleep. (4 marks + 16 marks)

Part (a) The stages of sleep

AO1	
AO1	

Part (b) Evolutionary explanation

AO1	
AO1	
AO2	
AO2	
AO2	
AO2	
AO2	
AO2 or IDA	
AO2 or IDA	
AO2 or IDA	

Answer plan 2

(a) Outline lifespan changes in sleep. (4 marks)

(b) Discuss **one** explanation for the functions of sleep. (4 marks + 16 marks)

Part (a) Lifespan

AO1	Babies, quiet and active sleep
AO1	Old age, SWS decreases to 5% of total sleep, REM decreases to 20%

Part (b) Restoration theory

AO1	SWS – growth hormone produced (van Cauter and Plat, 1996), immune system functionning reduced
AO1	REM – enables brain growth and neurotransmitters (e.g. monoamines) replenished
AO2	Sleep deprivation negative effects, e.g. Tripp not Gardner
AO2	Animal studies show fatal effects of lack of sleep, e.g. Rechtschaffen *et al.* (1983), rats on rotating disc
AO2	Methodological issues, e.g. case studies, microsleep
AO2	SWS and REM rebound support restoration effects, e.g. Ferrara *et al.* (1999), Empson (2002)
AO2	Exercise should increase sleep, e.g. Shapiro *et al.* (1981) but not Horne and Minard (1985)
AO2	Restoration approach can't explain e.g. why lack of consciousness necessary for sleep
IDA	Evolutionary approach explains e.g. phylogenetic signal, shows sleep patterns evolved (Capallini *et al.*, 2008)
IDA	Combined approach is best, e.g. distinction between core and optional sleep (Horne, 1988)

Answer plan 3

(a) Outline research into biological rhythms. (8 marks)

(b) Evaluate **one or more** explanations for the functions of sleep. (16 marks)

Part (a) Biological rhythms

AO1	Circadian, temporal isolation studies, e.g. Siffre (1975)
AO1	Aschoff and Wever (1976) WWII bunker
AO1	Ultradian, e.g. sleep stages (stages 1 and 2, 3, 4, SWS and REM)
AO1	Basic rest–activity cycle, Friedman and Fisher (1967) psychiatric patients eating/drinking

Part (b) Functions of sleep

AO2	Sleep deprivation negative effects, e.g. Tripp not Gardner
AO2	Animal studies show fatal effects, e.g. Rechtschaffen *et al.* (1983), rats on rotating disc
AO2	Methodological issues, e.g. case studies, microsleep
AO2	SWS and REM rebound support restoration effects, e.g. Ferrara *et al.* (1999), Empson (2002)
AO2	Exercise should increase sleep, e.g. Shapiro *et al.* (1981) but not Horne and Minard (1985)
AO2	Restoration approach can't explain e.g. why lack of consciousness necessary
IDA	Evolutionary approach explains e.g. phylogenetic signal, shows sleep patterns evolved (Capallini *et al.*, 2008)
IDA	Combined approach is best, e.g. core and optional sleep (Horne, 1988)

Model answer

(a) Outline lifespan changes in sleep. (4 marks)

Babies have immature versions of adult sleep. Quiet sleep is like slow wave sleep and active sleep is like REM but babies have proportionately much more REM sleep than adults have (about half of their sleep is active). Babies generally sleep more than adults (about 15 hours) and when they go to sleep their sleep is quite light (rather than the adult pattern of going into deep sleep). This explains why babies are so easily awoken.

At the other end of the spectrum, in old age, patterns change as well. Older adults have about the same amount of sleep than when they were younger but have less SWS and REM sleep. SWS decreases to about 5% of the total sleep time and REM decreases to 20%. The result may be that they feel less refreshed after a night's sleep and that's why they have naps.

> The notes for this essay (see facing page) just said 'babies, quiet and active sleep' but hopefully this will trigger you to think of other facts about infant sleep patterns.

> Part (a) of this answer is 143 words, just about the right amount for a question part worth 4 marks.

(b) Discuss **one** explanation for the functions of sleep. (4 marks + 16 marks)

One explanation for the functions of sleep is the restoration theory. Research has found that slow wave sleep (SWS) is linked to the production of various key proteins, such as growth hormone. One study found that the amount of growth hormones released correlated with the amount of SWS (van Cauter and Plat, 1996). Lack of SWS has also been associated with reduced immune function. Antibodies (another protein and key component of the immune system) are regenerated during SWS.

REM sleep (rapid eye movements) is also associated with brain growth. One clue comes from the fact that REM sleep is greater in babies whose brains are developing. Another clue comes from the fact that antidepressants suppress REM sleep. Antidepressants also enhance the production of monoamines (such as the neurotransmitter serotonin). This has been taken to imply that REM sleep promotes the production of neurotransmitters. If the neurotransmitters are enhanced by other means then there is less need for REM sleep.

> Each AO2 paragraph represents one point from the notes on the facing page and is about 50 words, producing the right amount of AO2 in total – here it is 460 words out of a total for the essay of 759 words.
>
> There should be twice as much AO2 as AO1. In this essay there is sufficient AO2 and probably a bit too much AO1.

Restoration theory is supported by research on the effects of sleep deprivation. If the function of sleep is to restore, then deprivation should have negative effects. Some well known case studies have been used as evidence. DJ Peter Tripp stayed awake for 201 hours and experienced hallucinations and paranoia. On the other hand wakeathon man Randy Gardner displayed no psychotic symptoms after 11 days without sleep.

Studies of animals support the fact that sleep deprivation has negative effects, even fatal. For example, Rechtschaffen *et al.* (1983) kept rats on a rotating disc and after 33 days they died. It is possible that their death was due to stress rather than lack of sleep.

There are other criticisms of this research. One issue is the use of case studies which makes it hard to make generalisations since individuals have unique characteristics – both Tripp and Gardner had special motivations to stay awake which may make their behaviour atypical. Another methodological issue relates to microsleep – it is difficult to properly control the fact that individuals may actually be getting some amounts of microsleep and therefore aren't actually sleep deprived.

> Further evaluation of the AO2 point adds elaboration, as in the last sentence of this paragraph. See the three-point rule for good AO2 on page 5.

Another line of support comes from studies of selective sleep deprivation. If people are deprived of SWS they show a need for more SWS on subsequent nights. This was demonstrated by using acoustic stimulation to wake sleepers as soon as brain waves showed SWS (Ferrara *et al.*, 1999). Similar REM rebound effects have also been observed with as much as 50% more REM sleep on subsequent nights after REM sleep deprivation (Empson, 2002). Such research suggests that both SWS and REM sleep perform some vital function.

> Each AO2 paragraph clearly starts with an AO2 lead-in phrase to make it clear that this is evaluation.

Another argument is that, if sleep is restorative, then increased exercise should increase the need for sleep. Shapiro *et al.* (1981) found that marathon runners slept 2 hours longer after a race. However, Horne and Minard (1985) found that a series of exhausting tasks led people to go to sleep faster but not longer.

Therefore, there is a reasonable amount of support for the restoration approach but there are a number of things it can't explain. For example, it doesn't explain why sleep involves a loss of consciousness – periods of rest could achieve the same effect.

There is a different approach to explaining the function of sleep – the evolutionary approach which can account for features of sleep that can't be explained by the restoration approach. For example, the 'phylogenetic signal' (similarity in sleep patterns between closely related species) shows sleep patterns evolved (Capallini *et al.*, 2008).

> Examiners often criticise students for tacking their IDA points onto the end of an answer. However, in the case of this essay, it makes sense to consider a contrasting approach at the end.

It may be that a combined approach is best, e.g. the idea of core and optional sleep proposed by Horne (1988). Core sleep equals SWS and is essential for restoration, whereas optional sleep is REM sleep (and some parts of NREM sleep) that keeps an animal safe during unproductive hours.

> Part (b) has 151 words of AO1 and 467 words AO2, again appropriate for the marks available.

Division 3 Disorders of sleep — Answer plans

Answer plan 1
Discuss explanations for **one or more** sleep disorders. (8 marks + 16 marks)

Disorder 1: Narcolepsy	
AO1	Malfunction of REM, paralysis, intrusion of REM sleep
AO2	REM patterns observed at start of episodes (Vogel, 1960)
AO2	Activity in REM brainstem neurons linked to cataplexy in dogs (Siegel, 1999)
AO1	Mutation in HLA, e.g. DQB1*0602 (Honda *et al.*, 1983)
AO2	HLA mutation not in all narcoleptics (Mignot *et al.*, 1997)
IDA	Biological vs psychological, e.g. disguises sexual fantasies (Lehrman and Weiss, 1943)

Disorder 2: Sleepwalking	
AO1	Incomplete arousal in SWS, delta and beta waves (found in SWS + awake state) present
AO1	Motor activity not inhibited, SWS immature (Oliviero, 2008)
AO2	Risk 10x greater in 1st degree relatives (Broughton, 1968)
AO2	Risk factors – sleep deprivation, alcohol, fever, SWS
IDA	Nature + nurture, diathesis (genetics) and sleep deprivation
IDA	Real-world application, defence in criminal trials

Work out your own plan for this question and then write your answer.
Discuss explanations of insomnia. (8 marks + 16 marks)

AO1	
AO1	
AO1	
AO1	
AO2	
AO2	
AO2	
AO2	
AO2	
AO2 or IDA	
AO2 or IDA	
AO2 or IDA	

Answer plan 2
Discuss explanations of narcolepsy. (8 marks + 16 marks)

Explanation 1	
AO1	Malfunction of REM, paralysis, intrusion of REM sleep
AO2	REM patterns observed at start of episodes (Vogel, 1960)
AO2	Activity in REM brainstem neurons linked to cataplexy in dogs (Siegel, 1999)

Explanation 2	
AO1	Mutation in HLA, e.g. DQB1*0602 (Honda *et al.*, 1983)
AO2	HLA mutation not in all narcoleptics (Mignot *et al.*, 1997)

Explanation 3	
AO1	Hypocretin maintains wakefulness. Abnormal gene in dogs (Lin *et al.*, 1999)
AO2	Abnormal levels confirmed in humans (Nishino *et al.*, 2000)
AO2	Family and twin studies indicate it is not inherited (Mignot, 1998)
IDA	Nurture, not nature. Low levels likely to be due to brain injury, diet, stress
AO2	Or may be auto-immune response – link to HLA

Explanation 4	
AO1	Psychological, disguises sexual fantasies (Lehrman and Weiss, 1943)
IDA	Biological approach is much more likely though not genetic, unlike e.g. sleep walking which is genetic

Answer plan 3
There are both biological and psychological explanations for sleep disorders.
(a) Outline explanations of sleep disorders. (8 marks)
(b) Evaluate explanations of sleep disorders. (16 marks)

Disorder 1: Narcolepsy	
AO1	Malfunction of REM, paralysis, intrusion of REM sleep
AO1	Mutation in HLA, e.g. DQB1*0602 (Honda *et al.*, 1983)
AO2	REM patterns observed at start of episodes (Vogel, 1960)
AO2	Activity in REM brainstem neurons linked to cataplexy in dogs (Siegel, 1999)
IDA	Biological vs psychological, e.g. disguises sexual fantasies (Lehrman and Weiss, 1943)

Disorder 2: Sleepwalking	
AO1	Incomplete arousal in SWS, delta and beta waves (found in SWS + awake state) present
IDA	Nature + nurture – diathesis (genetics) and sleep deprivation
IDA	Real-world application, defence in criminal trials

Disorder 3: Insomnia	
AO1	Underlying medical, psychiatric, environmental cause (secondary insomnia)
AO2	Twin studies show 50% due to genes (Watson *et al.*, 2006)
IDA	Nature–nurture, diathesis + environmental stressors (e.g. noise, too much coffee)
IDA	Real-world application, treat insomnia even if it is primary insomnia, e.g. depression may be cause by insomnia

Model answer

Discuss explanations of narcolepsy. (8 marks + 16 marks)

One explanation for narcolepsy is the malfunction of REM sleep, i.e. it intrudes into waking life. In the 1950s this was a popular idea because the characteristics of narcolepsy match those of REM sleep, such as body paralysis (lack of muscle tone, called 'cataplexy') and the intrusion of hallucinations.

There has been some research to support for this. For example, Vogel (1960) recorded the brain waves in one patient during their narcoleptic episodes. At the beginning of the narcoleptic episode there were brain waves similar to those found in REM sleep. However, observations of just one person are not very reliable or valid because individuals have unique characteristics.

Support also comes from animal studies. For example, Siegel (1999) studied one dog and found the same activity during the loss of muscle tone (cataplexy) as he found in REM sleep. However, again this was just one individual and it is possible that animal narcolepsy (and animal REM sleep) is different to humans even though the physiology is similar. Generally there is little research support for the REM malfunction explanation.

A more recent explanation for narcolepsy involves the HLA gene, the gene for human leukocyte antigen. This gene contributes to the body's immune response as antigens are an important component of the system. There is a mutation of this gene called HLA- DQBI*0602 which appears to be common in narcoleptics (Honda *et al.*, 1983).

This seemed a very promising idea, however the mutation isn't found in everyone with narcolepsy so it can't be the whole story. And Mignot *et al.* (1997) found that some people who don't suffer from narcolepsy do have the same mutation. This suggests that either the mutation has nothing to do with narcolepsy or that it only leads to narcolpsy when other conditions/abnormalities are present.

A third explanation relates to a different genetic mutation, this time related to the neurotransmitter hypocretin (which is also sometimes called orexin). This neurotransmitter is involved in the brain mechanisms that promote wakefulness, so it would make sense that an abnormality would affect a person's ability to stay awake. Lin *et al.* (1999) found that narcoleptic dogs had an abnormal gene related to the production of hypocretin, linking narcolepsy and hypocretin.

The research with dogs has been confirmed by human studies. For example, Nishino *et al.* (2000) tested the fluid in narcoleptics spine (cerebrospinal fluid) and found lower levels of hypocretin.

Research has found that these lower levels are not genetically-based. One study by Mignot (1998) looked at family members of narcoleptics and found that the condition doesn't appear to run in families. They also found that in the case of twins with one narcoleptic there was very little incidence of the co-twin also being a sufferer.

This raises the nature–nurture debate as the evidence appears to point to nurture rather than nature. Possible examples of environmental (nurture) causes are brain injury, diet or stress. For example, brain injury might affect the parts of the brain that produce hypocretin and this triggers narcolepsy. Stress is known to be important in triggering narcoleptic attacks so a person who has developed narcolepsy through brain injury might then experience episodes when stressed.

Another possible trigger is an auto-immune response. This is where the body's immune system turns on itself instead of fighting invading bacteria and viruses. This attack damages parts of the body. This could link the HLA explanation to the hypocretin explanation – so people with a defective HLA system develop narcolepsy because the result is a malfunction of the immune system which results in lowered hypocretin production. Whereas this may not happen for everyone with the defective gene.

There have been some attempts to offer a psychological explanation for narcolepsy. For example, Lehrman and Weiss (1943) proposed that the narcoleptic attack of sleepiness is a way to disguise sexual fantasies that a person might be having.

As we have seen all other explanations have been biological rather than psychological and there has been little if any support for psychological approaches. Therefore, we can conclude that it looks like narcolepsy is biologically caused but not as a consequence of nature – it is biological lifetime experiences that count. This can be contrasted with explanations for other sleep disorders, such as sleep walking, where the evidence points much more to a genetic basis.

Note that the essay does NOT begin with a definition for narcolepsy. Essays on sleep disorders will always be on explanations and definitions would gain no credit.

This answer wisely avoids wasting any time with an introduction of any kind and just plunges into the first explanation.

Always explain concepts (such as antigens) to demonstrate your understanding of psychology rather than just using a term you have just memorised. However, this only applies to terms you have introduced in your essay, it does not apply to a term, such as narcolepsy (see above).

When introducing an IDA point it's a good idea to make it clear to the examiner that this is an IDA point – using an IDA lead-in phrase.

It is also important to make sure your IDA is contextualised, i.e. not a general discussion of nature vs nurture but one that is set specifically in the context of narcolepsy.

In this essay the psychological explanation has been used as AO1 but if you look at answer plans 1 and 3 on the facing page you can see that it can be part of the AO2 content. Distinguishing between AO1 and AO2 simply relates to how you use material – this is why AO2 lead-in phrases are so important.

Knowledge about sleep walking has been used as effective AO2.

In total this essay is just over 700 words long – the AO2 content is 492 words (about 70% of the content).

Answer for you to mark

See page 170 for examiner's comments.

Question

(a) Outline **one** example of a circadian rhythm. (4 marks)
(b) (i) Outline explanations for sleep disorders. (4 marks)
(b) (ii) Evaluate explanations for sleep disorders. (16 marks)

Student answer

Part (a)

❶ *One example of the circadian rhythm is the sleep–wake cycle. There are internal (endogenous) biological clocks which have been shown to regulate the free running cycle of 24–25 hours (Siffre, Aschoff and Wever, Folkard). There are also external factors – called exogenous zeitgebers. These affect the sleep–wake cycle and include light, social factors (such as eating) and temperature.*

❷ *There are individual differences to this circadian rhythm but in general it is a determinist mechanism because people have no free will over it.*

(81 words)

AO1 mark scheme for part (a)
Candidates are likely to write about the sleep–wake cycle, and explain the role of endogenous and exogenous factors in this rhythm. The section should be marked bearing time constraints in mind.

4 marks is about 100–120 words.

Comments and marks for part (a) AO1

Guidance on marking is given on pages 6–11.

Mark	Knowledge and understanding	Accuracy	Organisation and structure
4	Reasonably thorough	Accurate	Coherent
3–2	Limited	Generally accurate	Reasonably coherent
1	Weak and muddled		
0	No creditworthy material		

Tick the terms you think apply to the student's answer.

The **AO1** mark I would give is ☐

Part (b) (i)

❸ *In older age people wake more often during their sleep. This is a form of insomnia. In fact it is a form of secondary insomnia because it is caused by other disorders, such as sleep apnoea.*

❹ *Narcolepsy is another sleep disorder. It is a genetic condition where a person falls asleep during the day where they may experience catalepsy.*

❺ *Gender is a potential explanation for sleeping disorders. Overweight males are prone to sleep apnoea which is a risk factor in developing insomnia. Young males are also more likely to suffer from sleep walking.*

(93 words)

AO1 mark scheme for part (b) (i)
Any sleep disorders would be creditworthy but the focus must be on explanations. Candidates can achieve full marks for one sleep disorder but must write about more than one explanation.

4 marks is about 100–120 words.

Comments and marks for part (b) (i) AO1

Mark	Knowledge and understanding	Accuracy	Organisation and structure
4	Reasonably thorough	Accurate	Coherent
3–2	Limited	Generally accurate	Reasonably coherent
1	Weak and muddled		
0	No creditworthy material		

The **AO1** mark I would give is ☐

Part (b) (ii)

6 The role of gender has been studied by Li et al. in Hong Kong. Women were found to be more likely to develop insomnia because of the levels of anxiety experienced in their normal lives. Housewives had the least risk. Men who had sleep apnoea developed secondary insomnia as a result of waking up because of breathing obstructions.

7 However, to generalise this to all men and suggest that all men with sleep apnoea would develop insomnia would be reductionist as in reality insomnia arises because of a collection of problems.

8 By having gender separation the research has higher reliability as gender differences are accounted for.

9 Gender and age have some links in developing sleep disorders. Research found that the change in hormones at adolescence is linked to disrupted circadian rhythms. This can lead to sleeping disorders. A methodological issue with testing explanations for sleep disorders is that it is hard to compare before a disorder has developed to after as there are too many confounding variables.

10 Another problem with research is the research is conducted on those referred to a disorder specialist. This means the findings may not represent the wider population.

11 The genetic predisposition for narcoplepsy has been supported from folk tales describing the effects of narcolepsy in the middle ages. Research is still being conducted to find the gene responsible.

12 Overall the explanations for sleep disorder are interconnected and can give a basis for why they develop. They do not look at all approaches, only biological ones which is a limitation. Ethical issues prevent indepth research being done.

(260 words)

AO2 mark scheme for part (b) (ii)

Analysis and evaluation would be creditworthy for any sleep disorders, not just those covered in part (b) (i). Research studies may be used to support or challenge explanations. Methodological issues may be examined and IDA points are creditworthy.

At least two explanations must be evaluated.

16 marks is about 400–480 words.

Comments and marks for part (b) (ii) AO2

Mark	Analysis and understanding	Focus	Elaboration	Line of argument	Issues/debates/ approaches	Quality of written communication
16–13	Sound	Well focused	Coherent	Clear	Used effectively	Fluent, effective use of terms
12–9	Reasonable	Generally focused	Reasonable	Evident	Reasonably effective	Clear, appropriate
8–5	Basic, superficial	Sometimes focused	Some evidence		Superficial reference	Lacks clarity, limited use of terms
4–1	Rudimentary, limited understanding	Weak, muddled and incomplete	Not effective	May be mainly irrelevant	Absent or muddled/ inaccurate	Often unconnected assertions, errors
0	No creditworthy material					

The **AO2** mark I would give is ☐

Chapter 2 Perception

There have been changes to the specification from September 2011 – therefore the updated specification details here are slightly different to those in some editions of the *A2 Complete Companion*.

Division 1 **Theories of perceptual organisation**	
	• **Gregory's top-down/indirect theory of perception**
	• **Gibson's bottom-up/direct theory of perception**

Possible exam questions for this division

Outline and evaluate Gregory's top-down/indirect theory of perception. (8 marks + 16 marks)	Questions may be set specifically on the theories named in the specification, so you should have a 8+16 mark version ready for both.
Discuss Gibson's bottom-up/direct theory of perception. (8 marks + 16 marks)	This theory is named in the specification, therefore questions may be set solely on this topic. See model answer on page 25.
Discuss **one** direct theory of perception (8 marks + 16 marks)	The question may identify the theory as direct or indirect, with no reference to Gregory or Gibson, so be prepared to make that link yourself.
Discuss **two** theories of perceptual organisation. (8 marks + 16 marks)	In this question you must cover both theories and therefore have to be careful to reduce your material to avoid stuffing too much into your essay and losing marks because there is insufficient depth (detail) for AO1 and elaboration for AO2. You won't have time to cover everything you know so be selective.
Discuss **two** theories of perceptual organisation. (8 marks + 16 marks)	Beware of the phrase 'theories of perceptual organisation' – this is the term used in the division title so exam questions may well be set on this rather than 'theories of perception'. When answering this question you could outline any two theories of perceptual organisation but they are likely to be Gregory and Gibson.
(a) Outline **one** direct and **one** indirect theory of perceptual organisation. (8 marks) (b) Consider whether direct or indirect theories provide the better explanation of perceptual organisation. (16 marks)	Part (a) is similar to the one above – an outline of the two theories you have studied. It is important to restrict your descriptions for each so you don't provide more than 8 marks worth in total. In part (b) you are required to evaluate the two theories. The question invites you to consider which is the better. In order to do this you should consider the strengths and/or weaknesses of each, i.e. evaluate them. By contrasting the two approaches you will be supplying IDA.
(a) Outline **one** direct theory of perceptual organisation. (4 marks) (b) Outline **one** study of perceptual development. (4 marks) (c) Evaluate research into perceptual development, including infant and cross-cultural studies. (16 marks)	Beware questions that span across several divisions and make sure, when answering such questions, that you focus on the specific demands of each part. In parts (a) and (b) make sure you write no more than required for a 4-mark question (about 150 words for each). In part (c) you must provide evaluation (and not any description). So your focus is on the value of the research and implications for understanding perceptual development. IDA is creditworthy only in part (c) of this question.

Division 2 **The development of perception**	
	• **The development of perceptual abilities, including depth/distance, visual constancies**
	• **Perceptual development, including infant and cross-cultural research**

Possible exam questions for this division

Discuss the development of depth/distance perception. (8 marks + 16 marks)	A discussion must include some description – in this case you could provide a description of the different kinds of depth/distance cues using research studies to illustrate this. The evaluation part of the answer is likely to include criticisms of the studies and the methodology used and may also present contrasting research evidence. Note that the content in the two bullet points in the specification is interwoven – when writing about depth/distance perception you will use infant and cross-cultural research studies.
(a) Explain the development of depth/distance perception. (4 marks) (b) Discuss the development of visual constancies. (4 marks + 16 marks)	The content of this division of the specification can be divided in many different ways. Your job is to supply an answer that reflects the allocation of marks and the wording of the question parts. In the case of the question on the left, just 4 marks describing depth distance perception, 4 marks describing visual constancies and 16 marks evaluating the latter.

(a) Outline **two or more** examples of visual constancies. (8 marks) (b) Evaluate research into perceptual development, including infant and cross-cultural studies. (16 marks)	In part (a) of this question only visual constancies are relevant. The focus of your answer should be on examples of visual constancy but you can use research studies (infant and cross-cultural ones) to illustrate these. In part (b) you can evaluate both depth/distance and/or visual constancies – but must include both infant and cross-cultural studies. See model answer on page 27.
Discuss the development of perceptual abilities, including infant and cross-cultural studies. (8 marks + 16 marks)	This question combines all possibilities for this division. As with the question above, this requires that you include both infant and cross-cultural studies – this time in both your description and evaluation. You can cover either depth/distance or visual constancies or both. In such cases you must guard against trying to include everything you know which would result in an answer that lacks detail and elaboration because of time constraints. See student answer on page 30.
Outline and evaluate **two or more** infant studies of perceptual development. (8 marks + 16 marks)	Questions may focus on any one of the four elements of this division – depth/distance, visual constancies, infant research (as in this question) or cross-cultural research. This means that, for each element, you need to prepare a 24-mark answer.

Division 3
Face recognition and visual agnosias

- **Bruce and Young's theory of face recognition, including case studies and explanations of prosopagnosia**

Possible exam questions for this division

Discuss Bruce and Young's theory of face recognition. (8 marks + 16 marks)	A straightforward question from the specification. The main danger here (as in every question) is writing too much description (AO1) and leaving insufficient time for the big marks from evaluation (AO2).
Discuss research into face recognition. (8 marks + 16 marks)	It is legitimate to use the words in the division title for an exam question. When answering this question you can use Bruce and Young's theory because 'research' refers to theories and/or studies. If you try to use research studies as your AO1 you may struggle with the AO2 – though you can always evaluate one research study with another, or evaluate the methodology of any research study.
Outline and evaluate **one or more** explanations of visual agnosias. (8 marks + 16 marks)	Again this essay title is taken from the division heading. You may only have studied prosopagnosia and therefore will just focus on this one example of a visual agnosia. The AO1 component of your answer must concern explanations. You would get no credit for a description of any research study unless your focus is on the implication of the study for the explanation. The AO2 component is likely to involve research studies and could involve an evaluation of these research studies.
Discuss explanations of prosopagnosia. (8 marks + 16 marks)	This question requires that you cover a minimum of two explanations for full marks. You can consider more than two if you feel you have time.
(a) Outline **two or more** case studies of prosopagnosia. (4 marks) (b) Discuss **one or more** explanations of prosopagnosia. (4 marks + 16 marks)	Case studies are explicitly included in the specification, so exam questions may ask you to write about such research. In part (b) only 4 marks are available for the description of explanations. The question is phrased so that you could just consider one explanation. See model answer on page 29.
(a) Outline and evaluate Bruce and Young's theory of face recognition. (4 marks + 8 marks) (b) Outline and evaluate **one or more** explanations of prosopagnosia. (4 marks + 8 marks)	Combination questions allow you to demonstrate your knowledge across the specification but you must be careful to stick to a strict limit of how much you write for each part of the question. You should write about 100–120 words for 4 marks worth and 200–240 for 8 marks. Note that each question part is worth the same number of marks, therefore your word length should be balanced appropriately across part (a) and part (b).

Division 1 Theories of perceptual organisation Answer plans

Answer plan 1
Outline and evaluate Gregory's top-down/indirect theory of perception. (8 marks + 16 marks)

Gregory's theory

AO1	Top-down necessary because visual input incomplete
AO1	Perception is an interaction between knowledge in the brain and sensory data, then tested against reality
AO2	Research support, e.g. Khorasani *et al.* (2007) Müller-Lyer
AO2	Not true for all illusions, e.g. Shopland and Gregory (1964) Necker cube reversals
AO1	Internal expectations based on past experience, e.g. Bruner *et al.* (1951) black hearts and red spades
AO2	Research support, e.g. Palmer (1975) objects in kitchen or Bruner and Minturn (1955) letter B
IDA	Real-world application, misidentification of passenger jet by US Navy due to expectations
AO1	'Misapplied' hypotheses lead to errors of perception, e.g. visual illusions, such as Müller-Lyer
AO2	Research support, people who don't live in carpentered environment don't 'see' some illusions (Segall *et al.*, 1963)
IDA	Contrasts with bottom-up approach, reconciled in terms of (1) visual conditions, (2) ventral and dorsal streams

Work out your own plan for this question and then write your answer.
Discuss **two** theories of perceptual organisation. (8 marks + 16 marks)

Theory 1

AO1	
AO1	
AO2	
AO2	
AO2	
AO2 or IDA	

Theory 2

AO1	
AO1	
AO2	
AO2	
AO2	
AO2 or IDA	

Answer plan 2
Outline and evaluate Gibson's bottom-up/direct theory of perception. (8 marks + 16 marks)

Gibson's theory

AO1	Optic flow, the further away the faster the flow
AO1	Ecological, e.g. depth/distance and texture gradient
AO1	Invariants, e.g. texture–gradient and horizon–ratio
AO1	Resonance and affordance (potential for action)
AO2	Research support, biological motion, e.g. babies (Fox and Daniel, 1982) and animals (Blake, 1993)
AO2	Research support, time-to-contact, e.g. Lee *et al.* (1982) long-jumpers and Lee (1980) gannets
AO2	Research support, movement, e.g. Wraga *et al.* (2000) Müller-Lyer illusion disappeared
AO2	Research support, visual illusions, e.g. Ames room can be explained directly using horizon-ratio
IDA	Nature and nurture, e.g. Gibson and Walk (1960) showed depth perception innate and thus direct but also indirect
IDA	Real-world application, design of robots
AO2	Limitations, can't explain effects of experience, e.g. Palmer (1975) objects in kitchen
IDA	Contrasts with bottom-up approach, reconciled in terms of (1) visual conditions, (2) ventral and dorsal streams

Answer plan 3
(a) Outline **one** direct and **one** indirect theory of perceptual organisation. (8 marks)
(b) Consider whether direct or indirect theories provide the better explanation of perceptual organisation. (16 marks)

Part (a) Direct and indirect theory

AO1	Top-down – perception is an interaction between knowledge in the brain and sensory data, then tested against reality
AO1	Internal expectations based on past experience, e.g. Bruner *et al.* (1951) black hearts and red spades
AO1	Bottom-up – optic flow, the further away the faster the flow
AO1	Ecological, e.g. depth/distance and texture gradient (an invariant)

Part (b) Evaluation

AO2	Research support, e.g. Khorasani *et al.* (2007) Müller-Lyer
AO2	Research support, e.g. Palmer (1975) objects in kitchen or Bruner and Minturn (1955) letter B
IDA	Real-world application, misidentification of passenger jet by US Navy
AO2	Research support, biological motion, e.g. babies (Fox and Daniel, 1982) and animals (Blake, 1993)
AO2	Visual illusions can be explained by both perspectives, e.g. carpentered environment and Ames room
IDA	Nature and nurture, e.g. Gibson and Walk (1960) showed depth perception innate and thus direct but also indirect
AO2	Limitations, top-down can't explain accuracy and bottom up can't explain effects of experience, e.g. Palmer (1975) objects in kitchen
IDA	Contrast approaches, reconciled in terms of (1) visual conditions, (2) ventral and dorsal streams

Model answer

Outline and evaluate Gibson's bottom-up/direct theory of perception. (8 marks + 16 marks)

One of the main ideas of Gibson's direct theory of perception is the optic flow. As you move forward, objects in front of you remain stationary whereas objects to the side flow past, the further away the faster the flow. This means you receive information about the environment directly from the images gathered by the eye without having to apply experience to interpret it. Movement is generally important in perception because we receive perceptual information as we move around the world.

Gibson's theory has been called an ecological theory because, according to Gibson, perceptual information is produced by the environment and that rich array is all we need to explain perception. One example is texture gradient – objects that are further away have a finer texture. This means that we can perceive depth/distance just from the visual information that reaches the eye.

Texture gradient is an example of an invariant, i.e. an aspect of the environment that doesn't change as we move about (whereas the optic flow does). Another example of an invariant that provides important perceptual information is the horizon–ratio relation – the proportion of an object above and below the horizon line is constant for objects of the same size standing on the same ground.

Resonance and affordance are also important concepts in Gibson's theory. Resonance refers to the idea that animals can 'pick up' perceptual information from the environment in the same way that a radio picks up radio waves. Affordance describes how the meaning of an object is directly perceived and provides the object's 'action potential', i.e. how it can be used. For example a handle looks like something to be grasped, i.e. it 'affords grasping'.

Gibson's theory is supported by the concept of biological motion, the ability to perceive movement directly from a changing array of dots. If small lights are placed on a moving body, observers can see movement as the array of lights changes. Even young babies (Fox and Daniel, 1982) and animals (Blake, 1993) respond appropriately when shown changing dots, which suggests this is an innate ability.

The theory is also supported by time-to-contact studies where animals/humans have to judge the response to be made when approaching an object. It can be seen in long jumpers who change stride length as they approach take-off (Lee *et al.*, 1982) and also in gannets who close their wings at a constant time when they are making a vertical dive into water (Lee, 1980). This judgment involves direct perception.

Further research support comes from studies which show that movement does affect perception. For example, Wraga *et al.* (2000) showed that the Müller-Lyer illusion disappeared when participants walked around a three-dimensional (3D) version. This meant that movement prevents the illusion which is perceived when the lines are viewed in two dimensions, and shows how movement is part of perception.

Visual illusions generally are used to support the indirect approach because, according to that view, perception is based on expectations which can be misapplied. However, Gibson's direct approach has also been used to explain visual illusions. For example, the Ames room illusion has been explained in terms of top-down processing (expectations about rectangular rooms) but could also be explained in terms of horizon–ratio relation because the illusion persists even without walls and floor. This shows that visual illusions may be understood within the bottom-up (direct) approach.

The tension between the direct and indirect approach in some ways reflects the nature–nurture debate. The direct approach takes the nature side of the debate, saying our perception is innate and not acquired through experience. For example, Gibson and Walk (1960) used the visual cliff apparatus to show that animals naturally develop depth perception around the time they are mobile – not through experience but because of a maturing innate system.

There are real-world applications of the direct approach, for example in designing autonomous robots that can learn about the meaning of objects in their environment. This is based on understanding of how people use perception to learn about objects in the world and use them appropriately.

We should also consider some limitations of the direct approach. For example, it cannot explain research on the effects of experience, such as Palmer (1975) demonstrated when showing people certain objects in different contexts. The context lets them to 'see' the objects differently.

It may be possible to reconcile the two different approaches. First of all the direct approach may explain perception in good visual conditions (e.g. daylight) whereas the indirect approach explains perception in ambiguous visual conditions. Second, the two approaches may reflect physiological differences in the perceptual system. The ventral stream deals with object recognition (top-down) whereas the dorsal stream deals with spatial/movement perception (bottom-up).

There is no need to begin an essay with a general introduction, just plunge straight in.

There is also no need to define any of the terms in the question, such as explaining what a bottom-up theory is.

Such introductions and definitions attract no credit.

Notice how each paragraph of this essay equates to one point in the plan. If each paragraph is about 50–60 words you should end up with the right length answer, appropriately proportioned with AO1 and AO2.

This essay could have been written with the AO2 interspersed with the AO1 but it is perhaps clearer for you, and clearer for the examiner reading your essay, to separate AO1 and AO2 in the way done here. This helps you keep an eye on whether you have supplied the right amounts of AO1 and AO2.

In this essay names and dates of researchers have been included. Neither are required but are a good way to provide detail and elaboration.

Try to start each AO2 paragraph with a lead-in sentence that makes it clear that this paragraph is an evaluation point. In your exam answer you won't be able to shade the AO2 material as we have done here but you need to make it obvious to the examiner that this paragraph is evaluation.

The total number of words in this essay is 780, split appropriately between AO1 (36%) and AO2 (64%).

Division 2 The development of perception Answer plans

Answer plan 1

Discuss the development of depth/distance perception. (8 marks + 16 marks)

Depth/distance perception

AO1	Infants – monocular cues, e.g. visual cliff (Gibson and Walk, 1960), motion parallax (Hofsten *et al.*, 1992)
AO2	Criticisms of visual cliff studies, e.g. age of infants. However, Campos *et al.* (1978) did find response in 2 month olds
AO2	Further support from young animals (Gibson and Walk, 1960)
AO1	Infants – binocular cues, e.g. Bower *et al.* (1970)
IDA	Nature vs nurture, not all perceptual processes innate, e.g perceptual completion not in two month olds (Ghim, 1990)
AO2	Methodological problems working with infants
AO1	Cross-cultural – pictorial clues, e.g. Hudson (1960)
IDA	Supports nurture approach because experience determines perceptual abilities
AO2	More recent research, e.g. Page (1970) found Zulus could interpret depth cues
AO1	Cross-cultural, Jahoda and McGurk (1974)
AO2	Methodological problems with infants and cross-cultural research
IDA	Cultural biases – imposed etics and assumption that perception same in all people (e.g. retinal pigmentation – Berry, 1971)

DIY

Work out your own plan for these questions and then write your answers.

(a) Explain the development of depth/distance perception. (4 marks)

(b) Discuss the development of visual constancies. (4 marks + 16 marks)

Part (a) Depth/distance perception

AO1	
AO1	

Part (b) Visual constancies

AO1	
AO1	
AO2	
AO2	
AO2	
AO2	
AO2	
AO2 or IDA	
AO2 or IDA	
AO2 or IDA	

Answer plan 2

(a) Outline **two or more** examples of visual constancies. (8 marks)

(b) Evaluate research into perceptual development, including infant and cross-cultural studies. (16 marks)

Part (a) Visual constancy

AO1	Shape constancy, e.g. Bower (1966) two month infants preferred slanted square even with changed retinal image
AO1	Also Allport and Pettigrew (1957) trapezoid illusion seen by urban not rural Zulus
AO1	Size constancy, e.g. Slater *et al.* (1990) newborn infants responded to new retinal image
AO1	Segall *et al.* (1963), Zulus couldn't 'see' Müller-Lyer illusion

Part (b) Perceptual development

IDA	Implications for nature–nurture debate
AO2	Some cross-cultural research doesn't support nurture, e.g. Jahoda and McGurk (1974)
AO2	Methodological problems in cross-cultural research
IDA	Imposed etics create cultural bias
AO2	Cross-cultural research assumes perception same in all people (e.g. retinal pigmentation – Berry, 1971)
AO2	Some infant research doesn't support nature, e.g. perceptual completion not in two month olds (Ghim, 1990)
AO2	Methodological problems working with infants
IDA	Nature–nurture issue – can't always tell whether a behaviour is due to an innate process

Answer plan 3

Outline and evaluate **two or more** infant studies of perceptual development. (8 marks + 16 marks)

Infant studies

AO1	Monocular cues, e,g. visual cliff (Gibson and Walk, 1960), motion parallax (Hofsten *et al.*, 1992)
AO1	Binocular cues, e.g. Bower *et al.* (1970)
AO1	Shape constancy, e.g. Bower (1966) two-month-old infants preferred slanted square even with changed retinal image
AO1	Size constancy, e.g. Slater *et al.* (1990) newborn infants responded to new retinal image
AO2	Criticisms of visual cliff studies, e.g. age of infants. However, Campos *et al.* (1978) response in 2 month olds
AO2	Support from young animals (Gibson and Walk, 1960)
AO2	Contrast with cross-cultural research, e.g. Hudson (1960) which shows experience matters
AO2	Bower, contrast with cross-cultural research, e.g. Allport and Pettigrew (1957) trapezoid window, shape constancy learned
AO2	Slater *et al.* supported by cross-cultural research, e.g. Jahoda and McGurk (1974) shows
AO2	Methodological problems working with infants
IDA	Nature vs nurture, not all perceptual processes innate, e.g perceptual completion not in two month olds (Ghim, 1990)
IDA	Nature–nurture issue – can't always tell whether a behaviour is due to an innate process

(a) Outline **two or more** examples of visual constancies. (8 marks)

One example is shape constancy, the ability to see the same shape (such as a rectangular table) even though the retinal image is distorted. Bower (1966) worked with infants aged two months who were conditioned by being rewarded to prefer a rectangle slanted at 45 degrees. They were then shown lots of different shapes and preferred the original shape even when the retinal image was different, showing shape constancy at an early age.

Shape constancy has also been demonstrated in cross-cultural research. For example Allport and Pettigrew (1957) used the trapezoid window illusion (window appears to swing back and forth instead of around because it is shaped like a trapezium). Zulus who live in rural areas without windows could not 'see' the trapezoid window illusion. Urban Zulus could see the illusion, suggesting that experience leads to shape constancy.

A second example of a visual constancy is size constancy, where an object looks the same size despite different retinal images due to distance. Slater *et al.* (1990) worked with newborn infants. The infants were habituated to certain sized cubes so these cubes should be less interesting to them. When shown two cubes that had the same retinal size but one was more distant, they still responded to the new one thus showing size constancy.

Size constancy has also been demonstrated in cross-cultural research. For example Segall *et al.* (1963) found Zulus were less susceptible to the Müller-Lyer illusion (line with outward fins looks longer). The illusion may be due to size constancy – experience with edges of rooms and buildings leads to seeing the outward fin line as more distant and therefore potentially bigger. Zulus would lack this experience because they lived in circular huts (not a carpentered environment). Therefore, their lack of experience means that this kind of size constancy had not developed.

In part (a) there is no requirement for any IDA points because these are only credited as part of evaluation (AO2).

The key criteria for AO1 are detail and breadth. Four studies are covered here (good breadth) and each is given in plentiful detail (good depth).

Trying to cover any more studies would result in less depth and therefore a lower mark because there is not a balance between depth and breadth.

(b) Evaluate research into perceptual development, including infant and cross-cultural studies. (16 marks)

The research described in part (a) relates to the nature–nurture debate. It appears to support both nature and nurture. The study by Bower implies that knowledge of shape constancy is innate whereas the research by Allport and Pettigrew implies that it is gained through experience. The same is true of the second two studies on shape constancy.

Implications count as AO2 – this first AO2 point looks at the implications of the research for the nature–nurture debate.

In general the cross-cultural studies support the nurture approach. However, this is not true of all cross-cultural studies. For example, Jahoda and McGurk (1974) tested children from Ghana and Scotland and found that although all children displayed some ability to interpret depth cues in pictures, children got better at this as they got older and Scottish children did better than Ghanian children. This shows that experience does matter.

There are problems with cross-cultural research. For example, participants and investigators, who rely on translators, may not understand each other. There is also the fact that these are natural experiments where the IV (experience) was not manipulated by the researcher and therefore we cannot claim the IV has caused the change in the DV (perception).

There is also the problem of imposed etics which lead to a cultural bias. Using tests or procedures developed in one country/culture may not be valid in the other culture, such as using the trapezoid illusion to test people unaccustomed to 3D pictures which therefore might not make sense to them. The bias is that we assume all people respond the same.

The issue of why imposed etics lead to cultural bias is explained clearly, making this an effective IDA point.

Notice also how the IDA point is contextualised. It is not just a general point about imposed etics but is related specifically to visual constancy.

These studies are all conducted assuming that the physical process of perception is the same in all people. However, the pigmentation of the retina has been found to vary with skin colour and is linked to difficulties in perceiving edges of objects (retinal pigmentation hypothesis). High pigmentation, found in African people, could explain why they are less likely to 'see' certain visual illusions.

Always follow the three-point rule as done here – state your point, provide evidence and explain the point you are making (so what?). The three point rule is explained on page 5.

Infant research generally supports the nature perspective but this is not true of all infant studies. For example, perceptual completion is not found in two month olds (Ghim, 1990). Perceptual completion involves bridging the gaps in a retinal image. This suggests that infants have some innate abilities but also some are gained through experience.

A major criticism of the research described in part (a) relates to those studies that used infants and such research has methodological problems. For example, the habituation technique assumes that an infant will express surprise at a novel object. This may be a false assumption. It is also possible that infants are responding to subtle cues from the researcher (investigator bias), or might be sleepy and that's why they fail to show interest rather than because they were habituated.

When considering evidence for nature or nurture it is not always easy to decide what counts as an innate process (nature). For example, just because a process is present at birth does not mean it is innate – an infant has experiences in the womb and may learn to coordinate some sensorimotor processes. Equally, just because an ability appears later in development it doesn't necessarily mean it is due to learning (nurture) because some innate abilities only appear when the nervous system is sufficiently developed.

A total word length of 824 words, with 303 words of AO1 and 521 words of AO2.

Although the content of part (a) is a bit overlong, the length of part (b) is perfectly appropriate – the danger in writing too much AO1 is leaving insufficient time for AO2 which should be a minimum of 400 words.

Division 3 Face recognition and visual agnosias Answer plans

Answer plan 1
Discuss research into face recognition. (8 marks + 16 marks)

Face recognition

AO1	Bruce and Young's theory (1986) is a serial model
AO1	Step 1 – structural encoding
AO1	Step 2 – either familiar faces (FRUs, PIN, NRU) or facial expression (expression, facial speech, directed visual)
AO1	Step 3 – cognitive system
AO2	Supporting research, e.g. Young *et al.* (1985) diary study
AO2	Supporting research from prosopagnosics who can decode emotional expressions but not faces (Groome, 2006)
AO2	Not supporting research, e.g. Stanhope and Cohen (1993) names not retrieved even with PIN information
AO2	Strengths – generates precise predictions which can be tested, distinguishes familiar/unfamiliar face processing
AO2	Limitations – components unclear, e.g. unfamiliar face processing and cognitive system
AO2	Updated model – Burton and Bruce (1993) connectionist IAC model, matches nervous system behaviour
IDA	Real-world application – identikits, facial biometric systems
AO2	Faces are special, e.g. FFA active (Kanwisher and Yovel, 2006), or aren't special, e.g. FFA active for expert identification (Gauthier *et al.*, 2000)

DIY

Work out your own plan for these questions and then write your answers.

(a) Outline and evaluate Bruce and Young's theory of face recognition. (4 marks + 8 marks)

(b) Outline and evaluate **one or more** explanations of prosopagnosia. (4 marks + 8 marks)

Part (a) Bruce and Young

AO1	
AO1	
AO2	
AO2	
AO2	
AO2 or IDA	

Part (b) Explanations of prosopagnosia

AO1	
AO1	
AO2	
AO2	
AO2	
AO2 or IDA	

Answer plan 2
Outline and evaluate **one or more** explanations of visual agnosias. (8 marks + 16 marks)

Visual agnosias

AO1	Different modules in the brain, e.g. faces, not faces; or for living and non-living things (Warrington and Shallice, 1984)
AO1	Fusiform face area (FFA) active when processing faces (e.g. Sergent *et al.*, 1992)
AO1	Agnosias aren't separate but on a continuum from configural to holistic processes (Farah, 1991)
AO1	A disconnection between perception and memory for face (Takahasi *et al.*, 1995)
AO2	Non-living things may be more familiar, when familiarity controlled there was no difference
AO2	Different models supported by infant research, e.g. Fantz (1961) preference for faces not same features mixed up
AO2	Some research challenges FFA as unique to faces, e.g. Gauthier *et al.* (2000) using car experts and Greebles
AO2	Continuum concept challenged, HJA – evidence of holistic and configural processing (Groome, 2006; Boulsen and Humphreys, 2002)
AO2	Based on case studies of abnormal individuals, lack validity because of uniqueness and contradictions
AO2	Contradictions in research may be due to lack of reliability in testing procedures
IDA	Ethics issues – confidentiality and intensive testing
IDA	Real-world application, relief for sufferers

Answer plan 3
(a) Outline **two or more** case studies of prosopagnosia. (4 marks)
(b) Discuss **one or more** explanations of prosopagnosia. (4 marks + 16 marks)

Part (a) Case studies

AO1	HJA (Riddoch *et al.*, 2003) individual features OK but not faces, copy but not name objects, search for letter T poor
AO1	VA (De Renzi and di Pellegrino,1998) recognised objects but not naming famous faces unless given names

Part (b) Explanations

AO1	Different modules in the brain, e.g. fusiform face area (FFA)
AO1	Subset of object recognition, continuum from configural to holistic processes (Farah, 1991)
AO2	Different models supported by infant research, e.g. Fantz (1961) preference for faces not same features mixed up
AO2	Some research challenges FFA as unique to faces, e.g. Gauthier *et al.* (2000) using car experts and Greebles
AO2	Continuum concept challenged, HJA – evidence of holistic and configural processing (Groome, 2006; Boulsen and Humphreys, 2002)
AO2	Alternative explanation – a disconnection between perception and memory for face (Takahasi *et al.*, 1995)
AO2	Based on case studies, lack validity because of contradictions, e.g. famers and cows (Bruyer *et al.*, 1983, and Assal *et al.*, 1984)
AO2	Contradictions in research may be due to lack of reliability in testing procedures
IDA	Ethics issues – confidentiality and intensive testing
IDA	Real-world application, relief for sufferers

Model answer

(a) Outline **two or more** case studies of prosopagnosia. (4 marks)

One case study looked at a man referred to as HJA who suffered brain damage as a result of a stroke (Riddoch *et al.*, 2003). HJA experienced agnosia generally but also prosopaganosia specifically. He also couldn't recognise faces but could recognise individual features of a face. He was able to copy and match objects but couldn't name them.

De Renzi and di Pellegrino (1998) studied VA who could recognise objects but was poor at naming famous faces from pictures. However, VA could match names of famous people to their photographs. VA probably did this by imagining the faces of famous people when presented with their names and then comparing this to the faces he was shown – so he wasn't really recognising the faces.

Coverage of just two detailed studies is sufficient for full marks in this section – one study would count as partial performance and would limit the marks given.

Both case studies are of prosopagnosics but including details of other disorders experienced is acceptable.

Part (a) is 123 words, just right for 4 marks worth (ideal range should be 100–120 words).

(b) Discuss **one or more** explanations of prosopagnosia. (4 marks + 16 marks)

One explanation for prosopagnosia is that there are different modules in the brain for different kinds of tasks. Face recognition may be associated with one particular region of the brain, the fusiform face area (FFA). This has found to be active when a person is processing faces but not when recognising other objects.

Another explanation is that face recognition is just a subset of object recognition generally. Farah (1991) proposed that all agnosias result from the disruption of two separate processes which lie on a continuum: (1) decoding structure (feature analysis, a kind of configural process) and (2) computing relationships among the parts (a holistic process).

It is vital to ensure that the AO1 component of part (b) is not too long as there are only 4 marks available.

The different modules explanation is supported by research with infants. For example, Fantz (1961) demonstrated that babies as young as four days old show a preference for a schematic face rather than the same features all jumbled up (or the same amount of dark and light). This shows that it is the unique configuration of a face rather than a complex pattern which is preferred.

Findings related to the FFA have not all supported unique face processing. For example, Gauthier *et al.* (2000) found that the FFA was also active when people who were experts were asked to distinguish between different types of birds or different types of car. It was also active if they were trained to be experts in distinguishing between computer-generated nonsense figures called Greebles.

Farah's concept of a continuum has not been supported by all research. For example, there is evidence from the case study of HJA that he showed evidence of both holistic and configural processing (Groome, 2006; Boutsen and Humphreys, 2002). According to the continuum model he should not have had the general problems he did.

An alternative suggestion from Takahashi *et al.* (1995) is that prosopagnosia might result from a disconnection between perception and memory for faces. This would explain why prosopagnosia affects the recognition of familiar faces in particular.

This linking sentence is crucial in order to attract credit for the AO2 point. If the paragraph just criticised case studies without explaining the link to the explanations its relevance would be marginal.

One problem with all of these explanations is that they tend to be based on case studies of abnormal people. Such research may lack validity because the studies are of unique individuals and often their abilities appear contradictory. For example one case study of a farmer found he couldn't recognise faces but could recognise his cows whereas another study found a farmer with prospagnoosia who couldn't recognise his cows (Bruyer *et al.*, 1983; Assal *et al.*, 1984).

The contradictions in research may be because it is difficult to reliably test any individual to be certain what they can and cannot do. Different researchers use different methods and patients may lack motivation to perform when tested (some may be quite depressed because of their condition which may mask their true abilities).

This paragraph is related to the previous paragraph but it is helpful to start a new paragraph to signal that it is a stand-alone AO2 point and thus should be credited as such.

There are also important ethical issues related to the research. First there is the matter of confidentiality, which is why only initials are used. Second there are concerns about psychological harm because patients may be subjected to intensive testing to fully establish what they can or can't do, and this continues for many years.

There are real-world applications for this research because it potentially could help people suffering from prosopagnosia. However, as yet there are no suggested cures though simply realising that you suffer from a known disorder may help. One woman reported that it came as a relief to find out that the problems she encountered weren't imaginary.

If you are making an IDA point it helps to make this very clear to the examiner by beginning the paragraph with an IDA lead-in sentence.

In part (b) the AO1 content is also within the appropriate range for 4 marks (106 words). The AO2 content is 458 words, again the right amount (400–480 words is the expected range).

Answer for you to mark

See pages 170–1 for examiner's comments.

Question

Discuss the development of perceptual abilities, including infant and cross-cultural studies. (8 marks + 16 marks)

Student answer

❶ A number of studies have been conducted which look at the development of perceptual abilities. Both infant and cross-cultural studies have been used to understand the development of these processes and in this essay I will look at a few of them.

❷ The first study I will examine is one by Gibson and Walk. They studied 36 six-month-old infants. The infants were placed on an apparatus which consisted of a glass surface with a checked pattern underneath which was made to look deeper on one side than the other, so it was if they were sitting on a cliff edge. If the babies were encouraged to crawl on to the deep side by their mothers they became very distressed but were not distressed if they crawled on to the apparently shallow side. This suggests that the development of depth perception is innate.

❸ Another study by Campos used a similar method to Gibson and Walk but this time they tested the heart rates of the infants to see how distressed they really were, and they also used two-month-old infants. The infants couldn't crawl themselves so they were wheeled across the cliff edge. They did show a slower heart rate, indicating interest but not distress, but it does show they could distinguish between both sides and again indicates that depth perception is innate. There were ethical issues that should be considered in this research because distress was caused to the babies.

❹ Another study of infant behaviour this time looked at the development of visual constancy. Bower showed infants a square and then showed them the square from a different angle so that it looked like a trapezium. This meant the visual image would be new to them and therefore if they did see it as new they should show more interest, and this would show they were not capable of visual constancy. They did show more interest.

❺ Slater also conducted some research on the development of visual constancies. Infants were shown cubes of different sizes. They were then shown two cubes side by side which looked the same size (same retinal image) but one was actually further away. The infants looked longer at the cube they were not familiar with. This suggests that the infants could tell the difference between cubes of different sizes.

❻ One cross-cultural study looked at perception of the trapezoid window illusion in Zulus. They are shown a trapezoidal window rotating which appears to reverse because it doesn't behave like a window should. The study found that Zulus who lived in rural areas did not see the illusion presumably because they did not have experience with rectangular windows whereas Zulus who lived in cities did see the illusion. They also found that Zulus were less affected by the Müller-Lyer illusion, possibly because they have less experience of learning depth cues in a rectangular world because their huts are circular and therefore they have less experience of straight lines. In such cross-cultural studies one problem is generalising this to other situations because there may be cultural bias.

❼ A study by Jahoda and McGurk tested children from Africa and Western children. The children were shown 2D images and asked to make a 3D model of what the image represented. The Western children coped better with making 3D models which suggests that it is Western culture that is responsible, i.e. it is their experience of buildings etc which helps us perceive depth cues whilst children from Africa have not learned to interpret these cues.

(577 words)

AO1 mark scheme

The key requirement is that studies must be described accurately.

Answers that only include either infant OR cross-cultural studies would count as partial performance and would receive a maximum of 6 marks.

Studies of non-human animals are acceptable as an example of infant perception.

There is no requirement to cover studies of depth perception as well as visual constancies and a focus on one or the other could still receive full marks.

8 marks is about 200–240 words.

Comments and marks for AO1

Guidance on marking is given on pages 6–11.

Mark	Knowledge and understanding	Range of material	Accuracy	Organisation and structure
8–7	Accurate and well-detailed	Good range	Depth and breadth	Coherent
6–5	Generally accurate and reasonably detailed	Range	Depth and/or breadth	Reasonably coherent
4–3	Basic, relatively superficial	Restricted		Basic
2–1	Rudimentary and may be muddled and/or inaccurate	Very brief or largely irrelevant		Lacking
0	No creditworthy material			

Tick the terms you think apply to the student's answer.

The **AO1** mark I would give is ☐

AO2 mark scheme

One approach to evaluation might be to relate the studies described to the nature/nurture debate, discussing the implications of each study to nature and/or nurture explanations of the development of perception.

Evaluation marks might also be gained through a consideration of methodological weaknesses or strengths of the studies described, such as problems conducting infant or cross-cultural research (including cultural bias).

Partial performance also applies to the AO2 mark – a maximum of 10 marks for answers that evaluate only infant or cross-cultural studies.

16 marks is about 400-480 words.

Comments and marks for AO2

Mark	Analysis and understanding	Focus	Elaboration	Line of argument	Issues/debates/ approaches	Quality of written communication
16–13	Sound	Well focused	Coherent	Clear	Used effectively	Fluent, effective use of terms
12–9	Reasonable	Generally focused	Reasonable	Evident	Reasonably effective	Clear, appropriate
8–5	Basic, superficial	Sometimes focused	Some evidence		Superficial reference	Lacks clarity, limited use of terms
4–1	Rudimentary, limited understanding	Weak, muddled and incomplete	Not effective	May be mainly irrelevant	Absent or muddled/ inaccurate	Often unconnected assertions, errors
0	No creditworthy material					

The **AO2** mark I would give is ☐

Chapter 3 Relationships

There have been changes to the specification from September 2011 – therefore the updated specification details here are slightly different to those in some editions of the *A2 Complete Companion*.

Division 1

The formation, maintenance and breakdown of romantic relationships

- **Theories of the formation, maintenance and breakdown of romantic relationships: for example, reward/need satisfaction, social exchange theory**

Possible exam questions for this division

Question	Comment
Discuss **two or more** theories of romantic relationships. (8 marks + 16 marks)	The term 'discuss' indicates that both AO1 and AO2 are required (and are worth 8 marks and 16 marks respectively). You are required to cover at least two theories (but see note below) and these should relate to 'romantic' relationships rather than other relationships, such as parent–child relationships or friendships.
Discuss **two or more** theories of the formation of romantic relationships. (8 marks + 16 marks)	'Two or more' does not indicate that more theories equals higher marks. Students often stretch themselves too thinly by trying to cover too many theories and end up with an answer that lacks depth, and so earns fewer marks. Be careful not to include too much AO1 here, and always remember the one-third AO1, two-thirds AO2 rule. This question, unlike the first one, requires you to focus only on the formation of relationships. Students often find it difficult to focus on just one aspect but the specification does identify formation, maintenance and breakdown separately so be prepared.
(a) Outline **one** theory of the formation of relationships (e.g. reward/need satisfaction). (8 marks) (b) Evaluate the theory outlined in part (a) in terms of relevant research evidence. (16 marks)	Part (a) of this question requires just one theory, so other theories would not receive credit. The example is not prescriptive, so you can choose your own, provided it is concerned with the 'formation' of relationships. In part (b) you should do more than just *describe* research evidence. You should also show how this research supports, challenges or in some other way illustrates the principles of your chosen theory. The golden rule here is 'Make it explicit'.
(a) Outline and evaluate **one** theory of the breakdown of romantic relationships. (4 marks + 8 marks) (b) Outline and evaluate the influence of culture on romantic relationships. (4 marks + 8 marks)	Part (a) is a mini-essay requiring both AO1 and AO2 content in the one-third/two-thirds format. Note that this only requires coverage of one theory and this must be a theory (e.g. Rollie and Duck) concerned with the *breakdown* of relationships. Part (b) is also a mini-essay requiring AO1 and AO2 in the same proportions as in part (a). However, this is on a slightly different topic (the influence of culture). Questions often adopt this 'modular' approach, so be flexible and prepared!
(a) Outline the influence of childhood on adult relationships. (4 marks) (b) Outline and evaluate **one** theory of the maintenance of relationships. (4 marks + 16 marks)	Questions may sometimes sample across different divisions (as here and above). Part (a) of this question requires a brief AO1 account of the influence of childhood on adult relationships (in about 100–200 words). Part (b) requires a mini-essay on one theory of the maintenance of relationships (e.g. social exchange theory), but note the mark division of 4 and 16, so the AO2 content should be four times the length of the AO1 content. See model answer on page 35.
Discuss **one** theory of the maintenance of romantic relationships and **one** theory of the breakdown of romantic relationships. (8 marks + 16 marks)	This question specifies *one* theory of the maintenance of romantic relationships and *one* theory of the breakdown of romantic relationships. Although covering only one of these theories would amount to partial performance (and would thus lose marks), there is no need to cover both in the same degree of detail (within reason). See student answer on page 40.

Division 2

Evolutionary explanations of human reproductive behaviour

- **The relationship between sexual selection and human reproductive behaviour**
- **Sex differences in parental investments**

Possible exam questions for this division

Question	Comment
Discuss the relationship between sexual selection and human reproductive behaviour. (8 marks + 16 marks)	The most obvious way to tackle this question is by looking at sexual selection and the origins of mate choice. Evaluation could then be in terms of research evidence and criticisms of the evolutionary approach to reproductive behaviour, with IDA offering alterative perspectives as a counterpoint. You must restrict yourself to *human* reproductive behaviour, so peacocks are only relevant as research support.

(a) Outline the relationship between sexual selection and human reproductive behaviour. (4 marks) (b) Discuss sex differences in parental investment. (4 marks + 16 marks)	In part (a) of this question, there are only 4 marks available for the AO1 content, so only a brief outline description (perhaps of selected 'highlights' of this explanation) is required in about 100–120 words. Part (b) requires a short AO1 account of sex differences in maternal and paternal investment (100–120 words), and a much lengthier (400–480 words) AO2 evaluation (perhaps in terms of research evidence, consequences or alternative perspectives). Both maternal and paternal investment must be covered in order to fulfil the requirement to discuss sex differences.
(a) Outline and evaluate the relationship between sexual selection and human reproductive behaviour. (4 marks + 8 marks) (b) Discuss sex differences in parental investment. (4 marks + 8 marks)	The first part of this question emphasises the need for flexibility in your exam preparation. The first question in this division called for a full 24-mark answer, but this part requires half that material, which could be achieved with a more selective focus or perhaps a less-detailed account of the same material. Be prepared! Part (b) requires the same amount of AO1 as in the previous question, but this time just half the amount of AO2. You should always have a 4 and 8 mark AO1 version of each topic, and an 8 and 16 AO2 version for that topic. See model answer on page 37.
Discuss sex differences in human parental investment. (8 marks + 16 marks)	As this question asks for sex differences, it is important that you do more than just detail maternal and paternal investment. There should be an attempt to consider the ways in which the investment of males and females differs, and the consequences of this differential parental investment. Note that this is restricted to human investment.
'Males invest less in any reproduction than females, and this has a profound impact on their behaviour.' Discuss sex differences in parental investment in humans. (8 marks + 16 marks)	There is a lesson here, and that is to answer the question, not the quotation. If you don't find the quotation particularly helpful, then just ignore it and focus your attention on the actual question instead. The answer required is the same as in the previous question, despite the fact this sort of question can easily catch out students. They might not recognise what it is asking for. They might not recognise they focus too much on the quotation and not enough on the question. However, this is actually a very friendly general question, because you could answer it in terms of sexual selection *or* parental investment, or both (although that might be a little ambitious).

Division 3
Effects of early experience and culture on adult relationships

- **The influence of childhood on adult relationships**
- **The influence of culture on romantic relationships**

Possible exam questions for this division

Describe and evauate the influence of childhood experiences on adult relationships. (8 marks + 16 marks)	There are different ways in which this question can be addressed, e.g. parent–child relationships (including attachment styles) and interactions with peers. Adolescence can be relevant to this question, but any answer should not concentrate on adolescence alone.
(a) Outline and evaluate the influence of childhood on adult relationships. (4 marks + 8 marks) (b) Outline and evaluate the influence of culture on romantic relationships. (4 marks + 8 marks)	Part (a) requires a more concise version of the answer to the previous question. Remember that a more concise version can involve either less detail (depth) or less breadth. If adopting the former approach, be careful not to make your answer too superficial. Part (b) has the same requirement but this time on a different topic – the influence of culture. Choosing what will be AO1 and AO2 takes practice and preparation here.
Discuss the influence of culture on romantic relationships. (8 marks + 16 marks)	When deciding what is going to be your AO2 content in any answer, and particularly here, it is a good idea to make it explicitly AO2 rather than just descriptive. To achieve this it is advisable to use lead-in phrases, such as 'there is a cultural bias in cross-cultural research'. See model answer on page 39.
'Many psychologists believe that an individual's childhood experiences act as a "blueprint for their adult relationships".' Discuss the influence of childhood on the development of subsequent adult relationships. (8 marks + 16 marks)	Questions occasionally include a quotation, but these are merely designed to stimulate your thought processes – however, you are answering the question and not the quotation so you should not worry about any subtleties in the quotation. Quotation apart, this question is the same as the first one in this division, and requires the familiar one-third/two-thirds proportion of AO1 and AO2. As a rough guide this means 220–240 words of AO1 and 400–480 words of AO2.
(a) Outline **one** way in which culture influences the development of romantic relationships. (4 marks) (b) Outline and evaluate the influence of childhood on adult relationships. (4 marks + 16 marks)	Part (a) of this question has a very specific requirement, i.e. an outline of one way in which culture influences relationships. This could be in terms of the individualism/collectivism distinction, voluntary, non-voluntary relationships, the importance of local rules and so on. Part (b) is essentially the same question as the opening question in this division. However, it needs half the AO1 content – it is vital to remember the mark division when planning any response.
Discuss the effects of early experience and culture on adult relationships. (8 marks + 16 marks)	Although not a likely question, this is certainly possible and could be answered using the same approach as outlined in the second question in this division. However, because these are not two separate part questions with separate mark divisions, this means that the two topics do not have to be evenly balanced.

Division 1 The formation, maintenance and breakdown of romantic relationships

Answer plans

Answer plan 1

(a) Outline **one** theory of the formation of relationships (e.g. reward/need satisfaction). (8 marks)

(b) Evaluate the theory outlined in part (a) in terms of relevant research evidence. (16 marks)

Part (a) Formation of relationships

AO1	We are attracted to people who provide direct reinforcement (operant conditioning)
AO1	This creates positive feelings (e.g. happiness, security)
AO1	We are attracted to people who are associated with pleasant events (classical conditioning)
AO1	They acquire positive value because of this association

Part (b) Evaluation

AO2	Griffitt and Guay (1969) support for direct reinforcement
AO2	Griffitt and Guay also support role of indirect reinforcement
AO2	Cate *et al.* (1982) reward level most important in determining relationship satisfaction
AO2	Hays (1985) *giving* rewards also linked to satisfaction
AO2	Lehr and Geher (2006) supported importance of reciprocal attraction in determining formation of relationships
IDA	Physiological approach – romantic love produces activation in brain reward circuits (Aron *et al.*, 2005)
IDA	Evolutionary reason for this love/brain reward association
IDA	Cultural bias – culture determines importance of rewards

DIY

Work out your own plan for this question and then write your answer.

Discuss **one** theory of the maintenance of romantic relationships and **one** theory of the breakdown of romantic relationships. (8 marks + 16 marks)

Maintenance of romantic relationships

AO1	
AO1	
AO2	
AO2	
AO2	
AO2 or IDA	

Breakdown of romantic relationships

AO1	
AO1	
AO2	
AO2	
AO2	
AO2 or IDA	

Answer plan 2

Discuss **two or more** theories of the formation of romantic relationships. (8 marks + 16 marks)

Theory 1: Reward/need satisfaction theory

AO1	We are attracted to people who provide direct reinforcement (operant conditioning)
AO1	We are attracted to people who are associated with pleasant events (classical conditioning)
AO2	Griffitt and Guay (1969) provide support for direct reinforcement and for indirect reinforcement
AO2	Cate *et al.* (1982) reward level most important in determining relationship satisfaction
AO2	Hays (1985) giving rewards also linked to satisfaction
IDA	Physiological approach – romantic love produces activation in brain reward circuits (Aron *et al.*, 2005)

Theory 2: Similarity

AO1	We are attracted to individuals with similar rather than dissimilar personalities and attitudes
AO1	Attitude alignment ensures similarity on important issues
AO2	Lehr and Geher (2006) supported importance of attitudinal similarity in liking of 'bogus stranger'
AO2	Similarity important because lessens chance of rejection and validates our own beliefs and attitudes
AO2	However, Rosenbaum (1986) claims dissimilarity more important in determining whether relationship will form
IDA	Dissimilarity-repulsion found to apply to different cultures suggesting it is a universal human characteristic

Answer plan 3

(a) Outline the influence of childhood on adult relationships. (4 marks)

(b) Outline and evaluate **one** theory of the maintenance of relationships. (4 marks + 16 marks)

Part (a) Influence of childhood

AO1	Early attachment style determines internal working model (Bowlby)
AO1	Children learn about relationships from their experiences with peers (Qualter and Munn, 2005)

Part (b) Maintenance of relationships

AO1	Social exchange theory – expectation that relationships will earn a 'profit' (i.e. rewards exceed costs incurred)
AO1	Relationships judged with reference to comparison levels (CL) and comparison level for alternatives (CLA)
AO2	CLA can explain why some women stay in abusive relationships (Rusbult and Martz, 1995)
AO2	Support for comparison levels idea (Simpson *et al.*, 1990)
AO2	But, equitable relationships more satisfactory than where one partner is over-benefitted (Stafford and Canary, 2006)
IDA	Real-world application, sexual deception part of exchange process (Marelich *et al.*, 2008) in intimate relationships
AO2	Theory criticised for ignoring social aspects of relationship
AO2	Men and women judge equity differently in marriages (Steil and Weltman, 1991), husband's career more important
AO2	Theories fail to predict outcome, inequity (underbenefit) only linked to divorce in women (DeMaris, 2007)
IDA	Cultural bias – exchange and equity may only apply to relationships in Western cultures (Moghaddam, 1998)

Model answer

(a) Outline the influence of childhood on adult relationships. (4 marks)

Bowlby claimed adult relationships are a continuation of early attachment styles, which create an internal working model of relationships. This leads the child to expect the same type of relationship (i.e. secure or insecure) in their adult relationships as they experienced in their relationship with their primary caregiver. Children may also learn appropriate behaviour toward others by modeling the behaviour of their primary caregiver, which guides their behaviour as adults.

Qualter and Munn (2005) suggest that children learn about relationships from their experiences with peers. Interactions with other children determine how the child thinks about him or herself, giving them a sense of their own value, and determining how they approach adult relationships (e.g. with confidence or with lowered expectations of being liked by others).

It is important to match the length of an answer to the number of marks available. You should have an 8 mark version on the influence of childhood on adult relationships but here must use only half of it (about 200–240 words).

Part (a) is 125 words, close to the appropriate range of 100–120 words for 4 marks..

(b) Outline and evaluate **one** theory of the maintenance of relationships. (4 marks + 16 marks)

Social exchange theory claims that in relationships, partners have the expectation that they will earn a 'profit', i.e. that the rewards gained from the relationship will be greater than the costs incurred. Commitment to a relationship is usually dependent on that relationship's profitability, with more profitable relationships being more durable and less likely to break down.

The comparison level (CL) is a way of judging the quality of the existing relationship against some standard. If the profitability of the existing relationship exceeds the CL, then the relationship is judged worthwhile. The individual may also develop a comparison level for alternatives (CLA). The individual may end the current relationship if the potential profitability of a new relationship is significantly higher than the profit level of the existing relationship.

Because part (a) was all AO1, that leaves just 4 more marks for AO1, and these have been addressed in the first part of the part (b) answer.

The idea of a CLA can explain why many women stay in abusive relationships. Rusbult and Martz (1995) claim that if investments are high (e.g. children, financial security) and potential alternatives are low (e.g. having nowhere to live or having no money to make it on their own), then a woman may consider staying in the abusive relationship to be more profitable than leaving it.

There is research support for the importance of comparison levels in relationships. Simpson *et al.*, (1990) found that people who were already in a relationship tended to give lower ratings of attractiveness to a member of the opposite sex than did people who were not already in a relationship. This suggests that new alternative relationships are judged as less profitable when an individual is committed to their existing partner.

However, the concept of social exchange appears to be an over-simplification of how real relationships are judged by individuals. Stafford and Canary (2006) found that marital satisfaction was lowest for individuals who considered themselves to be under-benefitted. However, those who considered themselves to be over-benefitted were less satisfied than those in more equitable relationships.

It is a good idea to write in paragraphs as it helps you to plan your answer as well keep an eye on the AO1/AO2 division. Each of these AO2 paragraphs equates to one point from the essay plan on the previous pages.

There are real-world applications. For example Marelich *et al.* (2008) has used the idea of social exchange to explain how sexual deception (e.g. appearing to be caring and/or committed) plays a key role the development of relationships. Potential profits for males included sexual intimacy and costs included guilt over the deception. For females, profits included approval and possible commitment from the male, and costs included unwanted sex or the threat of pregnancy.

Social exchange theory has been criticised for focusing only on the individual's perspective in a relationship, ignoring any social aspects of the relationship. These include the way in which partners communicate about events as well as the wider context of a relationship, e.g. within an extended family or social network. This theory suggests that individuals have only selfish concerns therefore may apply only to members of individualist cultures.

It is wise to make AO2 material look like AO2. This has been accomplished in these paragraphs by the use of lead-in phrases, such as 'Social exchange theory has been criticised…' and 'Research…has used the idea of social exchange to explain…'.

Research suggests that, although couples may prefer equitable relationships to profitable ones, men and women tend to judge the equity of a relationship differently. Steil and Weltman (1991) found that among working couples, both men and women tended to rate the husband's career as more important, yet this was not reversed when the woman earned more. The tendency for women, compared to men, to seek less for themselves in a relationship, makes equity less easy to judge.

A problem for exchange theory and its development, equity theory, is that they fail to predict whether real life relationships will be maintained or break down. DeMaris (2007) found that among 1,500 couples in the US, the only reliable indicator of divorce was a woman's sense of being under-benefitted. Other aspects of profitability or equity did not predict the likelihood of a relationship failing.

There is a cultural bias evident in this research. Moghaddam (1998) criticises the usefulness of 'economic' theories, such as social exchange or equity theory. He argues that these apply only to Western relationships, and even then to short-term relationships among individuals with high social mobility. This suggests that these theories do not represent a universal explanation of romantic relationships, therefore are culture-biased.

Part (b) has an appropriate distribution of AO1 (127 words) and AO2 (532 words).
For 4 marks there should be 100–120 words and for 16 marks 400–480 words.

Division 2 Evolutionary explanations of human reproductive behaviour

Answer plans

Answer plan 1
Discuss the relationship between sexual selection and human reproductive behaviour. (8 marks + 16 marks)

Sexual selection and reproductive behaviour	
AO1	Intrasexual selection – leads to competition and evolved preferences for casual sex and sex earlier in relationship
AO1	Intersexual selection – each sex has specific mate preferences, especially female choosiness
AO1	Men evolved greater desire for casual sex and sex earlier in relationship – no such evolutionary pressures for females
AO1	Sexual selection should favour a high level of choosiness in mate choice for both sexes, particularly among females
AO2	Logic of sexual selection ensures high-quality offspring
AO2	Short-term mating strategies adopted by men and women supported by Clarke and Hatfield (1989)
AO2	Female mate choice varies across menstrual cycle (Penton-Voak *et al.*, 1999)
AO2	An alternative explanation for male preference for younger women is based on social power (Kenrick *et al.*, 1996)
AO2	Research suffers problem of validity because restricted to mate preferences rather than real mate choices
AO2	However, study of actual marriages (Buss, 1989) confirmed predictions of sexual selection
AO2	Lap dancer study (Miller *et al.*, 2007) confirmed women most attractive while in fertile phase of menstrual cycle
IDA	Gender bias in short-term mating research – females may also profit from short-term mating (Greiling and Buss, 2000)

Work out your own plan for this question and then write your answer.
Discuss sex differences in parental investment. (8 marks + 16 marks)

Sex differences in parental investment	
AO1	
AO1	
AO1	
AO1	
AO2	
AO2	
AO2	
AO2	
AO2	
AO2 or IDA	
AO2 or IDA	
AO2 or IDA	

Answer plan 2
(a) Outline and evaluate the relationship between sexual selection and human reproductive behaviour. (4 marks + 8 marks)
(b) Discuss sex differences in parental investment. (4 marks + 8 marks)

Part (a) Sexual selection	
AO1	Intrasexual selection – leads to competition and evolved preferences for casual sex and sex earlier in relationship
AO1	Intersexual selection – each sex has mate preferences
AO2	Short-term mating strategies adopted by men and women supported by Clarke and Hatfield (1989)
AO2	Female mate choice varies across menstrual cycle (Penton-Voak *et al.*, 1999)
AO2	Low external validity – studies measure mate preference – Buss (1989) study of real marriages confirms predictions
IDA	Gender bias in short-term mating research – females also profit from short-term mating (Greiling and Buss, 2000)
Part (b) Sex differences in parental investment	
AO1	Larger investing sex will be more sexually discriminating, whereas sex with smaller investment competes for access
AO1	Female investment greater as eggs are more costly to produce than sperm and have greater parental certainty
AO2	Some women attempt to offset greater parental investment by cuckolding their partners but may risk partner violence
AO2	Belsky (1991) claims childhood experiences determine paternal investment rather than evolutionary factors
IDA	Comparative studies show little or no paternal investment in chimpanzees and bonobos
IDA	Physiological approach for differential costs of parental investment (Geher *et al.*, 2007)

Answer plan 3
(a) Outline the relationship between sexual selection and human reproductive behaviour. (4 marks)
(b) Discuss sex differences in parental investment. (4 marks + 16 marks)

Part (a) Sexual selection	
AO1	Intrasexual selection – leads to competition and evolved preferences for casual sex and sex earlier in relationship
AO1	Intersexual selection – each sex has mate preferences
Part (b) Sex differences in parental investment	
AO1	Larger investing sex will be more sexually discriminating, whereas sex with smaller investment competes for access
AO1	Female investment greater as eggs are more costly to produce than sperm and have greater parental certainty
AO2	Women may offset greater investment through cuckoldry
AO2	Cuckoldry carries risks, e.g. abandonment or mate violence
AO2	Belsky (1991) claims childhood experiences determine paternal investment rather than evolutionary factors
AO2	Buss *et al.* (1992) males concerned about sexual infidelity, females more concerned about emotional infidelity
AO2	Reid (1997) human males do contribute to parenting
AO2	Anderson (1999) paternal certainty may not be an issue
IDA	Comparative approach, studies show little or no paternal investment in chimpanzees and bonobos
IDA	Physiological approach for differential costs of parental investment (Geher *et al.*, 2007)

Model answer

(a) Outline and evaluate the relationship between sexual selection and human reproductive behaviour. (4 marks + 8 marks)

Intrasexual selection is the evolutionary process by which members of one sex (usually males) compete with each other for access to members of the opposite sex. Whatever characteristics that enable these males to compete successfully are then passed on to their offspring. Human males are also claimed to have a greater desire for short-term (i.e. casual) mating, and to seek sex earlier in a relationship because this increases their chances of reproductive success.

Intersexual selection involves one sex having preferences for mates that possess certain characteristics (such as good genes, attractiveness or resources). Human females are claimed to be particularly biologically 'pre-programmed' to attend to displays of indicators of male quality, and these males are then more likely to be chosen as mates.

The claim that males are more likely than females to seek short-term mating opportunities is supported in a study by Clarke and Hatfield (1989). They found that 75% of males agreed to have sex with an attractive stranger, whereas none of the females studied indicated the same willingness. This suggests that males have evolved mechanisms to increase their reproductive success, including a preference for sexual variety.

Research suggests female preference for particular types of male varies according to their position in their menstrual cycle. Penton-Voak *et al.* (1999) found females preferred a masculinised face during the most fertile phase and a more feminised face during less fertile phases. This suggests that females might choose a mate who showed kindness and cooperation, but mate with a high-quality male who possessed characteristics desirable in an offspring.

A problem for many studies in this area is that they lack external validity in that they measure mate preferences rather than actual mate choice (in which compromises are inevitably made). However, a study of actual marriages in 27 cultures (Buss, 1989) supported the mate choice hypotheses of sexual selection theory (i.e. males with resources tended to marry attractive females who were significantly younger than they were).

Most research suggests that males have evolved a preference for short-term mating, but this is gender-biased. Although short-term mating carries a high potential cost to the female, Greiling and Buss (2000) suggest that females could profit in a number of ways. They might use extra-marital mating to end a relationship with a poor-quality male or as a way of producing more genetically diverse offspring.

(b) Discuss sex differences in parental investment. (4 marks + 8 marks)

Parental investment theory predicts that the sex that makes the larger obligatory investment will be more discriminating in their choice of partner. The sex that makes the smaller investment will compete for access to the higher iinvesting sex. In humans, because females make a greater biological investment, they will be choosier in who they mate with, and males must compete for access to females.

Human females make a greater biological investment because they produce far fewer eggs over the course of their lifetime than the male produces sperm. Their greater investment can also be explained in terms of parental certainty, because in humans fertilisation is internal and the female is certain she is the mother of her child. The male, on the other hand, must always have some degree of parental uncertainty.

A consequence of these sex differences in parental investment is that some women may attempt to offset their greater parental investment by cuckolding their partners. This may be beneficial for them in that they receive additional social support from another male and maybe higher-quality genes for her offspring. However, this is not without risks. These include the possibility of her and her children being abandoned as well as the risk of violence against her by the current partner (Daly and Wilson, 1988).

Belsky (1991) claims that an evolutionary perspective of parental investment is limited because it ignores various personal and social conditions. He claims that childhood experiences, such as parental divorce are more likely to predict the degree to which men invest in the upbringing and care of their children.

There is support for sex differences in parental investment using the comparative approach where studies of non-human species are compared with humans. For example, studies of chimpanzees and bonobos have found little or no evidence of parental investment among males. This suggests that male parental investment is more likely to be due to cultural learning.

The physiological approach can be used to explain the differential costs of parental investment among males and females. A study by Geher *et al.* (2007) found that males showed greater ANS arousal when presented with scenarios that showed the real cost of parenting. Consistent with the predictions of parental investment theory, males appear biologically less prepared than females to deal with the issues associated with parenting.

Placing all the AO1 material first followed by AO2 helps you ensure you have written the right amounts of each. Time management is essential in a question like this where you have to provide 4 + 8 marks worth and then 4 + 8 marks worth. Thinking in this way will always be more effective than just presenting a general answer on the topic and hoping for the best!

Note how each paragraph in this essay mirrors the original answer plan.

Each AO2 point must be elaborated to gain maximum marks. Try to aim for 50–60 words for each point.

In this essay names and dates of researchers have been included. Neither are required but are a good way to provide detail and elaboration.

There is inevitably some overlap between the concepts of sexual selection and parental investment, but that's okay here because they are in two distinct part questions, so all relevant material will be marked on its merit.

The key issue is whether there is enough AO1 + AO2 in each half of the essay.

In parts (a) and (b) the AO1 count is 123 and 131 words respectively. For 4 marks we are looking for 100–120 words.

The AO2 counts are 268 and 251 words. For 8 marks we would expect 200–240.

So, overall there is well in excess of what would be required, but this is a model essay.

Division 3 Effects of early experience and culture on adult relationships

Answer plans

Answer plan 1

(a) Outline and evaluate the influence of childhood on adult relationships. (4 marks + 8 marks)

(b) Outline and evaluate the influence of culture on romantic relationships. (4 marks + 8 marks)

Part (a) Influence of childhood

AO1	Early attachment style determines internal working model
AO1	Children learn about relationships from their experiences with peers. This gives them a sense of their own value
AO2	Meta-analysis supports the link between attachment style and success in adult relationships (Fraley, 1998)
AO2	However, possible that attachment type determined by current relationship rather than attachment in childhood
AO2	Research (e.g. Simpson *et al.*, 2007) suggests early experiences do not determine adult relationships
IDA	Insight from psychopathology – some children find adult relationships difficult because of an attachment disorder

Part (b) Influence of culture

AO1	Relationships in Western and non-Western cultures differ in the degree to which they are voluntary or non-voluntary
AO1	Cultures differ in terms of the norms and rules that apply to the development of romantic relationships
AO2	Voluntary relationships not necessarily more successful
AO2	Romantic love an evolutionary adaptation, supported by anthropological evidence (Jankowiak and Fischer, 1992)
IDA	Argyle *et al.* (1986) found support for predictions of cultural differences in some relationship rules but not for others
IDA	Cultural bias in measurement of rules – the imposed etic

DIY

Work out your own plan for this question and then write your answer.

Describe and evaluate the influence of childhood experiences on adult relationships. (8 marks + 16 marks)

Influence of childhood

AO1	
AO1	
AO1	
AO1	
AO2	
AO2	
AO2	
AO2	
AO2	
AO2 or IDA	
AO2 or IDA	
AO2 or IDA	

Answer plan 2

Discuss the influence of culture on romantic relationships (8 marks + 16 marks)

Influence of culture

AO1	Relationships in Western and non-Western cultures differ in the degree to which they are voluntary or non-voluntary
AO1	Cultures differ in degree to which relationships reflect the interests of the individual or those of the family or group
AO1	Cultures differ in norms that apply to development of romantic relationships (e.g. norm of reciprocity) (Ma, 1996)
AO1	Cultures differ in rules for romantic relationships (e.g. social intimacy) (Argyle *et al.*, 1986)
AO2	Voluntary relationships not necessarily more successful
AO2	Research support for low divorce rates and high levels of love in non-voluntary relationships (Epstein, 2002)
AO2	Xiaohe and Whyte (1990) freedom of choice in relationships appears to promote marital stability
IDA	Romantic love an evolutionary adaptation, supported by anthropological evidence (Jankowiak and Fischer, 1992)
AO2	Norms – Moore and Leung (2001) difference between Anglo and Chinese students in romantic attitudes
AO2	Argyle *et al.* (1986) found support for predictions of cultural differences in some relationship rules but not for others
IDA	Cultural bias in measurement of rules – the imposed etic
IDA	May be a historical bias as many differences due to increasing urbanisation rather than cultural differences

Answer plan 3

(a) Outline one way in which culture influences the development of romantic relationships. (4 marks)

(b) Outline and evaluate the influence of childhood on adult relationships. (4 marks + 16 marks)

Part (a) Influence of culture

AO1	Relationships in Western and non-Western cultures differ in the degree to which they are voluntary or non-voluntary
AO1	Greater social mobility possible in urban cultures = greater degree of interaction with wider group and so more choice

Part (b) Influence of childhood

AO1	Early attachment style determines internal working model
AO1	Children learn about relationships from their experiences with peers. This gives them a sense of their own value
AO2	Meta-analysis supports the link between attachment style and success in adult relationships (Fraley, 1998)
AO2	However, possible that attachment type determined by current relationship rather than attachment in childhood
AO2	Longitudinal study (Simpson *et al.* 2007) expression of emotions in adulthood traced back to earlier experiences
AO2	However, Simpson *et al.* study also suggests that early experiences do not determine adult relationships
AO2	Madsen (2001) heavy dating patterns in adolescence associated with poorer quality adult relationships
AO2	Neeman *et al.* (1995) it is the timing of romantic relationships in adolescence that determines any influence
AO2	Many studies rely on highly restricted sample of individuals that makes it difficult to generalise to other groups
IDA	Insight from psychopathology – some children find adult relationships difficult because of an attachment disorder

Model answer

Discuss the influence of culture on romantic relationships. (8 marks + 16 marks)

Relationships in Western and non-Western cultures differ in the degree to which they are voluntary or non-voluntary, with Western cultures being characterised by a greater degree of social and geographical mobility than non-Western cultures. This means that individuals in Western cultures interact with a larger number of other people on a voluntary basis, thus giving them a greater choice of potential romantic partners.

Cultures differ in the degree to which relationships reflect the interests of the individual or the family or group. In individualist cultures, individual interests are considered more important, and romantic relationships are more likely to be formed on the basis of love and attraction. In collectivist cultures, on the other hand, relationships are more likely to reflect the interests of the family or the group.

Cultures differ in terms of norms that apply to development of romantic relationships. Norms act as guidelines for appropriate behaviour within a culture and dictate how people relate to and communicate with each other in the development of romantic relationships. Ma (1996) studied self-disclosure in Internet relationships. She found that American students self-disclosed sooner compared to East Asian students.

Cultures differ in terms of rules that apply to the development of romantic relationships. These include rules concerning courtesy and social intimacy. Argyle *et al.* (1986) examined relationship rules in the UK, Italy, Hong Kong and Japan and found that different relationship rules applied to these four cultures, although there were also similarities, e.g. concerning showing courtesy to a partner.

Although it might be expected that voluntary relationships based on love would produce more compatible partners and therefore be more successful, this is not necessarily the case, as in cultures where families play a key part in arranging a marriage, parents may be in a better position to judge compatibility as they are not blinded by romantic love.

There is research support for the view that non-voluntary relationships can work as well as, if not better than romantic relationships based on love and freedom of choice of partner. Epstein (2002) found that in cultures with reduced social mobility, non-voluntary relationships appeared to work very well, with lower divorce rates and higher levels of love between the partners.

In contrast to this finding, however, a Chinese study by Xiaohe and Whyte (1990) found that women who had freedom of choice and married for love were happier in their relationships than were women who were in arranged marriages. This study seems to support the claim that freedom of choice, as is more usual in Western cultures, appears to promote marital stability.

In terms of the evolutionary approach, romantic love may be an evolutionary adaptation that promotes reproduction and offspring survival in the human species. This claim is supported by anthropological research by Jankowiak and Fischer (1992), who found clear evidence of romantic love in most of the 166 non-Western tribal societies studied, thus suggesting it is universal and therefore the product of evolutionary rather than cultural factors.

The claim that cultures differ in their norms relating to romantic relationships is supported by a study by Moore and Leung (2001). They found differences between Anglo-Australian and Chinese-Australian students in their attitude to romantic relationships. For example, Anglo-Australian males were more casual about romantic relationships whereas Chinese-Australian males were as romantic as their female partners.

Argyle *et al.* (1986) found support for some of their predictions of cultural differences in some relationship rules (e.g. rules regarding intimacy) but not for others (e.g. the prediction that Japanese people place a greater emphasis on formalised gift exchange during the development of relationships). This suggests that many of the perceived differences between cultures are not supported by research.

There is a cultural bias in Argyle *et al.*'s research. The problem is that the list of rules, and the means of measuring them, was put together in a Western culture. This may have resulted in a failure to include rules that were specific to and important within a particular culture. This represents a cultural bias where a culturally specific idea or measure is applied to a culture where it is less relevant – an imposed etic.

There may also be a historical bias. The drift towards voluntary and temporary relationships appears to be a consequence of increasing urbanisation in the West over the last 50 years rather than differences in cultural norms and values. This would explain why non-Western relationships, such as China and India, have shown significant changes in the voluntary nature of relationships and increasing levels of divorce over this period.

> There is always the temptation to begin an answer such as this with material that is not creditworthy, such as a statement of intent or definitions of culture or romantic relationships. This answer avoids this.

> Cultures undoubtedly differ in all sorts of norms and rules, but it is essential to make it explicit that the norms and rules described here are related to the development of romantic relationships.

> This paragraph is an example of the three-point rule (see page 5). First, a critical point is identified (love as an evolutionary adaptation). Second, evidence is provided to support this point (Jankowiak and Fischer). Finally, the implications of this point are explained (love is the product of evolutionary rather than cultural factors).

> These last two paragraphs constitute the IDA content for this essay. Each is placed within an appropriate critical context and is sufficiently elaborated to ensure maximum credit. It is vital that you start such paragraphs with a clear indication to the examiner that this is IDA.

> This answer is 751 words long with 247 words of AO1 – almost exactly one-third. There are other, equally appropriate ways of laying out your AO1 and AO2, but make sure the balance between the two is the same as it is here.

Answer for you to mark

See page 171 for examiner's comments.

Question

Discuss **one** theory of the maintenance of romantic relationships and **one** theory of the breakdown of romantic relationships. (8 marks + 16 marks)

Student answer

❶ A theory of the maintenance of romantic relationships is social exchange theory. This is where a person wants to get as many rewards out of a relationship without having to put that much into it. For example, a man may want a very attractive wife and a woman wants a very rich man. This is rewarding for the individual and they experience this as profit.

❷ If a person feels they are not getting the rewards they want, or that the relationship is too costly for them (e.g. they do all the parenting or pay all the bills), they don't feel satisfied and the relationship might break down.

❸ There is also the idea of the comparison level, which is a way of comparing what a person has in their present relationship compared to what they have had in previous relationships. For example, they might keep going on about the previous wife's cooking and feel dissatisfied their new wife can't cook as well. Alternatively, they feel that their new wife is much better in other ways compared to their previous wife, so this increases their feelings of satisfaction.

❹ A related idea is the comparison level for alternatives. For example, Paul and Maria are married, then Paul meets a new woman, Susie, and falls in love with her. She is more attractive and more fun (i.e. she provides more rewards than Maria), but then the costs of leaving Maria (financial costs, investment in the children) are too high, so he stays with her.

❺ A problem for social exchange theory is that it doesn't really explain what goes on in real-life relationships, where people don't really keep a running total of rewards and costs, therefore it is an unrealistic theory and lacks validity. Usually people just get on with their relationships and although they may grumble to their friends, they don't expect to make a profit.

AO1 mark scheme

There is a requirement for two theories to be described here, one on maintenance and one on breakdown. Description of the formation of relationships would not receive credit.

Theories do not have to be presented in balance for full marks.

If only one theory is described partial performance applies with a maximum of 5 marks.

8 marks is about 200–240 words.

Tick the terms you think apply to the student's answer.

Comments and marks for AO1

Guidance on marking is given on pages 6–11.

Mark	Knowledge and understanding	Range of material	Accuracy	Organisation and structure
8–7	Accurate and well-detailed	Good range	Depth and breadth	Coherent
6–5	Generally accurate and reasonably detailed	Range	Depth and/or breadth	Reasonably coherent
4–3	Basic, relatively superficial	Restricted		Basic
2–1	Rudimentary and may be muddled and/or inaccurate	Very brief or largely irrelevant		Lacking
0	No creditworthy material			

The **AO1** mark I would give is ☐

6 *Another problem with social exchange theory is that people have been found to prefer equity in their relationships and are most satisfied when they get out of a relationship more or less what they put in. If they get too many rewards without many costs, then surprisingly they are not particularly satisfied with that relationship.*

7 *Moghaddam criticises social exchange theory because it only applies to Western cultures, and not to non-Western cultures such as China and Japan, where people are less concerned with what they as an individual can get out of a relationship. This means there is a cultural bias to the theory.*

8 *A theory of the breakdown of relationships is Rollie and Duck (2006). They claim that when a relationship breaks down, it goes through a series of different phases. These are intrapsychic, dyadic, social, grave-dressing and resurrection. The person goes from brooding about the relationship, to confronting the partner, to making it public, to offering their version of the break-up and finally to trying to learn from the break-up.*

9 *For example, if Paul and Maria do break-up, Maria may begin by resenting Paul because of his relationship with Susie. At this stage she doesn't say anything to him, but may then begin to discuss it with him, telling him about her unhappiness. In the next phase, if he doesn't clean up his act, she might start telling her family and friends. Finally, after the break-up, she can explain to other people that it was all his fault and then vow never to marry a good-looking man again and look for someone who is kinder and more considerate towards her.*

10 *Because relationship breakdown is a sensitive area, there are a number of ethical issues involved in its study. These include a possible invasion of privacy (these are personal matters) and the possibility of psychological harm as people have to relive a disturbing part of their life, which may well cause them significant distress. There is also the issue of confidentiality because one partner may give details of the other person's behaviour without their permission to do to.*

(656 words)

AO2 mark scheme

At least two theories must be evaluated for full marks. A partial performance penalty applies if only one explanation is evaluated (maximum of 10 marks).

Evaluation is likely to focus on research studies that support or challenge the explanations. It may also consider strengths and limitations of particular explanations.

16 marks is about 400–480 words.

Comments and marks for AO2

Mark	Analysis and understanding	Focus	Elaboration	Line of argument	Issues/debates/ approaches	Quality of written communication
16–13	Sound	Well focused	Coherent	Clear	Used effectively	Fluent, effective use of terms
12–9	Reasonable	Generally focused	Reasonable	Evident	Reasonably effective	Clear, appropriate
8–5	Basic, superficial	Sometimes focused	Some evidence		Superficial reference	Lacks clarity, limited use of terms
4–1	Rudimentary, limited understanding	Weak, muddled and incomplete	Not effective	May be mainly irrelevant	Absent or muddled/ inaccurate	Often unconnected assertions, errors
0	No creditworthy material					

The **AO2** mark I would give is ☐

Chapter 4 Aggression

There have been changes to the specification from September 2011 – therefore the updated specification details here are slightly different to those in some editions of the *A2 Complete Companion*.

Division 1 **Social psychological approaches to explaining aggression**	• **Social psychological theories of aggression, for example, social learning theory, deindividuation** • **Institutional aggression**

Possible exam questions for this division

Question	Comment
Discuss **two or more** social psychological theories of aggression. (8 marks + 16 marks)	'Two or more' does not indicate that more theories equals higher marks. Students often stretch themselves too thinly by trying to cover too many theories and end up with an answer that lacks depth, and so earns fewer marks. Be careful not to include too much AO1 here, and always remember the one-third AO1, two-thirds AO2 rule.
(a) Outline the role of hormonal mechanisms in aggression. (4 marks) (b) Outline and evaluate **one** social psychological theory of aggression. (4 marks + 16 marks)	In part (a) there are only 4 marks available, so this translates into about 100–120 words. Don't try to be too ambitious in your coverage. There is no credit for any evaluation. In part (b) there is again just four marks for AO1, so about 100–120 words. If choosing social learning theory, describe the *theory* and not just the Bobo doll studies. The AO2 content in part (b) should be four times the AO1 content (400–480 words).
(a) Outline **one** social psychological theory of aggression (e.g. social learning theory, deindividuation). (8 marks) (b) Evaluate the theory outlined in part (a) in terms of relevant research evidence. (16 marks)	In this question the AO1 content requires twice the detail required in the previous part (a). The two examples given in the question are just examples, and are not requirements of the question. In part (b) you should do more than just describe research evidence, you should show how this research supports, challenges or in some other way illustrates the principles of your chosen theory in this context. The golden rule here is 'Make it explicit'.
(a) Outline and evaluate **one** social psychological theory of aggression. (4 marks + 8 marks) (b) Outline and evaluate research into institutional aggression. (4 marks + 8 marks)	This question has a multitude of different requirements so it is always wise to plan any answer carefully so as to use your time profitably. Part (a) requires about 100–120 words of AO1 and 200–240 words of AO2. Part (b) also has the same word split, but this time your content should be linked to *research* (rather than explanations) relating to institutional aggression. See model answer on page 45.
Discuss institutional aggression. (8 marks + 16 marks)	This is a very general question on institutional aggression that could be addressed by explanations, research or a combination of both. Note also that there is a requirement to cover more than one explanation. Failure to do this would amount to 'partial performance', which would limit the number of marks awarded.
Discuss research into institutional aggression. (8 marks + 16 marks)	When preparing answers to possible questions it is a good idea to prepare for 'short' and 'long' versions of a topic, i.e. 4 +8 marks as earlier or 8 + 16 as in this question.

Division 2 **Biological explanations of aggression**	• **Neural and hormonal mechanisms in aggression** • **Genetic factors in aggressive behaviour**

Possible exam questions for this division

Question	Comment
Describe and evaluate neural mechanisms in aggression. (8 marks + 16 marks)	The term 'neural mechanisms' can be a little confusing, but the most obvious way of tackling this question would be the link between neurotransmitters (e.g. serotonin and dopamine) and aggression. Then research studies that address this link can be used as evaluation (AO2).
Describe and evaluate hormonal mechanisms in aggression. (8 marks + 16 marks)	There is the implication in this question (and in the previous one), that more than one 'mechanism' is required to avoid partial performance, therefore an answer should include a discussion of the role of both testosterone and cortisol.
Discuss neural **and** hormonal mechanisms in aggression. (8 marks + 16 marks)	The previous two questions have both required about 200–240 words of AO1 and 400–480 words of AO2. This is no different but now (ideally) it is 100–120 words of AO1 on neural mechanisms and 100–120 for AO1 on hormonal mechanisms, with the AO2 content of each likewise halved. See student answer on page 47.
Discuss neural **and/or** hormonal mechanisms in aggression. (8 marks + 16 marks)	Students are often nonplussed by the instruction 'and/or' in a question. There is no reason why this should be the case, as this very friendly question leaves the choice entirely up to you. An answer to this question could be restricted to just neural mechanisms or could include both (as in the previous question). If you do tackle both, then they should not be too imbalanced, otherwise one may be considered 'superficial' or 'lacking detail'.

Discuss genetic factors in aggressive behaviour. (8 marks + 16 marks)	It is sometimes difficult to decide what constitutes AO1 and AO2 in a question such as this. Some research studies will probably be used to illustrate how genetics influence aggression. Other research studies will be used as AO2, but their evaluative role needs to be made explicit by the use of lead-in phrases, such as 'There is research support for this'. See model answer on page 50.
(a) Outline genetic factors in aggressive behaviour. (4 marks) (b) Outline and evaluate neural **and/or** hormonal mechanisms in aggression. (4 marks + 16 marks)	This is another example of the wisdom of having two versions of each possible response. Rather than the 8 marks (and approximately 200–240 words) for AO1 in the previous question, part (a) of this question requires approximately 100–120 words of AO1. For part (b), it would be best to give your shortened version of either neural or hormonal mechanisms, plus your extended evaluation of the same.
Outline **one** social psychological theory of aggression. (4 marks) Outline and evaluate genetic factors in aggressive behaviour. (4 marks + 16 marks)	Questions such as this should not catch you out. The most effective way to tackle part (a) is to outline about two points relating to SLT and aggression, for a total of about 100–120 words. For part (b), there is another opportunity to use your shortened genetic factors answer for AO1 but your AO2 should be four times as long at about 400–480 words.

Division 3 Evolution and human aggression

- **Evolutionary explanations of human aggression, including infidelity and jealousy**
- **Evolutionary explanations of group display in humans, for example sport and warfare'**

Possible exam questions for this division

Discuss evolutionary explanations for infidelity **and/or** jealousy. (8 marks + 16 marks)	There is a clear link between infidelity and jealousy as a route to aggression in that one is a consequence of the other. As a result, it is virtually impossible to cover one without also covering the other.
(a) Outline and evaluate neural mechanisms in human aggression. (4 marks + 8 marks) (b) Outline and evaluate evolutionary explanations of human aggression. (4 marks + 8 marks)	We have met the component parts of part (a) before. Remember that there should be twice as much AO2 as AO1 so careful planning is essential. If you read the specification entry above, you will see that 'infidelity and jealousy' are included as evolutionary explanations of aggression. This makes answering this question pretty straightforward as it is simply a cut-down version of the answer above.
Describe and evaluate evolutionary explanations of human aggression. (8 marks + 16 marks)	The only difference between this question and the first one in this division is that the first one specifies the explanation(s), whereas this one does not. You could restrict yourself to a discussion of infidelity and/or jealousy, or include other explanations, e.g. the evolution of homicide. See model answer on page 49.
'Jealousy is one of the most powerful and potentially destructive emotions experienced in romantic relationships.' Discuss the role played by jealousy in the development of human aggression. (8 marks + 16 marks)	Questions occasionally include a quotation, but these are merely designed to stimulate your thought processes – however, you are answering the question and not the quotation so you should not worry about any subtleties in the quotation. Despite the fact that jealousy is mentioned on its own in this question, discussion will inevitably include infidelity, so the answer to this question will essentially be the same as the answer to the first question in this division.
(a) Outline **one** evolutionary explanation of group display in humans. (4 marks) (b) Outline and evaluate **one or more** evolutionary explanations of human aggression. (4 marks + 16 marks)	The specification mentions sport and warfare as examples of group display, but as these are only examples, other forms of group display are equally relevant. Part (a) requires description of just one area (e.g. sports, warfare, religion or lynch mobs). Part (b) is essentially the same answer as one of the above questions, but with half the AO1. One explanation is sufficient, although if you find it difficult to produce enough AO2 for one, you may choose to outline (and evaluate) two explanations.
Discuss evolutionary explanations of group display in humans, e.g. sport and warfare. (8 marks + 16 marks)	This is a very predictable question, as it is a straight translation of the specification entry into an examination question. Remember that sport and warfare are only suggestions, and not requirements and other forms of group display are fine. These explanations must be clearly 'evolutionary' in nature rather than general psychological explanations. There is a need for more than one explanation to avoid partial performance.
(a) Outline **one** evolutionary explanation of human aggression. (4 marks) (b) Outline and evaluate evolutionary explanations of **two** forms of group display in humans. (4 marks + 16 marks)	Questions may sample different topics within the same division (as here), or may sample across different divisions. Part (a) of this question requires a brief AO1 account of one evolutionary explanation (e.g. the infidelity/jealousy link). Part (b) is essentially the same question as above, but with half the AO1. Note that the same question can be asked in different ways.

Division 1 Social psychological approaches to explaining aggression

Answer plans

Answer plan 1

(a) Outline **one** social psychological theory of aggression. (e.g. social learning theory, deindividuation). (8 marks)

(b) Evaluate the theory outlined in part (a) in terms of relevant research evidence. (16 marks)

Part (a) Social psychological theory

AO1	SLT – aggressive behaviour is learned through observation and vicarious reinforcement
AO1	Mental representations required for learning to take place
AO1	Aggression is maintained as a result of direct reinforcement
AO1	Self-efficacy determined by successful use of aggression

Part (b) Evaluate

AO2	Research support from Bandura *et al.* (1961) Bobo doll
AO2	Bobo doll studies lack validity (demand characteristics) and real-world relevance (although there is a live clown study)
AO2	Context-dependent aggression can be explained by SLT
AO2	SLT explains aggression in absence of direct reinforcement
AO2	Research supports the importance of self-efficacy (Perry *et al.*, 1979) children high in confidence
IDA	Real-world application – link between televised boxing bouts and murder and assault rates (Philips, 1986)
AO2	Explains cultural differences in aggression (e.g. !Kung San)
IDA	Ethical issues make it difficult to test SLT experimentally

Work out your own plan for these questions and then write your answers.

(a) Outline and evaluate **one** social psychological theory of aggression. (4 marks + 8 marks)

(b) Outline and evaluate research into institutional aggression. (4 marks + 8 marks)

Part (a) Social psychological theory

AO1	
AO1	
AO2	
AO2	
AO2	
AO2 or IDA	

Part (b) Institutional aggression

AO1	
AO1	
AO2	
AO2	
AO2	
AO2 or IDA	

Answer plan 2

Discuss **two or more** social psychological theories of aggression. (8 marks + 16 marks)

Theory 1: Social learning theory (SLT)

AO1	Aggressive behaviour is learned through observation
AO1	Mental representations necessary for learning and expectation of reinforcement necessary for production
AO2	Research support from Bandura *et al.* (1961) Bobo doll
AO2	Bobo doll studies lack validity (demand characteristics) and real-world relevance (although there is a live clown study)
AO2	SLT explains aggression in absence of direct reinforcement
IDA	Ethical issues make it difficult to test SLT experimentally

Theory 2: Deindividuation

AO1	Leads to increase in behaviours that are normally inhibited by personal or social norms
AO1	Deindividuation aroused when individuals are in a state of anonymity (e.g. in large crowds)
AO2	Research support (Zimbardo, 1969) deindividuated participants were more aggressive
AO2	Does not always lead to aggression (Johnson and Downing, 1979), can also have prosocial consequences
AO2	Postmes and Spears (1998) meta-analysis fails to support claim that deindividuation more likely in large groups
IDA	Mann (1981) uses deindividuation to explain the mob behaviour found in 'the baiting crowd'.

Answer plan 3

Discuss explanations of institutional aggression. (8 marks + 16 marks)

Explanation 1: Importation model

AO1	Inmates in prison bring violent characteristics into prison
AO2	Research support for importation model among prison populations in US (Harer and Steffensmeier, 1996)

Explanation 2: Deprivation model

AO1	Aggression in prison a product of stressful and oppressive conditions
AO2	Research support for deprivation model, overcrowding and lack of privacy = violence (McCorkle *et al.*, 1995)
AO2	Deprivation model does not explain violence in all types of institution (e.g. Nijman *et al.*, 1999) in psychiatric wards
AO2	Deprivation model challenged by Poole and Regoli (1983) in juvenile institutions, pre-institutional levels of violence more important than institutional deprivation factors
IDA	Real-world application – changing deprivation conditions at HMP Woodhill decreased levels of violence (Wilson, 1998)

Explanation 3: Hazing

AO1	Causing other group members to suffer cruelty, abuse or humiliation as part of initiation ritual
AO1	May be due to situational influences, cultural notions of male toughness or conformity pressures
AO2	Research support – McCorkle (1992) in prisons
AO2	Problems in defining what is and what is not 'hazing'
IDA	Gender bias in claim that hazing is more likely to be caused by notions of male toughness, Allan (2002) claims females more likely to use psychological hazing

Model answer

(a) Outline **one** social psychological theory of aggression. (e.g. social learning theory, deindividuation). (8 marks)

According to social learning theory, children learn about aggressive behaviour by observing others acting aggressively. They also learn under what situations people are likely to be rewarded for their aggressive behaviour (vicarious reinforcement) and when they are punished. As a result, they learn how to perform aggressive acts and when it is appropriate, and when it isn't.

For social learning to take place the child must form a mental representation of the behaviour as well as an expectancy of any future outcome of them performing that behaviour. If opportunities for aggressive behaviour arise in the future, then the child may display that behaviour, provided the expectation of reward is greater than the expectation of punishment.

If a child is rewarded for their aggressive behaviour (e.g. by acquiring status or being praised by others), they become more likely to repeat that action in similar situations in the future. For example, a child who successfully bullies other children learns that aggression towards others is likely to produce rewards.

Children who are successful when using aggressive behaviour as a means to an end develop confidence (self-efficacy) in their ability to use aggression to achieve what they desire. However, children who are less successful in their use of this form of behaviour develop less self-efficacy relating to aggression and so turn to other forms of behaviour instead.

(b) Evaluate the theory outlined in part (a) in terms of relevant research evidence. (16 marks)

Social learning theory (SLT) is supported by Bandura *et al.* (1961). They found that children who observed a model behaving aggressively towards a Bobo doll were more likely to reproduce the same behaviours when they were later allowed to interact with the doll. This was particularly the case when they saw the adult rewarded for their aggressive behaviour, thus supporting the claim that the expectation of reward influences the likelihood of a behaviour being performed.

However, this study lacks validity because children may well have been aware of what was expected of them (demand characteristics) when they were allowed to play with the doll. The study also focuses on aggression toward a doll rather than real-life aggression, although a subsequent study using a live clown instead of a doll found similarly high levels of imitation among children.

A strength of this theory is that it can explain context-dependent aggression. People behave differently in different situations because they are rewarded for aggressive behaviour in some situations but not in others. This means that SLT is able to predict whether aggressive behaviour is likely in any specific situation dependent on previous experiences.

An additional strength is that SLT can explain aggressive behaviour in the absence of direct reinforcement, for example in the Bobo doll studies, at no point were the children directly reinforced for their own aggressive behaviour, and the concept of vicarious reinforcement is necessary to explain their actions.

There is research support for the idea of self-efficacy in the social learning of aggression. Perry *et al.* (1979) found that children who were described as highly aggressive by their peers also reported having greater confidence in their ability to use aggression to resolve conflicts than did children who were rated as less aggressive by their peers.

There are real-world applications in terms of evidence of the relevance of SLT to explain aggression outside the context of the laboratory. Philips found that murder and assault rates in the USA almost always increased in the week following a major televised boxing bout, suggesting that viewers were imitating some of the aggressive behaviour they had observed in the boxing.

A final strength of this theory of aggressive behaviour is that it can explain cultural differences in aggressive behaviour. For example, among the !Kung San people, aggressive behaviour is rare. Parents neither provide models for aggression (lack of opportunities for observational learning), nor do they reward aggressive behaviour in their children (lack of direct reinforcement). As a result, there is no motivation for the children to act aggressively.

Ethical issues make SLT difficult to test experimentally, as it is considered unethical to expose children to aggressive behaviour with the knowledge that they may then imitate those acts in their own behaviour. Thus, many of the hypotheses that form a part of this theory of aggression cannot be subjected to experimental validation.

There is a danger, when describing the social learning theory of aggression that you spend too long describing the Bobo doll studies instead. Part (a) focuses on the main points of the theory rather than dwelling on the studies that led to its development.

There should be an appropriate division between AO1 and AO2 in all questions. In this case Part (a) has to be all AO1. Any IDA would not be creditworthy as that is only relevant to AO2.

In this essay names and dates of researchers have been included. Neither are required but are a good way to provide detail and elaboration.

It is a good idea to write in paragraphs as it helps you to plan your answer as well as keep an eye on the AO1/AO2 division. Each of these paragraphs roughly equates to one point from the essay plan on the previous pages. And should be elaborated to roughly 50–60 words.

In order to use research evidence as AO2 it needs to be placed within an appropriate critical commentary, e.g. the relevance of Philips's study is made explicit rather than just being described.

Part (a) is all AO1 and Part (b) is all AO2. There are 223 words of AO1 and 475 words of AO2 for a total word count of about 700 words, and close to the one-third/two-thirds division necessary between AO1 and AO2, as well as sufficient amounts of each assessment objective.

Division 2 Biological explanations of aggression Answer plans

Answer plan 1
Describe and evaluate neural mechanisms in aggression. (8 marks + 16 marks)

Mechanism 1: Serotonin

AO1	Serotonin usually reduces aggression by inhibiting the firing of the amygdala in response to external events
AO1	Low levels of serotonin are associated with increased susceptibility to impulsive and aggressive behaviour
AO2	Research support – dexfenfluramine depletes serotonin and increases aggression (Mann *et al.*, 1990)
IDA	Gender bias in Mann *et al.* study – link was only for males.
AO2	Antidepressants raise serotonin and decrease aggression (Bond, 2005)
AO2	Animal studies – domestication of dogs associated with increases in serotonin levels (Popova *et al.*, 1991)

Mechanism 1: Dopamine

AO1	Increases in dopamine can produce increase in aggression
AO1	Demonstrated in studies, e.g. Lavine (1997) amphetamines, increase dopamine with associated increase in aggression
AO2	Research support – antipsychotics reduce dopamine levels and show decreased levels of aggression (Buitelaar, 2003)
AO2	Dopamine increase may be consequence rather than cause of aggression (Couppis and Kennedy, 2008)
AO2	Meta-analysis (Scerbo and Raine, 1993) serotonin but not dopamine differences in aggressive individuals
IDA	Neural explanations are reductionist in that they ignore the role of social learning in aggression (Bandura *et al.*, 1961)

Work out your own plan for this question and then write your answer.
Discuss genetic factors in aggressive behaviour. (8 marks + 16 marks)

Genetic factors

AO1	
AO1	
AO1	
AO1	
AO2	
AO2	
AO2	
AO2	
AO2	
AO2 or IDA	
AO2 or IDA	
AO2 or IDA	

Answer plan 2
Discuss neural **and** hormonal mechanisms in aggression. (8 marks + 16 marks)

Neural mechanisms

AO1	Serotonin usually reduces aggression by inhibiting the firing of the amygdala in response to external events
AO1	Increases in dopamine can produce increase in aggression
AO1	Research support – dexfenfluramine depletes serotonin and increases aggression (Mann *et al.*, 1990)
AO2	Animal studies – domestication of dogs associated with increases in serotonin levels (Popova *et al.*, 1991)
AO2	Meta-analysis (Scerbo and Raine, 1993) serotonin but not dopamine differences in aggressive individuals
IDA	Neural explanations are reductionist in that they ignore the role of social learning in aggression (Bandura *et al.*, 1961)

Hormonal mechanisms

AO1	Testosterone thought to increase aggressive behaviour through influence on brain areas that control aggression
AO1	High levels of cortisol inhibit testosterone and aggression
AO2	Evidence is inconclusive for link between testosterone and aggression (Albert *et al.*, 1993)
AO2	Importance of cortisol supported by McBurnett *et al.* (2000)
AO2	Although testosterone may be main hormonal influence, low cortisol levels increase likelihood of aggression
IDA	Gender bias – most studies of testosterone and aggression use small samples of prison males only

Answer plan 3
(a) Outline genetic factors in aggressive behaviour. (4 marks)
(b) Outline and evaluate neural **and/or** hormonal mechanisms in aggression. (4 marks + 16 marks)

Part (a) Genetic factors

AO1	Studies of adult twins suggest at least 50% of variance for aggression can be accounted for by genetic factors
AO1	MAOA regulates metabolism of serotonin in brain – low levels of MAOA found to be due to a defective gene

Part (b) Neural/hormonal mechanisms

AO1	Testosterone thought to increase aggressive behaviour through influence on brain areas that control aggression
AO1	High levels of cortisol inhibit testosterone and aggression
AO2	Evidence is inconclusive for link between testosterone and aggression (Albert *et al.*, 1993)
AO2	Importance of cortisol supported by McBurnett *et al.* (2000)
AO2	Methodological problems with measurement of cortisol
AO2	Although testosterone may be main hormonal influence, low cortisol levels increase likelihood of aggression
IDA	Gender bias – most studies of testosterone and aggression use small samples of prison males only
AO2	Archer *et al.* (2005) suggest link even stronger for women
AO2	Mazur (1985) claims testosterone affects dominance rather than aggression
AO2	Cortisol may make people less afraid of punishment, therefore less worried about using aggressive behaviour

Describe and evaluate neural mechanisms in aggression. (8 marks + 16 marks)

One of the neural mechanisms in aggression is the action of neurotransmitters on the brain, such as serotonin and dopamine. Serotonin plays an important role in social decision making by keeping aggressive social responses in check. Serotonin usually reduces aggression by inhibiting the firing of the amygdala, which might otherwise lead to impulsive or aggressive behaviour.

If there are low levels of serotonin in the brain, there is less inhibition of the amygdala. As a result, when it is stimulated by external events, it becomes more active, causing the person to act on their impulses, and making aggression more likely. Therefore, low levels of serotonin have been associated with an increased susceptibility to impulsive and aggressive behaviour.

The relationship between low levels of serotonin and aggression is supported by a study by Mann *et al.* (1990). They administered a drug (dexfenfluramine) to participants, which chemically depletes levels of serotonin in the brain. The researchers then used a questionnaire to assess hostility and aggression levels, which were raised after taking dexfenfluramine in males but not in females.

There may be a gender bias in this research. Although the Mann *et al.* study found a link between low levels of serotonin and aggression, this was not evident for the female participants. This suggests that the role of serotonin in aggression may be different for females compared to males and therefore there is a gender bias in human studies in this area.

Further evidence comes from the use of drugs that raise levels of serotonin in the brain, for example antidepressants. Bond (2005) found that in clinical studies, antidepressant drugs which elevate serotonin levels (e.g. SSRIs) also tend to have the effect of reducing irritability and impulsive aggression.

Evidence for the importance of serotonin in aggression comes from studies of non-human animals. Popova *et al.* (1991) found that among dogs that have been selectively bred for domestication and for an increasingly docile temperament, there has been a corresponding increase, over generations, of concentrations of brain serotonin. As a result, this suggests there is a link between low levels of serotonin and high levels of aggression.

There appears to be a link between dopamine and aggression in that increases in dopamine can produce an increase in levels of aggressive behaviour. For example, the increased rates of aggressive behaviour found in the schizophrenic population are believed to be the result of raised levels of dopamine in the brain.

The role of dopamine in aggression is also demonstrated in studies that have used amphetamines, which increase levels of dopamine. Lavine (1997) found that when participants were given amphetamines, there was a corresponding increase in their levels of aggression.

Evidence to support the importance of dopamine in aggression comes from studies using antipsychotics, which reduce dopamine levels in the brain. Buitelaar (2003) found that the use of antipsychotics successfully reduced the incidence of aggression among violent offenders.

However, evidence for the causal role of dopamine in aggression is inconclusive. A study by Couppis and Kennedy (2008) found that dopamine may be a consequence of aggressive behaviour rather than a cause. They suggest that some people may seek out aggressive encounters because dopamine is released as a positive reinforcer whenever they engage in aggressive behaviour.

There is research that challenges this link. Scerbo and Raine (1993) carried out a meta-analysis of studies that had examined neurotransmitter levels in antisocial children and adults. They found lower levels of serotonin in those individuals described as 'aggressive' but no difference in dopamine levels for these individuals when compared to 'normal' individuals.

The link between neural mechanisms, such as serotonin and dopamine and aggression can be criticised as being reductionist. The complexity of human behaviour means that biological explanations are insufficient on their own to explain the many different aspects of human aggression. For example, research by Bandura *et al* (1961) has shown that social learning can be a powerful influence on the aggressive behaviour of children.

Never waste time starting an essay with an introduction or definitions of terms, such as 'neural' or 'aggression'. None of this would gain marks.

There are two divisions in this question. The first is the AO1/AO2 division, as demonstrated by the 8/16 mark split. The second division is implied by the instruction 'neural mechanisms' in the plural. Coverage of two mechanisms (serotonin and dopamine) is enough to satisfy this requirement.

A key issue for IDA points is contextualisation. For example, you would not gain any credit for discussing gender bias in general. Your discussion must be firmly rooted in research on aggression.

There is no need for an equal division between the two neural mechanisms, although each should be sufficiently detailed.

There is lots of AO2 'language' in these two paragraphs (e.g. 'Evidence to support…', 'However…'). These are AO2 lead-in phrases which give the whole section an AO2 'feel', as well as ensuring that all the points are being used effectively as part of a critical commentary.

At just over 650 words, this is an ideal response to the question. Two neural mechanisms are covered in detail, and there is a clear distinction between AO1 and AO2, which are covered in the right proportion of approximately 1:2 (207 words AO1 and 448 words AO2).

Division 3 Evolution and human aggression Answer plans

Answer plan 1

Describe and evaluate evolutionary explanations of human aggression. (8 marks + 16 marks)

Explanation 1: Infidelity and jealousy

AO1	Adaptive value of aggression from sexual jealousy is to deter a mate from infidelity and minimise risk of cuckoldry
AO1	Males have evolved mate retention strategies including direct guarding and threats, that could lead to uxoricide
AO2	Research support (Shackelford *et al.*, 2005) correlation of use of mate retention strategies/violence against partner
AO2	Evolved homicide module theory (Duntley and Buss, 2005) explains why younger women killed – double loss
IDA	Explanation is gender-biased as focused solely on men
AO2	Social environment constantly changing so flexible behaviour more adaptive than such 'fixed' behaviours
IDA	Real-world application – use of mate retention is 'early warning signal' for violence

Explanation 2: Homicide

AO1	Male–male competition evolved because of lack of resources and inability to attract mates, Wilson and Daly (1985) 40% of Detroit murders by unemployed
AO1	Other motives – loss of status and sexual jealousy, Daly and Wilson (1988) 92% love-triangle murders male–male
AO2	A consequence is the evolution of anti-homicide defences
AO2	Ignores individual differences in male reaction to same adaptive problem (Buss and Shakleford, 1997)
AO2	Cannot explain cultural differences in use of violence, e.g. male violence for status in Yanomamo but not !Kung San

DIY

Work out your own plan for these questions and then write your answers.

(a) Outline **one** evolutionary explanation of human aggression. (4 marks)

(b) Outline and evaluate evolutionary explanations of two forms of group display in humans. (4 marks + 16 marks)

Part (a) Evolutionary explanation of aggression

AO1	
AO1	

Part (b) Evolutionary explanation of group display

AO1	
AO1	
AO2	
AO2	
AO2	
AO2	
AO2	
AO2 or IDA	
AO2 or IDA	
AO2 or IDA	

Answer plan 2

Discuss evolutionary explanations of group display in humans, e.g. sport and warfare. (8 marks + 16 marks)

Evolutionary explanation of group display

AO1	Cooperative group defence and antagonism to outsiders (e.g. lynch mobs) more common during social transition
AO1	Power-threat hypothesis – groups that pose threat to majority more likely to be subject to violent action
AO1	Costly signaling theory explains painful religious rituals
AO1	Xenophobia – adaptive to exaggerate threat from outsiders, evident in chants and banners of football crowds
AO2	Research support (Boyd and Richerson, 1990) for power of social conformity in group displays
AO2	Alternative explanation for behaviour of lynch mobs – deindividuation causing loss of self-regulation processes
AO2	Power-threat explanation challenged by study of lynchings in Brazil (Clark, 2006)
AO2	Costly signaling, research support – religious groups impose far more costly commitments of members than non-religious groups
AO2	Research support – Chen (2003) religious groups repay commitment through provision of 'social insurance'
AO2	Potential for greater inter-group hostility – groups with stricter practices have higher levels of intergroup conflict
AO2	Xenophobia, research support for football xenophobia (Foldesi, 1996)
IDA	Real-world application – has motivated club initiatives to stamp out xenophobia

Answer plan 3

(a) Outline **one** evolutionary explanation of human aggression. (4 marks)

(b) Outline and evaluate evolutionary explanations of **two** forms of group display in humans. (4 marks + 16 marks)

Part (a) Evolutionary explanation of aggression

AO1	Male–male competition evolved because of lack of resources and inability to attract mates, Wilson and Daly (1985) 40% of Detroit murders by unemployed
AO1	Other motives – loss of status and sexual jealousy, Daly and Wilson (1988) 92% love-triangle murders male–male

Part (b) Evolutionary explanation of group display

AO1	Costly signaling theory explains painful religious rituals
AO1	Xenophobia – adaptive to exaggerate threat from outsiders, evident in chants and banners of football crowds
AO2	Research support – religious groups impose far more costly commitments of members than non-religious groups
AO2	Research support – Chen (2003) religious groups repay commitment through provision of 'social insurance'
AO2	Adaptive significance is that group displays promote group cooperation and discourage free-riders from outside group
AO2	Potential for greater inter-group hostility – groups with stricter practices have higher levels of intergroup conflict
AO2	Research support for football xenophobia (Foldesi, 1996)
AO2	Research support – analysis of club and national football sides show more xenophobia toward national sides
IDA	Real-world application – has motivated club initiatives to stamp out xenophobia
AO2	An alternative explanation – football violence as 'career'

Model answer

Describe and evaluate evolutionary explanations of human aggression. (8 marks + 16 marks)

Aggression in men has an adaptive value. Men are more likely to experience sexual jealousy because of their fear of cuckoldry. Because they experience paternal uncertainty they are more at risk of cuckoldry, i.e. unwittingly investing resources in offspring that are not their own. Sexual jealousy and aggression, therefore, evolved to deter a female mate from sexual infidelity, and so minimising the risk of cuckoldry.

To achieve this, males have evolved a number of mate retention strategies which deter mates from infidelity. These include direct guarding or the threat of, or actual, violence against the partner. In extreme cases, the unintended consequence of male behaviour designed to deter the female partner from infidelity is that she dies (uxoricide).

Research support for the relationship between mate retention strategies and violence comes from a survey carried out by Shackelford *et al.* (2005). They found that men's use of mate retention strategies was positively correlated with violence scores. Women's responses confirmed this, with the use of mate retention strategies by their partners was positively correlated with their experience of violent behaviour toward them.

This explanation of uxoricide can't account for the fact that younger women have a much greater likelihood of being killed regardless of the age of their partner. However, the evolved homicide module theory (Duntley and Buss, 2005) can explain this, because a partner's infidelity carries a double loss for the male if the female is still of reproductive age. He both loses a partner (which damages his reproductive fitness) and another male gains a partner and increases their reproductive success.

A problem for this evolutionary explanation of aggression is that most studies of infidelity have focused solely on men's mate retention strategies and on male violence against women. This represents a gender-biased explanation, because women also practice mate retention strategies and carry out assaults on their partners as often as do men (Archer, 2000). This suggests that our current understanding of mate retention violence is limited because of the focus on males only.

A further problem for this perspective is that the social environment is constantly changing, so the only kind of mind that would be adaptive would be one that is flexible and responsive to these changes. Behaving in this manner may be adaptive in some circumstances but not in all.

This understanding can have a real-world application. The use of mate retention strategies by males can be used as an early indicator of potential partner violence, therefore it has a value for alerting others to intervene before actual violence against the partner can occur.

Aggression resulting in homocide may be explained in evolutionary terms. One factor is increased male–male competition, a response that evolves when there is a lack of resources and difficulties attracting long-term mates. An example of this can be seen in a study by Wilson and Daly (1985). They looked at homicides in Detroit and found that over 40% of those who committed the murders were unemployed.

Homicide can also be the result of sexual jealousy, for example Daly and Wilson (1988) found that for murders that occurred within 'love triangles', 92% were male–male, suggesting they were the result of male sexual jealousy.

A consequence for the evolution of man's tendency to commit murder in certain situations, is that humans have evolved anti-homicide defences. As a result of this, homicide becomes far more costly as a strategy in these situations because its success rate is then lower and increasingly dangerous for the person doing the killing.

There are also limitations of this evolutionary explanation, such as the fact that there are individual differences. Buss and Shackelford (1997) argue that it cannot explain why males react differently when faced with the same adaptive problem. The fact that some men react violently whereas others do not suggests violence is not a universal response to sexual jealousy.

Also, this perspective cannot explain why, if this was a universal human response to these situations, there are cultural differences in the importance of violence. For example, among the Yanomamo, male violence is required for males to achieve status, but among the !Kung San, aggression only leads to reputational damage.

What is not needed in this essay is a detailed account of the underlying theory of evolution, but rather an account of how this theory might explain human aggression. The plural 'explanations' suggests at least two areas must be covered as here.

Gender-biased in research is included as an IDA point. If you are making an IDA point it helps to make this very clear to the examiner by beginning the paragraph with an IDA lead-in sentence.

The evolution of homicide (murder) is included as a second explanation. Explanations do not need to be of the same length, but need to have sufficient detail to avoid being marked as 'superficial'.

In order to maximise AO2 marks, it is always necessary to elaborate each point being made (see three-point rule on page 5). Here, a point is made about there being cultural differences, and then the example shows why this is a problem for the evolutionary explanation.

There are 220 words of AO1 and 469 words of AO2, for a total of 689 words. There is ample material for both assessment objectives and an appropriate balance between them.

Answer for you to mark

See page 171 for examiner's comments.

Question

Discuss genetic factors in aggressive behaviour. (8 marks + 16 marks)

Student answer

1 There are two types of twin, monozygotic (MZ) twins who share the same genes, and dizygotic (DZ) twins who share only 50% of their genes. Psychologists study twins because if MZ twins are more alike than DZ twins in terms of aggressive traits, then this suggests that aggression is likely to be inherited.

2 Another way of investigating the influence of genetics is by looking at adopted children and their biological parents. If there is a similarity between the child and their biological parent, i.e. both are aggressive, then again this suggests that genetics has caused this similarity.

3 There is also the possibility of there being particular genes that lead people to become more violent. One of these is the MAOA gene. People who have one version of this gene tend to become more violent than people who have a different version. This was discovered in a Dutch family where all the men had one version of this gene and they were all more violent than normal people.

4 Research has found that people who commit violent crimes may be different to people who commit non-violent crimes, and this difference may be due to genetics.

5 There are a number of studies that have used twins. Miles and Carey (1997) looked at 24 studies involving twins or adopted children. They found that genetic influences were very important in these studies. Another meta-analysis carried out by Rhee and Waldman (2002) also found that genetic factors were very important in aggressive behaviour.

6 The genetic argument is also supported by real-life examples of violent individuals. Reggie and Ronnie Kray were identical twins who were also violent criminals and were responsible for a series of murders in the 1960s. Robert and Stephen Spahalski were twin brothers in the USA. They were raised together in childhood but separated afterwards. Both became serial killers.

7 There are problems with studies such as these. For one thing, researchers often have to rely on self-reports of aggression rather than measuring aggressive behaviour independently. Another problem is that with twin studies there are not that many identical twins who are raised apart, therefore it is a very limited sample.

8 There is also a sampling problem with studies that have looked at the role of particular genes in the development of aggressive behaviour in that these studies often are restricted to violent criminals. There are two major problems with this. First, violent criminals are not representative of people who carry out 'everyday' aggression. Second, some people who are sent to prison for one extremely violent offence (such as murder), do not necessarily have a history of violence.

9 However, the possibility that there may be a genetic basis to violent crime has led to the possibility of a real-life application of this research – genetic engineering. If we can identify the gene or genes responsible for violent behaviour, then it may be possible to knock out that particular gene and replace it with a different gene.

10 There are significant ethical issues involved with establishing a genetic basis to violent crime. For example, if someone is found to have a particular gene that is associated with aggression then they may be labeled as being a potential threat to society.

11 There is also an issue relating to free will. If aggressive behaviour is a product of our genes (i.e. determinism) rather than our free will, then this creates difficulties for knowing how to deal with violent criminals.

(560 words)

AO1 mark scheme

This is a broad area, and would include genetic abnormalities, twin studies, etc. Whichever approach is made, the link between genetic factors and aggressive behaviour should be explicit at all times.

Given the difficulties of describing genetic explanations, AO1 credit may be gained for straight descriptions of twin, family and adoption studies.

8 marks is about 200–240 words.

Guidance on marking is given on pages 6–11.

Comments and marks for AO1

Mark	Knowledge and understanding	Range of material	Accuracy	Organisation and structure
8–7	Accurate and well-detailed	Good range	Depth and breadth	Coherent
6–5	Generally accurate and reasonably detailed	Range	Depth and/or breadth	Reasonably coherent
4–3	Basic, relatively superficial	Restricted		Basic
2–1	Rudimentary and may be muddled and/or inaccurate	Very brief or largely irrelevant		Lacking
0	No creditworthy material			

The **AO1** mark I would give is ☐

Tick the terms you think apply to the student's answer.

AO2 mark scheme

Evaluation is likely to focus on research studies that support or challenge the factors identified. It may also consider strengths and limitations of particular explanations.

As with AO1, it is important that any evaluation is linked to aggression rather than being generic criticisms of genetic explanations.

16 marks is about 400–480 words.

Comments and marks for AO2

Mark	Analysis and understanding	Focus	Elaboration	Line of argument	Issues/debates/approaches	Quality of written communication
16–13	Sound	Well focused	Coherent	Clear	Used effectively	Fluent, effective use of terms
12–9	Reasonable	Generally focused	Reasonable	Evident	Reasonably effective	Clear, appropriate
8–5	Basic, superficial	Sometimes focused	Some evidence		Superficial reference	Lacks clarity, limited use of terms
4–1	Rudimentary, limited understanding	Weak, muddled and incomplete	Not effective	May be mainly irrelevant	Absent or muddled/ inaccurate	Often unconnected assertions, errors
0	No creditworthy material					

The **AO2** mark I would give is ☐

Chapter 5 Eating behaviour

There have been changes to the specification from September 2011 – therefore the updated specification details here are slightly different to those in some editions of the *A2 Complete Companion*.

Division 1 Eating behaviour

- **Factors influencing attitudes to food and eating behaviour, for example cultural influences, mood, health concerns**
- **Explanations for the success and failure of dieting**

Possible exam questions for this division

Question	Comment
Discuss **two or more** factors influencing attitudes to food and eating behaviour. (8 marks + 16 marks)	The instruction 'two or more' should not be taken as an invitation to present as many different factors as you can think of. The danger in that route is that your answer may become superficial and lacking in detail. Two factors, provided you can give sufficient detail for each, should be enough. See model answer on page 55.
Describe and evaluate research into factors influencing attitudes to food and eating behaviour (e.g. cultural influences, health concerns). (8 marks + 16 marks)	The term 'research' as it is used by AQA in examination questions, implies studies and/or explanations, so don't feel you have to restrict yourself just to the former. The answer to this question is essentially the same as the previous question. Don't be put off by the examples, they are simply that, i.e. *examples*.
(a) Outline **one** explanation for the success and/or failure of dieting. (4 marks) (b) Outline and evaluate **one or more** factors influencing attitudes to food and/or eating behaviour. (4 marks + 16 marks).	Part (a) of this question requires just a short outline description of *one* explanation of why dieting might succeed (or fail). There is no credit for any evaluation of this explanation, and the outline should be around 100–120 words. Part (b) would take some careful planning. There is an element of choice in how many factors you include. For example, the 'outline' component of this part might be just one factor or could be two (maximum 100–120 words) and the lengthier AO2 evaluative component could cover more than one factor (about 400–480 words).
'There are many different reasons why dieting may fail, including biological and social influences.' Discuss explanations for the success **and/or** failure of dieting. (8 marks + 16 marks)	Questions occasionally include a quotation, but these are merely designed to stimulate your thought processes – however, you are answering the question and not the quotation so you should not worry about any subtleties in the quotation. As is the case with all questions, you should carefully dissect the requirements of this one to work out exactly what is required. Here you need to discuss at least two explanations (just one would equate to partial performance).
(a) Outline **one** factor influencing attitudes to food and/or eating behaviour. (4 marks) (b) Outline and evaluate **one or more** explanations for the success **and/or** failure of dieting. (4 marks + 16 marks)	Part (a) of this question requires you to choose just one factor (e.g. cultural factors, mood, health concerns) and present a short (about 100–120 words) AO1 outline. Remember there is no AO2 required in part (a) and IDA is not creditworthy. Part (b) is similar in its requirements to the previous question. However, the AO1 content is half that in the previous question and there is the choice to cover just one explanation or more than one. Also the AO2 content should be four times as long as the AO1.
(a) Outline and evaluate **one or more** factors influencing attitudes to food and eating behaviour. (4 marks + 8 marks) (b) Outline and evaluate **one or more** explanations for the success **and/or** failure of dieting. (4 marks + 8 marks)	Part (a) is a mini-essay requiring both AO1 and AO2 content in the one-third/two-thirds format. Note that this gives you the choice to restrict your coverage to just one factor, or more than one. It is entirely up to you. Part (b) is also a mini-essay requiring AO1 and AO2 in the same proportions as in part (a). However, this is on a different topic, and given that there is the same number of marks for each part, they should be approximately the same length. Questions often adopt this 'modular' approach, so be flexible and prepared!

Division 2 Biological explanations of eating behaviour

- **Neural mechanisms involved in controlling eating behaviour**
- **Evolutionary explanations of food preference**

Possible exam questions for this division

Question	Comment
Discuss **two or more** neural mechanisms involved in controlling eating behaviour. (8 marks + 16 marks)	These mechanisms could include processes, such as homeostasis or different areas of the brain, such as the hypothalamus and amygdala. There is a requirement to cover at least two mechanisms. Failure to do this would amount to 'partial performance' and a loss of marks as a result.
Discuss research into neural mechanisms involved in controlling eating behaviour. (8 marks + 16 marks)	This question is virtually the same as the previous question, as the term 'research' as used by AQA allows for theories, explanations and/or research studies. The secret is not to be thrown by a change of wording.
Discuss evolutionary explanations of food preference. (8 marks + 16 marks)	There is no specified number of 'evolutionary explanations' in this question, although there might be in a different version of this question (e.g. 'Discuss two or more…'). Explanations of food preference should be discussed explicitly within an evolutionary context, but discussing evolution (e.g. the theory of natural selection) without reference to food preference would gain little credit. See model answer on page 57.

(a) Outline and evaluate **one or more** neural mechanisms involved in controlling eating behaviour. (4 marks + 8 marks) (b) Outline and evaluate evolutionary explanations of food preference. (4 marks + 8 marks)	The first part of this question emphasises the need for flexibility in your exam preparation. The first question in this division called for a full 24-mark answer, but this part requires half that material, which could be a more selective focus (hence 'one or more') or perhaps a less-detailed account of the same material. Be prepared! Part (b) requires half the amount of AO1 as in the previous question and also half the amount of AO2. You should always have a 4 and 8 mark AO1 version of each topic, and an 8 and 16 AO2 version for that topic.
(a) Outline and evaluate **one** neural mechanism involved in controlling eating behaviour. (4 marks) (b) Outline and evaluate evolutionary explanations of food preference. (4 marks + 16 marks)	This parted question again shows the need for flexibility in your examination preparation. The above question asked for 'one or more factors' for 4 marks, this one specifies just one – which should be covered in about 100–120 words. Part (b) of this question is the same as part (b) above except there is a requirement for twice as much AO2. You can always evaluate material that has not previously been described, and this is probably the best way of tackling this question.
(a) Discuss factors that influence attitudes to food. (4 marks + 8 marks) (b) Discuss neural mechanisms in controlling eating. (4 marks + 8 marks)	Questions frequently span different divisions, so don't be thrown by such a combination. We met part (a) in the last question of the previous division, and part (b) in an earlier question in this division. Preparing different versions of the same topic area (e.g. 4 or 8 marks for AO1 and 8 or 16 marks for AO2) is not only vital for effective examination performance, it is also useful as a way of processing the material and thus making it more memorable. Time management is also essential when responding to this question. Each part should take 15 minutes and should be approximately 300–360 words in length.

Division 3

Eating disorders

In relation to either anorexia nervosa or bulimia nervosa or obesity

- **Psychological explanations**
- **Biological explanations, including neural and evolutionary explanations**

Possible exam questions for this division

Discuss explanations of **one** eating disorder. (8 marks + 16 marks)	This question allows you to choose from anorexia nervosa, bulimia nervosa or obesity. The two (or more) explanations could be psychological and/or biological (including evolutionary explanations). You should make it clear which disorder you are discussing, and make all AO1 and AO2 explicitly relevant to that disorder.
Discuss psychological explanations of **one** eating disorder. (8 marks + 16 marks)	This is similar to the previous question except it specifies 'psychological' explanations rather than giving you the choice. Biological explanations could be used as part of a critical commentary, but would not receive credit if just described. All AO1 and AO2 must be explicitly relevant to the chosen disorder. See model answer on page 59.
Discuss **two or more** biological explanations of **one** eating disorder. (8 marks + 16 marks)	This is the 'biological' equivalent to the previous question. Both specify a plurality requirement ('explanations', 'two or more'). Both could be answered by two explanations or by more than two. The same advice as above applies.
(a) Outline and evaluate **one or more** psychological explanations of **one** eating disorder. (4 marks + 8 marks) (b) Outline and evaluate **one or more** biological explanations of **one** eating disorder. (4 marks + 8 marks)	A recurring piece of advice with these sample questions is the need for flexibility in your exam preparation. This is a case in point. If you were to prepare an answer to the above questions, you would probably have two psychological and two biological explanations. This question requires just one (or more) of each. So, make sure you have your full version of each question (as in the above questions) and your part version as here. Careful preparation will always pay dividends in the exam.
(a) Outline **one** biological explanation of **one** eating disorder. (4 marks) (b) Outline and evaluate **two** psychological explanations of **one** eating disorder. (4 marks + 16 marks)	Part (a) requires just a brief outline description of *one* biological explanation. Part (b) is the same as the second question in this division (see above) but the AO1 should be restricted to a brief (100–120 words) of those two explanations. The AO2 content is the same, i.e. four times the length of the AO1 component for this part.
(a) Outline **one** psychological explanation of **one** eating disorder. (4 marks) (b) Outline and evaluate evolutionary explanations of food preference. (4 marks + 16 marks)	This time part (a) requires just a brief outline description of *one* psychological explanation. Remember to make the focus of this explanation clear and don't include any evaluation, some explanations apply to more than one eating disorder, so make it explicitly clear how your chosen explanation applies to that particular disorder. Questions often span divisions, so part (b) of this question is the same as part (b) of the penultimate question in the previous division. Notice the 4+16 mark split, which means that any answer should be split accordingly in terms of word length. See student answer on page 60.

Division 1 Eating behaviour

Answer plans

Answer plan 1

Discuss **two or more** factors influencing attitudes to food and eating behaviour. (8 marks + 16 marks)

Factor 1: Cultural influences

AO1	Ethnicity – body dissatisfaction more characteristic of white than black or Asian women (Powell and Khan,1995), Ball and Kenardy (2002) – the 'enculturation effect'
AO1	Body dissatisfaction more common among middle class (Dornbusch *et al.*, 1984), healthy attitudes to food in higher income families (Goode *et al.*, 2008)
AO2	Research challenges ethnicity claim (Mumford *et al.*, 1991; Striegel-Moore *et al.*, 1995)
AO2	Research challenges social class claim (Story *et al.*, 1995)
AO2	Problems of generalisability – some studies use clinical and some sub-clinical populations
IDA	Cultural bias in research – cultural background influences attitudes to food and eating behaviour (Rozin *et al.*, 1999)

Factor 2: Mood

AO1	Anxiety experienced prior to bingeing (Wegner *et al.*, 2002)
AO1	Comfort eating – people in 'sad' mood likely to choose short-term pleasures of junk food (Garg *et al.*, 2007)
AO2	Anxiety/binge-eating link supported (Piomelli *et al.*, 2011)
AO2	However, does not explain why binge eating is reinforcing although possibly social negative reinforcement
AO2	Challenge to role of mood, eating chocolate more likely to prolong negative mood (Parker *et al.*, 2006)
IDA	Gender bias – most studies have concentrated on women to exclusion of homosexuality as risk factor (Siever, 1994)

DIY

Work out your own plan for these questions and then write your answers.

(a) Outline and evaluate **one or more** factors influencing attitudes to food and eating behaviour. (4 marks + 8 marks)

(b) Outline and evaluate **one or more** explanations for the success and/or failure of dieting. (4 marks + 8 marks)

Part (a) Factors influencing attitudes

AO1	
AO1	
AO2	
AO2	
AO2	
AO2 or IDA	

Part (b) Explanations for dieting

AO1	
AO1	
AO2	
AO2	
AO2	
AO2 or IDA	

Answer plan 2

Discuss explanations for the success and/or failure of dieting. (8 marks + 16 marks)

Explanation 1: Restraint theory

AO1	Disinhibition – attempting not to eat may increase the probability of eating
AO1	Boundary model – dieters take longer to feel hungry and therefore more food to reach state of satiety
AO2	Support for restraint theory (Wardle and Beales, 1988) but does not explain behaviour of restricting anorexics
IDA	Real-world application – can explain why treatments for obesity, which recommend restraint, often fail
AO2	Some cultural groups find it harder to diet because of greater central fat mass compared to other cultural groups
IDA	Psychology as science – many studies rely on anecdotal accounts of success or failure, so problems for reliability

Explanation 2: Role of denial

AO1	Attempting to suppress thoughts of food has the opposite effect, making them more prominent
AO1	Theory of ironic processes of mental control – as food is denied, it simultaneously becomes more attractive
AO2	Research support for greater preoccupation with food after attempts to suppress thoughts (Soetens *et al.*, 2006)
AO2	However, Wegner (1994) admits that 'ironic effects' found in research are 'detectable but not overwhelming'
IDA	Free will versus determinism – genetic mechanisms (e.g. gene for LPL) may determine failure for some dieters
AO2	Oestrogen inhibits LPL activity – explains why post-menopausal women have more difficulty with dieting

Answer plan 3

(a) Outline **one** explanation for the success and/or failure of dieting. (4 marks)

(b) Outline and evaluate **one or more** factors influencing attitudes to food and/or eating behaviour. (4 marks + 16 marks)

Part (a) Explanation of dieting

AO1	Disinhibition – Attempting not to eat may increase the probability of eating
AO1	Boundary model – dieters take longer to feel hungry and therefore more food to reach state of satiety

Part (b) Factors influencing atttiudes

AO1	Body dissatisfaction and related eating concerns more characteristic of white women and middle class individuals
AO1	Anxiety experienced prior to bingeing and sad mood more likely to result in comfort eating
AO2	Research challenges ethnicity claim (Mumford *et al.*, 1991)
AO2	Research challenges social class claim (Story *et al.*, 1995)
AO2	Problems of generalisability – some studies use clinical and some sub-clinical populations
IDA	Cultural bias in research – cultural background influences attitudes to food and eating behaviour (Rozin *et al.*, 1999)
AO2	Anxiety/binge-eating link supported (Piomelli *et al.*, 2011)
AO2	However, does not explain why binge eating is reinforcing although possibly social negative reinforcement
AO2	Eating chocolate more likely to prolong negative mood as part of emotional eating strategy (Parker *et al.*, 2006)
IDA	Gender bias – most studies have concentrated on women to exclusion of homosexuality as risk factor (Siever, 1994)

Model answer

Discuss **two or more** factors influencing attitudes to food and eating behaviour. (8 marks + 16 marks)

Research has found that ethnicity is an important cultural influence in body dissatisfaction and related eating concerns. Powell and Khan (1995) found these attitudes were more characteristic of white women than black or Asian women. Ball and Kenardy (2002) found that, regardless of ethnic background, the longer women spent in Australia, the more similar to women born in Australia were their attitudes to food and eating (the 'enculturation effect').

Social class is also an important cultural influence in dieting and body dissatisfaction. Dornbusch *et al.* (1984) found that among American adolescents, higher class females had a greater desire to be thin and were more likely to diet to achieve this compared to lower class females. Goode *et al.* (2008) also found that healthy attitudes to eating were more likely to be found among higher income families.

Other research challenges ethnicity as a factor in these attitudes. Mumford *et al.* (1991) found that the incidence of bulimia nervosa was higher among Asian schoolgirls than among white schoolgirls. Also, Striegel-Moore *et al.* (1995) found a greater drive to be thin among black girls than among white girls of the same age, which therefore challenges the claim that ethnicity is a key influence in the development of disordered eating.

Research challenges the claim that social class is important in developing attitudes to food and eating. Story *et al.* (1995) found that higher social class was actually associated with greater rather than lower body dissatisfaction and lower rates of behaviour designed to lose weight. Other studies have found no relationship between the two, thus suggesting that social class is not a reliable indicator of eating behaviour.

There is a generalisability problem with this research. Some research has studied clinical populations (i.e. people diagnosed with bulimia or some other eating disorder), whereas other studies have relied on sub-clinical populations (e.g. people with disordered attitudes to food, or comfort eaters). This therefore makes it difficult to generalise from one group to the other to determine the influence of different factors.

There is evidence of cultural bias. Rozin *et al.* (1999) found that different cultures had different attitudes to food. For example, Americans were more preoccupied with health issues related to food, whereas the French associated food with pleasure. This suggests that the measurement of attitudes to food and eating behaviour in one culture tells us little about attitudes in other cultures.

A second factor influencing attitudes towards food and eating behaviour is mood. For example, individuals with bulimia nervosa tend to experience anxiety prior to a binge-eating episode, despite the fact that binge-eating does not relieve the low-mood state. The same relationship between anxiety and binge-eating is also found in non-clinical populations. Wegner *et al.* (2002) found that people who binged tended to have low mood before and after binge-eating.

Another example of the influence of mood is that many people tend to comfort-eat when in a low mood. Garg *et al.* (2007) observed the food preferences of participants as they watched either an upbeat movie or a sad movie. They found that when they watched the upbeat movie, they were more likely to choose healthy snacks, but when watching a depressing movie they went for the short-term pleasure of junk food.

The relationship between anxiety and binge-eating is supported by research. However, Piomelli *et al.* (2011) found that consuming fats in the form of junk food triggers a binge-eating signal that makes the individual want to eat more of the same. This shows that although low mood may trigger the initial urge to binge, it is the consumption of fatty foods that sustains the episode.

However, the mood/bingeing relationship does not explain why binge-eating is reinforcing. However, there are a number of possible reasons why binge-eating might be reinforcing for an individual. These include social negative reinforcement, where bingeing is used to avoid interactions with others or to escape from their demands.

There are challenges to the view that low mood causes comfort-eating. For example, comfort-eating chocolate is more likely to prolong a negative mood when it is used as part of an emotional-eating strategy (Parker *et al.*, 2006). This challenges the view that low mood causes comfort-eating, as it suggests that it may not be that effective in overcoming a low mood.

There is a gender bias in research in this area. Most studies have concentrated only on women's attitudes to eating behaviour. However, studies (e.g. Siever, 1994) have shown that in men, homosexuality is a significant risk factor in the development of disordered eating attitudes and behaviour, a greater likelihood of dieting and more evidence of bulimic symptoms than in heterosexual men.

This essay has been written in a rather formulaic way. Such an approach is not required but it does ensure that two main factors are identified and each has one-third AO1 and two-thirds AO2. This amounts to 12 separate points (as identified in the plan on the facing page), each represented by its own distinct paragraph.

There is twice as much AO2 to AO1 material to reflect marks available. Each AO2 point should be elaborated to gain the maximum marks possible.

This paragraph is an example of the three-point rule in evaluation (see page 5). Ideally all AO2 paragraphs should follow this rule to ensure adequate elaboration and clarity.

You should try to make AO2 material look like AO2. This has been accomplished in these paragraphs by the use of lead-in phrases, such as 'The relationship between anxiety and binge-eating is supported by research...' and 'There is a gender bias in research in this area...'.

This answer is 770 words in length. With about 270 words of AO1 and 500 words of AO2, both assessment objectives are represented more than adequately and in the right proportion (one-third AO1/two-thirds AO2).

Division 2 Biological explanations of eating behaviour Answer plans

Answer plan 1

Discuss **two or more** neural mechanisms involved in controlling eating behaviour. (8 marks + 16 marks)

Neural mechanisms

AO1	Homeostatic mechanisms regulate food intake, dependent on glucose levels
AO1	Lateral hypothalamus (LH) – damage causes aphagia, stimulation through NPY brings about feeding behaviour
AO1	Ventromedial hypothalamus (VMH) – damage causes overeating, stimulation inhibits feeding
AO1	Amygdala selects foods on the basis of experience
AO2	Limitation of homeostatic mechanism is that it only reacts to rather than anticipates energy deficits
IDA	Evolutionary explanation rejects homeostasis, people eat because they develop taste for foods that promote survival
AO2	LH – Marie *et al.* (2005) manipulated NPY levels in mice, made no difference to feeding behaviour
IDA	Real-world application, targeting individuals at risk of increased levels of NPY a possible treatment for obesity
AO2	Gold (1973) claims that lesions to VMH only lead to overeating if lesion includes PVN
AO2	However, other research fails to support Gold's findings
IDA	Amygdala damage explains Klüver-Bucy syndrome
IDA	Real-world application, blocking body's response to ghrelin may prevent tendency to comfort-eat when stressed

Work out your own plan for these questions and then write your answers.

(a) Outline and evaluate **one or more** neural mechanisms involved in controlling eating behaviour. (4 marks + 8 marks)

(b) Outline and evaluate evolutionary explanations of food preference. (4 marks + 8 marks)

Part (a) Neural mechanisms

AO1	
AO1	
AO2	
AO2	
AO2	
AO2 or IDA	

Part (b) Evolutionary explanations

AO1	
AO1	
AO2	
AO2	
AO2	
AO2 or IDA	

Answer plan 2

(a) Outline and evaluate **one** neural mechanism involved in controlling eating behaviour. (4 marks)

(b) Outline and evaluate evolutionary explanations of food preference. (4 marks + 16 marks)

Part (a) Neural mechanism

AO1	Lateral hypothalamus – damage causes aphagia, stimulation through NPY brings about feeding behaviour
AO1	Ventromedial hypothalamus – damage causes overeating, stimulation inhibits feeding

Part (b) Evolutionary explanations

AO1	Early diets, preference for calorific rich foods and meat would have been adaptive within the EEA
AO1	Taste aversion would have had important survival value as would the medicine effect
AO2	Research support, e.g. Gibson and Wardle (2001) 4–5 year olds show preference for fruit and vegetables high in calories
IDA	Evidence from other species, chimpanzees (Stanford, 1999)
AO2	Cordain *et al.* (2006) early humans obtained calories from non-animal fats, but challenged by anthropological evidence
AO1	Challenged because it is likely that many food preferences developed because of cultural tastes and preferences
AO1	Taste aversions explained by biological preparedness (Seligman, 1970)
IDA	Real-world application, origins of taste aversion used to understand food avoidance during chemotherapy
AO2	This is supported by Bernstein and Webster (1980)
AO2	Many modern food preferences would not have been beneficial to early humans so would not have evolved

Answer plan 3

Discuss evolutionary explanations of food preference. (8 marks + 16 marks)

Evolutionary explanations

AO1	Adaptive problems faced by early humans in the EEA would have shaped food preferences
AO1	Bitter taste would have evolved to detect potentially harmful toxins in plants e.g. glucosinolates (Sandell and Breslin, 2006)
AO1	Preference for fatty foods, for calorific rich foods and meat would have been adaptive within the EEA
AO1	Taste aversion would have had important survival value as would the medicine effect
AO2	Research support, e.g. Gibson and Wardle (2001) 4–5-year-olds show preference for fruit and vegetables high in calories
IDA	Evidence from other species, chimpanzees (Stanford, 1999)
AO2	Cordain *et al.* (2006) early humans obtained calories from non-animal fats, but challenged by anthropological evidence
AO2	Challenged because it is likely that many food preferences developed because of cultural tastes and preferences
AO2	Taste aversions explained by biological preparedness (Seligman, 1970)
IDA	Real-world application, origins of taste aversion used to understand food avoidance during chemotherapy
AO2	This is supported by Bernstein and Webster (1980)
AO2	Many modern food preferences would not have been beneficial to early humans so would not have evolved

Model answer

Discuss evolutionary explanations of food preference. (8 marks + 16 marks)

One explanation of food preferences is that they were shaped by the envionment of early humans. The environment of evolutionary adaptation (EEA) refers to the environment in which human beings first evolved. The adaptive problems faced by early humans in the EEA would have shaped food preferences (e.g. for energy-rich foods) to ensure survival and natural selection would have ensured that these preferences were passed on to offspring.

An example of an evolved food preference is that the experience of bitter taste has evolved to detect potentially harmful toxins in plants. Sandell and Breslin (2006) screened 35 adults for the bitter taste receptor gene. Those with the sensitive form of this gene were more likely to experience toxic glucosinolates as bitter, which would explain why such genes are widespread in modern times.

Preference for fatty foods was also adaptive because the harsh conditions faced by early humans in the EEA meant that foods that provided energy resources were vital to survive. Early humans would therefore have evolved a preference for calorific rich foods, such as meat. A meat diet was full of nutrients, and became the catalyst for rapid brain growth.

Taste aversion is an evolved defensive mechanism that enables predators to survive encounters with prey with toxic defenses. When early humans experienced nausea after consuming toxic prey, they formed a long-lasting aversion to the taste and scent of this type of food. The medicine effect is a tendency for individuals to develop a preference for any food eaten prior to recovery from an illness.

There is research support for the evolved preference for high calorie foods. For example, Gibson and Wardle (2001) tested the preferences for specific fruits and vegetables among 4–5 year olds. They predicted that children would prefer foods that were rich in calories (such as bananas and potatoes) over other foods, which is what they found.

Evidence from comparative studies of closely related non-human species has supported the importance of saturated fats in the diets of early humans. Stanford (1999) studied chimpanzees in Gombe National Park. When these animals were close to starvation and managed to kill a monkey to eat, they went straight to the fattiest parts (e.g. the bone marrow) rather than the more nutritious flesh.

The importance of calories in early humans' diets is challenged by Cordain *et al.* (2006) who claim that early humans obtained calories from sources other than animal fats, and may even have been vegetarian. However, this in turn has been challenged by anthropological evidence, which has shown that all societies show a preference for animal fats, suggesting that this is a universal evolved preference.

The view that all food preferences are due to evolutionary factors is challenged by the fact that there are cultural differences in food likes and dislikes. Although there are some universal preferences, e.g. for sweet foods, these innate responses do not account for the broad range of food preferences found in different cultures. It is likely that these preferences (e.g. for spicy foods) developed because of cultural tastes and preferences.

Taste aversions can be explained by the concept of biological preparedness. Seligman (1970) claimed that each species has an evolved ability to learn certain associations more easily than others, particularly those that help that particular species to survive. This would explain why many humans develop a learned aversion to any food or drink that has made them sick.

A real-world application of taste aversion is to understand the food avoidance that is often found in children being treated for cancer. Some cancer treatments, such as radiotherapy and chemotherapy, have the side effect of causing gastrointestinal illness. When this illness is paired with eating a particular food such as ice cream, a taste aversion to that food can result.

This association was supported in a study by Bernstein and Webster (1980). They gave children undergoing chemotherapy a novel tasting ice cream prior to their chemotherapy. The children subsequently developed an aversion to that ice cream. Hospitals now give cancer patients a novel and a familiar food prior to chemotherapy. Because humans have an evolved avoidance of novel tastes, an aversion develops to the novel rather than to the familiar food.

However, not all food preferences can be explained in evolutionary terms as many modern food preferences (e.g. for low cholesterol foods) would not have been beneficial to early humans so would not have evolved. Similarly, many foods that would have been beneficial to early humans (e.g. high fat foods) are more likely to be avoided by modern humans.

There is a tendency for many students to waste time at the beginning of an essay by outlining their intentions and defining terms. There is no need to do this unless (as here) the definition is a key part of the answer and likely to earn marks. Outlining intentions ('In this essay I am going to…') will never earn marks.

Good answers aim for both breadth and depth. Four points, each of about 50–60 words is ideal as a way of picking up high AO1 marks.

This paragraph counts as IDA because it shows the value of comparative research where non-human behaviour is compared to human behaviour as a means of supporting one of the AO1 claims made earlier in the essay.

This real-world application also counts as an IDA point, but it is always a good idea to use an appropriate IDA lead-in phrase (e.g. 'A real-world application…') to make identification of this point more obvious.

In this essay names and dates of researchers have been included. Neither are required but are a good way to provide detail and elaboration.

This essay is about 750 words in length, with 255 words of AO1 and 499 words of AO2. Ideal word counts are about 100–120 AO1 words and 400–480 AO2 words so this is slightly longer than required.

Division 3 Eating disorders

Answer plans

Answer plan 1

(a) Outline and evaluate **one or more** psychological explanations of one eating disorder. (4 marks + 8 marks)

(b) Outline and evaluate **one or more** biological explanations of one eating disorder. (4 marks + 8 marks)

Part (a) Psychological explanation(s) for anorexia nervosa (AN)

AO1	Cultural ideals – Western standards of attractiveness contribute to body dissatisfaction
AO1	Media influences – portrayal of thin models in the media creates body image concerns and a 'drive to thinness'
AO2	Research challenges cultural ideals explanation (Hoek *et al.*, 1998) in Curacao, a Caribbean island
AO2	Evidence for media influences found in study of Fijian adolescents after introduction of TV (Becker *et al.*, 2002)
AO2	Real-world application – response of French fashion houses not to stereotype the 'thin ideal'
IDA	Ethical issues (e.g. privacy, lack of informed consent) in study of AN through chat rooms and newsgroups

Part (b) Biological explanation(s) for anorexia nervosa

AO1	Serotonin – disruption of serotonin levels leads to increased anxiety which may then trigger AN
AO1	Dopamine – increased dopamine activity alters the way people interpret pleasurable events (e.g. food)
AO2	Problem for serotonin explanation – SSRIs ineffective when used in the treatment of AN patients
AO2	Support for dopamine explanation – adolescent girls with AN had higher levels of dopamine waste products
IDA	Real-world application – possibility for treatment
IDA	Biological determinism – implication for insurance payouts

Work out your own plan for this question and then write your answer.

Discuss **two or more** biological explanations of one eating disorder. (8 marks + 16 marks)

Biological explanations

AO1	
AO1	
AO1	
AO1	
AO2	
AO2	
AO2	
AO2	
AO2	
AO2	
AO2 or IDA	
AO2 or IDA	
AO2 or IDA	

Answer plan 2

Discuss psychological explanations of **one** eating disorder. (8 marks + 16 marks)

Psychological explanation 1: Traumatic experience

AO1	Cooper *et al.* (2004) people with bulimia nervosa (BN) had early traumatic experiences that make them feel worthless
AO1	BN is then maintained by the 'circle of thoughts'
AO2	Research support – e.g. lack of parental bonding linked to development of dysfunctional beliefs (Leung *et al.*, 2000)
AO2	Evidence that binge-eating in BN is preceded by considerable distress (Abraham and Beaumont, 1982)
AO2	Dysfunctional beliefs also been shown to link to bingeing and vomiting symptoms (e.g. Waller *et al.*, 2000)
IDA	Real world application – implications for treatment of BN using CBT, but not always effective (Fairburn *et al.*, 1995)

Psychological explanation 2: Functional model

AO1	People engage in binge-eating as a way of coping with problems associated with self-image
AO1	Negative self-image and wish to escape from difficult life issues leads to a 'diffuse-avoidant identity style' (Wheeler *et al.*, 2001)
AO2	Support for functional theory, Polivy *et al.* (1994) stress-induced dieters consumed food regardless of palatability
AO2	Real-world application – target symptoms for treatment
IDA	Cultural bias – BN culture-bound (Keel and Klump, 2003)
IDA	Heterosexual bias – gay and bisexual men have higher risk factor (15%) for BN than lesbian (10%) or heterosexual (8%) women (Feldman and Meyer, 2003)

Answer plan 3

(a) Outline **one** biological explanation of **one** eating disorder. (4 marks)

(b) Outline and evaluate **two** psychological explanations of **one** eating disorder. (4 marks + 16 marks)

Part (a) Biological explanation

AO1	Sexual competition hypothesis – BN is a direct consequence of the evolved need to compete with other females in order to attract a mate
AO1	Obsession with weight an evolved adaptation to preserve a shape that is attractive to potential mates

Part (b) Psychological explanations

AO1	Cooper *et al.* (2004) BN result of traumatic experiences, worthlessness feelings maintained by 'circle of thoughts'
AO1	Functional model – binge-eating a way of coping with self-image problems, leads to a 'diffuse-avoidant identity style'
AO2	Research support, e.g. lack of parental bonding linked to development of dysfunctional beliefs (Leung *et al.*, 2000)
AO2	Evidence that binge-eating in BN is preceded by considerable distress (Abraham and Beaumont, 1982)
AO2	Dysfunctional beliefs also been shown to link to bingeing and vomiting symptoms (e.g. Waller *et al.*, 2000)
IDA	Real-world application – treatment of BN using CBT, but not always effective (Fairburn *et al.*, 1995)
AO2	Support for functional theory, Polivy *et al.* (1994) stress-induced dieters consumed food regardless of palatability
AO2	Real-world application – target symptoms for treatment
IDA	Cultural bias – BN culture-bound (Keel and Klump, 2003)
IDA	Heterosexual bias – gay and bisexual men have higher risk factor (15%) for BN than lesbian (10%) or heterosexual (8%) women (Feldman and Meyer, 2003)

Discuss psychological explanations of **one** eating disorder. (8 marks + 16 marks)

Cooper *et al.* (2004) claim people with bulimia nervosa have suffered early traumatic experiences. These experiences leave them feeling worthless and unlovable. When they later experience criticisms about their body shape or their weight, they try to lose weight in the belief that if they do so this will overcome their thoughts of worthlessness.

The individual's bulimia is maintained by a 'circle of thoughts'. First, they believe that binge-eating will make them feel better. This triggers a binge-eating episode until the thought that 'I will get fat' takes over. This triggers a purge to avoid the harm associated with the binge-eating episode. This leads to feelings of worthlessness, followed by binge-eating and the cycle is repeated.

Leung *et al.* (2000) provide research support for Cooper *et al.*'s cognitive model. They studied 66 women with a current eating disorder and found that failure to bond with parents was linked to the development of dysfunctional core beliefs, such as 'I am worthless'. The findings provide evidence that core beliefs are important factors in the development of eating disorders, such as BN.

Consistent with the claims of this model, Abraham and Beaumont (1982) found that binge-eating in BN is often preceded by feelings of considerable distress. They surveyed 32 bulimic patients and found that a high incidence of binge-eating was linked to situations where these individuals felt tense, anxious or lonely. This supports the claim that the characteristic bingeing of BN may be caused by extremes of low mood.

There is research evidence that dysfunctional beliefs link to bingeing and vomiting symptoms (e.g. Waller *et al.*, 2000). Waller *et al.* found that overeating (leading to purging) is considered a way of coping with the negative emotions that arise from activation of dysfunctional schemas thus further supporting the link between cognitions and binge-eating.

A real world application of this model is its implications for the treatment of BN. If BN is cognitively based, then it should be possible to treat it using a cognitively based therapy, such as CBT. Although there is some evidence that CBT is useful in reducing the symptoms of BN, it is not always effective, as Fairburn *et al.* (1995) found that at the end of treatment only 50% were symptom free.

The functional model states that people engage in binge-eating as a way of coping with problems associated with their self-image. By overeating, the individual can attribute any resulting distress to the overeating rather than to their low self-image. As a result, the binge-eating associated with BN is functional for individuals trying to deal with life stressors.

In an extension to the functional model, Wheeler *et al.* (2001) suggest that a negative self-image together with a desire to escape from difficult life issues leads to the development of a 'diffuse-avoidant identity style'. These individuals feel externally controlled, use emotion-focused rather than problem-focused coping strategies and avoid the exploration of identity issues. They maintain a negative self-image and feel socially isolated, which leads to BN.

There is research support for functional theory. Polivy *et al.* (1994) found that, compared to ordinary dieters, stress-induced dieters consumed larger quantities of food regardless of its palatability. This lends support to the claim that the primary purpose of binge-eating is to alleviate the stress associated with a negative self-image rather than the attractiveness of the food itself.

A real world application of this theory is in its implications for the treatment of BN. The development of a diffuse-avoidant identity style makes individuals susceptible to a number of different health and social problems. As a result, targeting the symptoms that might lead to this form of identity, such as self-consciousness and depression, is vital to prevent the development of BN.

Explanations of BN may well be culture biased. The fact that BN is more commonly found in Western cultures than non-Western cultures suggests that it is a culture-bound syndrome. Keel and Klump (2003) tested this claim with an analysis of the incidence of BN in Western and non-Western cultures, and their findings suggested that BN was a culture-bound syndrome.

Research into the causes of BN shows a heterosexual bias by focusing almost exclusively on heterosexual women. However, Feldman and Meyer (2007) estimated that 15% of gay and bisexual men suffer from an eating disorder, such as BN, compared to 10% of lesbian women or 8% of heterosexual women.

This question calls for explanations in the plural. The first two paragraphs in this essay are the AO1 content for the first explanation, followed by four paragraphs for its corresponding AO2. This pattern is then repeated for the second explanation. This ensures an appropriate balance in your answer.

Each point in the essay plan on the facing page has been expanded to about 50–60 words, thus producing an essay of the appropriate length and also with the appropriate balance between AO1 and AO2.

Usually you will need to provide an outline description of the material you have available in order to generate two 50–60 word paragraphs for each explanation. Occasionally you will need the full four paragraph version of this explanation. Be prepared for both possibilities when revising for your examinations. None of these questions should catch you unprepared.

The final two paragraphs count as IDA. Each point is linked specifically to the context of BN and is sufficiently elaborated to ensure maximum credit.

This answer is 723 words long. There are 239 words of AO1 and 484 words of AO2, providing ample AO1 and AO2 for 8 marks + 16 marks.

Answer for you to mark

See page 172 for examiner's comments.

Question

(a) Outline **one** psychological explanation of **one** eating disorder. (4 marks)

(b) Outline and evaluate evolutionary explanations of food preference. (4 marks + 16 marks)

Student answer

Part (a)

❶ *Anorexia nervosa could be due to exposure to thin models on TV and in magazines. We live in a society where we are surrounded by images of skinny models, such as Chloe Memiseric who is the face of Marc Jacobs. This causes young girls to feel they have to be skinny like the models, which can lead to anorexia.*

❷ *The fashion industry in France has responded to the damaging influence of the media by developing a charter where fashion houses agree to use a variety of different sized models and not to push the message that skinny is best. This aims to promote a healthier body image among girls and young women.*

(112 words)

Part (a) AO1 Mark scheme

There is a requirement for a brief description of one psychological explanation of one eating disorder (i.e. anorexia nervosa, bulimia nervosa or obesity). There are no marks available for a second psychological explanation, biological explanations, AO2 or IDA.

4 marks is about 100–120 words.

Comments and marks for part (a) AO1

Guidance on marking is given on pages 6–11.

Mark	Knowledge and understanding	Accuracy	Organisation and structure
4	Reasonably thorough	Accurate	Coherent
3–2	Limited	Generally accurate	Reasonably coherent
1	Weak and muddled		
0	No creditworthy material		

Tick the terms you think apply to the student's answer.

The **AO1** mark I would give is ☐

Part (b)

❸ *The first evolutionary explanation is the EEA, which stands for environment of evolutionary adaptation. This is thought to be about two million years ago, and was probably the African Savannah. This harsh environment is where human beings first emerged and lived as a separate species.*

❹ *A criticism of the EEA as an explanation of evolutionary food preferences is that not all preferences can be traced back to that period. For example there are many foods today that are preferred because they are healthy, and either would not have been available to early humans or would not have been eaten because in those days they had a completely different lifestyle.*

❺ *A second explanation is that early humans would have preferred fatty foods because fat could be converted into energy. They would also have preferred sweet tasting things for the same reason. That is why nowadays we like fatty foods like pizzas and burgers, and sweet tasting things, such as sugar and syrup.*

Part (b) AO1 Mark scheme

There is a requirement for a brief description of at least two evolutionary explanations of food preference.

Evolutionary explanations that are generic (i.e. not focused explicitly on food preferences) would gain little credit.

4 marks is about 100–120 words.

❻ A third explanation is the preference for meat. Meat was packed full of nutrients which could be converted into energy. This was essential for the very active lifestyle that early humans lived, and so preference for meat soon became an evolved preference. It is also thought that meat was important for brain growth, which would not have been possible with a vegetarian diet.

❼ Cordain et al. (2006) criticise the preference for meat explanation, claiming that early humans would not have eaten meat on a regular basis, therefore would have obtained all their nutrition and energy from other sources, such as fruits and nuts. However, Abrams (1987) disputes the claim that early humans might have been vegetarian, arguing that most societies across the world have a preference for meat.

❽ A final explanation is taste aversion. This is the ability of early humans to have learned very quickly to avoid any food that made them sick, because it might be poisonous. If they could avoid that food in the future then they would survive. Garcia et al. studied this effect in the laboratory and discovered that rats would avoid saccharin if they were made ill through radiation shortly after eating it. Taste aversion helps individuals survive and this ability is passed on to offspring.

❾ There is a practical application of taste aversion. Children who are having chemotherapy to treat cancer often develop taste aversion towards certain food that they eat round the time of their chemotherapy. However, it is the chemotherapy that is making them ill rather than the food. Despite this they still develop an aversion to the food and avoid it.

❿ One way to avoid this taking place is to feed the children with two types of food, one of which is unfamiliar. Because all animals have an evolved mistrust of unfamiliar foods, they are more likely to avoid the unfamiliar food and not any familiar food, so are more likely to eat their normal diet during treatment.

(485 words)

Part (b) AO2 mark scheme

This component of part (b) requires an evaluation of evolutionary explanations of food preferences. Although these are most likely to be the same explanations that were outlined in the AO1 component, this does not have to be the case, and more general criticisms of evolutionary explanations would also be creditworthy provided the focus remains on food preferences.

16 marks is about 400–480 words.

Comments and marks for part (b) AO1

Mark	Knowledge and understanding	Accuracy	Organisation and structure
4	Reasonably thorough	Accurate	Coherent
3–2	Limited	Generally accurate	Reasonably coherent
1	Weak and muddled		
0	No creditworthy material		

The **AO1** mark I would give is ☐

Comments and marks for part (b) AO2

Mark	Analysis and understanding	Focus	Elaboration	Line of argument	Issues/debates/ approaches	Quality of written communication
16–13	Sound	Well focused	Coherent	Clear	Used effectively	Fluent, effective use of terms
12–9	Reasonable	Generally focused	Reasonable	Evident	Reasonably effective	Clear, appropriate
8–5	Basic, superficial	Sometimes focused	Some evidence		Superficial reference	Lacks clarity, limited use of terms
4–1	Rudimentary, limited understanding	Weak, muddled and incomplete	Not effective	May be mainly irrelevant	Absent or muddled/ inaccurate	Often unconnected assertions, errors
0	No creditworthy material					

The **AO2** mark I would give is ☐

Chapter 6 Gender

There have been changes to the specification from September 2011 – therefore the updated specification details here are slightly different to those in some editions of the *A2 Complete Companion*.

Division 1 Psychological explanations of gender development	• Cognitive developmental theory, including Kohlberg • Gender schema theory

Possible exam questions for this division

Discuss Kohlberg's theory of gender development. (8 marks + 16 marks)	This 'blockbuster' question is an obvious one. It could be phrased differently (e.g. 'Discuss **one** cognitive developmental theory of gender development). Principal examiners do try to make questions as clear as possible but you have to be prepared for any wording that is on the specification.
Describe and evaluate gender schema theory. (8 marks + 16 marks)	The second most obvious question for this division would be on the second theory mentioned, gender schema theory. In this question (and the question above) it is important to heed the mark division and make sure you do write sufficient AO1 to gain the full 8 marks but at the same time, not to write too much so you have plenty of time for the 16 mark element. You should aim to write about 200–240 words of AO1 and 400–480 words of AO2.
(a) Outline and evaluate Kohlberg's theory of gender development. (4 marks + 8 marks) (b) Outline and evaluate gender schema theory as an explanation of gender development. (4 marks + 8 marks)	Questions may be parted to give candidates the opportunity to demonstrate their knowledge of both areas of this division. Since you should have lots to write on both theories (a 600 word answer for both), the main challenge will be cutting this down to match the mark allocations in this question. Time is very short in the exam so you should prepare your shorter answers in advance in order to avoid having to make decisions during the exam. See model answer on page 65.
Discuss **one** psychological theory of gender development. (8 marks + 16 marks)	This question leaves the choice to you about which theory to cover – but don't hedge your bets and do a bit of both as only one will be credited. You can always use the other theory as part of your evaluation (e.g. comparing approaches – a useful way to gain IDA marks). However, take great care to use the second theory as evaluation and not just some more description.

Division 2 Biological influences on gender	• The role of hormones and genes in gender development • Evolutionary explanations of gender • The biosocial approach to gender development including gender dysphoria

Possible exam questions for this division

Discuss the role of hormones **and/or** genes in gender development. (8 marks + 16 marks)	This is a straightforward lift from the specification with one alteration – you are given the choice of covering either hormones or genes or both. When answering this question it is important to focus on the *developmental* role of hormones and/or genes in gender.
Describe and evaluate evolutionary explanations of gender. (8 marks + 16 marks)	This is another obvious question that you should expect and therefore you should ensure that you have sufficient material for both AO1 and AO2. The biggest mistake that candidates make is to write about the theory of evolution in general and fail to link this to gender.
(a) Describe evolutionary explanations of gender. (8 marks) (b) Evaluate evolutionary explanations of gender. (16 marks)	You might think this question is essentially the same as the one above, and in many ways it is. One thing that catches candidates out is that they put IDA material in part (a) where it receives no credit. They also sometimes add evaluation points in part (a) which again gain no credit. In such parted questions you need to be very careful about where you place material. In addition, of course, it is important to write twice as much for part (b) (about 400–480 words) as for part (a).
Discuss the biosocial approach to gender development. (8 marks + 16 marks)	The 'biosocial approach' refers to theories that combine both biological and social explanations. The way the question (and specification) are phrased means that you could gain full marks just discussing one theory (there is no requirement for two). If you do wish to cover two be mindful of the problem that you may write too much AO1 and this almost inevitably means too little AO2, missing out on important marks.

Discuss biological influences on gender development. (8 marks + 16 marks)	A question could be set that covers all of the topics in this division and then the choice is yours about what to include. As pointed out earlier, the problem is that you will have far too much relevant material and will therefore need to make decisions about what to include. Perhaps it is best to restrict yourself to just one of the three topic areas in this division. If you do go for all three you must ensure sufficient depth/detail for all three topics – although there is a danger in such an answer of just becoming too superficial.
Discuss research on gender dysphoria. (8 marks + 16 marks)	In this question, and the one following one, you are required to discuss gender dysophoria. However, the first question is open-ended – you could include both research studies and explanations as part of your AO1. In the next question (below) you must focus on the biosocial approach as it applies to gender dysphoria, i.e. consider how both biological and psychosocial explanations can be combined. See model answer on page 67.
Describe and evaluate the biosocial approach to explaining gender dysophoria. (8 marks + 16 marks)	In this question gender dysphoria has been linked to the biosocial approach because that is how it appears in the specification. In this case research studies would not be a creditworthy part of the AO1 but could be used as part of your AO2. If you do use research studies for AO2 then you must restrict description of these studies to a bare minimum and focus on what the findings/conclusions tell us about biosocial explanations.
(a) Outline the role of genes in gender development. (8 marks) (b) Consider the extent to which the biosocial approach has explained gender development. (16 marks)	This question should alert you to the fact that questions may include elements from different topic areas; anything is possible. In part (b) here you have to supply only evaluation of the biosocial approach. You might find it difficult to leave out your description but you must force yourself to do this otherwise you are recklessly throwing away marks. Just imagine you have already written the AO1 part of the biosocial approach.
(a) Outline psychological and biological explanations of gender development. (8 marks) (b) Evaluate psychological and biological approaches of gender development. (16 marks)	It is also possible that exam questions will span divisions, as in the case of this question. Part (a) may appear a bit ambiguous because it clearly requires more than one explanation but it isn't clear whether one of each would be sufficient – given the total of 8 marks for the question part, it is reasonable to assume that one of each would be sufficient. You can do more if you wish but there is a risk that you'll end up writing too much and/or not giving enough detail. Part (b) is all AO2. Any evaluation provided in part (a) will not be credited (and this includes any IDA). You can include any theories in your evaluation, even if they haven't been covered in part (a). See student answer on page 70.

Division 3 Social influences on gender

- **Social influences on gender, for example the influence of parents, peers, schools, media**
- **Cultural influences on gender role**

Possible exam questions for this division

Describe and evaluate social influences on gender. (8 marks + 16 marks)	The specification includes four examples of social influences on gender but these are *examples* only and therefore not required in any exam answer. The principal examiner may include them as helpful guidance but always be aware that you don't have to include the examples in your answer.
Describe and evaluate social influences on gender. Some examples include the influence of parents, peers, schools, media. (8 marks + 16 marks)	This question is basically the same as the one above but the examples have been provided. Putting examples in a question is intended to be helpful but sometimes it confuses candidates because they think they must include all four examples – they are just examples.
Discuss cultural influences on gender role. (8 marks + 16 marks)	The likely approach to answering this question is to describe relevant studies for the AO1 content and evaluate these for AO2. Relevant studies would be those that have investigated the variations in gender role in different cultures. See model answer on page 69.
(a) Outline the biosocial approach to gender development. (4 marks) (b) Outline social influence on gender roles. (4 marks) (c) With reference to research studies, evaluate the influence of biosocial and social factors on gender roles. (16 marks)	This question again flags up the possibility that questions may be set on topics across divisions – part (a) concerns material from division 2 and parts (b) and (c) are related to this division. In part (c) you must focus on research studies only. It is important to avoid any description of the studies as this would not count as AO2. It is also important to remember the approximate word count for each part. About 100–120 words for part (a), the same for part (b) and a minimum of 400 words for part (c).

Division 1 Psychological explanations of gender development

Answer plans

Answer plan 1
Discuss Kohlberg's theory of gender development. (8 marks + 16 marks)

Kohlberg's theory

AO1	Theory based on Piaget's ideas about cognitive development, e.g. lack of internal logic and maturation
AO1	Stage 1 Gender labelling (2–3½ years), gender label based on appearance, but can change this if appearance changes
AO1	Stage 2 Gender stability (3½–4½ years), gender seen as consistent/stable over time but not across situations
AO1	Stage 3 Gender consistency, gender constant across time and situations, now learn gender-appropriate behaviour
AO2	Research support for gender labelling, e.g Thompson (1975) two-year-olds less able to identify their sex (76% vs 90%)
AO2	Research support for gender stability, e.g. Slaby and Frey (1975) no evidence until age 3 or 4 as predicted
AO2	Research support for gender consistency, e.g. Slaby and Frey (1975) interest in gender-appropriate models
AO2	Studies may lack internal validity, not testing what they intend to test, e.g. Bem (1989)
IDA	Alternative cognitive approach, e.g. gender schema theory
AO2	A compromise, Stangor and Ruble (1989) motivation related to constancy, memory related to schema
IDA	Limitations of cognitive developmental approach, e.g. thinking doesn't predict behaviour
IDA	Alternative biological approach, e.g. genes, hormones

DIY

Work out your own plan for these questions and then write your answers.

(a) Outline psychological and biological explanations of gender development. (8 marks)

(b) Evaluate psychological and biological approaches of gender development. (16 marks)

Part (a) Outline psychology and biological explanations

AO1	
AO1	
AO1	
AO1	

Part (b) Evaluate both

AO1	
AO2	
AO2	
AO2	
IDA	
AO2	
AO2 or IDA	
AO2 or IDA	
AO2 or IDA	

This essay comes from the selection given in division 2 (page 66), but we have included it here.

Answer plan 2
Describe and evaluate gender schema theory. (8 marks + 16 marks)

Gender schema theory

AO1	Martin and Halverson (1981), learning gender appropriate behaviour after gender labelling but before gender constancy
AO1	Children learn schemas through social interactions
AO1	Children focus on ingroup schemas and avoid outgroup behaviours
AO1	Fixed gender attitudes because they ignore information inconsistent with schemas
AO2	Gender stereotypes occurred without constancy (Martin and Little, 1990) not as Kohlberg suggested
AO2	Greater attention to information consistent with gender schemas (Martin and Halverson, 1983)
AO2	Greater attention to ingroup than outgroup schema (Bradbard *et al.*, 1986)
AO2	Children may be receptive to some gender inconsistent ideas (Gibbons *et al.*, 1996)
IDA	Alternative cognitive approaches, e.g. Kohlberg
AO2	A compromise, Stangor and Ruble (1989) motivation related to constancy, memory related to schema
IDA	Limitations of cognitive developmental approach, e.g. thinking doesn't predict behaviour
IDA	Alternative biological approach, e.g. genes, hormones

Answer plan 3
(a) Outline and evaluate Kohlberg's theory of gender development. (4 marks + 8 marks)
(b) Outline and evaluate gender schema theory as an explanation of gender development. (4 marks + 8 marks)

Part (a) Kohlberg's theory

AO1	Theory based on Piaget's ideas about cognitive development, e.g. maturation and lack of internal logic
AO1	Stages (1) gender labeling based on appearance, (2) gender stability over time, (3) gender consistency across time and situations, learn gender-appropriate behaviour
AO2	Research support for gender labelling, e.g Thompson (1975) two year olds less able to identify their sex (76% vs 90%)
AO2	Research support for gender stability, e.g. Slaby and Frey (1975) no evidence until age 3 or 4
AO2	Research support for gender consistency, e.g. Slaby and Frey (1975) interest in gender-appropriate models
AO2	Studies may lack internal validity, not testing what they intend to test, e.g. Bem (1989)

Part (b) Gender schema theory

AO1	Martin and Halverson (1981), learning gender appropriate behaviour before gender labelling but after gender constancy
AO1	Children learn schemas through social interactions
AO2	Gender stereotypes occurred without constancy (Martin and Little, 1990) not as Kohlberg suggested
AO2	Greater attention to information consistent with gender schemas (Martin and Halverson, 1983)
AO2	Greater attention to ingroup than outgroup schema (Bradbard *et al.*, 1986)
IDA	Limitations of cognitive developmental approach, e.g. thinking doesn't predict behaviour

Model answer

(a) Outline and evaluate Kohlberg's theory of gender development. (4 marks + 8 marks)

Kohlberg's concept of gender constancy comes from Piaget's ideas about cognitive development, for example maturation and a lack of internal logic when young. In early development children don't think logically, for example they are swayed by what things look like.

Kohlberg proposed a stage theory of gender development, based on the maturation of the child's ways of thinking. The first stage is gender labelling (2-3½ years), when children select a person's gender label based on appearance, but this can change if appearance changes. Stage 2 is gender stability (3½–4½ years). Children understand that gender is consistent/stable over time (e.g. boys grow into men) but lack understanding of constancy, i.e. it is not stable across situations. Stage 3 is gender consistency. Children realise that gender is constant across time and situations. Only at this point will children start to learn about gender-appropriate behaviour.

There is support for the gender labeling stage. Thompson (1975) found that two year olds were 76% correct in identifying their sex whereas three year olds were 90% correct. This supports Kohlberg's claim that children progressively become able to label their gender between the ages of 2 and 3.

Gender stability was investigated by Slaby and Frey (1975) who asked young children 'Were you a little girl or a little boy when you were a baby?' and 'When you grow up will you be a mummy or daddy?' Children did not recognise that these traits were stable over time until they were 3 or 4 years old, as Kohlberg had predicted.

Gender consistency was also considered by Slaby and Frey (1975). Those children high in gender constancy showed greatest interest in same-sex models. (Constancy is a combination of stability and consistency.) This suggests, as Kohlberg predicted, that an increasing sense of constancy leads children to pay more attention to gender-appropriate behaviour.

One problem for this research is the question of whether the researchers were actually testing what they intended to test. Bem (1989) demonstrated that it is genital knowledge rather than gender constancy which explains the findings. In her study many of those children who failed to display gender constancy (changed the gender label when the child was dressed in different clothes) actually also failed a genital knowledge test. This suggests that the research studies a lack of internal validity.

This is not an easy theory to write about in an outline without losing important details. It is desirable to go beyond a simple ages and stages outline and include some other details of the theory, as we have done here.

Notice how each AO2 paragraph starts with a lead-in sentence identifying the point and ends with a phrase or sentence explaining 'so what?'.

In this essay the AO1 and AO2 distributions need to be right for each part. In other words it would not be OK to have equal amounts of AO1 and AO2 in part (a) and make up for this with lots more AO2 in part (b) because each part is marked separately.

Part (a) has about 140 AO1 words and about 230 AO2 words, not the ideal 1:2 ratio but enough of each assessment objective.

(b) Outline and evaluate gender schema theory as an explanation of gender development. (4 marks + 8 marks)

Martin and Halverson (1981), like Kohlberg, believed that gender development involves acquiring information about one's own gender. However, Martin and Halverson argued that children start to learn about gender-appropriate behaviour before gender constancy is achieved. They claimed that basic gender identity (gender labelling) is sufficient for a child to identify him/herself as boy/girl and take an interest in what behaviours are appropriate.

Martin and Halverson explained gender development in terms of schemas, organised clusters of information about gender appropriate behaviour. Children learn these schemas from their interactions with people, such as learning about what toys are appropriate toys for each gender, what clothes to wear and so on.

There is research support for the view that gender stereotypes are acquired before constancy. Martin and Little (1990) found that children under the age of four showed no signs of gender constancy, but did display strong gender stereotypes about what boys and girls were permitted to do. This shows that they have acquired information about gender roles before Kohlberg suggested, in line with gender schema theory.

The concept of schemas is also supported by research that shows children do not simply pay more attention to consistent schemas but remember them better. Martin and Halverson (1981) found that when children were asked to recall pictures of people, children under six recalled more of the gender-consistent ones (such as a male fire-fighter or female teacher) than gender-inconsistent ones (such as a male nurse or female chemist).

The importance of schemas is shown in research by Bradbard *et al.* (1986). If gender schemas are important in acquiring information about gender then we would expect children to pay greater attention to information consistent with their gender schemas (about being a boy or a girl). Children aged between four and nine were told that gender neutral items (e.g. burglar alarm, pizza cutter) were either boy or girl items. Participants took a greater interest in toys labelled as ingroup (i.e. a boy was more interested in a toy labelled as a boy toy).

There are some obvious limitations to the cognitive developmental approach. One limitation is that there is evidence that the way we think may not be related to the way we behave. For example, Durkin (1995) observed that couples who agree to share domestic tasks in reality don't do it. In other words their intentions/thoughts don't match their actual behaviour.

When writing both parts (a) and (b) it is necessary to select certain aspects of each theory. If you try to describe everything you will end up with a superficial outline and fail to gain top marks.

IDA points only gain credit if they are made specifically relevant to the essay rather than being general points that could be placed in any essay.

Part (b) contains 108 words of AO1 and 286 words of AO2, so again the balance is not quite right (not 1:2) but there is more than sufficient content for each.

In total the answer is just about 780 words.

Division 2 Biological influences on gender Answer plans

Answer plan 1

Discuss the role of hormones **and/or** genes in gender development. (8 marks + 16 marks)

Hormones and/or gender

AO1	Genes are on chromosomes, most people are XX or XY
AO1	Chromosomal sex determines hormones which determine external genitalia and brain development
AO1	External genitalia affect sex typing and gender identity
AO1	Exposure to testosterone creates masculinised brain (Geschwind and Galaburda, 1987)
AO2	Evidence that biological sex not the main factor, e.g. Money and Ehrhardt (1972)
AO2	This evidence disputed by ultimate outcome of David Reimer case (Diamond and Sigmundsen, 1997)
AO2	Further supported by Reiner and Gearhardt (2004), 16 XY males born with almost no penis
IDA	Biological determinism challenged, e.g. Dessens *et al.* (2005) 250 cases of XY typed as females
IDA	Nature and nurture both involved
IDA	Real-world application, e.g. Olympics when determining sex
AO2	Methodological issues, e.g. case studies
AO2	Methodological issues, e.g. abnormal individuals

Work out your own plan for this question and then write your answer.

Discuss the biosocial approach to gender development. (8 marks + 16 marks)

Biosocial approach

AO1	
AO1	
AO1	
AO1	
AO2	
AO2	
AO2	
AO2	
AO2	
AO2 or IDA	
AO2 or IDA	
AO2 or IDA	

Answer plan 2

Describe and evaluate evolutionary explanations of gender. (8 marks + 16 marks)

Evolutionary explanations of gender

AO1	Division of labour enhanced reproductive success in EEA, men hunted, women did domestic duties and farmed
AO2	Consequence, meat-sharing hypothesis (Stanford, 1999)
IDA	Determinist approach, but in reality evolutionary theory combines both nature and nurture
AO1	Gender role behaviours related to adaptive reproductive strategies, e.g. men mate as frequently as possible
AO2	Research support, Buss (1989) 37 cultures
AO2	Research support, Waynforth and Dunbar (1995) personal ads, men seek attractiveness, women seek resources
AO1	E-S theory (Baron-Cohen, 2002) male hunters gained evolutionary advantage systematising, women better mothers through empathising
AO2	Research support, Baron-Cohen (2002) Systematising Quotient Questionnaire
AO2	Implication, autism is a product of an extreme male brain
AO1	Stress response, adaptive for men to fight or flight and for females to tend and befriend
AO2	Research support, Ennis *et al.* (2001) men increased cortisol during exams, women lower
IDA	Evolutionary approach criticised as speculative, some evidence is (e.g. Neanderthal extinction related to lack of gender roles) but also sound research support

Answer plan 3

Discuss research on gender dysphoria. (8 marks + 16 marks)

Gender dysphoria

AO1	Psychological explanation, mental illness (Coates *et al.*, 1991) defensive reaction to mother's depression
AO1	Prenatal exposure to male hormones, e.g. CAH causes mismatch of external genitalia and genetic sex
AO1	Transsexual androgen receptor gene (Hare *et al.*, 2009) causes under-masculinising of brain
AO1	Brain sex theory (Zhou *et al.*, 1995) BSTc smaller in MtF transsexuals than normal males
AO2	Psychological explanation, lack of research support, e.g. Cole *et al.* (1997) 435 gender dysphorics had no mental illness
AO2	Prenatal exposure, lack of support, e.g. Dessens *et al.* (2005) 250 cases of XY typed as females, 95% content with female role
AO2	Brain sex theory criticisms, e.g. Chung *et al.* (2002) difference develops after dysphoria
AO2	Support, e.g. Rametti *et al.* (2011) FtM individuals have brains similar to males before hormone therapy
AO2	Biological explanations not all genetic, e.g. environmental effect of DDT which contains oestrogen
IDA	Real-world application, helping intersexes
AO2	Methodological issues, e.g. different kinds of gender dysphoria require different explanations (Blanchard, 1985)
IDA	Socially sensitive research, may/may not help transsexuals

Model answer

Discuss research on gender dysphoria. (8 marks + 16 marks)

One psychological explanation is that gender dysphoria is related to mental illness caused by some childhood trauma or maladaptive upbringing. For example, Coates *et al.* (1991) studied one boy who developed gender dysphoria, proposing that this was a defensive reaction to the boy's mother's depression following an abortion. The trauma may have led to a cross-gender fantasy as a means of resolving the ensuing anxiety.

A second explanation is a biological one. Gender dysphoria may be caused by abnormal prenatal exposure to male hormones. Some genetic conditions cause a mismatch between hormones and genetic sex. For example. CAH (congenital adrenal hyperplasia) occurs when XY individuals (genetic female) have high levels of male hormones prenatally and develop a small penis, and may be sex-typed as male. In such cases the outcome may be gender dysphoria.

A further biological explanation is that some individuals are born with a transsexual gene. Hare *et al.* (2009) studied 112 MtF transsexuals and found a version of the androgen receptor gene that causes reduced action of the male sex hormone testosterone. This may have an effect on gender development in the womb (e.g. under-masculinising the brain) which would create dysphoria.

A third biological explanation is the brain sex theory. One region of the brain that has been studied is the BSTc. On average, the BSTc is twice as large in heterosexual men as in heterosexual women and contains twice the number of neurons. Zhou *et al.* (1995) found that the number of neurons in the BSTc of MtF transsexuals was similar to that of the females. It may be that the size of the BSTc correlates with preferred sex rather than biological sex.

However, there is little research support for psychological explanations. For example, Cole *et al.* (1997) studied 435 individuals experiencing gender dysphoria and reported that the range of psychiatric conditions displayed was no greater than found in a 'normal' population. This suggests that gender dysphoria is generally unrelated to mental illness, trauma or pathological families.

There has also not been consistent research support for abnormal exposure to male hormones. For example, Dessens *et al.* (2005) studied 250 genetic females with CAH who were raised as females. Despite prenatal exposure to male hormones 95% were content with their female gender role. The remaining 5% did experience gender dysphoria but generally prenatal exposure to male hormones did not show a clear relationship with dysphoria.

This brain sex theory was challenged by Chung *et al.* (2002) who noted that the differences in BSTc volume between men and women does not develop until adulthood, whereas most transsexuals report that their feelings of gender dysphoria began in early childhood. This suggests that the difference found in the BSTc could not be the cause of transsexualism but might perhaps be an effect.

On the other hand there has been research support. For example, Rametti *et al.* (2011) studied the brains of FtM transsexuals before they started transgender hormone therapy. In terms of amounts of white matter in their brains, the FtM individuals had a more similar pattern to individuals who share their gender identity (males) than those who share their biological sex (females).

Often people make the mistake of equating biology with genetics, but there are some biological explanations for gender dysphoria that are not genetic or even internal. For example, the insecticide DDT contains oestrogens which may mean that males are prenatally exposed to unduly high levels of these female hormones leading to a mismatch between genetic sex and hormone influences.

Understanding of gender dysphoria has real-world applications. It is very important in providing information about the effects of erroneous sex assignations and determining the best solutions. Various organisations campaign for the rights of intersex individuals and rely on research evidence to show both the biological and social influences on gender self-concepts.

One of the problems with this area of research is that there are different kinds of gender dysophoria. For example, Blanchard (1985) has proposed two distinct groups: 'homosexual transsexuals', who wish to change sex because they are attracted to men, and 'non-homosexual transsexuals', who wish to change sex because they are sexually aroused by the thought of themselves as a woman. Such differences suggest that there need to be different explanations.

One final consideration is the socially sensitive nature of this research. It may be good for transsexuals because if a biological cause is identified this may help other people to be more accepting about the needs of transsexuals (it is not their 'fault', it is simply in their biology). On the other hand if a biological cause is identified this might harm individuals born with the abnormality because it might be assumed (wrongly) that transsexualism is inevitable.

Note how this essay does not begin with a definition of gender dysphoria nor does it begin with an statement of what the essay intends to cover – neither of which would be creditworthy. There is no need to define the key term of the essay, in this case gender dysphoria. Similarly, general introductions add nothing.

Notice how research studies have been used in these two paragraphs as AO1.

Each point in the answer plan on the facing page has been expanded to about 50-60 words, thus producing an essay of the appropriate length and also with the appropriate balance between AO1 and AO2.

In this essay names and dates of researchers have been included. Neither are required but are a good way to provide detail and elaboration.

This explanation for gender dysphoria has been used as an effective critical point.

In total this essay is 781 words. About 35% is AO1 which is about the right proportion (half as much AO1 as AO2).

Division 3 Social influences on gender Answer plans

Answer plan 1

Describe and evaluate social influences on gender. (8 marks + 16 marks)

Social influences

AO1	Parents – differential reinforcement, e.g. fathers react negatively to sons' feminine behaviours (Idle *et al.*, 1993)
AO1	Peers – provide specific gender models and reinforce gender appropriate behaviour (Bandura, 1999)
AO1	Schools – socialise children, reinforce gender appropriate behaviour and act as role models
AO1	Media – gender stereotypes (Bussey and Bandura, 1999), more TV the more stereotypes (McGhee and Frueh, 1980)
AO2	Parents, research support, e.g. Smith and Lloyd (1978) babies presented as girl or boy, mothers selected a toy
AO2	Peers, research support, e.g. Lamb and Roopnarine (1979) peer reinforcement mainly a reminder
AO2	Schools, research support, e.g. Perry and Bussey (1979) same-sex modelling if behaviour not counter to stereotypes
AO2	Media, research support, e.g. Williams (1985) first exposure to TV led to increased gender stereotypes
IDA	Real-world application to change media representations, e.g. Pingree (1978) show women in non-traditional roles
IDA	Contrasts with the cognitive developmental approach
IDA	Ignores biological influences, e.g. hormones
AO2	Direct tuition may be more important, e.g. Martin *et al.* (1995) labelling of toys stronger than role model

DIY

Work out your own plan for these questions and then write your answer.

(a) Outline and evaluate social influences on gender. (4 marks + 8 marks)

(b) Outline and evaluate cultural influences on gender role. (4 marks + 8 marks)

Part (a) Social influences

AO1	
AO1	
AO2	
AO2	
AO2	
AO2 or IDA	

Part (b) Cultural influences

AO1	
AO1	
AO2	
AO2	
AO2	
AO2 or IDA	

Answer plan 2

Discuss cultural influences on gender role. (8 marks + 16 marks)

Cultural influences

AO1	Division of labour appears to be universal (Munroe and Munroe, 1975, e.g. childcare)
AO1	Male aggression higher in all cultures studied by Mead (1949) but also cultural relativism
AO1	Universal sex stereotypes (Williams and Best,1990)
AO1	Conformity highest in tightly knit, sedentary societies (Berry *et al.*, 2002)
AO2	Alternative explanation for universality, Eagly and Wood (1999) psychological differences due to social roles
AO2	Eagly and Wood's view supported by re-analysis of Buss (1989) data on mate preferences
AO2	Labour divisions are the same in most but not all cultures (Sugihara and Katsurada, 2002)
AO2	Alternative cultural explanation, conformity can be explained in terms of power (Schlegel and Barry, 1986)
AO2	Mead's research criticised by Freeman (1984) and his work criticised by Appell (1984)
IDA	Culture bias, Williams and Best criticised because possible imposed etic (questionnaire and concepts are Western)
AO2	General issues with cross-cultural research, e.g. natural experiments can't demonstrate causes (culture is IV)
IDA	Nature or nurture, biology or culture

Answer plan 3

(a) Outline the biosocial approach to gender development. (4 marks)

(b) Outline social influence on gender roles. (4 marks)

(c) With reference to research studies, evaluate the influence of biosocial and social factors on gender roles. (16 marks)

Part (a) Biological approach

AO1	Division of labour appears to be universal (Munroe and Munroe, 1975, e.g. childcare)
AO1	Male aggression higher in all cultures studied by Mead (1949) but also cultural relativism

Part (b) Social factors

AO1	Parents – differential reinforcement, e.g. fathers react negatively to sons' feminine behaviours (Idle *et al.*, 1993)
AO1	Media – gender stereotypes (Bussey and Bandura, 1999), more TV the more stereotypes (McGhee and Frueh, 1980)

Part (c) Assess influence

AO2	Evidence that biological sex not the main factor, e.g. Money and Ehrhardt (1972) importance of socialisation
AO2	This evidence disputed by ultimate outcome of David Reimer case (Diamond and Sigmundsen, 1997)
IDA	Biological determinism challenged, e.g. Dessens *et al.* (2005) 250 cases of XY typed as females
AO2	Methodological issues, e.g. case studies
AO2	Support for role of parents, e.g. Smith and Lloyd (1978) babies presented as girl or boy, mothers selected a toy
AO2	Research support, e.g. Williams (1985) first exposure to TV led to increased gender stereotypes
IDA	Real-world application, pressure on media, e.g. Pingree (1978)
IDA	Nature and nurture both involved

Model answer

Discuss cultural influences on gender role. (8 marks + 16 marks)

One aspect of gender roles is division of labour – men are hunters and women look after children and prepare food. Cross-cultural studies of gender show that every society has some division of labour and behaviour by gender (Munroe and Munroe, 1975). Childcare is sometimes shared but in no society is it the major responsibility of males. This universality suggests that gender roles are biological rather than cultural.

A second aspect of gender roles is differences in aggressiveness. Mead (1949) observed that in all three of the cultures she studied in Papua New Guinea the men were more aggressive than the women. Though she also observed differences between cultures where some women were more aggressive than women in other cultures. This has been described as cultural relativism – aggression is innate and universal but the degree to which these behaviours are expressed is relative to the particular culture.

Sex stereotypes affect gender roles. Williams and Best (1990) studied gender stereotypes in 30 different nations involving 2,800 university students as participants. There was a broad consensus across countries. Men were seen as more dominant, aggressive and autonomous, whereas women were more nurturant, deferent and interested in affiliation. This again points to biology rather than culture.

Conformity is also related to gender, across cultures there is a general consensus that women are more conformist than men. Perhaps less well known is that this difference varies across cultures. Berry *et al.* (2002) report that conformity differences between men and women are highest in tight, sedentary societies. This shows a cultural influence on gender role.

There is an alternative explanation for the universal division of labour. Eagly and Wood (1999) argue that this division is an indirect outcome of biological differences rather than a direct outcome. According to their biosocial theory physical differences (e.g. women bear children, men are stronger) lead to social role differences and it is these that create psychological differences. Thus social/cultural factors explain role division, aggressiveness and conformity.

Eagly and Wood (1999) supported their view by re-analysing Buss' (1989) data on sex differences in mate preferences (he found that men seek attractiveness and women seek resources). They found that when women have a higher status, then sex differences in mating preferences become less pronounced. This suggests that social roles are the driving force (rather than genetic/biological factors) in psychological sex differences.

However, in fact, the picture is more complicated. Labour divisions are the same in most but not all cultures. In some cultures men take more female roles. For example, Sugihara and Katsurada (2002) found Japanese men do not seek to be 'macho' types like Americans but instead value being well rounded in the arts, a trait normally regarded as feminine.

There is also an alternative explanation for the cultural differences in conformity. In societies where women contribute a lot to food accumulation (such as the nomadic societies) women are highly valued, allowed more freedom and generally less regarded as objects for male sexual and reproductive needs (Schlegel and Barry, 1986). This means that women occupy a higher position within the social group and therefore have more power and less need to conform to the demands of the powerful members of society. This further supports the role of cultural influences.

Mead's research has been criticised by Freeman (1984) who himself worked with native Samoans and was told that they had provided Mead with the information she wanted to hear. This suggests that her conclusions are not based on valid data. However, Freeman's version has also been criticised for being inaccurate (Appell, 1984).

The problem of cultural bias is an issue in research, such as the study by Williams and Best. They used a questionnaire designed by Western researchers containing Western concepts and stereotypes (imposed etics). These may not have the same meaning in other cultures and people may simply respond in terms of Westernised stereotypes rather than commenting on their real attitudes or behaviour. Therefore, the data collected may lack validity due to a cultural bias.

There are issues with cross-cultural research generally. For example, such research is essentially a natural experiment where the independent variable is culture. It is unjustified to conclude from such studies that culture (the IV) has caused any observable differences in behaviour (the dependent variable) because participants have not been randomly allocated to conditions.

The final question is whether it is nature or nurture, biology or culture. The fact that there are universals points to biology, but the fact that within these universals there are differences points to the role of social factors as being equally important. The final conclusion points to a complex interaction between both factors.

It is important to focus each paragraph on the two key features of the title – cultural influence and gender role – in order to ensure you are answering the question.

In this essay all of the AO1 has been placed first. An alternative approach would have been to put the appropriate AO2 points after each AO1 point, but the way we have done it means that the amounts of AO1 and AO2 are clear for you when reviewing your essay in an exam.

Alternative explanations can be AO2 as long as they are clearly used as evaluation, i.e. contrasted with the other explanation and this contrast is explained.

Some AO2 points may well be shorter. What matters is that it still contains sufficient elaboration for the point to be clear – see the three-point rule on page 5.

Each AO2 and IDA point begins with a lead-in phrase that makes it clear that this is AO2 or IDA.

There is almost exactly twice as much AO2 as AO1 in this essay – perfect! A total of 771 words divided into 259 AO1 and 512 AO2.

Answer for you to mark

See page 172 for examiner's comments.

Question

(a) Outline psychological and biological explanations of gender development. (8 marks)

(b) Evaluate psychological and biological approaches of gender development. (16 marks)

Student answer

Part (a

❶ One psychological explanation of gender is Kohlberg's gender constancy theory. There are three stages in this model. The first stage is gender labelling, when children are able to identify their gender. The second stage is gender stability, when they realise gender is stable over time. The third stage is gender consistency when they realise that it is also stable across situations. This theory was in part based on Piaget's idea of conservation because gender is conserved. Cross-cultural research has supported the idea of stages but some research has found that the ages may vary.

❷ A second psychological explanation is gender schema theory . Martin and Halverson suggested that children at the age of 3 have a basic gender identity and this enables them to start to develop schemas about gender role behaviour appropriate for their gender.

❸ There are a number of different biological explanations. The first one is genetics. Most people are born as XY or XX which is genetic sex. In normal males testosterone is produced which influences the development of external male genitalia and also affects the development of the brain. The development of genitalia affects sex typing at birth and subsequent socialisation. The masculinised brain creates an individual who tends to behave in a more male fashion e.g. systematising (Baron-Cohen).

(211 words)

AO1 mark scheme for part (a)

Answers covering one psychological approach plus one biological approach can gain full marks, though some students may cover more than one of each.

For marks in the top two bands both types of approach should be reasonably balanced.

Answers with only psychological OR biological approaches are showing partial performance, and would earn a maximum of 5 marks for AO1.

8 marks is about 200–240 words.

Tick the terms you think apply to the student's answer.

Comments and marks for part (a) AO1

Mark	Knowledge and understanding	Range of material	Depth and breadth	Organisation and structure
8–7	Accurate and well-detailed	Good range	Substantial evidence of depth and breadth	Coherent
6–5	Generally accurate and reasonably detailed	Range	Depth and/or breadth	Reasonably coherent
4–3	Basic, relatively superficial	Restricted	Generally accurate	Basic
2–1	Rudimentary and may be muddled and/or inaccurate	Very brief or largely irrelevant		Lacking
0	No creditworthy material			

Guidance on marking is given on pages 6–11.

The **AO1** mark I would give is ☐

Part (b)

4 The biological approach has strong support from research that began with Money and Ehrhardt. They studied identical twins. One twin had an accident during an operation and part of his penis was removed when he was an infant. John Money advised the family that the boy would do best by having his whole penis removed and being brought up as a girl because he believed that what mattered was the sex of rearing as long as you were told before the age of 2. At first everything appeared OK but in fact Brenda was deeply unhappy. When she was a teenager she was told the truth and decided to revert to being a boy and took the name David. He never fully recovered and eventually committed suicide. This case study shows that ultimately biological influences matter.

5 Another study that supported the biological approach was by Imperato-McGinley et al. They studied children from the Batista family who were born as females. In adolescence they suddenly developed a penis because they were insensitive to testosterone but the massive amounts during puberty produced a penis. The children accepted their gender change, thus supporting the stronger influence of biology.

6 There is also evidence that supports the psychological approach. For example Kohlberg's theory is supported by a study by Slaby and Frey. They asked young children whether they thought they were a boy or a girl when they were a baby. The children didn't know how to answer until they were about three or four, which shows that they didn't develop their gender identity/labelling until then, as Kohlberg had predicted.

7 On the other hand Martin and Little found evidence against Kohlberg but in favour of gender schema theory. They found that children under the age of 4 showed strong gender stereotypes despite the fact that they hadn't achieved gender constancy.

8 The biological approach largely ignores the psychological approach, therefore suggesting it is biological factors alone. There are some approaches labeled 'biosocial' which suggest it is a mixture of biology and socialisation. John Money's approach was a biosocial one because he said sex typing at birth is largely related to biological sex and this leads to gender socialisation.

9 These views can be related to the nature-nurture debate because they suggest gender is nature or nurture.

10 There are some people who are not happy with the gender assigned at birth. They may be genetically XY but wish to become a girl or vice versa. These people are said to have gender dysphoria which may be psychological or biological, i.e. due to upbringing or experience or due to some malfunction of the body.

11 After this review of the evidence it seems that biological explanations have more substantial evidence and therefore provide a better explanation.

(449 words)

AO2 mark scheme for part (b)

Evaluation is likely to rely on research evidence followed by a consideration of which approach has the better evidence.

Evaluation might also consider the extent to which either approach explains research observations of the nature of gender development.

16 marks is about 400–480 words.

Comments and marks for part (b) AO2

Mark	Analysis and understanding	Focus	Elaboration	Line of argument	Issues/debates/ approaches	Quality of written communication
16–13	Sound	Well focused	Coherent	Clear	Used effectively	Fluent, effective use of terms
12–9	Reasonable	Generally focused	Reasonable	Evident	Reasonably effective	Clear, appropriate
8–5	Basic, superficial	Sometimes focused	Some evidence		Superficial reference	Lacks clarity, limited use of terms
4–1	Rudimentary, limited understanding	Weak, muddled and incomplete	Not effective	May be mainly irrelevant	Absent or muddled/ inaccurate	Often unconnected assertions, errors
0	No creditworthy material					

The **AO2** mark I would give is ☐

Chapter 7 Intelligence and Learning

There have been changes to the specification from September 2011 – therefore the updated specification details here are slightly different to those in some editions of the *A2 Complete Companion*.

Division 1 Theories of intelligence

- **Psychometric theories, for example Spearman, Cattell, Thurstone**
- **Information processing theories, for example Sternberg, Gardner**

Possible exam questions for this division

Question	Guidance
Discuss **one or more** psychometric theories of intelligence. (8 marks + 16 marks).	In the specification, psychometric theories are qualified as being Spearman, Cattell and Thurstone, although there are others. The 'one or more' instruction invites you to either cover just the one theory in detail or more than one in less detail. If taking the latter route, make sure you don't spread yourself too thinly and err toward the superficial, which would limit your marks.
Discuss **one or more** information processing theories of intelligence. (8 marks + 16 marks).	This is the equivalent question for the second bullet point of this division. Note that Gardner's theory has been included as an 'information processing' theory in the specification. If choosing to write about Gardner's theory you should guard against lengthy descriptions of all the different 'intelligences' that make up Gardner's view of multiple intelligences and try to explain the overall approach as well.
(a) Outline and evaluate **one** psychometric theory of intelligence. (4 marks + 8 marks) (b) Outline and evaluate **one** information processing theory of intelligence. (4 marks + 8 marks)	You should be prepared for questions like this, where each part has AO1 and AO2. Remember that 4 marks + 8 marks should equate to 100–120 words of AO1 and 200–240 words of AO2. See model answer on page 75.
Outline and evaluate **two** theories of intelligence. (8 marks + 16 marks)	This very general question is effectively making the same demands as both of the questions above, and so the same material could be used to answer it.
(a) Outline **one** psychometric theory of intelligence, for example Spearman, Cattell or Thurstone. (4 marks) (b) Outline and evaluate the role of genetic factors in intelligence test performance. (4 marks + 16 marks)	Part (a) requires just a short outline description (100–120 words) of **one** psychometric theory of intelligence. Remember that the two examples are just a reminder of the theories you have studied count as psychometric theories. Don't be misled into thinking you have to outline both! Part (b) is from a completely different division. This should not throw you as such questions are common. We will look at this topic in division 3 on the facing page, but note the 4/16 split for AO1/AO2, which equates to about 100–120/200–240 words.

Division 2 Animal learning and intelligence

- **Simple learning (classical and operant conditioning) and its role in the behaviour of non-human animals**
- **Intelligence in non-human animals, for example self-recognition, social learning, Machiavellian intelligence**

Possible exam questions for this division

Question	Guidance
Discuss the role of classical conditioning **and/or** operant conditioning in the behaviour of non-human animals. (8 marks + 16 marks)	This question asks for the role of classical conditioning and/or operant conditioning in the behaviour of non-human animals. You should have a full answer to each topic area (i.e. an 8/16 mark version) which you might use here. But you should also have a more restricted version (i.e. a 4/8 mark version) for each and you might prefer to use that. Note that this question does not ask about the nature of classical and operant conditioning but their role in the behaviour of non-human animals. See model answer on page 77.
(a) Outline and evaluate the role of classical conditioning in the behaviour of non-human animals. (4 marks + 8 marks) (b) Outline and evaluate the role of operant conditioning in the behaviour of non-human animals. (4 marks + 8 marks)	In this question you have to use your restricted 4/8 version for each of the different types of conditioning. You will need to be very careful with your time management, as it is easy to get carried away with part (a), leaving very little time for part (b).
(a) Outline the main features of classical conditioning. (4 marks) (b) Outline and evaluate the role of operant conditioning in the behaviour of non-human animals. (4 marks + 16 marks)	By creating full and part versions of each topic area, you should then be able to recombine them to fulfil the requirements of almost any question that you might face in the exam. In this case you simply use your restricted 4-mark version for classical conditioning (about 100–120 words) for part (a). For part (b) you would use your restricted AO1 version and your full AO2 version for operant conditioning. Your time management should also reflect the mark divisions.

Outline and evaluate **two** explanations of simple learning in the behaviour of non-human animals. (8 marks + 16 marks)	This general question asks you to describe (AO1) the main features of classical and operant conditioning and then evaluate (AO2) these two explanations of 'simple' learning, perhaps even mentioning their value in the explanation of animal behaviour.
(a) Outline the role of operant conditioning in the behaviour of non-human animals. (4 marks) (b) Outline and evaluate evolutionary factors in the development of human intelligence. (4 marks + 16 marks)	Questions such as this can often throw a student, because the topic areas are completely unrelated. This is not unusual in an examination question, so you should be prepared for it. Part (a) requires a brief account (about 100–120 words) of the role of operant conditioning in the behaviour of non-human animals (e.g. foraging or positive reinforcement training), and part (b) covers an area from the next division.
'Animal intelligence may be a matter of simple conditioning, or it may be more than that.' Describe and evaluate evidence for intelligence in non-human animals. (8 marks + 16 marks)	Questions with quotations look more challenging but they aren't. The quotation is simply to guide you into how you might approach your answer, it is not intended to mislead. This quotation is not that helpful as it may convince some students that they have to discuss whether conditioning is sufficient to explain animal behaviour, which is not the case. If a quotation confuses, simply ignore it, read the question and answer that.
(a) Outline and evaluate the role of classical conditioning in the behaviour of non-human animals. (4 marks + 8 marks) (b) Discuss evidence for intelligence in non-human animals. (4 marks + 8 marks)	This question combines material from the other questions in the division. Part (a) is the restricted version of the classical conditioning question from earlier and part (b) would be a restricted version of your answer to the above question. Answering questions such as this takes thorough preparation, careful reading and diligent time management. As you will see in the following plans and essays, working in terms of 12 chunks for each question makes your planning a lot easier.

Division 3 Human intelligence

- **Evolutionary factors in the development of human intelligence, for example ecological demands, social complexity, brain size**
- **Genetic and environment factors associated with intelligence test performance, including the influence of culture**

Possible exam questions for this division

Discuss evolutionary factors involved in the development of human intelligence. (8 marks + 16 marks)	There is guidance in the specification as to what would be considered appropriate material for this question, including ecological demands (e.g. finding food), social complexity (e.g. group size) and brain size. The question implies that at least two of these should be covered in your answer. Note that the question asks for 'human intelligence' rather than 'non-human intelligence' as in the previous division.
Discuss **two or more** evolutionary factors involved in the development of human intelligence (e.g. ecological demands, social complexity, brain size). (8 marks + 16 marks)	This question requires exactly the same material as in the previous question, yet it looks quite different. By reading both questions carefully, as well as the advice for the previous question, it should become obvious that they are the same. You have the choice of just covering two factors or more than two, but take care not to spread yourself too thinly and making your answer superficial and lacking in detail.
Describe and evaluate genetic factors associated with intelligence test performance. (8 marks + 16 marks)	This question requires a discussion of how genetic factors have been shown to influence intelligence test performance. This would most probably be achieved through a description (AO1) and evaluation (AO2) of twin and adoption studies and specific genes for intelligence. Don't worry too much about the expression 'intelligence test performance', this is simply to identify a focus on measurable intelligence rather than more abstract meanings of the term.
Describe and evaluate environmental factors associated with intelligence test performance. (8 marks + 16 marks)	This question focuses on the influence of environmental factors, e.g. family, culture, education. You could mention genetic factors only if you are using this as part of a critical commentary that is explicitly focused on the role of environmental factors. Simply describing research on genetic factors would not receive credit.
(a) Outline and evaluate genetic factors associated with intelligence test performance. (4 marks + 8 marks) (b) Outline and evaluate environmental factors associated with intelligence test performance. (4 marks + 8 marks)	This is another example of how questions can make a multitude of demands and the effective student will be flexible enough to meet those demands. As well as having a full 24-mark essay version for these two topics, you should also have a shorter, more tightly focused 12 mark (in total) version of each of these two topics. As a target, when preparing for this sort of question, you would have 100–120 words of AO1 and 200–240 words of AO2 for each part of the question. See student answer on page 80.
(a) Outline and evaluate evolutionary factors involved in the development of human intelligence. (4 marks + 8 marks) (b) Outline and evaluate the influence of culture on intelligence test performance. (4 marks + 8 marks)	Part (a) of this question is a restricted version of the first question in this division. There are two main ways to achieve this. First, you could cover less (e.g. just two ecological demands) and second, you could cover the same breadth of material in less detail. Part (b) is similar to part (b) in the question above, but with an important difference. Although it is also on environmental factors, it is only on one specific environmental factor – culture. Therefore, other environmental factors would not be relevant. See model answer on page 79.

Division 1 Theories of intelligence Answer plans

Answer plan 1
(a) Outline and evaluate **one** psychometric theory of intelligence. (4 marks + 8 marks)
(b) Outline and evaluate **one** information processing theory of intelligence. (4 marks + 8 marks).

Part (a) Psychometric theory

AO1	Cattell's (1987) multifactor theory – crystallised (Gc) and fluid intelligence (Gf) acquired vs innate
AO1	Investment theory – people with high capacity for Gf acquire Gc knowledge at faster rates (Cattell, 1987)
AO2	Theory explains what typically happens over individual's lifetime – Gc rises whereas Gf falls (McArdle *et al.*, 2000)
AO2	Flynn effect (1987) increase in Gf over generations, but Raven (2000) much smaller increases in Gc over time
IDA	Application – psychometric IQ tests unfair because of coaching, 40% improvement (Bunting and Mooney, 2001)
IDA	Cultural bias in IQ tests when using tests devised by white Americans with black Americans and immigrants

Part (b) Information processing theory

AO1	Gardner (1983) multiple intelligences (MI) many different abilities count, e.g. spatial, musical, interpersonal
AO1	Criteria for inclusion as 'intelligence' include distinct developmental history
IDA	Real-world application, e.g. Douglas *et al.* (2008) teaching methods focusing on MI had many positive effects
AO2	However, Gardner's theory is difficult to test scientifically
AO2	Implications for assessment – assessment should involve multiple measures rather than one single measure of IQ
IDA	Cultural bias – Chan (2004) mathematical intelligence more highly valued in China than bodily-kinaesthetic or natural

Work out your own plan for this question and then write your answer.
Discuss **one or more** information processing theories of intelligence. (8 marks + 16 marks)

Information processing theory

AO1	
AO1	
AO1	
AO1	
AO2	
AO2	
AO2	
AO2	
AO2 or IDA	
AO2 or IDA	
AO2 or IDA	

Answer plan 2
Discuss **one or more** psychometric theory of intelligence. (8 marks + 16 marks)

Theory 1: Spearman

AO1	Intelligence test performance explained in terms of specific abilities (*s*) and general intelligence (*g*)
AO2	Neurophysiological evidence for '*g*' (Duncan *et al.*, 2000)
AO2	Spearman committed error of reification (Gould, 1981)

Theory 2: Cattell

AO1	Crystallised intelligence (Gc) acquired knowledge/skills; fluid intelligence (Gf) reasoning/problem-solving ability
AO1	Investment theory – people with high capacity for Gf acquire Gc knowledge at faster rates (Cattell, 1987)
AO2	Theory explains what typically happens over individual's lifetime – Gc rises whereas Gf falls (McArdle *et al.*, 2000)
AO2	Flynn effect (1987) increase in Gf over generations, but Raven (2000) much smaller increases in Gc over time

Theory 3: Guilford

AO1	Intelligence is the result of 150 abilities in three groups (operations, contents, products)
AO2	Important contribution to understanding of intelligence including broad view and detailed enough to be tested
AO2	Unnecessarily complicated, lacking parsimony and difficult to construct IQ tests to measure all the components
AO2	Psychometric IQ tests seen as unfair because of coaching in middle-class schools (Bunting and Mooney, 2001)
IDA	Cultural bias in IQ tests when using tests devised by white Americans with other cultural groups

Answer plan 3
(a) Outline **one** information processing theory of intelligence, for example Sternberg or Gardner. (4 marks)
(b) Outline and evaluate the role of genetic factors in intelligence test performance. (4 marks + 16 marks)

Part (a) Information processing theory

AO1	Gardner (1983) believed many different abilities could count as intelligence, e.g. spatial, musical, interpersonal
AO1	Criteria for inclusion as 'intelligence' include distinct developmental history

Part (b) Genetic factors

AO1	Malouff *et al.* (2008) – meta-analysis of twin studies, half variation in IQ due to genetics, Horn *et al.* (1979) impact of family decreases with age, impact of genetics increases
AO1	Hill *et al.* (1999) IGF2R gene for high intelligence
AO2	Problems with twin studies in that they may overestimate heritability of intelligence (Kamin and Goldberger, 2002)
AO2	Twins not a representative group, scoring on average 4 IQ points lower than singletons (Voracek and Haubner, 2008)
AO2	Supporting evidence – adopted children increasingly resemble biological mothers (Plomin and DeFries, 1983)
AO2	However, some contradictory findings (Schiff *et al.*, 1978)
IDA	Sub-cultural bias – Turkheimer *et al.* (2003) claim same gene can have different effects in different environments
AO2	Genetic 'influences' may be due to selective placement – children adopted into similar environments to their own
AO2	IGF2R gene cannot cause high IQ on its own therefore other factors must be involved
IDA	Research into high IQ gene is 'socially sensitive' as it could marginalise those who do not possess these genes

(a) Outline and evaluate **one** psychometric theory of intelligence. (4 marks + 8 marks)

Cattell (1987) claimed that intelligence had two distinct components. Crystallised intelligence (Gc) consists of acquired knowledge and skills, such as vocabulary and general knowledge, the result of cultural and educational experiences. Fluid intelligence (Gf) refers to reasoning and problem-solving ability. This is not dependent on experience and is the raw material for the development of Gc.

Cattell believed that people with a high capacity for Gf acquire Gc at faster rates. He called this relationship 'investment'. In his investment theory he proposes that Gf is therefore an inborn capacity for intelligence, which when invested in through education and experience, leads to a higher level of Gc.

A strength of Cattell's view of intelligence is that it appears better able to explain what really happens over an individual's lifespan. Research has shown that Gc typically rises over an individual's lifespan whereas Gf usually falls (McArdle *et al.*, 2000). Early theories that focused on one unchanging general intelligence (*g*) appear to underestimate the complexity of cognitive changes throughout the lifespan.

The distinction between Gc and Gf is supported by the Flynn effect. Flynn (1987) discovered that IQ scores have increased steadily over the previous 50 years. However, Flynn only used measures of fluid intelligence. Raven (2000) confirmed Flynn's findings, but found much smaller increases or even decreases in vocabulary and other measures of crystallized intelligence over the same period.

One real-world application of psychometric theories is IQ tests used for educational selection. However, such tests may not be a fair measure of ability because of the practice of coaching carried out in some middle-class schools. Bunting and Mooney (2001) found that children coached for nine months prior to their 11-plus exam typically improved their scores by 40% yet many later struggled to keep up with the academic demands of a grammar school education.

There is evidence of a cultural bias in IQ tests when using tests devised by one cultural group with other groups. For example, in 1921, the US army used psychometric IQ tests in their selection process. These showed that white Americans scored significantly higher than European immigrants and black Americans. However, the poor scores found in the immigrant and black groups were a result of the cultural bias of the test items used to test them rather than differences in intelligence.

You are not required to write essays in this rather formulaic way, however this is an effective way to ensure that all aspects are covered. Parts (a) and (b) need to be of approximately equal length and each should have one-third AO1 and two-thirds AO2. You should have 12 separate points, each represented by its own distinct paragraph.

There is twice as much AO2 to AO1 material to reflect the different number of marks available. Each point should be elaborated to about 50–60 words to gain the maximum marks possible (see the three-point rule on page 5).

In part (a) there are 106 words of AO1 and 286 words of AO2 for a total of 392 words.

(b) Outline and evaluate **one** information processing theory of intelligence (4 marks + 8 marks)

Gardner (1983) believed many different abilities could count as intelligence, identifying eight different forms. These included spatial intelligence, which is an understanding of spatial relationships between things, such as the ability to read maps. Musical intelligence includes skills, such as the ability to play an instrument or read music, and interpersonal intelligence includes an ability to understand the motivations and intentions of others.

Gardner also proposed a number of criteria to identify whether a specific ability was sufficient to be regarded as an 'intelligence'. These criteria include distinct developmental history. For example, for linguistic intelligence, spoken language develops quickly and to reasonably high levels in all people, whereas mathematical skills develop more slowly and not to the same high level in all individuals.

There have been successful real-world applications of Gardner's theory. For example, Douglas *et al.* (2008) found that, compared to formal teaching methods, such as direct instruction, teaching methods that concentrated more on developing multiple intelligences produced significant increases in students' academic, social and emotional well-being.

Despite the success of such applications, there is a general lack of research support. One reason for this may be many of the hypotheses generated by Gardner's theory remain difficult to test. Therefore, the theory lacks evidence to confirm its validity. This limits its acceptability as a 'scientific' theory of intelligence.

Gardner's theory has important implications for assessment in education. Gardner claimed that assessment should not rely on just one measure of IQ, which is the case with many tests used in education, but should involve multiple measures. He believed that a single measure of intelligence can only rank children and provides too little information for educational intervention to help them.

There is a cultural bias in this theory as demonstrated by relative importance of different forms of intelligence in different cultures. For example, in China, mathematical intelligence is very highly valued whereas other forms of intelligence, such as bodily-kinaesthetic and natural intelligence are valued significantly lower (Chan, 2004). This suggests that although the different forms of intelligence may exist, they do not have the same importance in all cultures.

Effective AO1 is often about knowing what to leave out as much as what to include. Just a flavour of the different forms of intelligence is fine, there is no need to include all of them.

You should try to make AO2 material look like AO2. This has been accomplished in these paragraphs by the use of lead-in phrases, such as 'There have been successful real-world applications…' and 'Gardner's theory has important implications…'.

In part (b) there are 124 words of AO1 and 225 words of AO2, reasonably close to the ideal 1:2 ratio and sufficient evidence of each assessment objective.

Division 2 Animal learning and intelligence Answer plans

Answer plan 1

Discuss evidence for intelligence in non-human animals. (8 marks + 16 marks)

Intelligence in non-human animals

AO1	Intelligence an adaptation to problem solving in large groups through Machiavellian intelligence
AO1	Formation of alliances determines power in social groups
AO1	Self-recognition indicates intelligence, demonstrated in studies of chimpanzees (Gallup, 1970)
AO1	Self-recognition also found in dolphins (Reiss and Marino, 2001) and killer whales (Defour and Marten, 2001)
AO2	Support for existence of Machiavellian intelligence in Barbary macaque monkeys (Deag and Crook, 1971)
AO2	Consequence of Machiavellian intelligence is 'arms race' of social intelligence within a particular species
AO2	Machiavellian intelligence evident in macaques but they fail on another criterion of intelligence – self-recognition
IDA	Biological approach – positive correlation between tactical deception and neocortex volume (Byrne and Corp, 2004)
AO2	Dunbar (1992) neocortex size correlates with group size
IDA	Evolutionary similarities in self-recognition between dolphins and chimpanzees, result of large brains
AO2	Heyes (1998) argues little reliable evidence that self-recognition evident in all primate species
IDA	Implications of self-recognition among non-human species relate to ethical issues and rights in their treatment

Work out your own plan for this question and then write your answer.

Outline and evaluate **two** explanations of simple learning in the behaviour of non-human animals. (8 marks + 16 marks)

Two explanations of simple learning

AO1	
AO1	
AO1	
AO1	
AO2	
AO2	
AO2	
AO2	
AO2	
AO2 or IDA	
AO2 or IDA	
AO2 or IDA	

Answer plan 2

Discuss the role of classical **and/or** operant conditioning in the behaviour of non-human animals. (8 marks + 16 marks)

Classical conditioning (CC)

AO1	Training animals for release by using compound conditioning to avoid association between humans and food
AO1	Reproductive success increased if animal responds to any CS that occurs prior to mating
IDA	Ethical issues with compound conditioning – increase in stress due to under-stimulation (Goldblatt, 1993)
AO2	Critical that animals don't learn responses that they transfer to the wild and which would endanger them (Bauer, 2004)
AO2	Support for importance of CC in reproductive success, Matthews *et al.* (2007) male quail had 2× number of eggs
AO2	For CC to be adaptive, CS and CR must occur together regularly, therefore one must be predictive of the other

Operant conditioning (OC)

AO1	Important in foraging behaviour (e.g. woodpeckers)
AO1	Positive reinforcement training (PRT), e.g. desensitisation and cooperative feeding
AO2	Research support for OC in foraging monkeys, Agetsuma (1999) foraging more frequent in patches when reinforced
AO2	Support for desensitisation training, Clay *et al.* (2009) macaques showed reduction in fearful behaviour
IDA	PRT deals with ethical issues and alleviates stress associated with research satisfies Welfare Act requirements
AO2	Research support for PRT – dominant chimps trained not to steal subordinates' food (Bloomsmith *et al.*, 1994)

Answer plan 3

(a) Outline and evaluate the role of classical conditioning in the behaviour of non-human animals. (4 marks + 8 marks)

(b) Discuss evidence for intelligence in non-human animals. (4 marks + 8 marks)

Part (a) Classical conditioning (CC)

AO1	Training animals for release by using compound conditioning to avoid association between humans and food
AO1	Reproductive success increased if animal responds to any CS that occurs prior to mating
IDA	Ethical issues with compound conditioning – increase in stress due to under-stimulation (Goldblatt, 1993)
AO2	Critical that animals don't learn responses that they transfer to the wild and which would endanger them (Bauer, 2004)
AO2	Support for importance of CC in reproductive success, Matthews *et al.* (2007) male quail had 2× number of eggs
AO2	For CC to be adaptive, CS and CR must occur together regularly, therefore one must be predictive of the other

Part (b) Intelligence in non-human animals

AO1	Intelligence an adaptation to problem-solving in large groups through Machiavellian intelligence and alliances
AO1	Self-recognition indicates intelligence, demonstrated in studies of chimpanzees (Gallup, 1970)
AO2	Support for existence of Machiavellian intelligence in Barbary macaque monkeys (Deag and Crook, 1971)
IDA	Biological approach – positive correlation between tactical deception and neocortex volume (Byrne and Corp, 2004)
AO2	Heyes (1998) argues that there is little reliable evidence that self-recognition evident in all primate species
IDA	Implications of self-recognition among non-human species relate to ethical issues and rights in their treatment

Discuss the role of classical **and/or** operant conditioning in the behaviour of non-human animals. (8 marks + 16 marks)

In animals that must be kept in captivity prior to release, classical conditioning is used to ensure an association does not form between humans and food, which would put the animals in danger when returned to the wild. Compound conditioning combines a human presence with a more appropriate stimulus, such as an auditory stimulus. This becomes a more reliable predictor because it always precedes food whereas humans do not.

The learned association between a conditioned and unconditioned stimulus possibility is that it increases reproductive success. For example, a CS that occurs before mating (e.g. a signal from the female) serves to predict mating opportunities and therefore would increase an animal's reproductive success if they can respond appropriately to the CS.

The use of compound conditioning can create ethical problems, in that it can be undesirable to totally isolate many species completely from humans. Goldblatt (1993) carried out a review of research on captive animal stress and concluded that understimulating environments, including those totally devoid of human contact were more likely to be associated with stress responses in a wide range of species.

As an ethical issue in this type of research, Bauer (2004) argues that is critical that captive animals do not learn associations that they transfer to the wild and which would endanger them. In order to protect the well-being of these animals, researchers cannot rely on learned associations between humans and food extinguishing naturally, therefore they must prevent them from being learned in the first place.

There is research support for the importance of classical conditioning in reproductive success in a laboratory study using male quail (Matthews *et al.*, 2007). Matthews *et al.* found that male birds who received a signal (a conditioned stimulus) prior to a mating opportunity fertilised more than double the number of eggs compared to males who did not receive a signal prior to mating.

The adaptive value of classical conditioning is demonstrated by the fact that to be adaptive in the behaviour of non-human animals, a conditioned stimulus and unconditional stimulus must occur together regularly, so that one is predictive of the other. Occasional CS-UCS associations would not lead to learning, however, because they would not be reliably predictive in the natural environment.

Operant conditioning has an important role in the behaviour of non-human animals as they forage in their environment. For example, woodpeckers are reinforced for pecking a certain tree if they find insects there. As a result they are more likely to return to that tree in the future. When the supply of insects becomes exhausted, this response is gradually extinguished and the bird moves to a new patch.

Positive reinforcement training (PRT) is used to enhance the care and well-being of animals used in research. Desensitisation pairs positive rewards with procedures that cause fear so that they become less frightening and less stressful. In cooperative feeding, dominant animals are rewarded for allowing subordinate animals to feed and subordinate animals are rewarded for being 'brave' enough to accept food in the presence of dominant animals.

There is research support for the role of operant conditioning in foraging. Agetsuma (1999) manipulated the quality of food patches in the environments of Japanese monkeys. Consistent with the prediction of operant conditioning, subsequent foraging visits were more frequent to the high quality patches than to the low quality patches.

There is research support for desensitisation training. Clay *et al.* (2009) used this technique to desensitise rhesus macaques from feeling fearful in the presence of humans. The individual macaques that received positive reinforcement whenever they were in the laboratory environment subsequently showed less fearful behaviour than did control group macaques that were simply exposed to the same environment without any reinforcement.

Ethical issues are a concern of PRT because it aims to reduce the stress that arises in research participation. It also satisfies the requirements of the Animal Welfare Act, which include to protect against suffering and to allow animals the opportunity to exhibit normal behaviour patterns.

There is research support for the role of reinforcement in cooperative feeding. Bloomsmith *et al.* (1994) used PRT to train dominant chimpanzees not to chase and steal subordinate's food by reinforcing behaviours incompatible with chasing and stealing (e.g. sitting still while feeding). This had the desired effect of decreasing aggression from dominants and submission from subordinates during feeding periods.

There is a tendency for many students to waste time at the beginning of an essay by outlining their intentions and defining terms. There is no need to do this and so definitions of classical (and operant) conditions, or explanations of their mechanisms are unnecessary. Likewise, outlining intentions ('In this essay I am going to…') will not earn marks.

This paragraph counts as IDA because it discusses ethical issues that might arise using compound conditioning.

Good AO1 aims for both breadth and depth. Four points in total in this answer (2 for classical and 2 for operant conditioning), each of about 50–60 words is ideal as a way of demonstrating sufficient breadth while still having time for detail (depth) picking up high AO1 marks.

This paragraph also counts as IDA (PRT overcomes ethical issues and satisfies legal requirements). As far as possible IDA points should be woven into your commentary (as here) rather than just added as an afterthought.

They should also begin with a clear lead-in phrase so the examiner is clear that this is IDA.

This essay is 720 words in length, with 254 words of AO1 and 466 words of AO2, fairly close to the one-third AO1/two-thirds AO2 required in an effective answer to this question.

Division 3 Human intelligence Answer plans

Answer plan 1

Describe and evaluate genetic factors associated with intelligence test performance. (8 marks + 16 marks)

Genetic factors

AO1	Twin studies, e.g. Malouff *et al.* (2008) meta-analysis of 400 twin studies – half variation in IQ due to genetics
AO1	Adoption studies, e.g. Horn *et al.* (1979) impact of family decreases with age, impact of genetics increases
AO1	Hill *et al.* (1999) IGF2R gene for high intelligence
AO1	Curtis *et al.* (2008) studied DNA of children, found six genetic markers influencing IQ test scores
AO2	Problems with twin studies in that they may overestimate heritability of intelligence (Kamin and Goldberger, 2002)
AO2	Twins not a representative group, scoring on average 4 IQ points lower than singletons (Voracek and Haubner, 2008)
AO2	Supporting evidence – adopted children increasingly like biological mothers with age (Plomin and DeFries, 1983)
AO2	However, some contradictory findings (Schiff *et al.*, 1978)
IDA	Sub-cultural bias – Turkheimer *et al.* (2003) claim same gene can have different effects in different environments
AO2	Genetic 'influences' may be due to selective placement – children adopted into similar environments to their own
AO2	IGF2R gene cannot cause high IQ on its own therefore other factors must be involved
IDA	Research into high IQ gene is 'socially sensitive' as it could marginalise those who do not possess these genes

Work out your own plan for this question and then write your answer.

Discuss evolutionary factors involved in the development of human intelligence. (8 marks + 16 marks)

AO1	
AO1	
AO1	
AO1	
AO2	
AO2	
AO2	
AO2	
AO2	
AO2 or IDA	
AO2 or IDA	
AO2 or IDA	

Answer plan 2

Describe and evaluate environmental factors associated with intelligence test performance. (8 marks + 16 marks)

Environmental factors

AO1	Class – Mackintosh (1998) children of SES Class I scored 10 IQ points higher than Class V, Belmont and Marolla (1973) first born and from smaller families higher IQ
AO1	Ceci (1991) meta-analysis, regular school attendance = higher IQ, Perry Preschool Project boosted achievement
AO1	Culture – group socialisation theory (Harris, 1995) experiences outside home (e.g. peers) more important
AO1	Ethnicity and IQ – Herrnstein and Murray (1994) claim immigrants to US created downward pressure on IQ levels
AO2	Support for influence of SES, Schiff *et al.* (1978) found moving infants from low to high SES family raised IQ level
AO2	Blake (1989) – birth order effect only short-lived
AO2	Group socialisation theory rejected by Pinker (2002) who claims little influence of peers on intelligence
AO2	Herrnstein and Murray (1994) argue that attempts to raise IQ through compensatory education are doomed to failure
IDA	Physiological explanation for poverty and low intelligence, Kishiyama *et al.* (2008) deficiency in prefrontal cortex
AO2	Contradictory claims by Ceci and Hernnstein and Murray explained by failure to define what is an 'improvement'
AO2	Herrnstein and Murray base their view on concept of IQ as '*g*' but this is challenged by theorists, such as Gardner
IDA	Greenfield (1997) argues that IQ tests are culture-biased and lead to invalid conclusions

Answer plan 3

(a) Outline and evaluate evolutionary factors involved in the development of human intelligence. (4 marks + 8 marks)

(b) Outline and evaluate the influence of culture on intelligence test performance. (4 marks + 8 marks)

Part (a) Classical conditioning (CC)

AO1	Ecological demands – finding and extracting food, evidence of tool use (e.g. among !Kung San)
AO1	Social complexity – Machiavellian intelligence (Whiten and Byrne, 1988), meat-sharing hypothesis (Stanford, 1999)
AO2	Dunbar (1992) significant relationship between neocortex volume and social but not environmental complexity
AO2	Byrne (1995) group size can't explain why chimpanzees more intelligent than monkeys as both live in large groups
AO2	Social complexity research support, e.g. Mitani and Watts (2001) chimpanzees shared meat with males
IDA	Hill and Kaplan (1988) evidence of meat sharing among Ache, Wrangham (1975) meat sharing just saves energy

Part (b) Culture (an environmental factor)

AO1	Group socialisation theory (Harris, 1995) experiences outside the home (e.g. peer groups) more important
AO1	Ethnicity and IQ – Herrnstein and Murray (1994) claim immigrants to US created downward pressure on IQ levels
AO2	Group socialisation theory rejected by Pinker (2002) who claims little influence of peers on intelligence
AO2	Herrnstein and Murray base their view on concept of IQ as '*g*' but this is challenged by theorists, such as Gardner
IDA	Physiological explanation for poverty and low intelligence. Kishiyama *et al.* (2008) deficiency in prefrontal cortex
IDA	Greenfield (1997) argues that IQ tests are culturally biased and lead to invalid conclusions

(a) Outline and evaluate evolutionary factors involved in the development of human intelligence. (4 marks + 8 marks)

Ecological demands are aspects of the environment that a species must adapt to in order to survive. One of these is the need to find food. Early humans had an increased cognitive demand on them to monitor food supplies that were only available at certain times and in certain locations. Tool use is also an indication of intelligence, and the most successful hunter gatherers, such as the !Kung San show elaborate tool use whereas less successful groups do not.

Whiten and Byrne (1988) claim the evolution of intelligence in humans was primarily driven by the need to deal with the problems posed by other group members, which led to the development of Machiavellian intelligence. The meat-sharing hypothesis (Stanford, 1999) claims that meat could be used to forge alliances and to persuade females to mate. Strategic meat sharing requires considerable cognitive abilities to keep a running score of debts and credits.

There is research support for the importance of social complexity as an influence for the development of human intelligence. Dunbar (1992) analysed the relationship between environmental complexity and social complexity with neocortex volume (an indication of the intelligence of a species). He found a significant relationship between neocortex volume and social complexity but not between neocortex volume and environmental complexity. This suggests that the social demands of group living had shaped human intelligence more than ecological demands.

However, Byrne (1995) claims that social complexity based on group size alone cannot explain why apes, such as chimpanzees, are more intelligent than monkeys, as both live in groups of similar size and complexity. Byrne suggests that the social challenges of group living may be more significant to apes than to monkeys, leading to higher intelligence in ape species (including humans).

There is further research support for social complexity as an influence. Mitani and Watts (2001) found that, in a comparative species, male chimpanzees were more likely to share meat with other males than with females. This is important in forging alliances as hunting is more successful when carried out in groups.

There is further evidence to support the meat-sharing hypothesis. Hill and Kaplan (1988) found that in the Ache people meat is shared outside of the family, with skilled hunters being rewarded with sexual favours from females. Wrangham (1975) suggests a simpler explanation for this. Males must expend considerable energy defending a kill, so by sharing with others, they can eat without interruption.

(b) Outline and evaluate the influence of culture on intelligence test performance. (4 marks + 8 marks)

In her group socialisation theory, Harris (1985) claims that, as children grow older, they are less influenced by experiences within the family environment family, and more influenced by life outside the home (e.g. peer groups). These cultural influences determine the degree to which children engage in intellectual pastimes and therefore the development of their intelligence.

Herrnstein and Murray (1994) claim that ethnicity has a significant influence on intelligence. They found that immigrants to the US had IQ levels that were significantly lower than US residents. They argued that as more and more immigrants came into the US, this created a downward pressure on intelligence levels and an increase in the social problems typically associated with people with low IQ.

The group socialisation theory is rejected by Pinker (2002) who claims that peer group influence is a possible explanation for some behaviours, such as smoking, but there is little, if any, evidence of the influence of peers on the development of intelligence. He argues that identical twins share the same genes, family environments and peer groups, yet the correlation between them is still only 50%. This indicates that peer group influences alone cannot account for why they are different.

Herrnstein and Murray's argument for the influence of ethnicity is weakened by their belief that 'g' can be accurately measured by IQ tests This belief is challenged by Gardner (1983), who argues that intelligence is multidimensional and so attempts to measure it with a single IQ test would be meaningless.

The physiological approach offers an explanation for the relationship between poverty and low intelligence. Kishiyama *et al.* (2008) found that children with low SES backgrounds differed from children with higher SES backgrounds in the efficiency with which their prefrontal cortex handled problem-solving tasks, with children from low SES backgrounds showing a reduced response to novel stimuli.

Greenfield (1997) argues that assessing the IQ of people from cultures or sub-cultures other than the one in which a test was developed represents a cultural bias. She claims that this inevitably influences any results when these tests are used and leads to invalid conclusions about the measure of IQ in such groups.

There is always a danger, when seeing the word 'evolutionary' in a question, to charge into a discussion of natural selection and other evolutionary 'factors' without relating these to the question topic – here it is human intelligence. An answer that is related to evolutionary factors in general would receive little credit.

Each point in the essay plan on the facing page has been expanded to about 50–60 words, thus producing an essay of the appropriate length and also with the appropriate balance between AO1 and AO2.

In this essay names and dates of researchers have been included. Neither are required but are a good way to provide detail and elaboration.

If your time management has been appropriate, you should reach part (b) after about 15 minutes of writing. It is best to move on to part (b) after that time, and leave a gap because you can always come back if you have time and add anything else that occurs to you for your answer to part (a).

These last two paragraphs count as IDA. Each point has been clearly related to the topic of culture and intelligence test performance, rather than being a generic IDA point, which would gain little credit.

Part (a) is 401 words long, with 150 words of AO1 and 251 of AO2.

Part (b) is 357 words long, with 119 words of AO1 and 238 of AO2.

Although there is a slightly greater proportion of AO1 to AO2 in part (a) and the opposite in part (b), there are sufficient amounts of both AO1 and AO2 in each part.

Answer for you to mark

See page 173 for examiner's comments.

Question

(a) Outline and evaluate genetic factors associated with intelligence test performance. (4 marks + 8 marks)

(b) Outline and evaluate environmental factors associated with intelligence test performance. (4 marks + 8 marks)

Student answer

Part (a)

❶ Twin studies have been used to study whether intelligence is the result of genetic factors. There are two types of twin, monozygotic (MZ) and dizygotic (DZ). MZ share 100% of their genes, whereas DZ twins share 50% of their genes. Twins are used because if MZ twins are more similar in terms of their intelligence, then this suggests that this must be due to their greater genetic similarity. This argument is even more powerful if the twins have been reared apart because they would not have shared the same environments.

❷ An influential twin study was by Bouchard and McGue who found that for MZ twins reared apart, their concordance rate was .72, but for DZ twins reared together, the concordance rate was lower at .60. A meta-analysis of 400 studies by Malouff et al. confirmed the importance of genetic factors, finding that just under half of the variance in IQ scores could be explained in terms of genetic factors.

❸ Another method used in the study of genetic factors is the adoption study. These studies compare adopted children with their adopted and their biological parents. If the adopted children are more alike, in terms of intelligence, then this indicates a strong genetic influence. The Texas Adoption Project (Horn et al.) measured the intelligence of children and their biological and adoptive mothers at ten year intervals. When they first measured them, the children were more similar to their adoptive than biological mothers, suggesting that environmental effects were stronger than genetic effects.

❹ A problem with the use of twins is that they may not be a representative group. A study by Voracek and Haubner looked at all studies that had compared twins with singletons (non-twins). They found that, on average, twins scored 4.2 IQ points lower than singletons. The reason for this was not entirely clear, although it does suggest that using twins to assess the development of intelligence may not be entirely appropriate.

❺ Kamin and Goldberger claim that twin studies may overestimate the heritability of intelligence, particularly those that compare MZ twins reared together with DZ twins reared together. They claim that, because MZ twins are identical, they tend to be treated more similarly, therefore their environments as well as their genes are also more similar than the environments of DZ twins, meaning that it is almost impossible to disentangle the relative contribution of genes and environment in their IQ similarity.

❻ Although the Texas Adoption Project initially found that children were more like their adoptive than biological parents, when they were assessed again as adolescents, the children were more like their biological parents. This supports the importance of genetic influences, which appear to get stronger with age.

(440 words)

AO1 mark scheme for part (a)

The AO1 content for this part of the question is a brief outline of influence of genetic factors on IQ. The word 'factors' should be taken to indicate more than one research area, e.g. twin studies, adoption studies or specific intelligence genes.

Failure to focus on more than one 'factor' should be taken to indicate partial performance, with a corresponding reduction in marks.

4 marks should be about 100–120 words.

AO2 mark scheme for part (a)

Evaluation may be achieved by considering research that either supports or challenges the claim that genetic factors are involved in the development of intelligence. Merely describing such studies does not, on its own, constitute AO2, but these should be built into a critical commentary.

There are other ways of evaluating this material (e.g. by examining methodological difficulties of using twin studies in this area), but these should be explicitly focused on intelligence to be creditworthy.

8 marks should be about 200–240 words.

Part (b)

7 Mackintosh used evidence from the British National Child Development Study to show that socioeconomic status (SES) was influential in determining a child's intelligence. Even when factors, such as area of residence were taken into account, children with fathers in SES Class I still scored, on average, 10 IQ points higher than children with fathers who were SES Class V.

8 A second factor is education, with research showing that children who had regular attendance at school scored higher on IQ tests, and that IQ scores tended to go down over the long summer break from school.

9 A third factor is ethnicity, for example Herrnstein and Murray claimed that the average IQ in the US was depressed by the number of immigrants coming into the country, with immigrants scoring lower on IQ tests than resident Americans.

10 There are a number of reasons why SES should make a difference. It can be explained by the fact that high SES families have access to better resources (e.g. the Internet) and have more positive attitudes to education.

11 The belief that education can improve IQ scores is supported by the Perry Preschool Project which found that when children living in poverty were given compensatory education, it raised their educational achievement.

12 A problem for any study that compares the IQ of members of different cultures is that they use a test that is mainly suited to members of their own culture. As a result, members of other groups do badly, which is a cultural bias.

(244 words)

AO1 mark scheme for part (b)

This is the other side of the genetics and IQ debate, i.e. the role of environmental factors. This could include education, culture and family environment, or just one of these.

4 marks should be about 100–120 words

AO2 mark scheme for part (b)

Although the most obvious way of providing AO2 evaluation is through an examination of research support for the role of environment and culture, there are other possible routes, for example, by examining the cultural bias inherent in IQ testing across cultural and sub-cultural groups, or applications of this research.

8 marks should be about 200–240 words

Comments and marks for part (a) AO1 and part (b) AO1

Mark	Knowledge and understanding	Accuracy	Organisation and structure
4	Reasonably thorough	Accurate	Coherent
3–2	Limited	Generally accurate	Reasonably coherent
1	Weak and muddled		
0	No creditworthy material		

The **AO1** mark I would give part (a) is ☐

The **AO1** mark I would give part (b) is ☐

Comments and marks for part (a) AO2 and part (b) AO2

Mark	Analysis and understanding	Focus	Elaboration	Line of argument	Issues/debates/ approaches	Quality of written communication
8–7	Sound	Well-focused	Coherent	Clear	Used effectively	Fluent, effective use of terms
6–5	Reasonable	Generally focused	Reasonable	Evident	Reasonably effective	Clear, appropriate
4–3	Basic, superficial	Sometimes focused	Some evidence		Superficial reference	Lacks clarity, limited use of terms
2–1	Rudimentary, limited understanding	Weak, muddled and incomplete	Not effective	May be mainly irrelevant	Absent or muddled/ inaccurate	Often unconnected assertions, errors
0	No creditworthy material					

The **AO2** mark I would give part (a) is ☐

The **AO2** mark I would give part (b) is ☐

Chapter 8 Cognition and development

There have been changes to the specification from September 2011 – therefore the updated specification details here are slightly different to those in some editions of the *A2 Complete Companion*.

Division 1 Development of thinking	• **Theories of cognitive development, including Piaget and Vygotsky** • **Applications of cognitive development theories to education**

Possible exam questions for this division

Discuss Piaget's theory of cognitive development. (8 marks + 16 marks)	Two theories of cognitive development are named in the specification, so either could form the basis of a 24-mark question. You will undoubtedly have difficulty restricting yourself to 8 marks worth (about 200–240 words) describing Piaget's theory as there is so much to write. Therefore, this is something you should practice beforehand.
Discuss Vygotsky's theory of cognitive development. (8 marks + 16 marks)	The same comments as above apply to this question.
Describe and evaluate applications of cognitive development theories to education. (8 marks + 16 marks)	This is another question that can be lifted straight from this part of the specification. As part of the evaluation you can consider the research support for the theories on which the applications are based – but take care to make such evaluation relevant to the applications.
(a) Outline Piaget and Vygotsky's theories of cognitive development. (8 marks) (b) Evaluate these theories of cognitive development. (16 marks)	It is possible that an exam question will ask for very brief outlines of both theories, as here. It helps to be prepared for such questions by deciding how to write a very brief version of each theory (about 100–120 words for each). In part (b) you must evaluate both theories, though this need not be in balance for full marks. Any IDA material must be in part (b) to attract credit and will not be exported from part (a) if placed there.
(a) Outline Piaget's theory of cognitive development. (8 marks) (b) Consider ways in which research into cognitive development has been applied to education. (16 marks)	This is a tricky question because part (a) and (b) are divorced from each other. Part (a) is straightforward enough but in part (b) you must focus solely on evaluation as it is entirely AO2. Therefore, you would not *describe* any research (theories and/or studies) but consider how this has been applied. For example, Piaget's stages (a part of his theory) have been applied to education by considering what kind of teaching methods are appropriate at different ages. You might assess these applications by using research studies that provide evidence of the effectiveness of the applications.
(a) Outline and evaluate Vygotsky's theory of cognitive development. (4 marks + 8 marks) (b) Outline and evaluate how Vygotsky's theory has been applied to education. (4 marks + 8 marks)	Various part questions can be constructed from the specification, as in this question which could equally be set with reference to Piaget's theory. With such part questions the big task is reducing your material to fit the demands of the question and ensuring that you present appropriate amounts of AO1:AO2 in both parts of the question. See model answer on page 85.

Division 2 Development of moral understanding	• **Kohlberg's theory of moral understanding**

Possible exam questions for this division

Discuss Kohlberg's theory of moral understanding. (8 marks + 16 marks)	This is a topic where students often have far too much descriptive material. The 'ages and stages' part of Kohlberg's theory could take much more than 200 words to describe so you need to reduce this significantly in order to have time to describe other aspects of the theory – and also to have time for AO2. See model answer on page 87.
(a) Outline Kohlberg's theory of moral understanding. (4 marks) (b) Outline and evaluate Vygotsky's theory of cognitive development. (4 marks + 16 marks)	It is possible that a question on Kohlberg's theory of *moral* development could be combined with a question on one of the theories of *cognitive* development. Questions that span different divisions (in this case division 1 and division 2) are relatively common in AQA psychology examinations. This essay also serves to remind you that all topics should be prepared in a shorter version (4+8) as well as the long version (8+16).

(a) Outline Piaget's theory of cognitive development. (8 marks) (b) To what extent has Kohlberg's theory of moral understanding been supported by research evidence? (16 marks)	It is also possible that a question may involve a division of skills here so you are asked to describe Piaget's theory and then evaluate Kohlberg's theory. Part (b) has been phrased in a less usual way ('To what extent ...') but basically is asking for an evaluation of the theory. For top marks, you possibly would be required to reach a conclusion about whether or not research evidence does support the theory. Questions where the evaluation is not linked to the description are difficult because it is hard to resist doing some description. You must imagine that you have already written the descriptive part.

Division 3

Development of social cognition

- **Development of the child's sense of self, including Theory of Mind**
- **Development of children's understanding of others, including perspective-taking, for example Selman**
- **Biological explanations of social cognition, including the role of the mirror neuron system**

Possible exam questions for this division

Discuss the development of the child's sense of self. (8 marks + 16 marks)	This division of the specification produces a series of obvious 'blockbuster' questions, i.e. where the whole 24 marks is focused on one topic. You should be able to prepare well for these blockbuster questions because you know they are coming, but should also prepare for shorter versions worth 4 + 8 marks. See student answer on page 90.
Discuss the development of the child's sense of self, including Theory of Mind. (8 marks + 16 marks)	This question is almost the same as the one above, except Theory of Mind has been added (as in the specification entry). You may well have included it in your answer to the question above anyway so the answers may well be the same.
Discuss the development of children's understanding of others. (8 marks + 16 marks)	Some students may muddle this topic with the first because both topics (development of sense of self and development of an understanding of others) concern early childhood development. However, the specification clearly identifies them as separate topics and you should ensure, when revising, that you are clear about what to include in each answer. It is perfectly acceptable to focus solely on perspective-taking when answering this question.
Discuss the development of children's understanding of others, including perspective taking. (8 marks + 16 marks)	The specification here has the word 'including' for perspective taking. This means that it could be specified in the question or could even form a stand-alone question (see below). The last part of this specification entry says 'for example Selman'. This is not an 'including' and therefore would not be specified in an exam question.
Describe and evaluate biological explanations of social cognition. (8 marks + 16 marks)	This is the third topic area in this division that could be asked in one of two forms – as here or as in the next question which specifically refers to the mirror neuron system. Beware that the question asks for explanations and not simply a description of, for example, the mirror neuron system. See model answer on page 89.
'Mirror neurons are thought to contribute to our Theory of Mind and our ability to understand others.' Describe and evaluate the role of the mirror neuron system in social cognition. (8 marks + 16 marks)	Sometimes questions start with a quotation. There is usually no requirement to address the quotation but the intention is to offer you some 'inspiration' when answering the question. In this case the quotation suggests that you *might* make reference to the Theory of Mind and understanding others when answering this question, but this is not a requirement.
(a) Outline and evaluate the development of Theory of Mind. (4 marks + 8 marks) (b) Outline and evaluate the development of perspective taking. (4 marks + 8 marks)	There are a number of combinations possible in this division and this is one of them, as is the next one. There are so many topics in this division that it is desirable for the principal examiner to set questions that cover a few of the topics in part questions rather than use the blockbuster questions. This is why it is so important to be able to reduce your material for questions worth, for example, 4 rather than the full 8 marks, and 8 rather than the full 16 marks. The key issue is that you must not lose detail so don't aim to cover everything, just choose a few rather carefully selected key points and explain these well.
(a) Explain Theory of Mind. (4 marks) (b) Explain the mirror neuron system. (4 marks) (c) Evaluate biological explanations of social cognition. (16 marks)	The injunction 'explain' is not commonly used but suits this question well. 'Explain' can signify AO1 or AO2 but in this case is clearly AO1 because part (c) is AO2. In any case it should be clear what is required – a description of these concepts that provides deeper understanding of what they mean. This might include examples and/or research studies. Each explanation should be about 100–120 words.
(a) Describe and evaluate the role of the mirror neuron system in social cognition. (4 marks + 8 marks) (b) Outline and evaluate Kohlberg's theory of moral understanding. (4 marks + 8 marks)	Questions can also be set across divisions, as is the case in this question. Both elements of this question are ones that you have met before, and therefore you should be well prepared to answer such a question.

Answer plan 1
Discuss Piaget's theory of cognitive development. (8 marks + 16 marks)

Piaget's theory

AO1	Key points – maturation, qualitative differences
AO1	Key mechanisms – schema, assimilation, accommodation, equilbration, operations
AO1	Stage 1 sensori-motor (0–2), e.g. object permanence, stage 2 pre-operational (2–7), e.g. egocentricism
AO1	Stage 3 concrete (7–11), e.g. conservation, stage 4 formal (11+), e.g. abstract hypothetico-deductive reasoning
IDA	Nativists claim infants can do more, e.g. Baillargeon and DeVos (1991) used carrot behind window
AO2	Research support for egocentrism (three mountains) but Hughes (1975) children could cope with policeman doll
AO2	Research support for conservation (e.g. with counters) but Samuel and Bryant (1984) two questions may confuse
AO2	Research support for formal logic (beaker problem) but Wason and Shapiro (1971) 10% university students can
AO2	Limitations, e.g. tasks unrealistic, sample-biased (middle class, Western), ignores social factors
AO2	Strengths, e.g. qualitative differences supported by research
IDA	Real-world application to education, e.g. readiness, value of disequilibrium, importance of self-discovery
IDA	Contrast with Vygotsky, e.g. cultural vs individualist approach, but also similarities (Glassman, 1999)

Work out your own plan for this question and then write your answer.
Describe and evaluate applications of cognitive development theories to education. (8 marks + 16 marks)

Application to education

AO1	
AO1	
AO1	
AO1	
AO2	
AO2	
AO2	
AO2	
AO2	
AO2 or IDA	
AO2 or IDA	
AO2 or IDA	

Answer plan 2
Discuss Vygotsky's theory of cognitive development. (8 marks + 16 marks)

Vygotsky's theory

AO1	Elementary and higher mental functions, role of culture
AO1	The role of others – experts
AO1	Semiotics, the role of language and stages (preintellectual speech, egocentric speech, inner speech)
AO1	Zone of proximal development (ZPD)
AO2	Research support for role of culture, e.g. Gredler (1992) primitive counting system in Papua New Guinea
AO2	Research support for scaffolding, e.g. Wood and Middleton (1975) pyramid task and continigent regulations
AO2	Research support for language, e.g. Carmichael *et al.* (1932), challenged by Sinclair-de-Zwart (1969)
AO2	Research support for ZPD, e.g. McNaughton and Leyland (1990) mothers working with jigsaw puzzles
AO2	Limitations, e.g. social influences overplayed, not conducive to research (hard to operationalise)
AO2	Strengths, e.g. positive approach because suggests ways to assist learner
IDA	Real-world application to education, e.g. collaborative learning, peer tutoring, scaffolding
IDA	Contrast with Piaget, e.g. cultural vs individualist approach, but also similarities (Glassman, 1999)

Answer plan 3
(a) Outline and evaluate Vygotsky's theory of cognitive development. (4 marks + 8 marks)
(b) Outline and evaluate how Vygotsky's theory has been applied to education. (4 marks + 8 marks)

Part (a) Vygotsky's theory

AO1	The role of culture and others – experts
AO1	Zone of proximal development (ZPD) and scaffolding
AO2	Research support for role of culture, e.g. Gredler (1992) primitive counting system in Papua New Guinea
AO2	Research support for ZPD, e.g. McNaughton and Leyland (1990) mothers working with jigsaw puzzles
AO2	Limitations, e.g. social influences overplayed, not conducive to research (hard to operationalise)
IDA	Contrast with Piaget, e.g. cultural vs individualist approach, but also similarities (Glassman, 1999)

Part (b) Application to education

AO1	Collaborative learning, shared understandings
AO1	Peer tutoring creates motivation to learn as expert guides you through ZPD
AO2	Research support, e.g. Gokhale (1995) better performance on critical thinking test
AO2	Research support, e.g. Cohen *et al.* (1982) though best for tutor (Cloward, 1967)
IDA	Culture bias, most appropriate in collectivist societies, e.g. Stigler and Perry (1999) compared US and Asian schools
AO2	Comparison with traditional methods, Bennett (1976) found active learning less good

(a) Outline and evaluate Vygotsky's theory of cognitive development. (4 marks + 8 marks)

The main theme of Vygotsky's theory is that social/cultural interaction plays a fundamental role in cognitive development. Culture is transmitted through language and by 'experts', i.e. people with greater knowledge. This refers to parents, teachers and even peers who have greater knowledge. These experts provide problem-solving experiences where the expert gradually transfers responsibility for learning to the child.

The zone of proximal development (ZPD) is the distance between the child's actual development level as determined by independent problem solving and the level of potential development as determined through problem solving under adult guidance or in collaboration with more capable peers. The role of the expert is to guide the child through this zone using the process of scaffolding, providing temporary support when it is needed.

The importance of culture is supported by research. Gredler (1992) cited the primitive counting system used in Papua New Guinea as an example of how culture can limit cognitive development. Counting is done by starting on the thumb of one hand and going up the arm and down to the other fingers, ending at 29. This system makes it very difficult to add and subtract large numbers, a limiting factor for development in this culture.

Evidence for the ZPD was produced in a study by McNaughton and Leyland (1990). They observed young children working with their mothers on jigsaw puzzles of increasing difficulty, and then a week later observed the children working on their own. The children reached a higher of level of difficulty with their mothers (their potential ability) then when working on their own (their current ability) so defining their ZPD.

There are limitations with this theory, for example, Vygotsky may have overplayed the importance of the social environment – if social influence was all that was needed to advance cognitive development then learning would be a lot faster than it is. Another limitation is that this theory does not lend itself as readily to experimentation as Piaget's because the concepts are more difficult to operationalise. This makes it difficult to 'prove' the theory.

The Vygotskian/cultural approach can be contrasted with the Piagetian/individualist approach. The two theories represent different styles of learning and different kinds of learner. Vygotsky was a communist believing in the power of society in the development of the individual; Piaget was a product of individualist European society. However, the theories also have similarities; both emphasise the interactionist character of development, the importance of scientific thought and the learner as active rather than passive (Glassman, 1999).

(b) Outline and evaluate how Vygotsky's theory has been applied to education. (4 marks + 8 marks)

Collaborative learning is one example of how Vygotsky's theory has been applied to education. Collaborative learning refers to a method of learning in which students at various performance levels work together in small groups toward a common goal. This links to Vygotsky's work because of the emphasis on shared understandings. When people work collaboratively, they bring their own perspectives to the activity, and so are better able to generate a solution.

Peer tutoring is another example of applying Vygotsky's theory. Vygotsky suggested that children move through the ZPD because of the intervention of 'experts', i.e. the 'more knowledgeable other' (MKO). Although the MKO is often a teacher or older adult, this is not necessarily the case. A child's peers may be the individuals with more knowledge or experience, and therefore may act as the MKO.

There is research support for the value of collaborative learning. For example, Gokhale (1995) found that students who participated in collaborative learning subsequently performed better on an individual critical-thinking test than students who studied individually.

There is also research support for the value of peer tutoring. Cohen *et al.* (1982) found improvements in both tutees' and tutors' academic and social development (e.g. Cohen *et al.* 1982). However, a consistent finding is that it is most effective for peer tutors (Cloward, 1967) presumably because, in order to teach something, you need an increased understanding.

One issue related to the Vygotskian approach is culture bias. This approach may be more appropriate in collectivist settings because true sharing is the basis of such cultures. This is not to say that group work is not possible in individualist societies but in settings where children are encouraged to be more competitive and self-reliant, groupwork may be less effective. For example, Stigler and Perry (1990) compared American and Asian schools and found in latter that maths was more effectively taught by group work than in individualist American schools.

A further criticism of the approach is that it may not be as effective as traditional methods. Bennet (1976) found that more traditional, formal, teacher-oriented approaches lead to higher attainment levels than the kind of active learning advocated by Vygotsky. This may be because 'formal' teachers spend more time on core topics and because active learning requires more sensitivity and experience from teachers.

The task here is to select two features of Vygotsky's theory and provide a detailed description of each, rather than trying to cover everything you know about Vygotsky's theory at a superficial level, which would not attract marks in the top band. You are always seeking a balance between depth and breadth in order to achieve high marks for AO1.

Some AO2 points are shorter than others but you should always aim to follow the three-point rule (see page 5).

In this essay names and dates of researchers have been included. Neither are required but are a good way to provide detail and elaboration.

This part of the question has an appropriate AO1:AO2 division with 125 words of AO1 and 290 words of AO2. 100–120 words of AO1 and 200–240 words of AO2 is appropriate for 4+8 marks.

Organisation and structure are important criteria for AO1. This tends to be easier to achieve in a parted question but even here paragraphs help improve this skill. Each paragraph is based on the plan on the facing page. Using a plan like this helps you keep track of how much AO1 and AO2 you have included, and ensures you get the ratio right.

You can see at a glance that part (b) also has an appropriate division of AO1 and AO2 (135:245 words). It helps you to keep an eye on the balance in your own answers if you do all AO1 first followed by all the AO2.

Division 2 Development of moral understanding Answer plans

Answer plan 1
Discuss Kohlberg's theory of moral understanding. (8 marks + 16 marks)

Kohlberg's theory

AO1	Key point – focus on moral decision-making process rather than behaviour, moral dilemmas with boys aged 10–16
AO1	Stages are invariant, universal, progressively more logical consistency; combine maturity + disequilibrium + empathy
AO1	Preconventional (accept rules of authority), conventional (understand need for social order)
AO1	Post-conventional (abstract moral principles)
AO2	Colby *et al.* (1983) original sample interviewed, showed a continuing decrease in stages 1 and 2
AO2	Further support from Walker *et al.* (1987)
AO2	Relationship between principles and behaviour supported by Kohlberg (1975) but not Burton (1976)
AO2	Dilemmas lack realism, Gilligan (1982) real-life dilemmas
IDA	Gender bias, Gilligan (1982) proposed a different stage theory emphasising principles of care
IDA	Culture bias, Snarey and Kelio (1991) stage 3 mainly industrialised societies
IDA	Real-world application, Cluster Schools where moral decision-making encouraged
AO2	Conclusion – some research evidence but lacks validity

Work out your own plan for these questions and then write your answers.

(a) Outline and evaluate Piaget's theory of cognitive understanding. (4 marks + 4 marks)

(b) Outline and evaluate Kohlberg's theory of moral development. (4 marks + 12 marks)

Part (a) Piaget's theory

AO1	
AO1	
AO2	
AO2 or IDA	

Part (b) Kohlberg's theory

AO1	
AO1	
AO2	
AO2	
AO2	
AO2 or IDA	
AO2 or IDA	
AO2 or IDA	

Answer plan 2
(a) Outline Kohlberg's theory of moral understanding. (4 marks)

(b) Outline and evaluate Vygotsky's theory of cognitive development. (4 marks + 16 marks)

Part (a) Kohlberg's theory

AO1	Stages are invariant, universal, progressively more logical consistency, maturity + disequilibrium + empathy
AO1	Preconventional (accept rules of authority), conventional (understand need for social order), post-conventional (abstract moral principles)

Part (b) Vygotsky's theory

AO1	The role of culture and others – experts
AO1	Zone of proximal development (ZPD) and scaffolding
AO2	Research support for role of culture, e.g. Gredler (1992) primitive counting system in Papua New Guinea
AO2	Research support for scaffolding, e.g. Wood and Middleton (1975) pyramid task and contingent regulations
AO2	Research support for language, e.g. Carmichael *et al.* (1932), challenged by Sinclair-de-Zwart (1969)
AO2	Research support for ZPD, e.g. McNaughton and Leyland (1990) mothers working with jigsaw puzzles
AO2	Limitations, e.g. overplayed social influences, not conducive to research (hard to operationalise)
AO2	Strengths, e.g. positive approach because suggests ways to assist learner
IDA	Real-world application to education, e.g. collaborative learning, peer tutoring, scaffolding
IDA	Contrast with Piaget, e.g. cultural vs individualist approach, but also similarities (Glassman, 1999)

Answer plan 3
(a) Outline Piaget's theory of cognitive development. (8 marks)

(b) To what extent has Kohlberg's theory of moral understanding been supported by research evidence. (16 marks)

Part (a) Piaget's theory

AO1	Key points – maturation, qualitative differences
AO1	Key mechanisms – schema, assimilation, accommodation, equilbration, operations
AO1	Stage 1 sensori-motor (0–2), e.g. object permanence, stage 2 pre-operational (2–7), e.g. egocentricism
AO1	Stage 3 concrete (7–11), e.g. conservation, stage 4 formal (11+), e.g. abstract hypothetico-deductive reasoning

Part (b) Kohlberg's theory

AO2	Colby *et al.* (1983) original sample interviewed, continuing decrease in stages 1 and 2
AO2	Further support from Walker *et al.* (1987)
AO2	Relationship between principles and behaviour supported by Kohlberg (1975) but not Burton (1976)
AO2	Dilemmas lack realism, Gilligan (1982) real-life dilemmas
IDA	Gender bias, Gilligan (1982) proposed a different stage theory emphasising interpersonal concerns
IDA	Culture bias, Snarey and Kelio (1991) stage 3 mainly industrialised societies
IDA	Real-world application, Cluster Schools where moral decision-making encouraged
AO2	Conclusion – some research evidence but lacks validity

Model answer

Discuss Kohlberg's theory of moral understanding. (8 marks + 16 marks)

Kohlberg focused particularly on the way that children think about moral decisions rather than on their moral behaviour. Kohlberg (1966) constructed a stage theory based on extensive interviews that he conducted with boys aged 10–16.

There are certain key features of the theory. The stages are invariant and universal, i.e. people everywhere go through the same stages in the same order. Second, each new stage represents a more logically consistent form of understanding and one that is qualitatively different to the previous stage. Finally, moral maturity is achieved through a combination of biological maturation (like Piaget's ideas), disequilibrium (noticing weaknesses in the existing style of thinking) and gains in empathy (perspective-taking).

The stage theory is divided into three levels, each further subdivided into two stages. The first level is pre-conventional. Children accept the rules of authority figures and judge actions by their consequences. Actions that result in punishments are judged as bad, those that bring rewards are judged as good. The second level is conventional. Individuals continue to believe that conformity to social rules is desirable, but not out of self-interest. Maintaining the current social system ensures positive human relationships and social order.

The final stage is post-conventional where the individual moves beyond unquestioning compliance with the norms of their own social system. They now define morality in terms of abstract moral principles that apply to all societies and situations. This level may be an unrealistic ideal, especially the final 6th stage of universal ethical principles, which is not achieved by many.

There is research support from Kohlberg's original study and also from Colby *et al.* (1983) who re-interviewed Kohlberg's original participants regularly over 20 years. The data from this study confirmed that stage 1 and 2 reasoning decreases with age while stage 4 and 5 reasoning increases.

There is further research support from Walker *et al.* (1987). They interviewed 80 children (boys and girls). Six year olds were at stage 1 or 2 whereas by age 15 most children had reached stage 3. A further sample of adults (average age 40) were tested and were mainly between stages 3 and 4, with only 3% between stages 4 and 5.

One criticism of this research is that the moral principles may have little to do with moral behaviour. Kohlberg did predict that those who reason in a more mature fashion should show more morally mature behaviour. He found some support for this in a study (1975) where 15% of college students at the post-conventional stage cheated on a test whereas 70% of those at the pre-conventional stage did. However, Burton (1976) found that people only behave consistently with their moral principles on some kinds of moral behaviour, such as cheating or sharing toys and concluded that it is likely that factors other than moral principles affect moral behaviour, such as the likelihood of punishment or the nature of the situation.

Another criticism is that the moral dilemmas used to assess moral thinking lacked realism. Kohlberg's evidence is not based on real life decisions and in addition the moral dilemmas (such as Heinz and the chemist) may have made little sense to young children. Gilligan (1982) conducted research interviewing people about their own moral decisions and found quite different results.

Gilligan also criticised Kohlberg for gender bias in his theory which is not surprising since he wrote the dilemmas from a male perspective and also used boys' responses to construct his theory. Kohlberg's dilemmas are based on a male morality of justice whereas Gilligan's stage theory is based on principles of care.

Kohlberg's theory has also been criticised for its culture bias. Kohlberg's moral dilemmas are rooted in Western moral principles but he did find evidence of similar moral reasoning in other cultures. However, Snarey and Keljo (1991) found that post-conventional understanding occurs mainly in more developed, industrialised societies. This may occur because diverse communities pose more conflicts, which promotes moral development because individuals have to question moral standards.

A real-world application of Kohlberg's work is the idea of creating democratic groups (Cluster Schools) in schools and prisons where people had the power to define and resolve disputes within their group, encouraging moral development.

In conclusion, the research evidence on the surface seems supportive but there are a number of issues with the methodology which suggest the means of assessment is not valid. Nevertheless his ideas have had influence and the basic concept of a stage theory of moral development remains unchallenged.

Strictly speaking it would make more sense to have three separate paragraphs for the three different levels, but we have made it two to fit in with our 'pattern' of four AO1 paragraphs.

We also might have omitted one of the earlier paragraphs but this gives the answer a nice balance – some more general, overview points rather than focusing too much on the levels.

There is no need to describe each individual stage. This would result in too much detail and too little range.

Note how each AO2 point begins with a clear lead-in phrase to alert the examiner that this is evaluation. In the exam your AO2 won't be shaded in colour so you need other means of flagging it up to the examiner, hence the importance of these phrases.

IDA points should also be clearly flagged for the examiner using IDA lead-in phrases. It is also important to ensure the IDA point is not general i.e. could be placed equally well in any essay.

Conclusions can be pointless because they are often little more than a summary. In this case we have analysed the evidence and produced a genuine conclusion.

There are 742 words in total, of which 253 are AO1 – which is an almost perfect 34%!

Division 3 Development of social cognition Answer plans

Answer plan 1
Discuss the development of the child's sense of self. (8 marks + 16 marks)

Sense of self

AO1	Subjective self-awareness – 2 months sense of personal agency, 5 months recognise own face
AO1	Objective self-awareness – Lewis and Brooks-Gunn (1979) used mirror test, self-recognition by 2 years (66%)
AO1	Psychological self – children age 4–5 just use physical features for self-description
AO1	Theory of Mind (ToM) by 4 years, false-belief task
AO2	Research support, e.g. Bahrick and Watson (1985) videos of leg movements
AO2	Research support, e.g. Legerstee *et al.* (1998) pictures of own and other faces
AO2	Objective self-awareness individual differences, develops faster in securely attached infants (Pipp *et al.*, 1992)
IDA	Link to intelligence in non-human animals (self-recognition)
AO2	Psychological self, cultural differences, Western 10–11 years use more psychological terms (Van den Heuvel *et al.*, 1992)
AO2	Individual differences, securely attached children rate selves more highly (Verschueren and Marcoen, 1999)
AO2	ToM link with autism, deficit (Baron-Cohen *et al.*, 1985)
IDA	Nature and nurture, innate ToM module but also affected by experience (Perner *et al.*, 1994) faster in large families

DIY

Work out your own plan for these questions and then write your answers.

(a) Outline and evaluate the development of Theory of Mind. (4 marks + 8 marks)

(b) Outline and evaluate the development of perspective-taking. (4 marks + 8 marks)

Part (a) Theory of Mind

AO1	
AO1	
AO2	
AO2 or IDA	

Part (b) Perspective-taking

AO1	
AO1	
AO2	
AO2	
AO2	
AO2 or IDA	
AO2 or IDA	
AO2 or IDA	

Answer plan 2
Discuss the development of children's understanding of others. (8 marks + 16 marks)

Understanding of others

AO1	Imitation and understanding intentions in infants
AO1	Perceptual perspective-taking, Piaget three mountains
AO1	Role-taking, conceptual perspective-taking related to ToM, Selman's stages
AO1	Deception, can plant a false belief, e.g. hiding disappointment about a present (Cole, 1986)
AO2	Research evidence, Meltzoff and Moore (1977)
AO2	Research evidence, Carpenter *et al.* (1998) gaze following
AO2	Distinction between knowing about someone's internal state and their mental state (True ToM) (Wellman and Wolley, 1990)
IDA	Nature, invariant stages (biological) and innate ToM module supported by autistics (Hobson, 1984)
IDA	Nurture, experience matters, e.g. sensory impairments (Eide and Eide, 2006), family size (Perner *et al.*, 1994)
IDA	Evolutionary approach to understanding deception, Machiavellian intelligence is adaptive
IDA	Real-world application, social skills training programmes (Smith and Pelligrini, 2008)
IDA	Real-world application, used with prisoners

Answer plan 3
Describe and evaluate biological explanations of social cognition. (8 marks + 16 marks)

Explanation 1: Theory of Mind Module (ToMM)

AO1	Set of beliefs held by each of us about what is in someone else's mind (Baron-Cohen, 1995)
AO2	Research support, autistic children (Baron-Cohen *et al.*, 1995), conceptual perspective-taking (Hobson, 1984)
AO2	Neurophysiological support (Stone, 2007), e.g. amygdala and OFC, but ToMM not one specific region
IDA	Nature and nurture, ToM not just biology, also affected by experience (Perner *et al.*, 1994) faster in large families

Explanation 2: Mirror neuron system (MNS)

AO1	Neurons in frontal premotor cortex respond when performing an action and when watching someone else
AO1	MNS explains perspective taking, empathy and prosocial behaviour (Eisenberg, 2000)
AO1	MNS explains language acquisition, Binofsky *et al.* (2000) Broca's area, helps learning speech sounds
AO2	Evidence for MNS, e.g. Iacoboni *et al.* (2001) intentions as well as motor activity ('why' as well as 'what')
AO2	Research evidence, Iacoboni *et al.* (2005) fMRI showed MN activity when Ps watching intention not just action film
AO2	Iacoboni (2007) also recorded 300 individual cells, identifying 34 mirror neurons
AO2	Gopnik (2007) it's a myth because evidence mainly from animals and behaviour is too complex for simple MNS
IDA	Nature and nurture, MNS part biological but may also arise through experience (learn by association) (Gopnik)
IDA	Real-world application, train autistics through imitation practice (Slack, 2007)

Model answer

Describe and evaluate biological explanations of social cognition. (8 marks + 16 marks)

Theory of Mind (ToM) is an intuitive set of beliefs held by each of us about what is in someone else's mind, i.e. understanding what someone else is thinking. Baron-Cohen (1995) proposed that ToM may have a biological basis. He proposed that there is a ToM module (ToMM) in the brain, which matures around the age of four.

There is research evidence for the idea of an innate, biological ToMM from the study of autistic children. Children with this disorder cannot cope with a false-belief task which involves understanding what someone else is thinking (Baron-Cohen *et al.*, 1995). Hobson (1984) found that autistic children performed at the same level as children of the same mental age on the three mountains task – so they could cope with perceptual perspective-taking but ultimately do not develop conceptual perspective-taking. This suggests that there is something biological underlying conceptual perspective-taking.

There is neurophysiological evidence to support the ToMM. Stone (2007) reports that evidence has been found in many areas of the brain including the amygdala and the orbitofrontalcortex (OFC). The fact that so many regions have been identified suggests that the ToMM is not one specific region but many regions may contribute to it.

We can consider nature and nurture. ToM Is not solely determined by biology. For example, research shows that it appears earlier in children from large families (Perner *et al.*, 1994). Having a large family and especially older siblings means that a child is challenged to think about the intentions of others when resolving conflicts.

More recently researchers have identified the mirror neuron system (MNS). This system may explain many aspects of social cognition. Basically the MNS consists of a collection of neurons in the frontal, premotor cortex that respond when a person performs an action but also respond when a person watches someone else perform an action. Essentially it enables a person to experience the actions of another as if they were performing the action themselves.

The mirror neuron system has been used to explain imitation of another person's actions. This would just involve motor activity. But it is also suggested that the MNS can explain perspective taking where an understanding of intentions is required. It could further be used to explain empathy, where an individual is able to experience the emotions of another person. Eisenberg (2000) proposed that empathy lay at the root of prosocial behaviour.

The MNS has also been used to explain language acquisition, an important part of social behaviour. Binkofski *et al.* (2000) used brain imaging techniques to demonstrate the existence of mirror neurons in Broca's area which is involved in speech production. The MNS may assist in the imitation of speech sounds which is an important component of language acquisition.

Research evidence originally came from monkeys but has also been found in humans. For example, Iacoboni *et al.* (2005) used fMRI to record neuron activity in participants watching films clips of items you might have at a tea party. The highest level of mirror neuron activity was recorded when participants were watching an intention clip (e.g. a person was intending to drink their tea or to clear up) rather than just an action clip. This shows that what was encoded was not just 'what' but also 'why' (i.e. ToM).

However, evidence from imaging studies only relates to general neuron activity. Iacoboni (2007) also recorded the activity of almost 300 individual neurons in the frontal lobes of epileptic patients and identified 34 mirror neurons activated by both performance and observation. This supports the presence of specific mirror neurons responding to the mental states of another.

There are criticisms of the mirror neuron concept. Gopnik (2007) suggests it is a myth. She claims that the only real evidence is derived from non-human animal studies. These studies may not generalise to humans since non-human animals, arguably, do not have ToM. She also argues that it is hard to believe that systems as complex as altruistic behaviour or ToM could be explained simply by a MNS.

Perhaps a better approach is to think in terms of nature and nurture. The original suggestion was that the MNS is an innate system. Gopnik suggests instead that the MNS might arise as a result of experience because neurons learn by association – when two events are associated the neurons for each event form a connection. An infant's first experience is to see a hand moving (its own) and at the same time experience that hand moving. This creates a mirror connection, acquired through experience rather than being innate.

There are real-world applications of this knowledge. For example, if a malfunction of the MNS explains why some people have certain autistic behaviours (failing to understand what others are thinking) and this can be learned through experience, then it might be possible to strengthen the MNS in autistics using activities that require the imitation of others (Slack, 2007).

The content of this essay is divided into two sections, one on the Theory of Mind module and the other on mirror neurons.

With each of these sections, the focus is on *explanations* for social cognition.

When in doubt always add 'This suggests that …' at the end of an AO2 paragraph to make your point clear, as described in the three-point rule (page 5).

It is tempting to include evidence from the original animal studies on mirror neurons but this would not be relevant to 'explanations'.

You may feel that a study makes little sense unless you describe it but such description doesn't gain AO2 credit beyond the briefest outline to make the study identifiable.

The AO1:AO2 ratio of this answer is not as immediately clear as the one on the previous spread where the first third was all AO1. In this essay the number of paragraphs is a useful guide to how much AO1 and AO2 you have done. There should be 12 paragraphs with, on average 50–60 words.

The total length of this essay is 812 words, with 257 words AO1 (32%). Just for the record, each paragraph, on average, is 67 words, so slightly longer than usual.

Answers for you to mark

See page 173 for examiner's comments.

Question

Discuss the development of the child's sense of self. (8 marks + 16 marks)

Student answer

1 A key feature of a child's development of a sense of self is the Theory of Mind. Wimmer and Perner created the Sally Anne test as a means of assessing whether someone can cope with false beliefs. What happens is that first of all the participant is shown two dolls called Sally and Anne. Second, Sally puts a ball in her basket. Next Sally leaves the room and Anne moves the ball to her basket. When Sally returns the participant is asked where Sally will think the ball is. If the participant says in Sally's box then they possess a Theory of Mind. Wimmer and Permer found that two to three years olds tended to answer wrong and say this is because the younger children don't understand that Sally doesn't know that Anne moved the ball. Since the child knows where the ball is he/she presumes Sally does too. By the age of three or four children can answer correctly, therefore demonstrating that they have a Theory of Mind.

2 Baron-Cohen did a similar study this time looking at how autistic children performed. There were in fact three groups in his study – autistic children, normal children, and Down's Syndrome children (lower IQ). Despite the fact that the Down's syndrome children had the lowest IQ, the group that couldn't cope with the task were the autistic children. A few autistic children managed to get the task right but all the others couldn't do it. This shows that the task isn't related to intelligence. It is likely to be related to social factors.

3 This relates to the nurture side of the nature–nurture debate because it is explaining Theory of Mind in terms of social factors. Though on the other hand Baron-Cohen has suggested that Theory of Mind is due to biological factors.

4 There is some research support for the nurture side. Perner did another study this time looking at children from families with a lot of children or a just a few children. Perner found that those children from very large families developed Theory of Mind at an earlier age than children from smaller families. It is probably because children in larger families have a lot more occasions when they are interacting with people and this might explain why they developed Theory of Mind more quickly. This would go against Baron-Cohen's idea that Theory of Mind is biological because it seems to be related to experience instead.

5 There is another way to test Theory of Mind which is called the Smartie Tube test. A child is shown a tube of Smarties and asked what is inside. The child is then shown that in fact a pencil is inside. Then they are asked what they think another child would answer when asked the question about what is inside. A child without a Theory of Mind would say that there is a pencil inside because they can't separate what is in their mind from what is in someone else's mind. Children at about the age of 4 can cope correctly with this task, demonstrating they have a Theory of Mind.

6 One criticism of this research is that the reason children may find the task difficult is because their language is very underdeveloped, and therefore they get confused. So it isn't because they lack a Theory of Mind but because their language skills are poor.

(555 words)

AO1 mark scheme

The two most likely approaches to answering this question, given the specification entry for this topic, are (1) a chronology of a child's developing sense of separateness and (2) the development of Theory of Mind (ToM).

Candidates can look at one particular aspect of the development of self, e.g. ToM or self-awareness (as assessed by the mirror test). Alternatively, candidates might look at a number of different behaviours and their developmental sequence.

Answers should clearly illustrate the developmental aspect of this question.

8 marks is about 200-240 words.

Comments and marks for AO1

Mark	Knowledge and understanding	Range of material	Depth and breadth	Organisation and structure
8–7	Accurate and well-detailed	Good range	Substantial evidence of depth and breadth	Coherent
6–5	Generally accurate and reasonably detailed	Range	Depth and/or breadth	Reasonably coherent
4–3	Basic, relatively superficial	Restricted	Generally accurate	Basic
2–1	Rudimentary and may be muddled and/or inaccurate	Very brief or largely irrelevant		Lacking
0	No creditworthy material			

The **AO1** mark I would give is ☐

Tick the terms you think apply to the student's answer.

AO2 mark scheme

Research evidence is most likely to be the main source of AO2 marks.

Methodological evaluation of these studies may be a further source of AO2 but credit may only be gained if the implications of such criticisms for the theory are explicit.

A further route to AO2 is to consider alternative explanations, for example failure on ToM tasks may be due to language problems rather than perspective taking. However, such alternative explanations are only creditworthy if part of a sustained critical commentary.

Individual differences may be considered as well as the role of parents and peers in development.

16 marks is about 400–480 words.

Guidance on marking is given on pages 6–11.

Comments and marks for AO2

Mark	Analysis and understanding	Focus	Elaboration	Line of argument	Issues/debates/ approaches	Quality of written communication
16–13	Sound	Well-focused	Coherent	Clear	Used effectively	Fluent, effective use of terms
12–9	Reasonable	Generally focused	Reasonable	Evident	Reasonably effective	Clear, appropriate
8–5	Basic, superficial	Sometimes focused	Some evidence		Superficial reference	Lacks clarity, limited use of terms
4–1	Rudimentary, limited understanding	Weak, muddled and incomplete	Not effective	May be mainly irrelevant	Absent or muddled/ inaccurate	Often unconnected assertions, errors
0	No creditworthy material					

The **AO2** mark I would give is ☐

Chapter 9 Psychopathology: Schizophrenia

There have been changes to the specification from September 2011 – therefore the updated specification details here are slightly different to those in some editions of the *A2 Complete Companion*.

Division 1 Overview	• **Clinical characteristics of schizophrenia**
	• **Issues surrounding the classification and diagnosis of schizophrenia, including reliability and validity**

Possible exam questions for this division

Question	Comment
(a) Outline clinical characteristics of schizophrenia. (8 marks) (b) Explain issues associated with the classification **and/or** diagnosis of schizophrenia. (16 marks)	Questions may ask for a description of the clinical characteristics of schizophrenia – note that the maximum mark for such questions is 8. Questions will not ask you to evaluate the clinical characteristics, therefore questions on clinical characteristics will always be paired with an evaluation of something else. In this question 'issues associated with classification and/or diagnosis' is all AO2 (evaluation), i.e. you do not need to provide descriptions of the issues.
Discuss issues surrounding the classification and diagnosis of schizophrenia. (8 marks + 16 marks)	An alternative possibility is that issues associated with classification and/or diagnosis require description and evaluation. In this case you should help the examiner by providing a clear *description* of each issue. Descriptions of classification systems, such as *DSM*, will not be creditworthy. Issues that are not related to schizophrenia will also not be creditworthy. See model answer on page 95.
(a) Outline clinical characteristics of schizophrenia. (4 marks) (b) Explain issues associated with the classification **and/or** diagnosis of schizophrenia. (10 marks) (c) Outline and evaluate **one** psychological explanation for schizophrenia. (4 marks + 6 marks)	The total number of marks available for clinical characteristics may be less than the full 8 marks, so be prepared for a shorter answer. In part (a) you should present a list of characteristics appropriate for 4 marks, i.e. about 100–120 words. Part (b) in this question is all AO2. The final part is taken from other divisions of this chapter and requires attention to the mark split – usually you are asked to write twice as much AO2 as AO1, which is not the case here. You can follow the pattern used in this book and aim to write two paragraphs of AO1 and three of AO2 where each paragraph is 50–70 words.

Division 2 Explanations	• **Biological explanations of schizophrenia, for example genetics, biochemistry**
	• **Psychological explanations of schizophrenia, for example behavioural, cognitive, psychodynamic and socio-cultural**

Possible exam questions for this division

Question	Comment
'There is a variety of different biological explanations for schizophrenia, ranging from genetic to biochemistry and also including neuroanatomy, viruses and evolutionary factors.' Discuss biological explanations of schizophrenia. (8 marks + 16 marks)	Questions sometimes start with a quotation. The intention here is to remind you of the breadth of material that you might include in your answer. However, don't be led astray – it does not mean that you have to cover all of these different biological factors. The question itself states that you must do at least two for full marks but two would be sufficient. It would be creditworthy to evaluate explanations that have not been described, particularly if used to compare and contrast. See student answer on page 100.
Describe **two or more** psychological explanations of schizophrenia. (8 marks + 16 marks)	The specification provides four examples of psychological explanations – but these are examples only. Exam questions on this specific bullet point of the specfication will only ask for psychological explanations and will not specify which ones. See model answer on page 97.
(a) Outline and evaluate **one or more** biological explanations for schizophrenia. (4 marks + 8 marks) (b) Discuss **one or more** psychological explanations for schizophrenia. (4 marks + 8 marks)	The only two kinds of question in this division are about (1) biological explanations and (2) psychological explanations. You may be asked for one, two, at least one, or two or more. What this boils down to is that learning two explanations for each will be sufficient. You will notice from the selection of questions on this spread that the maximum marks for one psychological/biological explanation is 4 marks description + 8 marks evaluation (blockbuster questions on one explanation have not been set – they are possible but unlikely). In total this means that you need about 100–120 words description for each of the four different explanations (two psychological and two biological) and about 200–240 words evaluation of each of these four explanations.

(a) Outline **one** psychological explanation and **one** biological explanation for schizophrenia. (8 marks) (b) Evaluate explanations for schizophrenia. (16 marks)	There are many variations on the same theme. Here both explanations are described in part (a) and the evaluation is all in part (b). In the previous question psychological and biological explanations were separated. You could use exactly the same material in the two answers but just arranged differently.
(a) Outline **one or more** biological explanations of schizophrenia and **one or more** psychological explanations of schizophrenia. (8 marks) (b) Evaluate biological and psychological explanations of schizophrenia. (16 marks)	In this question you have the option to cover more than one explanation of each type. There is a danger in trying to write about more than one of each – you will probably sacrifice depth for breadth and thus would not achieve a mark in the top band because your answer would lack detail.
(a) Outline at least **one** biological explanation of schizophrenia and at least **one** psychological explanation of schizophrenia. (8 marks) (b) Consider whether psychological or biological approaches provide the better explanation of schizophrenia. (16 marks)	This variation has a slightly different part (b). In such a question it is likely that marks in the top band would only be awarded if your answer does address the question of which kind of explanation is better. Your answer is likely to be based on the relative quality of research evidence for each explanation.
(a) Outline clinical characteristics of schizophrenia. (4 marks) (b) Outline **one** psychological explanation of schizophrenia. (4 marks) (c) Evaluate psychological explanations of schizophrenia. (16 marks)	Questions are likely to span the divisions in order to include part questions on clinical characteristics and/or issues associated with classification and/or diagnosis. In such cases attend carefully to the number of marks available and construct your answers appropriately. Here 4 marks worth would be about 100–120 words.

Division 3 Therapies

- **Biological therapies for schizophrenia, including their evaluation in terms of appropriateness and effectiveness**
- **Psychological therapies for schizophrenia, for example behavioural, psychodynamic and cognitive-behavioural, including their evaluation in terms of appropriateness and effectiveness**

Possible exam questions for this division

Discuss biological therapies for schizophrenia. (8 marks + 16 marks)	When a question is open-ended, as here (as opposed to parted questions) you need to be especially careful to reflect the mark division in your answer – about 200–240 words of description and 400–480 words of evaluation.
Outline and evaluate **two or more** psychological therapies for schizophrenia. (8 marks + 16 marks)	The question possibilities for therapies are the same as for explanations – biological and/or psychological and never more than two of each *required*.
(a) Outline at least **one** biological therapy for schizophrenia and at least **one** psychological therapy for schizophrenia. (8 marks) (b) Evaluate biological and psychological therapies for schizophrenia in terms of appropriateness and effectiveness. (16 marks)	The specification suggests that you should evaluate therapies in terms of appropriateness and effectiveness, so it is worth being prepared for a question that uses such terms. See model answer on page 99.
'There are two key factors that help in evaluating therapies – whether they are effective and whether they are appropriate.' Outline and evaluate **two or more** therapies used in the treatment of schizophrenia. (8 marks +16 marks)	When a questions says 'two or more' this means you can gain credit if more than two therapies are described/evaluated but two would be sufficient to gain full marks. The danger of trying to write about more than two is that you inevitably lose depth and elaboration in your answer, and this means you may not get marks in the top band because your answer would lack detail and elaboration.
(a) Outline clinical characteristics of schizophrenia. (4 marks) (b) Briefly describe **one** psychological therapy for schizophrenia. (4 marks) (c) Evaluate psychological therapies for schizophrenia. (16 marks)	This is another example of a question set across the divisions. Candidates are often tempted to write more than required for parts (a) and (b) whereas the big marks are from part (c). In questions on psychopathology there are no 'specific' marks for IDA so it is not required but, if included, such comments would gain AO2 credit.

Division 1 Overview

Answer plans

On Unit 4 there is no requirement for issues debates and approaches (IDA). If such material is included it would gain AO2 credit – if suitably contextualised.

Answer plan 1

(a) Outline clinical characteristics of schizophrenia. (8 marks)

(b) Explain issues associated with the classification **and/or** diagnosis of schizophrenia. (16 marks)

Part (a) Clinical characteristics

AO1	Duration – two months of two or more positive symptoms
AO1	Delusions, e.g. fear of persecution, inflated belief of power
AO1	Hallucinations, e.g. auditory (e.g. voices), visual (e.g. ghosts) or tactile (e.g. insects)
AO1	No possibility of mood disorder or organic cause (e.g. drugs)

Part (b) Issues

AO2	Inter-rater reliability low, e.g. Whaley (2001) found +.11
AO2	Cultural differences, same description 60% diagnosed by US psychiatrists, only 2% of UK (Copeland *et al.*, 1971)
AO2	Reliability, diagnosis, demonstrated by Rosenhan (1973) sane in insane places
AO2	Tested further in follow-up study, found only 21% detection rate
AO2	Comorbidity – first rank symptoms found in other disorders, e.g. depression (Bentall *et al.*, 1988)
AO2	May be a spectrum of psychosis rather than discrete condition (Allardyce *et al.*, 2001)
AO2	Low predictive validity, some recover previous level of functioning (20%) but 40% never recover
AO2	Outcome influenced more by gender (Malmberg *et al.*, 1998) or social skills (Harrison *et al.*, 2001)

DIY

Work out your own plan for these questions and then write your answers.

(a) Outline clinical characteristics of schizophrenia. (4 marks)

(b) Briefly describe **one** psychological therapy for schizophrenia. (4 marks)

(c) Evaluate psychological therapies for schizophrenia. (16 marks)

Part (a) Clinical characteristics

AO1	
AO1	

Part (b) One psychological therapy

AO1	
AO1	

Part (c) Evaluate psychological therapies

AO2	
AO2	
AO2	
AO2	
AO2	
AO2	
AO2	
AO2	

Answer plan 2

Discuss issues surrounding the classification and diagnosis of schizophrenia. (8 marks + 16 marks)

Issues

AO1	Reliability, classification – compare clinicians' diagnoses
AO2	Inter-rater reliability low, e.g. Whaley (2001) found +.11
AO2	Cultural differences, same description 60% diagnosed by US psychiatrists, only 2% UK (Copeland *et al.*, 1971)
AO1	Reliability, diagnosis – situation rather than illness
AO2	Evidence from Rosenhan (1973) sane in insane places
AO2	Tested further in follow-up study, found only 21% detection rate
AO1	Validity, comorbidity suggests classification is not a 'real' category because not distinct
AO2	First rank symptoms found in other disorders, e.g. depression (Bentall *et al.*, 1988)
AO2	May be a spectrum of psychosis rather than discrete condition (Allardyce *et al.*, 2001)
AO1	Predictive validity, predicts outcome following treatment confirming value of the diagnosis
AO2	Low predictive validity, some recover previous level of functioning (20%) but 40% never recover
AO2	Outcome influenced more by gender (Malmberg *et al.*, 1998) or social skills (Harrison *et al.*, 2001)

Answer plan 3

(a) Outline clinical characteristics of schizophrenia. (4 marks)

(b) Explain issues associated with the classification **and/or** diagnosis of schizophrenia. (10 marks)

(c) Outline and evaluate **one** psychological explanation for schizophrenia. (4 marks + 6 marks)

Part (a) Clinical characteristics

AO1	Delusions, e.g. fear of persecution, inflated belief of power
AO1	Hallucinations, e.g. auditory (e.g. voices), visual (e.g. ghosts) or tactile (e.g. insects)

Part (b) Explain issues

AO2	Inter-rater reliability low, e.g. Whaley (2001) found +.11
AO2	Cultural differences, same description 60% diagnosed by US psychiatrists, only 2% of UK (Copeland *et al.*, 1971)
AO2	Reliability, diagnosis, demonstrated by Rosenhan (1973) sane in insane places
AO2	Comorbidity – first rank symptoms found in other disorders, e.g. depression (Bentall *et al.*, 1988)
AO2	May be a spectrum of psychosis rather than discrete condition (Allardyce *et al.*, 2001)

Part (c) One psychological explanation

AO1	Life events (stressors) act as trigger, e.g. death of close relative
AO1	Research, e.g. Brown and Birley (1968) found 2× as many stressful events prior to schizophrenic episode
AO2	Prospective studies (e.g. Hirsch *et al.*, 1966) life events have cumulative effect preceding relapse
AO2	Not all evidence supportive, e.g. Van Os *et al.* (1994) after major life event patients had lower incidence of relapse
AO2	Correlational evidence, early symptoms could be causal

Discuss issues surrounding the classification and diagnosis of schizophrenia. (8 marks + 16 marks)

One issue related to classification and diagnosis is reliability. Reliability refers to the consistency of a measuring instrument, such as DSM (the Diagnostic and Statistical Manual) that is used when diagnosing schizophrenia. Reliability can be measured in terms of whether two independent assessors give similar scores (inter-rater reliability). High reliability is indicated by a high positive correlation.

Inter-rater reliability has been assessed for diagnoses of schizophrenia and found to be relatively low. This was especially true for early versions of DSM but it was hoped that later revisions of DSM would prove more reliable. However, more recent versions have continued to produce low inter-rater reliability scores. For example, Whaley (2001) found only a small positive correlation of +.11 between different raters.

Differences in cultural interpretations also pose a threat to the reliability of the diagnosis of schizophrenia. A research study by Copeland *et al.* (1971) gave a description of a patient showing clinical characteristics associated with schizophrenia to US and UK psychiatrists. Of the US psychiatrists, 69% diagnosed schizophrenia, whereas only 2% of the UK psychiatrists gave the same diagnosis. This suggests that the diagnostic criteria had quite a different meaning in different cultures and therefore are not reliable when used in different cultural settings.

Reliability is also an issue for diagnosis. This was raised by Rosenhan (1973) who claimed that situational factors were more important in determining the ultimate diagnosis of schizophrenia, rather than any specific characteristics of the person.

Rosenhan demonstrated this in his well-known study called 'Sane in insane places'. He arranged for 'pseudopatients' to present themselves to psychiatric hospitals claiming to be hearing voices (a symptom of schizophrenia). All were diagnosed with schizophrenia and admitted, despite the fact they displayed no further symptoms during their hospitalisation. Throughout their stay, none of the staff recognised that they were actually normal.

The unreliability of diagnosis was further demonstrated in a follow-up study by Rosenhan. Psychiatrists at several mental hospitals were told to expect pseudopatients over a period of several months. This resulted in a 21% detection rate by the psychiatrists, even though none were actually sent. This shows that the diagnostic criteria used by psychiatrists could not reliably identify a person with schizophrenia.

A second issue is validity which concerns both classification and diagnosis. For example, there is the issue of comorbidity which is related to the validity. Comorbidity refers to the extent that two (or more) conditions co-occur (such as schizophrenia and depression) and therefore the extent to which the condition is 'real' and distinct.

One way to avoid the issue of comorbidity is to just use first-rank symptoms of schizophrenia when diagnosing (e.g. delusions or halluciantions). However, Bentall *et al.* (1988) claim that many of the first-rank symptoms of schizophrenia are also found in other disorders (e.g. depression and bipolar disorder). This makes it difficult to separate schizophrenia as a distinct disorder from other disorders and suggests that schizophrenia is not a distinct condition.

It may be more realistic to suggest that there is no such discrete disorder as schizophrenia but instead there is a spectrum of psychotic symptoms. Allardyce *et al.* (2001) claim that symptoms used to characterise schizophrenia do not define a specific disorder because its symptoms are also found in other categories of psychosis described in DSM and therefore there should just be a psychotic spectrum.

Another aspect of validity is predictive validity. Predictive validity demonstrates the validity of a diagnosis by demonstrating that it can predict scores on some criterion measure. If a disorder has high predictive validity then it should be clear how the disorder would develop and how people would respond to treatment.

Research has found low predictive validity for schizophrenia. Some patients (about 20%) do recover their previous level of functioning but 40% never really recover. This much variation in the prognosis suggests that the original diagnosis lacked predictive validity. It means that diagnosis was not helpful in dealing with the course of schizophrenia.

Research has shown that other factors may be more influential on the ultimate outcome of having schizophrenia. For example, it seems more to do with gender (Malmberg *et al.*, 1998) and psychosocial factors, such as social skills, academic achievement and family tolerance of schizophrenic behaviour (Harrison *et al.*, 2001).

Some exam questions on the topic of 'issues related to classification and diagnosis' are just AO2. Others are AO1 and AO2, as is the case here. When both AO1 and AO2 are required it is vital to make the AO1 component clearly separate from the AO2. Many students lose AO1 marks because clear division is missing.

This essay requires that both classification and diagnosis are discussed, whereas some essay titles don't (they say 'and/or').

You can keep track of the relative amounts of AO1 and AO2 by sticking to your plan – have four AO1 paragraphs and eight AO2 paragraphs, each 50–60 words on average.

With this topic there is a fine line between AO1 and AO2 – AO1 is a description of the issue and AO2 is any commentary on the issue, such as research evidence, implications, ways of dealing with the issue and so on. Always try to use AO2 lead-in phrases for the AO2 paragraphs.

In total this essay is 704 words, with 195 words of AO1 content and 506 of AO2. The ratio is not the ideal 1:2 but what matters is that there is sufficient of each assessment objective. Given that AO1 is difficult to achieve with this topic, this is quite acceptable.

Answer plans

Answer plan 1

Discuss biological explanations of schizophrenia. (8 marks + 16 marks)

Biological explanations

AO1	Genetic factors, based on family studies, e.g. Gottesman (1991) greater genetic relatedness, greater risk
AO1	Twin studies, e.g. meta-analysis by Joseph (2004) found 40% concordance for MZ twins and 7% for DZ
AO1	Dopamine hypothesis, excess D_2 receptors result in more dopamine neurons firing, leads to thought disturbance
AO1	Enlarged ventricles, Torrey (2002) 15% bigger
AO2	Maladaptive genetic traits selected out but may be adaptive, e.g. group splitting hypothesis (Stevens and Price, 2000)
AO2	Concordance rates may only reflect environmental differences, MZ twins treated more similarly
AO2	Alternative is adoption studies, e.g. Tienari *et al.* (2000) 7% children with biological schizophrenic mothers vs 2%
AO2	Methodological problems with adoption studies, e.g. schizophrenia spectrum disorder used
AO2	Dopamine support from amphetamine use and L-dopa
AO2	May be consequence rather than cause, e.g. Haracz (1982) post-mortem study
AO2	Inconsistent evidence for enlarged ventricles, e.g. Copolov and Crook (2000) meta-analysis, over 90 CT studies
AO2	May be an effect, e.g. Lyon *et al.* (1981) found correlation with dose of antipsychotics

DIY

Work out your own plan for these questions and then write your answers.

(a) Outline at least **one** biological explanation of schizophrenia and at least **one** psychological explanation of schizophrenia. (8 marks)

(b) Evaluate biological and psychological explanations of schizophrenia. (16 marks)

Part (a) Biological and psychological explanations

AO1	
AO1	
AO1	
AO1	

Part (b) Evaluate biological and psychological explanations

AO2	
AO2	
AO2	
AO2	
AO2	
AO2	
AO2	
AO2	

Answer plan 2

Describe **two or more** psychological explanations of schizophrenia. (8 marks + 16 marks)

Psychological explanations

AO1	Cognitive, starts biologically but symptoms require interpretation
AO1	Lack of validation from others causes feelings of persecution and delusional beliefs
AO1	Life events (stressors) act as trigger, e.g. death of close relative
AO1	Research, e.g. Brown and Birley (1968) found 2× as many stressful events prior to schizophrenic episode
AO2	Cognitive – biological support, e.g. Meyer-Linderberg *et al.* (2002) linked excess dopamine and working memory
AO2	Implications for treatment, Yellowlees *et al.* (2002) virtual hallucinations to learn to deal with unreal ones
AO2	Life events – retrospective studies (e.g. Brown and Birley, 1968), may have faulty recall
AO2	Prospective studies (e.g. Hirsch *et al.*, 1966) life events have cumulative effect preceding relapse
AO2	Not all evidence supportive, e.g. Van Os *et al.* (1994) after major life event patients had lower incidence of relapse
AO2	Correlational evidence, early symptoms could be causal
AO2	Biological explanations have stronger support, e.g. genetic studies (Gottesman, 1991)
AO2	Best explanation is diathesis-stress model, e.g. genetic vulnerability triggered by life events

Answer plan 3

(a) Outline and evaluate **one or more** biological explanations for schizophrenia. (4 marks + 8 marks)

(b) Discuss **one or more** psychological explanations for schizophrenia. (4 marks + 8 marks)

Part (a) Biological explanations

AO1	Genetic factors, based on family studies, e.g. Gottesman (1991) greater genetic relatedness, greater risk
AO1	Twin studies, e.g. meta-analysis by Joseph (2004) found 40% concordance for MZ twins and 7% for DZ
AO2	Maladaptive genetic traits selected out but may be adaptive, e.g. group splitting hypothesis (Stevens and Price, 2000)
AO2	Concordance rates may only reflect environmental differences, MZ twins treated more similarly
AO2	Alternative is adoption studies, e.g. Tienari *et al.* (2000) 7% in children with biological schizophrenic mothers vs 2%
AO2	Methodological problems with adoption studies, e.g. schizophrenia spectrum disorder used

Part (b) Psychological explanations

AO1	Life events (stressors) act as trigger, e.g. death of close relative
AO1	Research, e.g. Brown and Birley (1968) found 2× as many stressful events prior to schizophrenic episode
AO2	Retrospective studies (e.g. Brown and Birley, 1968), may be subject to faulty recall
AO2	Prospective studies (e.g. Hirsch *et al.*, 1966) life events have cumulative effect preceding relapse
AO2	Not all evidence supportive, e.g. Van Os *et al.* (1994) after major life event patients had lower incidence of relapse
AO2	Correlational evidence, early symptoms could be causal

Model answer

Describe **two or more** psychological explanations of schizophrenia. (8 marks + 16 marks)

The cognitive explanation acknowledges the role of biological factors in schizophrenia, suggesting that the basis of the condition is abnormal brain activity producing visual and auditory hallucinations. Further features of the disorder emerge as people try to make sense of the hallucinations.

When schizophrenics first experience voices and other worrying sensory experiences, they turn to others to confirm the validity of what they are experiencing. Other people fail to confirm the reality of these experiences, so the schizophrenic comes to believe that others must be hiding the truth. They begin to reject feedback from those around them and develop delusional beliefs that they are being manipulated and persecuted by others.

An alternative psychological explanation is that stressful life events cause the onset of schizophrenia. Events such as the death of a close relative act as a trigger. The individual may have a biological predisposition for schizophrenia but only some people with such a predisposition will develop the disorder – those who experience stressors.

Brown and Birley (1968) found that, prior to a schizophrenic episode, patients reported twice as many stressful life events compared to a healthy control group, who reported a low and unchanging level of stressful life events over the same period. This illustrates the link between stressors and the onset of schizophrenia.

There is biological evidence to support the cognitive explanation. Meyer-Linderberg *et al.* (2002) found a link between excess levels of dopamine in the prefrontal cortex and dysfunctions of working memory. Working memory dysfunction is associated with the cognitive disorganisation typically found in schizophrenics. This supports the idea that biological factors underlie some of the early symptoms of schizophrenia.

The cognitive approach has real-world applications as the basis for a form of therapy. Yellowlees *et al.* (2002) have trialled a machine that can deliver 'virtual' auditory and visual hallucinations, such as hearing the TV tell you to kill yourself, or one person's face morphing into another. The intention is to show schizophrenics that their hallucinations are not real. As yet, however, there is no evidence that this will provide a successful treatment.

The research by Brown and Birley was a retrospective study where data is collected after events have occurred. In other words, once a person had developed schizophrenia they are asked about events leading up to the onset. It is quite likely that recall would be negatively affected by events surrounding the onset of schizophrenia so such evidence may be unreliable.

Prospective studies are preferable, where people are studied after the onset of the disorder. Hirsch *et al.* (1996) followed 71 schizophrenic patients over a 48-week period. It was clear that life events made a significant cumulative contribution in the 12 months preceding relapse rather than having a more concentrated effect in the period just prior to the schizophrenic episode. This does support the retrospective research.

However, not all research supports the importance of life stressors. For example, Van Os *et al.* (1994) reported no link between life events and the onset of schizophrenia. In the prospective part of the study, patients who had experienced a major life event went on to have a lower incidence of relapse rather than an increased risk as predicted.

One criticism of this research is that it is correlational. Therefore, we cannot infer a causal relationship between stressful life events and schizophrenia. It could be that the early symptoms of the disorder (e.g. erratic behaviour) were the cause of the major life events (e.g. divorce, loss of a job). As a result, it is possible that the stressful major life events that are evident in the lives of some schizophrenics might be the consequence rather than the cause of the disorder.

In general the biological explanations probably have better research support than psychological ones. There is a large body of evidence, for example, supporting the role of genetic factors, such as the research by Gottesman (1991) which showed that the greater the degree of genetic relatedness, the greater the risk of schizophrenia.

However, the best solution is probably the diathesis stress model which combines both biological and psychological approaches. The diathesis stress model suggests that people have a vulnerability for schizophrenia (diathesis) but the disorder only manifests itself when triggered by life events (a stressor). The same model can be applied to the cognitive explanation where a biological diathesis only turns into schizophrenia if a person misinterprets other people's behaviour (a kind of stressor).

Candidates often start an essay on explanations of schizophrenia by giving a quick outline of the clinical characteristics. This would gain no credit in any essay unless part of the question specifically asked for clinical characteristics.

Just plunge straight in.

You might be tempted to produce just two paragraphs for the AO1 content (one on cognitive explanations and one on life events). Writing four paragraphs, as here, helps you keep your eye on how much you have written because you should know what a 50-word paragraph looks like.

Remember that there is no requirement for IDA in Unit 4 but if you do introduce such points they are creditworthy as AO2.

If you are using an alternative explanation as AO2, a small amount of description is necessary but focus on the relative strengths/weaknesses.

Notice how many of these AO2 points end with a 'so what' statement, making the point crystal clear to the examiner (see the three-point rule on page 5).

A total of 733 words, with slightly less than 1/3 AO1 but enough at 213 words. For 8 marks there should be 200–240 words of AO1.

Division 3 Therapies

Answer plans

Answer plan 1

Discuss biological therapies for schizophrenia. (8 marks + 16 marks)

Biological therapies

AO1	Conventional antipsychotics lower dopamine levels by blocking receptors
AO1	Atypical antipsychotics, only temporarily occupy dopamine receptors therefore fewer side effects
AO1	ECT for e.g. catatonic schizophrenia, rapid alleviation
AO1	Procedure – unilateral, barbiturate, nerve-blocking agent, small current creates seizure
AO2	Effectiveness, conventional antipsychotics, e.g. Davis *et al.* (1980) 29 studies, 19% relapse if on drug, 55% if placebo
AO2	Appropriateness, 30% of people getting conventional antipsychotics get tardive dyskineasia, irreversible in 75%
AO2	Effectiveness, atypical antipsychotics, e.g. Leucht *et al.* (1999) meta-analysis found these superior to conventional
AO2	Placebo trials not a fair test because of drug withdrawal effects (Ross and Read, 2004)
AO2	Appropriateness, fewer side effects
AO2	Use of medication reduces motivation to seek other help (Ross and Read, 2004)
AO2	ECT effectiveness, e.g. Greenhalgh *et al.* (2005) meta-analysis, ECT no better than antipsychotics
AO2	Appropriateness – may be useful during acute phase but significant risks

Work out your own plan for these questions and then write your answers.

(a) Outline and evaluate **one** psychological therapy for schizophrenia. (4 marks + 8 marks)

(b) Outline and evaluate **one** biological therapy for schizophrenia. (4 marks + 8 marks)

Part (a) One psychological therapy

AO1	
AO1	
AO2	
AO2	
AO2	
AO2	

Part (b) One biological therapy

AO1	
AO1	
AO2	
AO2	
AO2	
AO2	

Answer plan 2

Outline and evaluate **two or more** psychological therapies for schizophrenia. (8 marks + 16 marks)

Psychological therapy 1: Cognitive behavioural therapy (CBT)

AO1	CBT, challenges distorted beliefs and delusions
AO1	Techniques – trace origin of symptoms, evaluate content of e.g. delusions, develop alternatives
AO2	Effectiveness can decrease positive symptoms Gould *et al.* (2001) meta-analysis of 7 studies
AO2	Combined with antipsychotics more effective, e.g. Kuipers *et al.* (1997) and lower patient drop out
AO2	Appropriateness, CBT aims to reduce rather than eliminate distressing beliefs, preferable as safety behaviours
AO2	CBT not suitable for everyone, some people don't engage

Psychological therapy 2: Psychoanalysis

AO1	Making unconscious conflicts conscious
AO1	Techniques – gain patient trust, replace punishing conscience, patient takes active control
AO2	Effectiveness, e.g. Gottdiener (2000) but small sample
AO2	However, May (1968) found better with antipsychotics, and antipsychotics alone better
AO2	But Karon and VandenBos (1981) found opposite
AO2	Appropriateness, lengthy and costly though may overall be cost effective (Karon and VandenBos, 1981)

Answer plan 3

(a) Outline at least **one** biological therapy for schizophrenia and at least **one** psychological therapy for schizophrenia. (8 marks)

(b) Evaluate biological and psychological therapies for schizophrenia in terms of appropriateness and effectiveness. (16 marks)

Part (a) Biological and psychological therapies

AO1	Conventional antipsychotics, lower dopamine by blocking receptors
AO1	Atypical antipsychotics, only temporarily occupy dopamine receptors
AO1	CBT, challenges distorted beliefs and delusions
AO1	Techniques – trace origin of symptoms, evaluate content of e.g. delusions, develop alternatives

Part (b) Evaluate biological and psychological therapies

AO2	Effectiveness, conventional antipsychotics, e.g. Davis *et al.* (1980) 29 studies, 19% relapse if on drug, 55% if placebo
AO2	Appropriateness, 30% of people receiving conventional antipsychotics get tardive dyskineasia, irreversible in 75%
AO2	Effectiveness, atypical antipsychotics, e.g. Leucht *et al.* (1999) meta-analysis found these superior to conventional
AO2	Use of medication reduces motivation to seek other help (Ross and Read, 2004)
AO2	CBT effectiveness can decrease positive symptoms Gould *et al.* (2001) meta-analysis of 7 studies
AO2	Combined with antipsychotics more effective, e.g. Kuipers *et al.* (1997) and lower patient drop out
AO2	Appropriateness, CBT aims to reduce rather than eliminate distressing beliefs, preferable as safety behaviours
AO2	Not suitable for everyone, some people don't engage

Model answer

(a) Outline at least **one** biological therapy for schizophrenia and at least **one** psychological therapy for schizophrenia. (8 marks)

One biological therapy for schizophrenia is the use of conventional antipsychotics. These drugs reduce the effects of dopamine and so reduce the symptoms of schizophrenia. They bind to dopamine receptors but do not stimulate them, thus blocking their action. By reducing stimulation of the dopamine system in the brain, conventional antipsychotics can eliminate the hallucinations and delusions experienced by people with schizophrenia.

Atypical antipsychotics also act on dopamine receptors, and thus on dopamine levels. However, they only temporarily occupy the dopamine receptors and then rapidly dissociate to allow normal dopamine transmission. It is this characteristic which is thought to be responsible for the lower levels of side effects associated with atypical antipsychotics (e.g. tardive dyskinesia).

One psychological therapy is cognitive behavioural therapy (CBT). The aim of the therapy is to challenge a schizophrenic's distorted beliefs, such as believing their thoughts are being controlled by somebody or something else. It is these distorted beliefs that are thought to cause their maladaptive behaviour, such as hallucinations or delusions. CBT is used to help the patient identify and correct the distorted or maladaptive beliefs.

A CBT therapist first of all traces the origins of the patient's symptoms to see how they might have developed. Then the therapist evaluates the content of any delusions or voices and considers how they can be tested to demonstrate that they are not real. Jointly therapist and patient develop their own alternatives to previous maladaptive beliefs.

Since you are allowed to cover more than one biological therapy there is no need to identify these two antipsychotics under one umbrella of 'drug treatments', but you would have to do this if the question only asked for one biological therapy.

When describing a therapy, such as CBT it is important to make your description as specific as possible to the treatment of schizophrenia, otherwise you will receive reduced credit.

(b) Evaluate biological and psychological therapies for schizophrenia in terms of appropriateness and effectiveness. (16 marks)

The effectiveness of conventional antipsychotics has been demonstrated in research studies. For example, Davis *et al.* (1980) reviewed 29 relevant studies and found that relapse occurred only in 19% of people with schizophrenia who continued using conventional antipsychotics. In contrast 55% of those whose drugs were replaced by a placebo relapsed and displayed schizophrenic symptoms again.

In terms of appropriateness, one of the problems with conventional antipsychotics is the serious side effects associated with such durgs. For example, tardive dyskinesia (uncontrollable movements of the lips, tongue, face, hands and feet) occurs in about 30% of people taking conventional antipsychotics and for 75% this effect is irreversible.

The effectiveness of atypical antipsychotics has also been demonstrated in research. For example, Leucht *et al.* (1999) conducted a meta-analysis and found that atypical antipsychotics were not only effective but they were superior to conventional antipsychotics.

One limitation with the use of drugs as a treatment for schizophrenia has been put forward by Ross and Read (2004). They argue that being prescribed medication reinforces the view that there is 'something wrong with you'. This reduces schizophrenics' motivation to look for other possible causes, such as life stressors. If they did find alternative causes they could then use them to reduce their suffering.

The effectiveness of CBT has been demonstrated in research studies, such as Gould *et al.* (2001). They conducted a meta-analysis of seven other studies and found in all of them that CBT had decreased the positive symptoms of schizophrenia.

However, most of the studies of the effectiveness of CBT have combined CBT with antipsychotic medication. Kuipers *et al.* (1997) found a significant reduction in positive symptoms (hallucinations, delusions) following having CBT combined with antipsychotic medication. They also found that there was a lower rate of patient drop-out when these two types of treatment were combined.

In terms of appropriateness, CBT aims to help a person to create less distressing explanations for their psychotic beliefs rather than eliminate distressing beliefs altogether. This is good because patients may want to keep some behaviours because they act as a safety net, especially certain negative symptoms, such as affective flattening (reduced emotional expression).

Another issue related to appropriateness is the fact that CBT is not suitable for everyone. Some people don't engage sufficiently with the processes of analysing their thinking. This means that their maladaptive thinking doesn't change and the therapy is ineffective.

Some of these AO2 points are rather long whereas others are short. The average length is 50 words which is just right.

Definitions of specialist psychological terms (such as tardive dyskenisia) may be creditworthy if it is a term you have introduced into an essay, but keep it brief.

Many of these AO2 paragraphs begin with similar wording – don't feel you have to be creative with your writing, just make the point as clear as possible using AO2 lead-in phrases.

Part (a) is all AO1 and about 238 words, more than requird for 8 marks (100–120 is sufficient). The danger with writing too much AO1 is there is not sufficient time for AO2.

Part (b) is all AO2 and is just about right at 395 words, 400–480 is the range for 16 marks.

Answer for you to mark

See page 173 for examiner's comments.

Question

'There is a variety of different biological explanations for schizophrenia, ranging from genetic to biochemistry and also including neuroanatomy, viruses and evolutionary factors.'

Discuss biological explanations of schizophrenia. (8 marks + 16 marks)

Student answer

❶ There are four main biological explanations of schizophrenia – genetic, neuroanatomical, biochemical or viral. I am going to cover the first three of these in my essay.

❷ The genetic explanation proposes that schizophrenia is inherited or at least that there is a significant genetic component. Family, twin and adoption studies have been used to investigate this genetic explanation. However, such studies never have 100% concordance so it can't be all genetic.

❸ One example of a twin study is by Joseph who pooled together the findings from all the studies conducted before 2001 and found a concordance rate of 40% for MZ twins compared to only 7% for DZ twins. However, there are problems with this kind of research because often the measures used in the different studies are different and therefore they can't really be compared. Nevertheless other research studies show that there is usually a big difference between MZ and DZ twins supporting the genetic argument.

❹ Twin studies are better than family studies because they control the genetic component better. In family studies the similarities might be due to sharing the same environment but in twin studies they both share the same environment too and yet there are wide differences. The thing may be that MZ twins actually have more similar environments because they are treated similarly because they look the same. DZ twins may be different gender and treated quite differently.

❺ Another way to investigate genetic explanations is adoption studies. These have the advantage of cutting out any environmental component because biological relatives are separated early in life. Tienari conducted a study known as the Finnish adaption study where he looked at children who had been adopted and who had biological mothers who had been diagnosed with schizophrenia. This study found that almost 7% of the adopted children who had biological mothers diagnosed with schizophrenia also developed schizophrenia themselves whereas only 2% of those in a control group (biological mother was not schizophrenic) developed schizophrenia.

❻ This study would appear to conclusively show the link between schizophrenia and genes. There are also problems with this kind of research. For example, many of the adults were diagnosed at a time when the classification and diagnosis of schizophrenia was less reliable.

❼ Neuroanatomical explanations are where some aspect of the brain appears to be abnormal. Brain scans suggest that people with schizophrenia may have enlarged ventricles in their brain and a reduction in brain tissue. This has also been observed in post-mortem studies.

❽ One problem with this explanation is that cause and effect can't be established. It could be that the ventricles are an effect rather than a cause of the disorder. And in fact one study found that some normal individuals also had enlarged ventricles. It could be that the enlarged ventricles act as a kind of predisposing factor.

9 *The biochemical approach suggests that neurotransmitters in the brain may be responsible. The dopamine hypothesis proposes that schizophrenia is caused by excess levels of the neurotransmitter dopamine at the synapses where dopamine is the main neurotransmitter.*

10 *The evidence for this comes from drugs, such as amphetamines. When this drug is given to normal people it produces symptoms similar to schizophrenia, such as hallucinations. The drug has the effect of increasing dopamine levels in the brain.*

11 *There is also evidence from people who suffer from Parkinson's disease. They have low levels of dopamine but the drug they take (L-dopa) increases the dopamine levels. If people without Parkinson's disorder take L-dopa they again have symptoms like schizophrenia, such as hallucinations.*

12 *However, one problem with this dopamine hypothesis is that not every patient with schizophrenia who takes drugs to reduce dopamine levels has their symptoms reduced, and also the symptoms are not shown by everyone who takes drugs that increase levels of dopamine. This means that dopamine can't be the only explanation.*

(629 words)

AO1 mark scheme

Given the difficulties of describing genetic explanations, AO1 credit may be gained for straight descriptions of twin, family and adoption studies.

The question requires a minimum of two explanations. There is no requirement to cover all of the explanations mentioned in the quotation.

If only one explanation is described partial performance applies with a maximum of 5 marks.

8 marks is about 200-240 words.

AO2 mark scheme

At least two explanations must be evaluated for full marks. A partial performance penalty applies if only one explanation is evaluated (maximum of 10 marks).

Evaluation is likely to focus on research studies that support or challenge the explanations. It may also consider strengths and limitations of particular explanations.

A consideration of the effectiveness of any therapy derived from a particular explanation could count as evaluation, but not the description of such therapies.

16 marks is about 400–480 words.

Comments and marks for AO1

Tick the terms you think apply to the student's answer.

Mark	Knowledge and understanding	Range of material	Depth and breadth	Organisation and structure
8–7	Accurate and well-detailed	Good range	Substantial evidence of depth and breadth	Coherent
6–5	Generally accurate and reasonably detailed	Range	Depth and/or breadth	Reasonably coherent
4–3	Basic, relatively superficial	Restricted	Generally accurate	Basic
2–1	Rudimentary and may be muddled and/or inaccurate	Very brief or largely irrelevant		Lacking
0	No creditworthy material			

Guidance on marking is given on pages 6–11.

The **AO1** mark I would give is ☐

Comments and marks for part AO2

Mark	Analysis and understanding	Focus	Elaboration	Line of argument	Quality of written communication
16–13	Sound	Well focused	Coherent	Clear	Fluent, effective use of terms
12–9	Reasonable	Generally focused	Reasonable	Evident	Clear, appropriate
8–5	Basic, superficial	Sometimes focused	Some evidence		Lacks clarity, limited use of terms
4–1	Rudimentary, limited understanding	Weak, muddled and incomplete	Not effective	May be mainly irrelevant	Often unconnected assertions, errors
0	No creditworthy material				

The **AO2** mark I would give is ☐

On Unit 4 there is no requirement for issues, debates and approaches (IDA). If such material is included it would gain AO2 credit – if suitably contextualised.

Chapter 10 Psychopathology: Depression

There have been changes to the specification from September 2011 – therefore the updated specification details here are slightly different to those in some editions of the *A2 Complete Companion*.

Division 1 Overview	**• Clinical characteristics of depression** **• Issues surrounding the classification and diagnosis of depression, including reliability and validity**

Possible exam questions for this division

(a) Outline clinical characteristics of depression. (8 marks) (b) Explain issues associated with the classification **and/or** diagnosis of depression. (16 marks)	Questions may ask for a description of the clinical characteristics of depression. Note that the maximum mark for such questions is 8. Questions will not ask you to evaluate the clinical characteristics, therefore questions on clinical characteristics will always be paired with an evaluation of something else. In this case 'issues associated with classification and/or diagnosis' is all AO2 (evaluation), i.e. you do not need to provide descriptions of the issues.
Discuss issues surrounding the classification and diagnosis of depression. (8 marks + 16 marks)	An alternative possibility is that issues associated with classification and/or diagnosis require description and evaluation. In this case you should help the examiner by providing a clear *description* of each issue. Descriptions of classification systems, such as *DSM*, will not be creditworthy. Issues that are not related to depression will also not be creditworthy. See model answer on page 105.
(a) Outline clinical characteristics of depression. (4 marks) (b) Explain issues associated with the classification **and/or** diagnosis of depression. (10 marks) (c) Outline and evaluate **one** psychological explanation for depression. (4 marks + 6 marks)	The total number of marks available for clinical characteristics may be less than the full 8 marks, so be prepared for a shorter answer. In part (a) you should present a list of characteristics appropriate for 4 marks, i.e. about 100–120 words. Part (b) in this question is all AO2. The final part is taken from other divisions of this chapter and requires attention to the mark split – usually you are asked to write twice as much AO2 as AO1, which is not the case here. You can follow the pattern used in this book and aim to write two paragraphs of AO1 and three of AO2 where each paragraph is 50–70 words.

Division 2 Explanations	**• Biological explanations of depression, for example genetics, biochemistry** **• Psychological explanations of depression, for example behavioural, cognitive, psychodynamic and socio-cultural**

Possible exam questions for this division

'There is a variety of different biological explanations for depression, ranging from genetic to biochemistry and also including neuroanatomy and evolutionary factors.' Discuss biological explanations of depression. (8 marks + 16 marks)	Questions sometimes start with a quotation. The intention here is to remind you of the breadth of material that you might include in your answer. However, don't be led astray – it does not mean that you have to cover all of these different biological explanations. The question itself states that you must do at least *two* for full marks but two would be sufficient. It would be creditworthy to evaluate explanations that have not been described, particularly if used to compare and contrast. See model answer on page 107.
Describe **two or more** psychological explanations of depression. (8 marks + 16 marks)	The specification provides four examples of psychological explanations – but these are examples only. Exam questions set on this bullet point of the specification will only ask for psychological explanations and will not specify which ones.
(a) Outline and evaluate **one or more** biological explanations for depression. (4 marks + 8 marks) (b) Discuss **one or more** psychological explanations for depression. (4 marks + 8 marks)	The only two kinds of question in this division are about (1) biological explanations and (2) psychological explanations. You may be asked for one, two, at least one, or two or more. What this boils down to is that learning two explanations for each will be sufficient. You will notice from the selection of questions on this spread that the maximum marks for one psychological/biological explanation is 4 marks description + 8 marks evaluation (blockbuster questions for one explanation have not been set – they are possible but unlikely). In total this means that you need about 100–120 words description for each of the four different explanations (two psychological and two biological) and about 200–240 words evaluation of each of these four explanations.
(a) Outline at least **one** biological explanation of depression and at least one psychological explanation of depression. (8 marks) (b) Evaluate biological and psychological explanations of depression. (16 marks)	There are many variations on the same theme. Here both explanations are described in part (a) and the evaluation is all in part (b). In the previous question psychological and biological explanations were separated. You could use exactly the same material in the two answers but just arranged differently. See student answer on page 110.

(a) Outline **one or more** biological explanations of depression and **one or more** psychological explanations of depression. (8 marks) (b) Evaluate biological and psychological explanations of depression. (16 marks)	In this question you have the option to cover more than one explanation of each type. There is a danger in trying to write about more than one of each – you probably will sacrifice depth for breadth and thus would not achieve a mark in the top band because your answer would lack detail.
(a) Outline at least **one** biological explanation of depression and at least **one** psychological explanation of depression. (8 marks) (b) Consider whether psychological or biological approaches provide the better explanation of depression. (16 marks)	This variation has a slightly different part (b). In such a question it is likely that marks in the top band would only be awarded if your answer does address the question of which kind of explanation is better. Your answer is likely to be based on the relative quality of research evidence for each explanation.
(a) Outline clinical characteristics of depression. (4 marks) (b) Outline **one** psychological explanation of depression. (4 marks) (c) Evaluate psychological explanations of depression. (16 marks)	Questions are likely to span the divisions in order to include part questions on clinical characteristics and/or issues associated with classification and/or diagnosis. In such cases attend carefully to the number of marks available and construct your answers appropriately. Here 4 marks worth would be about 100–120 words.

Division 3 Therapies

- **Biological therapies for depression, including their evaluation in terms of appropriateness and effectiveness**
- **Psychological therapies for depression, for example behavioural, psychodynamic and cognitive-behavioural, including their evaluation in terms of appropriateness and effectiveness**

Possible exam questions for this division

Discuss biological therapies for depression. (8 marks + 16 marks)	When a question is open-ended, as here (as opposed to parted questions) you need to be especially careful to reflect the mark division in your answer – about 200–240 words of description and 400–480 words of evaluation.
Outline and evaluate **two or more** psychological therapies for depression. (8 marks + 16 marks)	The question possibilities for therapies are the same as for explanations – biological and/or psychological and never more than two of each *required*.
(a) Outline at least **one** biological therapy for depression and at least **one** psychological therapy for depression. (8 marks) (b) Evaluate biological and psychological therapies for depression in terms of appropriateness and effectiveness. (16 marks)	The specification suggests that you should evaluate therapies in terms of appropriateness and effectiveness, so it is worth being prepared for a question that uses such terms. See model answer on page 109.
'There are two key factors that help in evaluating therapies – whether they are effective and whether they are appropriate.' Outline and evaluate **two or more** therapies used in the treatment of depression. (8 marks +16 marks)	When a questions says 'two or more' this means you can gain credit if more than two therapies are described/evaluated but two would be sufficient to gain full marks. The danger of trying to write about more than two is that you inevitably lose depth and elaboration in your answer, and this means you may not get marks in the top band because your answer might lack detail and elaboration.
(a) Outline clinical characteristics of depression. (4 marks) (b) Briefly describe **one** psychological therapy for depression. (4 marks) (c) Evaluate psychological therapies for depression. (16 marks)	This is another example of a question set across the divisions. Candidates are often tempted to write more than required for parts (a) and (b) whereas the big marks are from part (c). In questions on psychopathology there are no 'specific' marks for IDA so it is not required but, if included, such comments would gain AO2 credit, if relevant.

Division 1 Overview

Answer plans

On Unit 4 there is no requirement for issues debates and approaches (IDA). If such material is included it would gain AO2 credit – if suitably contextualised.

Answer plan 1

(a) Outline clinical characteristics of depression. (8 marks)

(b) Explain issues associated with the classification **and/or** diagnosis of depression. (16 marks)

Part (a) Clinical characteristics

AO1	Main symptoms either depressed mood or loss of interest
AO1	Physical symptoms – difficulties in sleeping, shift in activity level and appetite, loss of energy and great fatigue
AO1	Psychological symptoms – negative self concept, worthlessness, difficulty concentrating, thoughts of death or suicide
AO1	Should show distress and be present for minimum of 2 weeks
AO2	Keller *et al.* (1995) 524 depressives assessed at 6 months, inter-rater reliability 'fair to good'
AO2	Lack of reliability due to range of DSM criteria (nine items), and lack of agreement on diagnostic threshold
AO2	Cultural bias – Karasz (2005) European Americans diagnosed as requiring help but not South Asian
AO2	Test–retest, Keller *et al.* (2005) found 'poor to fair'
AO2	Beck's inventory, test–retest +.88 correlation (Visser *et al.*, 2006)
AO2	Comorbidity, McCullough *et al.* (2003) 681 patients diagnosed with e.g. MDD and dysthymia, overlap in symptoms
AO2	Validity, Van Weel-Baumgarten *et al.* (2006) GPs less objective because know patient and family history
AO2	Stirling *et al.* (2001) 50% increase in GP consultation time resulted in a 32% increase in the accuracy

DIY

Work out your own plan for these questions and then write your answers.

(a) Outline clinical characteristics of depression. (4 marks)

(b) Briefly describe **one** psychological therapy for depression. (4 marks)

(c) Evaluate psychological therapies for depression. (16 marks)

Part (a) Clinical characteristics

AO1	
AO1	

Part (b) One psychological therapy

AO1	
AO1	

Part (c) Evaluate psychological therapies

AO2	
AO2	
AO2	
AO2	
AO2	
AO2	
AO2	
AO2	

Answer plan 2

Discuss issues surrounding the classification and diagnosis of depression. (8 marks + 16 marks)

Issues

AO1	Inter-rater reliability – compare clinicians' diagnoses
AO2	Keller *et al.* (1995) 524 depressives assessed at 6 months, inter-rater reliability 'fair to good'
AO2	Lack of reliability due to range of DSM criteria (nine items), and lack of agreement on diagnostic threshold
AO2	Cultural bias – Karasz (2005) European Americans diagnosed as requiring help but not South Asian
AO1	Test–retest, diagnosis should remain constant
AO2	Keller *et al.* (2005) found 'poor to fair test–retest
AO2	Beck's inventory, correlation of +.88 (Visser *et al.*, 2006)
AO1	Validity, comorbidity suggests classification is not a 'real' category because not distinct
AO2	McCullough *et al.* (2003) 681 patients diagnosed with e.g. MDD and dysthymia, had overlap in symptoms
AO1	Validity of diagnosis, better by psychiatrist than GP
AO2	Van Weel-Baumgarten *et al.* (2006) GPs less objective because know patient and family history
AO2	Stirling *et al.* (2001) 50% increase in GP consultation time resulted in a 32% increase in the accuracy

Answer plan 3

(a) Outline clinical characteristics of depression. (4 marks)

(b) Explain issues associated with the classification **and/or** diagnosis of depression. (10 marks)

(c) Outline and evaluate **one** psychological explanation for depression. (4 marks + 6 marks)

Part (a) Clinical characteristics

AO1	Main symptoms either depressed mood or loss of interest and pleasure
AO2	Physical (e.g. difficulties in sleeping, loss of appetite) and psychological – worthlessness, thoughts of death

Part (b) Explain issues

AO2	Inter-rater reliability, Keller *et al.* (1995) 524 depressives assessed at 6 month, inter-rater reliability 'fair to good'
AO2	Cultural bias – Karasz (2005) European Americans diagnosed as requiring help but not South Asian
AO2	Test–retest, Keller *et al.* (2005) found 'poor to fair'
AO2	Comorbidity, McCullough *et al.* (2003) 681 patients diagnosed with e.g. MDD and dysthymia, overlap in symptoms
AO2	Validity, Van Weel-Baumgarten *et al.* (2006) GPs less objective because know patient and family history

Part (c) One psychological explanation

AO1	Cognitive, e.g. Beck (1967) negative triad (self, world, future), cognitive bias in thinking
AO1	Learned helplessness, depressive attributional style (Abrahamson *et al.*, 1978), internal, stable, global
AO2	Research support, e.g. Bates *et al.* (1999) depressed participants given negative thought statements became more depressed
AO2	Effective therapy, e.g. Butler and Beck (2000) 14 meta-analyses, 80% of adults benefited from cognitive therapy
AO2	Research support, Hiroto and Seligman (1975) group with no control, later didn't turn off noise

Model answer

Discuss issues surrounding the classification and diagnosis of depression. (8 marks + 16 marks)

One issue related to classification and diagnosis is reliability. Reliability refers to the consistency of a measuring instrument, such as DSM (the Diagnostic and Statistical Manual) which is used when diagnosing depression. Reliability can be measured in terms of whether two independent assessors give similar scores (inter-rater reliability). High reliability is indicated by a high positive correlation.

Inter-rater reliability has been assessed for diagnoses of depression and found to be reasonable. For example, Keller *et al.* (1995) recruited 524 depressed individuals from different clinical sites. Each was interviewed using the DSM criteria and interviewed again 6 months later to establish reliability. Results showed that inter-rater reliability was 'fair to good'.

Inter-rater reliability is possibly lower than desirable. This may be due to the fact that for a diagnosis of depression to be given on DSM, a minimum of five out of nine symptoms must be present. When the severity of the disorder is such that it is at the diagnostic threshold, a disagreement between clinicians of just one item (e.g. whether an individual is sufficiently lethargic to denote a shift in activity levels) could mean the difference between giving a diagnosis of MDD or a less serious disorder.

There are cultural biases in diagnosis. For example, Karasz (2004) gave a vignette describing depressive symptoms to New Yorkers who were South Asian or European Americans. Only the latter group identified the problem as being biological and requiring 'professional' help. This suggests that some cultural groups won't seek help for depression.

Reliability of diagnosis can also be assessed using the test–retest method where the same patient is tested twice over a period of time to demonstrate whether the scores on a classification measure remain consistent. We would expect scores to remain relatively constant over a short period of time so there should be a strong positive correlation between two scores from the same person – if the test is reliable.

In terms of diagnoses of depression, test–retest results indicate low reliability. For example, Keller *et al.* (1995) found 6-month test–retest reliability was 'fair' for dysthymia, but 'poor to fair' for major depression. It is possible that 6 months is a long period over which to expect scores to remain constant for a disorder like depression so the variability is not because the measurement is unreliable, it's because the person's mental state has changed.

Test–retest reliability has also been calculated for Beck's Depression Inventory (BDI), one of the most popular diagnostic tools for evaluating depression. For example, Visser *et al.* (2006) assessed patients for depression using the BDI, producing a test–retest correlation of +.88. This suggests that the BDI is a reliable measure of the severity of depressive symptoms.

A second issue is validity, which concerns both classification and diagnosis. For example, there is the issue of comorbidity, which is the extent that two (or more) conditions co-occur, such as different subtypes of depression, and therefore the extent to which the conditions are 'real'.

There is research support for comorbidity of different types of depression, McCullough *et al.* (2001) compared 681 patients who had been diagnosed with various types of depression, including major depressive disorder (MDD) and dysthymia. They found considerable overlap in their symptoms, responses to treatment and other variables that made it difficult to justify distinct forms of depressive illness.

Another issue concerning the validity of diagnosis is the question of who carries out the diagnosis. For most people, a diagnosis of depression is given by their local GP rather than by a psychiatrist, which may affect the validity of the diagnosis.

There are arguments to explain why GP diagnoses might lack validity. Van Weel-Baumgarten *et al.* (2006) suggest that diagnoses made by GPs may be less objective because they are based on previous knowledge of the patient and family history rather than the actual presenting symptoms (necessary for DSM diagnosis).

There is research support for the lack of validity of GP diagnoses. Stirling *et al.* (2001) found that the average consultation time for a GP to diagnose depression was just over 8 minutes, whereas for psychiatrist it was 1 hour. A 50% increase in GP consultation time resulted in a 32% increase in the accuracy of diagnosis for depression.

Some exam questions on the topic of 'issues related to classification and diagnosis' are just AO2. Others are AO1 and AO2, as is the case here. When both AO1 and AO2 are required it is vital to make the AO1 component clearly separate from the AO2. Many students lose AO1 marks because clear division is missing.

This essay requires that both classification and diagnosis are discussed, whereas some essay titles don't (they say 'and/or').

You can keep track of the relative amounts of AO1 and AO2 by sticking to your plan – have four AO1 paragraphs and eight AO2 paragraphs each about 50–60 words. This ensures that your essay has the right proportions of each.

Note how each paragraph in this essay mirrors the original answer plan.

This use of paragraphs helps you keep a track of how much AO1 and AO2 you have covered, and also helps the examiner to read your answer because each separate point is clear.

This answer is just about 700 words in length, 70% of which is AO2. There are just over 200 words of AO1 which is sufficient content for that skill.

Division 2 Explanations

Answer plans

Answer plan 1

Discuss biological explanations of depression. (8 marks + 16 marks)

Biological explanations

AO1	Genetic – based on family studies, e.g. Harrington *et al.* (1993) 20% in first degree relatives, 10% 'normal'
AO1	Twin studies, e.g. McGuffin *et al.* (1996) 48% concordance for MZ, 20% for DZ; adoption, e.g. Wender (1986)
AO1	Neurotransmitter – low noradrenaline (Bunney *et al.*, 1965)
AO1	Low serotonin demonstrated by efficacy of SSRIs, also Delgado *et al.* (1990) diet low in tryptophan
AO2	Genetic, research support, e.g. Zhang *et al.* (2005) mutant serotonin gene 10× more common in depressives
AO2	Low concordance due to comorbidity, Kendler *et al.* (1992) rates rose when looking at GAD and depression
AO2	Evolutionary significance, an 'honest' signal of need; Buist-Bouwman *et al.* (2004) higher levels of functioning
AO2	Diathesis-stress, supported by Kendler *et al.* (1995) higher concordance with relatives who had stressors in their lives
AO2	Research support for noradrenaline, e.g. Leonard (2000) drugs that increase levels, reduce depression
AO2	SNRIs even more effective than SSRIs (Kraft *et al.*, 2005)
AO2	Serotonin, pesticide, depression link (Amr *et al.*, 1993)
AO2	Tryptophan effects not observed in non-depressives

DIY

Work out your own plan for these questions and then write your answers.

(a) Outline at least **one** biological explanation of depression and at least **one** psychological explanation of depression. (8 marks)

(b) Evaluate biological and psychological explanations of depression. (16 marks)

Part (a) Biological and psychological explanations

AO1	
AO1	
AO1	
AO1	

Part (b) Evaluate biological and psychological explanations

AO2	
AO2	
AO2	
AO2	
AO2	
AO2	
AO2	
AO2	

Answer plan 2

Describe **two or more** psychological explanations of depression. (8 marks + 16 marks)

Psychological explanations

AO1	Psychodynamic – loss of loved one, extended mourning
AO1	Loss creates anger which is then turned inwards
AO1	Cognitive, e.g. Beck (1967) negative triad (self, world, future), cognitive bias in thinking
AO1	Learned helplessness, depressive attributional style (Abrahamson *et al.*, 1978), internal, stable, global
AO2	Psychodynamic, research support, e.g. Barnes and Prosen (1985) depression scores high in men whose fathers died
AO2	Further support Bifulco *et al.* (1992) children who lost their mothers later more likely to become depressed
AO2	However, Paykel and Cooper (1992) only 10% who experience early loss go on to become depressed
AO2	Psychodynamic theories lack effectiveness, though communication may be a problem
AO2	Cognitive research support, e.g. Bates *et al.* (1999) depressed participants given negative thought statements became more depressed
AO2	Effective therapy, e.g. Butler and Beck (2000) 14 meta-analyses, 80% of adults benefited from cognitive therapy
AO2	Research support, Hiroto and Seligman (1975) no control group later didn't turn noise off
AO2	Research support, Miller and Seligman (1974) depressed students performed worst of all on a similar task

Answer plan 3

(a) Outline and evaluate **one or more** biological explanations for depression. (4 marks + 8 marks)

(b) Discuss **one or more** psychological explanations for depression. (4 marks + 8 marks)

Part (a) Biological explanations

AO1	Genetic – based on family studies, e.g. Harrington *et al.* (1993), 20% in first degree relatives, 10% 'normal'
AO1	Twin studies, e.g. McGuffin *et al.* (1996) 48% concordance for MZ, 20% for DZ; adoption, e.g. Wender (1986)
AO2	Genetic, research support, e.g. Zhang *et al.* (2005) mutant serotonin gene 10× more common in depressives
AO2	Low concordance due to comorbidity, Kendler *et al.* (1992) rates rose when looking at GAD and depression
AO2	Evolutionary significance, an 'honest' signal of need; Buist-Bouwman *et al.* (2004) higher levels of functioning
AO2	Diathesis-stress, supported by Kendler *et al.* (1995) higher concordance with relatives who had stressors in their lives

Part (a) Psychological explanations

AO1	Cognitive, e.g. Beck (1967) negative triad (self, world, future), cognitive bias in thinking
AO1	Learned helplessness, depressive attributional style (Abrahamson *et al.*, 1978), internal, stable, global
AO2	Research support, e.g. Bates *et al.* (1999) depressed participants given negative thought statements became more depressed
AO2	Effective therapy, e.g. Butler and Beck (2000) 14 meta-analyses, 80% of adults benefited from cognitive therapy
AO2	Research support, Hiroto and Seligman (1975) group with no control, later didn't turn off noise
AO2	Research support, Miller and Seligman (1974) depressed students performed worst of all on a similar task

Discuss biological explanations of depression. (8 marks + 16 marks)

One biological explanation for depression is that it is an inherited condition, i.e. it's in your genes. The source for this suggestion is family studies of depression. Having a first-degree relative with depression appears to be a risk factor for depression. For example, Harrington *et al.* (1993) found that around 20% of first-degree relatives of a proband with depression also have depression compared to 10% of general population.

Another source of data on a genetic basis for depression comes from twin and adoption studies. McGuffin *et al.* (1996) found 46% concordance rates for MZ twins and 20% for DZ twins. Wender *et al.* (1986) found that biological relatives of adopted individuals were more likely to be hospitalised for severe depression compared to biological relatives of a non-depressed group. Both sources of evidence indicate that depression has a substantial heritable component.

A second biological explanation for depression is that it relates to neurotransmitters. Depression can be caused by a deficiency of the neurotransmitter noradrenaline in the brain. For example, Bunney *et al.* (1965) found that waste products associated with noradrenaline are low in depressed individuals.

Depression can also be caused by a deficiency of serotonin in the brain. Evidence comes from the discovery that SSRIs, which selectively block the re-uptake of serotonin from the synaptic gap, reduce the symptoms of depression. Also Delgado *et al.* (1990) gave depressed patients a diet that lowered tryptophan (a precursor of serotonin) levels. They found the majority of the depressed patients experienced a return of their symptoms, suggesting that reduced serotonin might well be a cause.

There is research to support a genetic explanation. A mutant gene that starves the brain of serotonin has been found to be 10 times more common in depressed patients than in normal individuals (Zhang *et al.*, 2005). This suggests that one of the things that might be inherited is a disposition to have low levels of serotonin and this is what predisposes an individual to experience depression.

Low concordance rates may be explained in terms of comorbidity. It is possible that people inherit a vulnerability for a wider range of disorders than depression alone, which would explain the relatively low concordance rates for depression alone. For example, Kendler *et al.* (1992) found a higher incidence of mental disorders in twins of depressed probands when looking at depression and generalised anxiety disorder than when looking at just depression.

Depression may have an evolutionary significance. The fact that depression is so widespread suggests that it may have some adaptive significance. Buist-Bouwman *et al.*, (2004) found that individuals reported higher levels of psychological functioning after their depression than beforehand. As depression is costly for the individual, it serves as an 'honest' signal of need so that others in the social network respond by providing much-needed help and support for the individual, leading to better psychological functioning.

Genetic explanations can be understood within the diathesis-stress model, where genetic inheritance acts as a diathesis. There is research support for this model in relation to depression. Kendler *et al.* (1995) found that among the siblings of depressed probands, the highest level of depression was found in those who, together with this genetic predisposition (diathesis), had also been exposed to significant negative life events (stressors).

There is research support for the role of noradrenaline in depression. For example, Leonard (2000) showed that drugs that lowered noradrenaline levels bring about depressive states while those that increase noradrenaline levels show antidepressant effects.

Further support for the role of noradrenaline comes from the success of treatments using SNRI, a dual serotonin-noradrenaline re-uptake inhibitor. Kraft *et al.* (2005) treated patients with major depression with SNRI. The patients showed a significantly more positive response than those treated with a placebo, thus strengthening the link between the depletion of these neurotransmitters and the development of depressive symptoms.

There is research support for the role of serotonin. For example, Amr *et al.* (1993) found an association between high-level exposure to pesticides which increase serotonin levels and an increased risk of depression.

A problem for the serotonin explanation is that tryptophan depletion studies have used patients who are in remission from depression. Individuals who have no history of depression tend not to show any mood changes following tryptophan depletion, despite the fact that it alters the same mood regulating areas of the brain. This suggests that the effect of tryptophan isn't quite so straightforward.

Candidates often start an essay on explanations of depression by giving a quick outline of the clinical characteristics. This would gain no credit in any essay unless part of the question specifically asked for clinical characteristics.

Just plunge straight in.

You might be tempted to produce just two paragraphs for the AO1 content (one on genetic explanations and one on neurotransmitters). Writing four paragraphs, as here, helps you keep your eye on how much you have written because you should know what a 50-word paragraph looks like.

Notice how many of these AO2 points end with a 'so what' statement (e.g. 'This suggests that ...') making the point crystal clear to the examiner (see the three-point rule on page 5).

Always take care to use an AO2 lead-in phrase to make it clear to the examiner that this is evaluation and not description.

Remember there is no requirement for IDA in Unit 4 but if you do introduce such points they are creditworthy as AO2.

You could use an alternative psychological explanation as a form of AO2 but, if you do make sure you do no more than a brief description of the alternative explanation and mainly focus on the relative strengths/weaknesses.

In this essay there are 261 words of AO1 and 469 words of AO2, close to the desired 1:2 proportions and certainly enough content for each assessment objective.

Division 3 Therapies

Answer plans

Answer plan 1

Discuss biological therapies for depression. (8 marks + 16 marks)

Biological therapies

AO1	Antidepressants, e.g. tricyclics (TCAs) reabsorb serotonin and noradrenaline into the presynaptic cell
AO1	SSRIs block re-uptake of just serotonin, e.g. Prozac
AO1	ECT for severe depression and possible suicide, fast acting
AO1	Procedure – unilateral, barbiturate, nerve-blocking agent, small current creates seizure
AO2	Antidepressants effectiveness, both TCAs and SSRIs better than placebo (Arroll *et al.*, 2005)
AO2	SSRIs may only be effective in cases of severe depression (Kirsch *et al.*, 2008) but may be because low expectations
AO2	Appropriateness, lack effectiveness with children and adolescents (e.g. Geller *et al.*, 1992)
AO2	Publication bias, Turner *et al.* (2008) may mislead doctors
AO2	ECT effectiveness, real ECT better than sham ECT (e.g. Gregory *et al.*, 1985)
AO2	ECT better than antidepressants for short-term (Scott, 2004) over 1,000 patients
AO2	Appropriateness, side effects, e.g. permanent anxiety, may be alleviated by unilateral ECT (Sackheim *et al.*, 2000)
AO2	May be best for elderly, Mulsant *et al.* (1991) meta-analysis, 83% improvement

DIY

Work out your own plan for these questions and then write your answers.

(a) Outline and evaluate **one** psychological therapy for depression. (4 marks + 8 marks)

(b) Outline and evaluate **one** biological therapy for depression. (4 marks + 8 marks)

Part (a) One psychological therapy

AO1	
AO1	
AO2	
AO2	
AO2	
AO2 or IDA	

Part (b) One biological therapy

AO1	
AO1	
AO2	
AO2	
AO2	
AO2	

Answer plan 2

Outline and evaluate **two or more** psychological therapies for depression. (8 marks + 16 marks)

Psychological therapy 1: Cognitive behavioural therapy (CBT)

AO1	Identify and alter maladaptive cognitions and behaviours
AO1	Thought catching, challenge and replace thoughts; behavioural activation
AO2	Effectiveness, Robinson *et al.* (1990) CBT superior to waiting list group but not placebo
AO2	Effectiveness depends on therapist competence and belief (drop out rate of 8%, Hunt and Andrews, 2007)
AO2	Appropriateness, good for all ages and best with antidepressants (March *et al.*, 2007)
AO2	Good on computer/over phone thought not as good as face-to-face, but does reduce drop-out (Mohr *et al.*, 2005)

Psychological therapy 2: Psychodynamic interpersonal therapy (PIT)

AO1	Hobson (1985) therapeutic relationship important, thinking in the present
AO1	Techniques exploratory rational, shared understanding, feelings, focusing, insight, sequencing, change
AO2	Effectiveness, Paley *et al.* (2008) equivalent to CBT though effect of life events not controlled
AO2	Barkham *et al.* (1996) symptoms recurred with PIT
AO2	Appropriateness, particularly for dysfunctional relationships (Guthrie, 1999)
AO2	Reduces stresses associated with remission

Answer plan 3

(a) Outline at least **one** biological therapy for depression and at least **one** psychological therapy for depression. (8 marks)

(b) Evaluate biological and psychological therapies for depression in terms of appropriateness and effectiveness. (16 marks)

Part (a) Biological and psychological therapies

AO1	Antidepressants, e.g. tricyclics (TCAs) reabsorb serotonin and noradrenaline into the presynaptic cell
AO1	SSRIs block re-uptake of just serotonin, e.g. Prozac
AO1	CBT – identify and alter maladaptive cognitions and dysfunctional behaviours
AO1	Thought catching, challenge and replace thoughts; behavioural activation

Part (b) Evaluate biological and psychological therapies

AO2	Antidepressants effectiveness, both TCAs and SSRIs better than placebo (Arroll *et al.*, 2005)
AO2	SSRIs may only be effective in cases of severe depression (Kirsch *et al.*, 2008) but may be because low expectations
AO2	Appropriateness, lack effectiveness with children and adolescents (e.g. Geller *et al.*, 1992)
AO2	Publication bias, Turner *et al.* (2008) may mislead doctors
AO2	CBT effectiveness, Robinson *et al.* (1990) CBT superior to waiting list group but not placebo
AO2	Effectiveness depends on therapist competence and belief (drop out rate of 8%, Hunt and Andrews, 2007)
AO2	Appropriateness, good for all ages and best with antidepressants (March *et al.*, 2007)
AO2	Good on computer/over phone thought not as good as face-to-face, but does reduce drop-out (Mohr *et al.*, 2005)

Model answer

(a) Outline at least **one** biological therapy for depression and at least **one** psychological therapy for depression. (8 marks)

Psychoactive drugs are a biological therapy used to treat depression, such as tricyclics (TCAs). These block the transporter mechanism that reabsorbs serotonin and noradrenaline into the presynaptic cell after it has fired. As a result, more neurotransmitters are left in the synapse, prolonging their action.

Another drug that is used is selective serotonin re-uptake inhibitors (SSRIs). Instead of blocking the re-uptake of different neurotransmitters, they block mainly serotonin and so increase the availability of serotonin at the synapse. Evidence comes from the success of SSRIs, such as Prozac, which reduce the symptoms of depression.

One of the most popular psychological treatments for depression is cognitive behavioural therapy (CBT). CBT emphasises the role of negative (maladaptive) thoughts and cognitions in the origins and maintenance of depression. The aim of CBT is to identify and alter these negative cognitions, as well as any dysfunctional behaviours that may be contributing to the depression. CBT is focused on current problems and current dysfunctional thinking.

One of the key aspects of CBT is thought catching. Depressed individuals have negative thoughts and they are taught to challenge these and replace them with more constructive ones, thus reducing the symptoms of their depression. This should lead to a change in behaviour, becoming more active (behavioural activation). A characteristic of depression is that depressed people no longer participate in activities that they previously enjoyed. Being active leads to rewards that act as an antidote to depression.

Since you are allowed to cover more than one biological therapy there is no need to identify these two antidepressants under one umbrella of 'drug treatments' but you would have to do this if the question only asked for one biological therapy.

When describing a therapy such as CBT it is important to make your description as specific as possible to depression, otherwise you will receive reduced credit.

(b) Evaluate biological and psychological therapies for depression in terms of appropriateness and effectiveness. (16 marks)

The effectiveness of both TCAs versus SSRIs have been demonstrated. Arroll *et al.* (2005) found they both produce a more significant reduction in depressive symptoms compared to a placebo.

However, other research suggests that SSRIs may only be effective in cases of severe depression. Kirsch *et al.* (2008) reviewed clinical trials of SSRIs and concluded that only in cases of the most severe depression was there any significant advantage to using SSRIs over a placebo. This may be because, among the severely depressed, there is no expectation that anything will work, thus removing any placebo effect.

Research studies indicate that antidepressants are not appropriate for children and adolescents. For example, Geller *et al.* (1992) found no superiority over placebos for antidepressants in children and adolescents. This may have something to do with developmental differences in brain chemistry.

One problem with this research on drug treatments is that there appears to be a publication bias. Turner *et al.* (2008) claim that research that shows a positive outcome of antidepressant treatment is more likely to be published, thus exaggerating the benefits of antidepressant drugs. The implication of this is that doctors may be led into inappropriate treatment decisions that may not be in the best interests of patients.

The effectiveness of CBT for depression was demonstrated in a meta-analysis by Robinson *et al.* (1990). Their conclusion was that CBT was superior to no-treatment control groups. However, when these control groups were divided into waiting list (i.e. no treatment at all) and placebo groups, CBT was not significantly more effective than placebos at reducing depressive symptoms.

The apparent effectiveness of CBT depends on various factors. For example, the competence of the therapist; a less competent therapist will have less impact on changing the thoughts and feelings of someone with depression. There is also an issue with belief in the therapist; drop-out rates are as high as 8% which suggests that depressed patients may lack belief in the therapy (Hunt and Andrews, 2007).

CBT is appropriate for many different age groups, such as elderly populations, juveniles and depressed adolescents. When combined with antidepressants, CBT is particularly effective at reducing the symptoms of depression and reducing suicidal thoughts and behaviour (March *et al.*, 2007).

Alternative approaches to CBT are both appropriate and successful. Mohr *et al.* (2005) carried out a meta-analysis of 12 studies and found that psychotherapy conducted over the phone significantly reduced the symptoms of depression compared to a non-treatment control group, although it was only half as effective as face-to-face psychotherapy. A particular advantage of computer-based and phone-based psychotherapy is the low drop-out compared to face-to-face CBT.

Some of these AO2 points are rather long whereas others are short. The average length is 50 words which is just right.

Some of these AO2 paragraphs begin with similar wording – don't feel you have to be creative with your writing, just make the point as clear as possible using AO2 lead-in phrases.

More detail of Robinson *et al.*'s research could have been included but the danger is providing too much description, which won't gain AO2 credit.

Part (a) is all AO1 and about 240 words, slightly more than required for 8 marks (100–120 words would be sufficient).

Part (b) is almost twice as much as the AO1 (as it should be) at about 435 words.

Answer for you to mark

See page 174 for examiner's comments.

Question

(a) Outline at least **one** biological explanation of depression and at least **one** psychological explanation of depression. (8 marks)

(b) Evaluate biological and psychological explanations of depression. (16 marks)

Student answer

Part (a)

❶ One biological explanation of depression is that it is caused by your genes. You inherit genes from your parents and share them with your sisters and brothers and family generally. This means that you should find that people who are related to each other would be more likely to suffer from depression, which is what research has shown. Research has looked at twins and close family members and found that depression is more common in an MZ twin if the other has it than a DZ twin, and more common in families if one person has it.

❷ Another biological explanation is based on neurotransmitters. The neurotransmitters noradrenaline and serotonin may play a role in depression. Low levels of both have been found in depressed people.

❸ One psychological explanation has been put forward by Beck who suggested depression is due to the way you think. He suggested that depressed people have faulty schemas about themselves, the world and the future. A depressed person comes to expect that things will always go wrong because they had early experiences of failure. So they expect the same in similar situations.

❹ Another psychological explanation comes from Freud who also said it is to do with early experiences but he said it was particularly early experiences of loss. You get depressed when you are older because it reminds you of the earlier loss.

(224 words)

AO1 mark scheme for part (a)

Answers must contain at least one of each kind of explanation for full marks but these do not have to be balanced.

Descriptions of research studies may count as AO1.

There is a depth/breadth trade off – candidates writing about more than one biological or psychological explanation will necessarily provide less detail but gain credit for the breadth of their answer.

8 marks is about 200–240 words.

Tick the terms you think apply to the student's answer.

Comments and marks for AO1

Mark	Knowledge and understanding	Range of material	Depth and breadth	Organisation and structure
8–7	Accurate and well-detailed	Good range	Substantial evidence of depth and breadth	Coherent
6–5	Generally accurate and reasonably detailed	Range	Depth and/or breadth	Reasonably coherent
4–3	Basic, relatively superficial	Restricted		Basic
2–1	Rudimentary and may be muddled and/or inaccurate	Very brief or largely irrelevant		Lacking
0	No creditworthy material			

The **AO1** mark I would give is ☐

Guidance on marking is given on pages 6–11.

Part (b)

5 Genetic explanations are supported by research studies, for example Harrington found that 20% of relatives of people who have depression also had depression, compared to just 10% in the general population. This does show that there is a genetic basis for depression. Twin studies provide further support this, for example McGuffin found a concordance rate of 46% for MZ twins compared with only 20% for DZ twins. MZ twins share 100% of their genes so this evidence is good support for the genetic explanation.

6 One problem with the genetic research is related to the nature–nurture issue. It could be that having depression is not because of the genes but because you are sharing the same environment as your relatives. So it is not necessarily the genes but it could also be the environment.

7 The twin studies don't take into account that MZ twins might be closer because they are more similar and also treated more similarly by other people. So it is again nurture as well as nature.

8 Beck's psychological explanation has been supported by research which found that depressed people did have more faulty ways of thinking.

9 Bifulco has produced evidence that supports Freud's theory because she found that people who had experienced loss when they were younger did tend to be more likely to become depressed later. However, some depressives have not experienced loss so Freud's theory can't be fully correct.

10 One problem for all explanations is that the research is often correlational so you can't tell what is cause and what is effect. This is the case with the neurotrasmitter explanation because it could be that low levels of these neurotransmitters are the effect rather than the cause.

11 Another issue is that there probably isn't one simple explanation and in fact neither biological or psychological is the only explanation. It is likely that both of them are involved. So people have a biological predisposition for depression but it is only when they have certain environmental/psychological experiences that the depression occurs. Thus it is a mixture of the biological and the psychological.

12 Overall there are many different kinds of explanation for depression and they all have strengths and limitations.

(355 words)

AO2 mark scheme for part (b)

Both biological and psychological explanations must be evaluated for full marks but again not necessarily in balance. A partial performance penalty applies if only one explanation is evaluated (maximum of 10 marks).

Explanations that were not described in part (a) can be evaluated in part (b).

Evaluation might compare the relative strengths/weaknesses of the two approaches or consider how they might be combined, as suggested by the diathesis-stress model.

16 marks is about 400–480 words.

Comments and marks for AO2

Mark	Analysis and understanding	Focus	Elaboration	Line of argument	Quality of written communication
16–13	Sound	Well focused	Coherent	Clear	Fluent, effective use of terms
12–9	Reasonable	Generally focused	Reasonable	Evident	Clear, appropriate
8–5	Basic, superficial	Sometimes focused	Some evidence		Lacks clarity, limited use of terms
4–1	Rudimentary, limited understanding	Weak, muddled and incomplete	Not effective	May be mainly irrelevant	Often unconnected assertions, errors
0	No creditworthy material				

The **AO2** mark I would give is ☐

On Unit 4 there is no requirement for issues, debates and approaches (IDA). If such material is included it would gain AO2 credit – if suitably contextualised.

Chapter 11 Psychopathology: Phobic disorders

There have been changes to the specification from September 2011 – therefore the updated specification details here are slightly different to those in some editions of the *A2 Complete Companion.*

Division 1 Overview	• **Clinical characteristics of phobic disorders** • **Issues surrounding the classification and diagnosis of phobic disorders, including reliability and validity**

Possible exam questions for this division

(a) Outline clinical characteristics of phobic disorders. (8 marks) (b) Explain issues associated with the classification **and/or** diagnosis of phobic disorders. (16 marks)	Questions may ask for a description of the clinical characteristics of phobic disorders – note that the maximum mark for such questions is 8. Questions will not ask you to evaluate the clinical characteristics, therefore questions on clinical characteristics will always be paired with an evaluation of something else. In this case 'issues associated with classification and/or diagnosis' is all AO2 (evaluation), i.e. you do not need to provide descriptions of the issues.
Discuss issues surrounding the classification and diagnosis of phobic disorders. (8 marks + 16 marks)	An alternative possibility is that issues associated with classification and/or diagnosis require description and evaluation. In this case you should help the examiner by providing a clear *description* of each issue. Descriptions of classification systems, such as *DSM*, will not be creditworthy. Issues that are not related to phobic disorders will also not be creditworthy. See model answer on page 115.
(a) Outline clinical characteristics of phobic disorders. (4 marks) (b) Explain issues associated with the classification **and/or** diagnosis of phobic disorders. (10 marks) (c) Outline and evaluate **one** psychological explanation for phobic disorders. (4 marks + 6 marks)	The total number of marks available for clinical characteristics may be less than the full 8 marks, so be prepared for a shorter answer. In part (a) you should present a list of characteristics appropriate for 4 marks, i.e. about 100–120 words. Part (b) in this question is all AO2. The final part is taken from other divisions of this chapter and requires attention to the mark split – usually you are asked to write twice as much AO2 as AO1, which is not the case here. You can follow the pattern used in this book and aim to write two paragraphs of AO1 and three of AO2 where each paragraph is 50–70 words.

Division 2 Explanations	• **Biological explanations of phobic disorders, for example genetics, biochemistry** • **Psychological explanations of phobic disorders, for example behavioural, cognitive, psychodynamic and socio-cultural**

Possible exam questions for this division

'There is a variety of different biological explanations for phobic disorders, ranging from genetic to biochemistry and also including neuroanatomy and evolutionary factors.' Discuss biological explanations of phobic disorders. (8 marks + 16 marks)	Questions sometimes start with a quotation. The intention here is to remind you of the breadth of material that you might include in your answer. However, don't be led astray – it does not mean that you have to cover all of these different biological explanations. The question itself states that you must do at least *two* for full marks but two would be sufficient. It would be creditworthy to evaluate explanations that have not been described, particularly if used to compare and contrast. See model answer on page 117.
Describe **two or more** psychological explanations of phobic disorders. (8 marks + 16 marks)	The specification provides four examples of psychological explanations – but these are examples only. Exam questions set on this bullet point of the specification will only ask for psychological explanations and will not specify which ones.
(a) Outline and evaluate **one or more** biological explanations for phobic disorders. (4 marks + 8 marks) (b) Discuss **one or more** psychological explanations for phobic disorders. (4 marks + 8 marks)	The only two kinds of question in this division are about (1) biological explanations and (2) psychological explanations. You may be asked for one, two, at least one, or two or more. What this boils down to is that learning two explanations for each will be sufficient. You will notice from the selection of questions on this spread that the maximum marks for one psychological/biological explanation is 4 marks description + 8 marks evaluation (blockbuster questions for one explanation have not been set – they are possible but unlikely). In total this means that you need about 100–120 words description for each of the four different explanations (two psychological and two biological) and about 200–240 words evaluation of each of these four explanations.

(a) Outline **one** psychological explanation and **one** biological explanation for phobic disorders. (8 marks) (b) Evaluate explanations for phobic disorders. (16 marks)	There are many variations on the same theme. Here both explanations are described in part (a) and the evaluation is all in part (b). In the previous question psychological and biological explanations were separated. You could use exactly the same material in the two answers but just arranged differently.
(a) Outline **one or more** biological explanations of phobic disorders and **one or more** psychological explanations of phobic disorders. (8 marks) (b) Evaluate biological and psychological explanations of phobic disorders. (16 marks)	In this question you have the option to cover more than one explanation of each type. There is a danger in trying to write about more than one of each – you probably will sacrifice depth for breadth and thus would not achieve a mark in the top band because your answer would lack detail.
(a) Outline at least **one** biological explanation of phobic disorders and at least **one** psychological explanation of phobic disorders. (8 marks) (b) Consider whether psychological or biological approaches provide the better explanation of phobic disorders. (16 marks)	This variation has a slightly different part (b). In such a question it is likely that marks in the top band would only be awarded if your answer does address the question of which kind of explanation is better. Your answer is likely to be based on the relative quality of research evidence for each explanation.
(a) Outline clinical characteristics of phobic disorders. (4 marks) (b) Outline **one** psychological explanation of phobic disorders. (4 marks) (c) Evaluate psychological explanations of phobic disorders. (16 marks)	Questions are likely to span the divisions in order to include part questions on clinical characteristics and/or issues associated with classification and/or diagnosis. In such cases attend carefully to the number of marks available and construct your answers appropriately. Here 4 marks worth would be about 100–150 words.

Division 3 Therapies

- **Biological therapies for phobic disorders, including their evaluation in terms of appropriateness and effectiveness**
- **Psychological therapies for phobic disorders, for example behavioural, psychodynamic and cognitive-behavioural, including their evaluation in terms of appropriateness and effectiveness**

Possible exam questions for this division

Discuss biological therapies for phobic disorders. (8 marks + 16 marks)	When a question is open-ended, as here (as opposed to parted questions) you need to be especially careful to reflect the mark division in your answer – about 200–240 words of description and 400–480 words of evaluation.
Outline and evaluate **two or more** psychological therapies for phobic disorders. (8 marks + 16 marks)	The question possibilities for therapies are the same as for explanations – biological and/or psychological and never more than two of each required.
(a) Outline at least **one** biological therapy for phobic disorders and at least **one** psychological therapy for phobic disorders. (8 marks) (b) Evaluate biological and psychological therapies for phobic disorders in terms of appropriateness and effectiveness. (16 marks)	The specification suggests that you should evaluate therapies in terms of appropriateness and effectiveness, so it is worth being prepared for a question that uses such terms. See model answer on page 119
'There are two key factors that help in evaluating therapies – whether they are effective and whether they are appropriate.' Outline and evaluate **two or more** therapies used in the treatment of phobic disorders. (8 marks +16 marks)	When a questions says 'two or more' this means you can gain credit if more than two therapies are described/evaluated but two would be sufficient to gain full marks. The danger of trying to write about more than two is that you inevitably lose depth and elaboration in your answer, and this means you may not get marks in the top band because your answer would lack detail and elaboration.
(a) Outline clinical characteristics of phobic disorders. (4 marks) (b) Briefly describe **one** psychological therapy for phobic disorders. (4 marks) (c) Evaluate psychological therapies for phobic disorders. (16 marks)	This is another example of a question set across the divisions. Candidates are often tempted to write more than required for parts (a) and (b) whereas the big marks are from part (c). In questions on psychopathology there are no 'specific' marks for IDA so it is not required but, if included, such comments would gain AO2 credit if relevant. See student answer on page 120.

Division 1 Overview

Answer plans

On Unit 4 there is no requirement for issues, debates and approaches (IDA). If such material is included it would gain AO2 credit – if suitably contextualised.

Answer plan 1
(a) Outline clinical characteristics of phobic disorders. (8 marks)
(b) Explain issues associated with the classification **and/or** diagnosis of phobic disorders. (16 marks)

Part (a) Clinical characteristics

AO1	Fear – marked and persistent, excessive or unreasonable
AO1	Patient has self-awareness of excessive nature of the fear
AO1	Avoidance or distress interferes with normal functioning
AO1	Duration – in individuals under age 18 years the duration of symptoms is at least 6 months

Part (b) Issues

AO2	Inter-rater reliability, e.g. SCID-1 +.72 (Skyre *et al.*, 1991)
AO2	Not always high, e.g. Kendler *et al.* (1999) because poor recall, different interpretation of symptoms by clinicians
AO2	Validity, comorbidity high, e.g. with other phobias and depression (Kendler *et al.*, 1993)
AO2	Concurrent validity high, e.g. Mattick and Clarke (1998) social phobia scale
AO2	Construct validity, e.g. Beidel *et al.* (1989) SPAI correlates positively with behavioural measures of phobia
AO2	Gender bias, female stereotypes lead to bias (Worrell and Remer, 2003)
AO2	Culture bias, e.g. TKS in Japan would not be diagnosed in UK
AO2	Social desirability bias may be helped by computer diagnosis

DIY

Work out your own plan for these questions and then write your answers.
(a) Outline clinical characteristics of phobic disorders. (4 marks)
(b) Briefly describe **one** psychological therapy for phobic disorders. (4 marks)
(c) Evaluate psychological therapies for phobic disorders. (16 marks)

Part (a) Clinical characteristics

AO1	
AO1	

Part (b) One psychological therapy

AO1	
AO1	

Part (c) Evaluate psychological therapies

AO2	
AO2	
AO2	
AO2	
AO2	
AO2	
AO2	
AO2	

Answer plan 2
Discuss issues surrounding the classification and diagnosis of phobic disorders. (8 marks + 16 marks)

Issues

AO1	Inter-rater reliability, compare clinicians' diagnoses
AO2	High for SCID-1, e.g. +.72 (Skyre *et al.*, 1991)
AO2	Not always high, e.g. Kendler *et al.* (1999) because poor recall, different interpretation of symptoms
AO1	Validity, comorbidity, suggests not a 'real' category
AO2	High comorbidity with other phobias and depression (Kendler *et al.*, 1993)
AO1	Concurrent and construct validity
AO2	Supported, e.g. Mattick and Clarke (1998) social phobia scale
AO2	Supported, e.g. Beidel *et al.* (1989) SPAI correlates with behaviour
AO1	Validity – gender and culture bias, social desirability bias
AO2	Gender bias, female stereotypes lead to bias (Worrell and Remer, 2003)
AO2	Culture bias and interviewer expectation, e.g. TKS and interviewer expectations in Japan would not be diagnosed in UK
AO2	Social desirability bias may be avoided by computer diagnosis

Answer plan 3
(a) Outline clinical characteristics of phobic disorders. (4 marks)
(b) Explain issues associated with the classification **and/or** diagnosis of phobic disorders. (10 marks)
(c) Outline and evaluate **one** psychological explanation for phobic disorders. (4 marks + 6 marks)

Part (a) Clinical characteristics

AO1	Fear – marked and persistent, excessive or unreasonable
AO1	Avoidance or distress interferes with normal functioning

Part (b) Explain issues

AO2	Inter-rater reliability, e.g. SCID-1 +.72 (Skyre *et al.*, 1991)
AO2	Not always high, e.g. Kendler *et al.* (1999) because poor recall, different interpretation of symptoms
AO2	Validity, comorbidity high, e.g. Kendler *et al.* (1993)
AO2	Concurrent validity, e.g. Mattick and Clarke (1998) social phobia scale
AO2	Construct validity, e.g. Beidel *et al.* (1989) SPAI correlates with behaviour

Part (c) One psychological explanation

AO1	Behavioural – two process theory (Mowrer, 1947)
AO1	E.g. Little Albert (Watson and Rayner, 1920)
AO2	Research support, e.g. Sue *et al.* (1994) dog phobics report being bitten by dog
AO2	However, not everyone has a traumatic memory (DiNardo *et al.*, 1988), might be repressed (Ost, 1987)
AO2	Can't explain biological preparedness, e.g. Bregman (1934) couldn't condition fear to a bell

Model answer

Discuss issues surrounding the classification and diagnosis of phobic disorders. (8 marks + 16 marks)

One issue related to diagnosis is reliability. Reliability refers to the consistency of a measuring instrument, such as SCID-I, a semi-structured interview used in the diagnosis of phobias. Reliability can be measured in terms of whether two independent assessors give similar scores (inter-rater reliability).

There is research evidence that suggests SCID-I has high reliability. Skyre *et al.* (1991) assessed inter-rater reliability for diagnosing social phobia by asking three clinicians to assess over 50 patient interviews obtained using SCID-I. There was high inter-rater agreement (+.72) showing that the diagnosis of phobia is reliable. This may be the case because using SCID requires extensive training.

In contrast Kendler *et al.* (1999) did not find that the reliability for diagnosing phobias was always high. Kendler *et al.* used face-to-face and telephone interviews to assess individuals with phobias and found low reliability over time (test–retest). They suggest this might be because of poor recall by participants of their fears, for example, people tend to overexaggerate fears when recalling previous distress. Also low reliability might be because some clinicians decide that the severity of a symptom exceeds the clinical threshold whereas other clinicians might not.

A second issue is validity, which concerns both classification and diagnosis. For example, there is the issue of comorbidity, which is the extent that two (or more) conditions co-occur (such as phobias co-occuring with depression or different kinds of co-occuring phobias which are classified as distinct) and therefore the extent to which the conditions are 'real'. If, for example, social and animal phobias, do tend to co-occur this suggests that they are not separate entities and therefore should not be classified as separate disorders.

Some research has found evidence of comorbidity in phobic disorders. For example, Kendler *et al.* (1993) reported high levels of comorbidity between social phobias, animal phobias and generalised anxiety disorder, and also with depression, i.e. people were often diagnosed with more than one of these disorders. This questions the validity of different kinds of phobias as a separate disorder.

Two further aspects of validity are concurrent and construct validity. Concurrent validity establishes validity by comparing one method of diagnosis with another, previously validated method of diagnosis. Construct validity measures the extent that a test measures a target construct.

There is evidence of concurrent validity for methods of diagnosing phobic disorders. For example, Mattick and Clarke (1998) showed that their Social Phobia Scale (SPS) correlated well with other standard measures (varying between +.5 and +.7).

There is also evidence to support the construct validity of methods of diagnosing phobic disorders. For example, the Social Phobia and Anxiety Inventory (SPAI) correlates well with behavioural measures of social phobia (e.g. ease of public speaking) and lacks association with behaviours unrelated to social phobia (Beidel *et al.*, 1989).

There are other issues related to validity. For example, there is the issue that clinicians may be gender-biased or culture-biased when making a diagnosis, i.e. they have an unintentional tendency to certain kinds of diagnosis. A diagnosis may also lack validity if the clinician affects the responses given by a participant (e.g. social desirability bias). People prefer to present themselves in a positive light so, when answering questions in an interview, a patient may give a more socially acceptable answer especially when they don't want to appear odd or mentally ill.

Gender bias in the diagnosis of phobias has been supported by Worrell and Remer (2003). They suggest that women are more likely to be diagnosed with specific phobias because of gender stereotypes, i.e. clincians perceive women as more likely to be fearful and therefore are more likely to diagnose a phobia.

Culture bias can be seen in classification systems. For example, in Japan there is a condition called TKS. It is a social phobia where people are afraid of embarrassing others in social situations. In the UK a person exhibiting such symptoms would not be diagnosed with a social phobia, indicating the effect of cultural experiences on the classification (and ultimately diagnosis) of a disorder.

The issue of social desirability bias in diagnosis may be dealt with by using computer diagnosis. Computerised scales for assessing phobic disorders may be preferable because the presence of another person can create fears of negative evaluation. Computerised scales also mean there is less of an effect of interviewer expectations on the patient's answers.

Some exam questions on the topic of 'issues related to classification and diagnosis' are just AO2. Others are AO1 and AO2, as is the case here. When both AO1 and AO2 are required it is vital to make the AO1 component clearly separate from the AO2. Many students lose AO1 marks because clear division is missing.

This essay requires that both classification and diagnosis are discussed, whereas some essay titles don't (they say 'and/or').

You can keep track of the relative amounts of AO1 and AO2 by sticking to your plan – have four AO1 paragraphs and eight AO2 paragraphs each about 50–60 words. This ensures that your essay has the right proportions of each.

With this topic there is a fine line between AO1 and AO2 – AO1 is a description of the issue and AO2 is any commentary on the issue, such as research evidence, implications, ways of dealing with the issue and so on. Always try to use AO2 lead-in phrases for the AO2 paragraphs.

Remember there is no requirement for IDA in Unit 4 but if you do introduce such points they are creditworthy as AO2.

In total this essay is 719 words, with 258 words of AO1 content. Given that AO1 is difficult to achieve with this topic, this is not bad going!

Division 2 Explanations

Answer plans

Answer plan 1

Discuss biological explanations of phobic disorders. (8 marks + 16 marks)

Biological explanations

AO1	Genetic – high levels of ANS arousal inherited (adrenogenic theory)
AO1	Dopamine pathways, maybe some people more easily conditioned; abnormal serotonin increases anxiety
AO1	Evolutionary – ancient fears adaptive to ancestors in EEA
AO1	Prepotency (before direct experience) and preparedness (Seligman, 1970)
AO2	Family and twin studies, e.g. Fyer *et al.* (1995) probands' relatives 3× incidence, Torgerson (1983) MZ twins 5× DZ
AO2	Such studies don't control environmental component
AO2	Some phobias more genetic component, e.g. Kendler *et al.* (1992) 67% agoraphobia, 47% animal phobias
AO2	Evidence for ANS arousal, e.g. Biederman *et al.* (1993) children with behavioural inhibition
AO2	Research support for prepotency, e.g. Öhman and Soares (1994) greater SNS response to ancient fears
AO2	Research support for preparedness, e.g. Mineka *et al.* (1984) monkeys conditioned to snake not flower
AO2	Doesn't explain clinical phobias (Merckelbach *et al.*, 1988)
AO2	Simpler explanation, expectancy bias (Davey, 1995) expectations about fear-relevant stimuli

DIY

Work out your own plan for these questions and then write your answers.

(a) Outline at least **one** biological explanation of phobic disorders and at least **one** psychological explanation of phobic disorders. (8 marks)

(b) Evaluate biological and psychological explanations of phobic disorders. (16 marks)

Part (a) Biological and psychological explanations

AO1	
AO1	
AO1	
AO1	

Part (b) Evaluate biological and psychological explanations

AO2	
AO2	
AO2	
AO2	
AO2	
AO2	
AO2	
AO2	

Answer plan 2

Describe **two or more** psychological explanations of phobic disorders. (8 marks + 16 marks)

Psychological explanations

AO1	Psychodynamic – conscious expression of repressed conflicts, displaced onto neutral thing
AO1	E.g. Little Hans (Freud, 1909) fear of horses
AO1	Behaviourist – two process theory (Mowrer, 1947)
AO1	E.g. Little Albert (Watson and Rayner, 1920)
AO2	Little Hans case study limitations, e.g. unique case, biased reporting by father
AO2	Can explain Hans' phobia in terms of conditioning
AO2	Research support, e.g. Bowlby (1973) agoraphobics had early childhood conflicts
AO2	Can explain why some therapies (e.g. systematic desensitisation) fail, not dealing with conflicts
AO2	Behaviourist research support, e.g. Sue *et al.* (1994) dog phobics report being bitten by dog
AO2	However, not everyone has a traumatic memory (DiNardo *et al.*, 1988) though might be repressed (Ost, 1987)
AO2	Can account for cultural differences
AO2	Can't explain biological preparedness, e.g. Bregman (1934) couldn't condition fear to a bell

Answer plan 3

(a) Outline and evaluate **one or more** biological explanations for phobic disorders. (4 marks + 8 marks)

(b) Discuss **one or more** psychological explanations for phobic disorders. (4 marks + 8 marks)

Part (a) Biological explanations

AO1	Genetic – high levels of ANS arousal inherited (adrenogenic theory)
AO1	Dopamine pathways, maybe some people more easily conditioned; abnormal serotonin increases anxiety
AO2	Family and twin studies, e.g. Fyer *et al.* (1995) probands' relatives 3× incidence, Torgerson (1983) MZ twins 5× DZ
AO2	Such studies don't control environmental component
AO2	Some phobias more genetic component, e.g. Kendler *et al.* (1992) 67% agoraphobia, 47% animal phobias
AO2	Evidence for ANS arousal, e.g. Biederman *et al.* (1993) children with behavioural inhibition

Part (b) Psychological explanations

AO1	Behavioural – two process theory (Mowrer, 1947)
AO1	E.g. Little Albert (Watson and Rayner, 1920)
AO2	Research support, e.g. Sue *et al.* (1994) dog phobics report being bitten by dog
AO2	However, not everyone has a traumatic memory (DiNardo *et al.*, 1988) though might be repressed (Ost, 1987)
AO2	Can account for cultural differences
AO2	Can't explain biological preparedness, e.g. Bregman (1934) couldn't condition fear to a bell

Discuss biological explanations of phobic disorders. (8 marks + 16 marks)

One biological explanation for phobic disorders is that they are inherited, i.e. it's in your genes. For example, some people may be innately more prone to arousal of the autonomic nervous system (ANS). High levels of arousal in the ANS creates increased amounts of adrenaline and this leads to an oversensitive fear response. This has been called the adrenogenic theory.

Additional theories concern dopamine pathways in the brain that predispose some people to be more readily conditioned so that they are likely to acquire phobias more easily (the behavioural explanation says phobias are acquired through conditioning). Or abnormal serotonin activity may be responsible because this neurotransmitter is related to anxiety since it modulates those areas of the brain involved in the fear response, such as the amygdala.

A second biological explanation is that phobic disorders are adaptive, i.e. the evolutionary approach. Some stimuli are more likely to be feared than others, such as snakes, heights and darkness because these stimuli reflected very real danger to our ancestors in the environment of evolutionary adaptation (EEA). Most modern-day phobias are exaggerations of these ancient fears.

Experiencing anxiety after an event has happened would not be an adaptive response, therefore animals have evolved a response to potential threats. This is called prepotency and refers to the tendency to respond anxiously to e.g. snake-like movement. Prepotency would be coupled with preparedness. Seligman (1970) argued that animals are biologically prepared to rapidly learn an association between particular (i.e. potentially life-threatening) stimuli and fear, and once learned this association is difficult to extinguish.

Innate, genetic explanations are supported by family and twin studies. For example, Fyer *et al.* (1995) found that probands had three times as many relatives who also experienced phobias compared to normal controls. Torgersen (1983) compared MZ and same-sex DZ twin pairs where one proband had an anxiety disorder. Such disorders were five times more frequent in MZ twin pairs. Both studies suggest that phobic disorders have a genetic basis.

One of the problems with family and twin studies is that they don't control for shared experiences. MZ twins are likely to share more similar experiences (environments) than DZ twins because, for example, they are likely to have more similar interests even when reared apart (interests often are related to inherited tendencies).

There is evidence that some phobias have a greater genetic component than others. For example, Kendler *et al.* (1992) found a heritability rate of 67% for agoraphobia but only 47% for animal phobias. This might explain why rates are generally lower for phobias than other mental disorders, such as depression. This suggests that some phobias may have a genetic cause whereas others don't.

There is evidence to support the role of ANS arousal. Children who showed signs of behavioural inhibition at birth (a tendency to withdraw from unfamiliar people, objects and situations) were found to later have higher ANS activity and develop significantly more anxiety disorders (Biederman *et al.*, 1983). This indicates a link between innate ANS sensitivity and phobias.

There is also research support for prepotency. Öhman and Soares (1994) showed that people who were fearful of snakes or spiders showed a greater fear response (SNS activity measured by GSR) when shown masked (not immediately recognisable) pictures of snake/spiders. This shows that people respond to prepotent signals.

There is also research support for preparedness. Mineka *et al.* (1984) found that Rhesus monkeys rapidly develop a fear of snakes if they see another Rhesus monkey showing fear towards a snake but the same doesn't happen if fear was shown towards a flower. So they responded to an ancient fear, supporting Seligman's concept of preparedness.

One problem with evolutionary explanations of phobias is that they may explain 'everyday' fears but not clinical phobias. Merckelbach *et al.* (1988) found that most of the clinical phobias in their sample were rated as not ancient fears (i.e. 'non-prepared' rather than prepared fears).

An alternative, simpler explanation has been proposed by Davey (1995). He has suggested that expectancy bias can explain the research findings. An expectancy bias is an expectation that fear-relevant stimuli (such as dangerous situations) will produce negative consequences in the future. There is no need to invoke past evolutionary history. This explains why there are some modern phobias (e.g. phobia of hypodermic needles).

Candidates often start an essay on explanations of phobic disorders by giving a quick outline of the clinical characteristics. This would gain no credit in any essay unless part of the question specifically asked for clinical characteristics.

Just plunge straight in.

You might be tempted to produce just two paragraphs for the AO1 content (one on genetic explanations and one on evolutionary explanations). Writing four paragraphs, as here, helps you keep your eye on how much you have written because you should know what a 50-word paragraph looks like.

Notice how many of these AO2 points end with a 'so what' statement (e.g. 'This suggests that ...') making the point crystal clear to the examiner (see the three-point rule on page 5).

Don't be afraid to be repetitive using AO2 lead-in phrases ('There is also research support …'). The most important thing is to make it clear to the examiner that this is an AO2 point.

If you are using an alternative explanation as AO2, a small amount of description is necessary but focus on the relative strengths/weaknesses.

A total of 710 words, with slightly more than 1/3 AO1 but there is enough AO2 (453 words) for full marks – 400–480 words is the appropriate range for 16 marks.

Division 3 Therapies

Answer plans

Answer plan 1

Discuss biological therapies for phobic disorders. (8 marks + 16 marks)

Biological therapies

AO1	Benzodiazepines (BZs) – lock on GABA receptors on receiving neuron, chloride ions decrease sensitivity
AO1	Beta-blockers (BBs) – bind to heart receptors, reducing effect of adrenaline released by stress response
AO1	Antidepressants – SSRIs increase serotonin at synapse, regulates mood
AO1	Psychosurgery, e.g. capsulotomy functionally removes part of limbic system (regulates mood), also DBS
AO2	BZs effectiveness, e.g. Kahn *et al.* (1986) better than placebo, Hildago *et al.* (2001) better than SSRIs
AO2	BBs effectiveness, e.g. Liebowitz *et al.* (1985)
AO2	BBs may block fearful memories (Kindt *et al.*, 2009)
AO2	SSRIs effectiveness, e.g. Katzelnick *et al.* (1995) self-rated anxiety, Choy and Schneider *et al.* (2008) preferred method
AO2	Appropriateness drugs – limitations, e.g. not a cure, side effects of BZs (memory), addiction BZs, informed consent
AO2	Appropriateness drugs – strengths, e.g. no effort, BBs have fewer problems
AO2	Psychosurgery effectiveness, e.g. Ruck *et al.* (2003) success but negative symptoms too (e.g. suicide)
AO2	Appropriateness psychosurgery, rarely suitable, Szasz (1978) illogical to treat psyche

DIY

Work out your own plan for these questions and then write your answers.

(a) Outline and evaluate **one** psychological therapy for phobic disorders. (4 marks + 8 marks)

(b) Outline **and** evaluate one biological therapy for phobic disorders. (4 marks + 8 marks)

Part (a) One psychological therapy

AO1	
AO1	
AO2	
AO2	
AO2	
AO2	

Part (b) One biological therapy

AO1	
AO1	
AO2	
AO2	
AO2	
AO2	

Answer plan 2

Outline and evaluate **two or more** psychological therapies for phobic disorders. (8 marks + 16 marks)

Psychological therapy 1: Systematic desensitisation

AO1	Relaxation, counterconditioning and reciprocal inhibition (Wolpe)
AO1	Desensitisation hierarchy, covert or in vivo (overt)
AO2	Effectiveness, e.g. McGrath *et al.* (1990) 75% success
AO2	In vivo better than other forms (Menzies and Clarke, 1993)
AO2	Limitations, e.g. symptom substitution, not good for prepared fears (Öhman *et al.*, 1975)
AO2	Strengths, can be self-administered, little effort

Psychological therapy 2: Rational emotive behaviour therapy

AO1	ABC model (Ellis), activating event, irrational belief, self-defeating consequences
AO1	Disputing – logical, empirical, pragmatic
AO2	Effectiveness, e.g. Ellis (1957) 90% success, Engels *et al.* (1993) meta-analysis, NICE (2004) CBT best
AO2	Appropriateness, e.g. not suitable for all
AO2	Irrational beliefs may not be counterproductive, e.g. sadder but wiser effect (Alloy and Abrahmson, 1979)
AO2	Ethical considerations, e.g. aggressive and judgemental therapy

Answer plan 3

(a) Outline at least **one** biological therapy for phobic disorders and at least **one** psychological therapy for phobic disorders. (8 marks)

(b) Evaluate biological and psychological therapies for phobic disorders in terms of appropriateness and effectiveness. (16 marks)

Part (a) Biological and psychological therapies

AO1	Benzodiazepines (BZs) – lock on GABA receptors on receiving neuron, chloride ions decrease sensitivity
AO1	Beta-blockers (BBs) – bind to heart receptors, reducing effect of adrenaline released by stress response
AO1	Systematic desensitisation (SD) – relaxation, counterconditioning and reciprocal inhibition (Wolpe)
AO1	Desensitisation hierarchy, covert or in vivo (overt)

Part (b) Evaluate biological and psychological therapies

AO2	BZs effectiveness, e.g. Kahn *et al.* (1986) better than placebo, Hildago *et al.* (2001) better than SSRIs
AO2	BBs effectiveness, e.g. Liebowitz *et al.* (1985), Kindt *et al.* (2009) fearful memories
AO2	Appropriateness drugs – limitations, e.g. not a cure, side effects of BZs (memory), addiction BZs, informed consent
AO2	Appropriateness drugs – strengths, e.g. no effort, BBs have fewer problems
AO2	SD effectiveness, e.g. McGrath *et al.* (1990) 75% success rates
AO2	In vivo better (Menzies and Clarke, 1993)
AO2	Limitations, e.g. symptom substitution, not good for prepared fears (Öhman *et al.*, 1975)
AO2	Strengths, can be self-administered, little effort

Model answer

(a) Outline at least **one** biological therapy for phobic disorders and at least **one** psychological therapy for phobic disorders. (8 marks)

One biological therapy is anti-anxiety drugs which treat phobias by reducing anxiety levels. Benzodiazepines (BZs) slow down the activity of the central nervous system by enhancing the activity of GABA, a neurotransmitter that has a general quietening effect on many of the neurons in the brain. It does this by locking into GABA receptors on the outside of receiving neurons, which opens a channel to increase the flow of chloride ions into the neuron. Chloride ions make it harder for the neuron to be stimulated by other neurotransmitters.

Beta-blockers (BBs) reduce anxiety by reducing the activity of adrenaline (part of the sympathetic response to stress). BBs bind to receptors on the cells of the heart and other parts of the body that are usually stimulated during arousal. By blocking these receptors, it is harder to stimulate these cells so the heart beats slower and blood vessels do not contract so easily, resulting in a fall in blood pressure, and less feeling of anxiety.

The way the question is phrased means that one example of each is enough for full marks. The danger in trying to cover more than one is that you end up with breadth but less depth. Therefore, here we have focused on one example of each approach – although it could be argued that BZs and BBs are actually two different biological therapies!

One psychological therapy is systematic desensitisation (SD). Wolpe developed a technique where the feared stimulus is re-introduced gradually using a process of counter-conditioning. The patient is taught relaxation techniques and then given the opportunity to experience the feared stimulus while relaxed, forming a new association that runs counter to the original association. Wolpe also called this 'reciprocal inhibition' because the relaxation inhibits the anxiety.

A key element of the therapy is the desensitisation hierarchy. The therapist and patient construct a series of imagined scenes, each one progressively more fearful. They then work through this hierarchy, relaxing and mastering each stage before moving on to the next. This approach is called 'covert' desensitisation but it can also be overt or 'in vivo' where the feared stimulus is not simply imagined by is directly experienced.

The description of systematic desensitisation given here, in two paragraphs, shows how much you need to cover for 4 marks.

(b) Evaluate biological and psychological therapies for phobic disorders in terms of appropriateness and effectiveness. (16 marks)

BZs have been shown to be effective. For example, Kahn *et al.* (1986) found that BZs were better than just using a placebo treatment, which suggests they have some pharmacological value. Hildago *et al.* (2001) found that BZs had better results than SSRIs.

Research has also shown that BBs can be an effective treatment for phobias. For example, Liebowitz *et al.* (1985) demonstrated that BBs provide an effective means of anxiety control. Kindt *et al.* (2009) found that BBs also suppress memory and suggest in particular that they may interfere with the emotional content of memories. Therefore, an additional advantage is that BBs lead to forgetting of fearful memories that would reduce subsequent anxiety in the same situation.

Notice how the evidence from Kindt *et al.* is described and then elaborated further to explain the point made. This is important for AO2 credit.

In terms of appropriateness, there are limitations to drug treatments. First of all, drugs can't provide a complete treatment as they focus on symptoms. This may lead to symptom substitution because the real cause isn't dealt with and a new set of symptoms may appear. A second issue is side effects. BZs in particular are linked to problems, such as increased aggressiveness and long-term impairment of memory. BZs have also been linked to addiction. Finally there is the issue of informed consent because patients are not always informed about the fact that drugs may not actually be much better than placebos. Therefore, they are not giving truly informed consent.

Some of these AO2 points are rather long whereas others are short. The average length is 50 words which is just right.

When considering appropriateness it is also relevant to think of the strengths of drug therapies. They offer an easy solution for patients, requiring little effort. And some drug treatments (such as BBs) have fewer problems with, for example, side effects and addiction. So not all drug treatments have the same limitations.

SD has also been demonstrated through research to be effective, for example McGrath *et al.* (1990) found about 75% of phobic patients recover when treated with SD.

More detail of McGrath *et al.*'s research could have been included but the danger is providing too much description, which won't gain AO2 credit.

Other research has compared the effectiveness of covert methods of SD with in vivo methods. Menzies and Clarke (1993) found that in vivo techniques worked better probably because contact with the real stimulus transfers better to real life.

There are some limitations with SD. First of all symptom substitution may again be a problem. Just because a person stops feeling afraid of an object doesn't mean their underlying problem has disappeared. A further issue is that the SD may not work as well with prepared fears, i.e. those with an underlying evolutionary component (such as fear of spiders or the dark) (Öhman *et al.*, 1975).

The strengths of SD are that in general it is quick and requires less effort on the patient's part than other psychotherapies (such as REBT) where patients have to play a more active part in their treatment. A further strength of SD is that it can be self-administered, a method that has proved successful with, for example, social phobia.

Part (a) of this essay is about 300 words, quite a long section. Part (b) is just over 450 words which is sufficient for the AO2 part even though here it is not twice as much as the AO1.

Answer for you to mark

See page 174 for examiner's comments.

Question

(a) Outline clinical characteristics of phobic disorders. (4 marks)

(b) Briefly describe **one** psychological therapy for phobic disorders. (4 marks)

(c) Evaluate psychological therapies for phobic disorders. (16 marks)

Student answer

Part (a)

❶ According to the DSM a diagnosis of phobia is made if a person fulfils certain criteria. This enables a distinction to be made between an ordinary fear as opposed to a clinical phobia. First, the person is suffering excessive and unreasonable fear. Second, an individual does recognise that their behaviour is irrational. Third, the behaviour (fear) should interfere with the person's day-to-day living, such as work, relationships and leisure activities. Finally the fear should last for a significant period of time. In children this should be for more than 6 months. Panic attacks may accompany a phobia which will lead to irrational behaviour and even crying in children.

(108 words)

AO1 mark scheme for part (a)

No credit would be given for a description of different types of phobic disorder.

Acceptable clinical characteristics might include: physiological, behavioural, emotional and cognitive signs/ symptoms; incidence and prevalence; course and prognosis; and/or diagnostic criteria.

4 marks is about 100–120 words.

Comments and marks for part (a) AO1

Tick the terms you think apply to the student's answer.

Mark	Knowledge and understanding	Accuracy	Organisation and structure
4	Reasonably thorough	Accurate	Coherent
3–2	Limited	Generally accurate	Reasonably coherent
1	Weak and muddled		
0	No creditworthy material		

The **AO1** mark I would give is ☐

Part (b)

❷ One psychological therapy that is used to treat phobias is systematic desensitisation. This method started with Joseph Wolpe who suggested that the key to overcoming a phobia is relaxation. If you are feeling anxious then practicing relaxation will help overcome the fear. This is because anxiety and relaxation can't occur at the same time. This is the idea of counterconditioning. The argument is that originally the fear has been conditioned and then, if a new conditioning experience happens where the object is paired with relaxation, a new link is learned.

❸ An example of this is the original work that was done with cats. The cats were placed in a box and they were given an electric shock. Not surprisingly this resulted in them avoiding the box. Food was later placed near the box and then the cats gradually got to feel comfortable about the box. The cats were counterconditioned because they no longer feared the box.

❹ Wolpe then used this idea to create systematic desensitisation. There are several stages to this process where the person creates a hierarchy going from something that is not very fearful to something that is very fearful and couldn't confront before without feeling very anxious. There are different kinds of desensitisation where either the feared thing is imagined (called covert) or where the actual thing is confronted (called in vivo). There is also flooding where there is no hierarchy.

(234 words)

AO1 mark scheme for part (b)

If candidates outline more than one therapy, credit should be given to the one that attracts the most marks.

Explanations of a biological therapy would receive no credit.

4 marks is about 100–120 words.

Record mark for part (b) on facing page.

Guidance on marking is given on pages 6–11.

Comments and marks for part (b) AO1

Mark	Knowledge and understanding	Accuracy	Organisation and structure
4	Reasonably thorough	Accurate	Coherent
3–2	Limited	Generally accurate	Reasonably coherent
1	Weak and muddled		
0	No creditworthy material		

The **AO1** mark I would give is ☐

Part (c)

5 *Research studies have looked at the effectiveness of systematic desensitisation and confirmed that it is an effective way to treat phobias. A significant number of people respond well to treatment and have recovered from their phobia. It has been found that this is particularly true when in vivo methods are used where the actual thing is confronted rather than the covert method.*

6 *Research has also found that systematic desensitisation may work better on some fears rather than others. It seems that in particular it doesn't work so well with ancient fears, such as fear of the dark or fear of snakes or spiders, things that would have been dangers in the distant past.*

7 *A further criticism of systematic desensitisation is that it deals with symptoms only. It just aims to get rid of the anxiety and fear that a person is experiencing. But the phobia may have a deeper cause. For example, Freud suggested that the cause might be a repressed feeling and because the actual cause doesn't get treated repressed feelings may lead to new symptoms.*

8 *A strength of the approach is that it can be managed by the phobic without even having to go to a therapist. A person can just go through the hierarchy themselves.*

9 *Ellis proposed a different kind of therapy which he called Rational Emotive Behaviour Therapy (REBT). The aim of this therapy is to deal with a phobia by changing the way a person thinks. Phobics have been found to have delusional thoughts about themselves and about the world around them and also the future. Ellis' therapy aims to alter such irrational thoughts through his ABC model – A is the Activating Event, B is the belief which leads to C the consequence.*

10 *This therapy has been shown to be effective because it targets the cause of the phobia. However, REBT is not suitable for everyone. REBT takes a long time and has been criticised for being too logical. REBT has also been criticised for being unethical too because it is quite aggressive.*

11 *Both approaches may be criticised for being reductionist and determinist because they reduce a complex behaviour to something simple and suggest that doing the therapy should cause recovery, which it doesn't.*

(366 words)

AO2 mark scheme for part (c)

Credit would be given for the evaluation of any psychological therapy, not just the one described in part (b).

No credit would be given for the description of other therapies.

Evaluation is likely to involve a consideration of effectiveness and appropriateness (strengths and weaknesses) of any psychological therapy.

16 marks is about 400–480 words.

Comments and marks for part (c) AO2

Mark	Analysis and understanding	Focus	Elaboration	Line of argument	Quality of written communication
16–13	Sound	Well focused	Coherent	Clear	Fluent, effective use of terms
12–9	Reasonable	Generally focused	Reasonable	Evident	Clear, appropriate
8–5	Basic, superficial	Sometimes focused	Some evidence		Lacks clarity, limited use of terms
4–1	Rudimentary, limited understanding	Weak, muddled and incomplete	Not effective	May be mainly irrelevant	Often unconnected assertions, errors
0	No creditworthy material				

The **AO2** mark I would give is ☐

On Unit 4 there is no requirement for issues, debates and approaches (IDA). If such material is included it would gain AO2 credit – if suitably contextualised.

Chapter 12 Psychopathology: Obsessive compulsive disorder

There have been changes to the specification from September 2011 – therefore the updated specification details here are slightly different to those in some editions of the *A2 Complete Companion*.

Division 1 Overview	
	• **Clinical characteristics of obsessive compulsive disorder**
	• **Issues surrounding the classification and diagnosis of obsessive compulsive disorder, including reliability and validity**

Possible exam questions for this division

Question	Guidance
(a) Outline clinical characteristics of obsessive compulsive disorder. (8 marks) (b) Explain issues associated with the classification **and/or** diagnosis of obsessive compulsive disorder. (16 marks)	Questions may ask for a description of the clinical characteristics of obsessive compulsive disorder – note that the maximum mark for such questions is 8. Questions will not ask you to evaluate the clinical characteristics, therefore questions on clinical characteristics will always be paired with an evaluation of something else. In this case 'issues associated with classification and/or diagnosis' is all AO2 (evaluation), i.e. you do not need to provide descriptions of the issues.
Discuss issues surrounding the classification and diagnosis of obsessive compulsive disorder. (8 marks + 16 marks)	An alternative possibility is that issues associated with classification and/or diagnosis require description and evaluation. In this case you should help the examiner by providing a clear *description* of each issue. Descriptions of classification systems, such as *DSM*, will not be creditworthy. Issues that are not related to obsessive compulsive disorder will also not be creditworthy. See model answer on page 125.
(a) Outline clinical characteristics of obsessive compulsive disorder. (4 marks) (b) Explain issues associated with the classification **and/or** diagnosis of obsessive compulsive disorder. (10 marks) (c) Outline and evaluate **one** psychological explanation for obsessive compulsive disorder. (4 marks + 6 marks)	The total number of marks available for clinical characteristics may be less than the full 8 marks, so be prepared for a shorter answer. In part (a) you should present a list of characteristics appropriate for 4 marks, i.e. about 100–120 words. Part (b) in this question is all AO2. The final part is taken from other divisions of this chapter and requires attention to the mark split – usually you are asked to write twice as much AO2 as AO1, which is not the case here. You can follow the pattern used in this book and aim to write two paragraphs of AO1 and three of AO2 where each paragraph is 50–70 words.

Division 2 Explanations	
	• **Biological explanations of obsessive compulsive disorder, for example genetics, biochemistry**
	• **Psychological explanations of obsessive compulsive disorder, for example behavioural, cognitive, psychodynamic and socio-cultural**

Possible exam questions for this division

Question	Guidance
'There is a variety of different biological explanations for obsessive compulsive disorder, ranging from genetic to biochemistry and also including neuroanatomy and evolutionary factors.' Discuss biological explanations of obsessive compulsive disorder. (8 marks + 16 marks)	Questions sometimes start with a quotation. The intention here is to remind you of the breadth of material that you might include in your answer. However, don't be led astray – it does not mean that you have to cover all of these different biological explanations. The question itself states that you must do at least *two* for full marks but two would be sufficient. It would be creditworthy to evaluate explanations that have not been described, particularly if used to compare and contrast. See model answer on page 127.
Describe **two or more** psychological explanations of obsessive compulsive disorder. (8 marks + 16 marks)	The specification provides four examples of psychological explanations – but these are examples only. Exam questions set on this bullet point of the specification will only ask for psychological explanations and will not specify which ones.
(a) Outline and evaluate **one or more** biological explanations for obsessive compulsive disorder. (4 marks + 8 marks) (b) Discuss **one or more** psychological explanations for obsessive compulsive disorder. (4 marks + 8 marks)	The only two kinds of question in this division are about (1) biological explanations and (2) psychological explanations. You may be asked for one, two, at least one, or two or more. What this boils down to is that learning two explanations for each will be sufficient. You will notice from the selection of questions on this spread that the maximum marks for one psychological/biological explanation is 4 marks description + 8 marks evaluation (blockbuster questions for one explanation have not been set – they are possible but unlikely). In total this means that you need about 100–120 words description for each of the four different explanations (two psychological and two biological) and about 200–240 words evaluation of each of these four explanations.

Question	Comment
(a) Outline **one** psychological explanation and **one** biological explanation for obsessive compulsive disorder. (8 marks) (b) Evaluate explanations for obsessive compulsive disorder. (16 marks)	There are many variations on the same theme. Here both explanations are described in part (a) and the evaluation is all in part (b). In the previous question psychological and biological explanations were separated. You could use exactly the same material in the two answers but just arranged differently.
(a) Outline **one or more** biological explanations of obsessive compulsive disorder and **one or more** psychological explanations of obsessive compulsive disorder. (8 marks) (b) Evaluate biological and psychological explanations of obsessive compulsive disorder. (16 marks)	In this question you have the option to cover more than one explanation of each type. There is a danger in trying to write about more than one of each – you probably will sacrifice depth for breadth and thus would not achieve a mark in the top band because your answer would lack detail.
(a) Outline at least **one** biological explanation of obsessive compulsive disorder and at least **one** psychological explanation of obsessive compulsive disorder. (8 marks) (b) Consider whether psychological or biological approaches provide the better explanation of obsessive compulsive disorder. (16 marks)	This variation has a slightly different part (b). In such a question it is likely that marks in the top band would only be awarded if your answer does address the question of which kind of explanation is better. Your answer is likely to be based on the relative quality of research evidence for each explanation.
(a) Outline clinical characteristics of obsessive compulsive disorder. (4 marks) (b) Outline **one** psychological explanation of obsessive compulsive disorder. (4 marks) (c) Evaluate psychological explanations of obsessive compulsive disorder. (16 marks)	Questions are likely to span the divisions in order to include part questions on clinical characteristics and/or issues associated with classification and/or diagnosis. In such cases attend carefully to the number of marks available and construct your answers appropriately. Here 4 marks worth would be about 100–150 words.

Division 3 Therapies

- **Biological therapies for obsessive compulsive disorder, including their evaluation in terms of appropriateness and effectiveness**
- **Psychological therapies for obsessive compulsive disorder, for example behavioural, psychodynamic and cognitive-behavioural, including their evaluation in terms of appropriateness and effectiveness**

Possible exam questions for this division

Question	Comment
Discuss biological therapies for obsessive compulsive disorder. (8 marks + 16 marks)	When a question is open-ended, as here (as opposed to parted questions) you need to be especially careful to reflect the mark division in your answer – about 200–240 words of description and 400–480 words of evaluation.
Outline and evaluate **two or more** psychological therapies for obsessive compulsive disorder. (8 marks + 16 marks)	The question possibilities for therapies are the same as for explanations – biological and/or psychological and never more than two of each required.
(a) Outline at least **one** biological therapy for obsessive compulsive disorder and at least **one** psychological therapy for obsessive compulsive disorder. (8 marks) (b) Evaluate biological and psychological therapies for obsessive compulsive disorder in terms of appropriateness and effectiveness. (16 marks)	The specification suggests that you should evaluate therapies in terms of appropriateness and effectiveness, so it is worth being prepared for a question that uses such terms. See model answer on page 129.
'There are two key factors that help in evaluating therapies – whether they are effective and whether they are appropriate.' Outline and evaluate **two or more** therapies used in the treatment of obsessive compulsive disorder. (8 marks +16 marks)	When a question says 'two or more' this means you can gain credit if more than two therapies are described/evaluated but two would be sufficient to gain full marks. The danger of trying to write about more than two is that you inevitably lose depth and elaboration in your answer, and this means you may not get marks in the top band because your answer would lack detail and elaboration.
(a) Outline clinical characteristics of obsessive compulsive disorder. (4 marks) (b) Briefly describe **one** psychological therapy for obsessive compulsive disorder. (4 marks) (c) Evaluate psychological therapies for obsessive compulsive disorder. (16 marks)	This is another example of a question set across the divisions. Candidates are often tempted to write more than required for parts (a) and (b) whereas the big marks are from part (c). In questions on psychopathology there are no specific marks for IDA so it is not required but, if included, such comments would gain AO2 credit, if relevant. See student answer on page 130.

Division 1 Overview

Answer plans

On Unit 4 there is no requirement for issues, debates and approaches (IDA). If such material is included it would gain AO2 credit – if suitably contextualised.

Answer plan 1

(a) Outline clinical characteristics of obsessive compulsive disorder. (8 marks)

(b) Explain issues associated with the classification **and/or** diagnosis of obsessive compulsive disorder. (16 marks)

Part (a) Clinical characteristics

AO1	Obsessions, recurrent and intrusive, marked distress and more than everyday worries, e.g. germs
AO1	More than everyday worries about real-life problems
AO1	Compulsions, repetitive, time-consuming and rigid
AO1	Compulsions don't reduce obsessions

Part (b) Issues

AO2	Inter-rater reliability high for Y-BOCS, e.g. Woody *et al.* (1995), and children's version (Scahill *et al.*, 1993)
AO2	Test–retest, e.g. Kim *et al.* (1990) good in short-term but Woody *et al.* (1995) found less reliable after 50 days
AO2	Validity, comorbidity, e.g. Rosenfeld *et al.* (1992) higher Y-BOCS for OCD patients
AO2	Poor discrimination with depression (Woody *et al.*,1995)
AO2	Diagnostic scales culture-biased, e.g. Williams *et al.* (2005) differences between white and black Americans
AO2	Evidence for universality, e.g. Matsunaga *et al.* (2008)
AO2	Social desirability bias, supported by Anthony and Barlow (2004), makes OCD difficult to assess, computerised scales may help
AO2	Improve validity by interviewing friends/family

Work out your own plan for these questions and then write your answers.

(a) Outline clinical characteristics of obsessive compulsive disorder. (4 marks)

(b) Briefly describe **one** psychological therapy for obsessive compulsive disorder. (4 marks)

(c) Evaluate psychological therapies for obsessive compulsive disorder. (16 marks)

Part (a) Clinical characteristics

AO1	
AO1	

Part (b) One psychological therapy

AO1	
AO1	

Part (c) Evaluate psychological therapies

AO2	
AO2	
AO2	
AO2	
AO2	
AO2	
AO2	
AO2	

Answer plan 2

Discuss issues surrounding the classification and diagnosis of obsessive compulsive disorder. (8 marks + 16 marks)

Issues

AO1	Inter-rater reliability, compare clinicians' diagnoses, test–retest
AO2	Inter-rater reliability high for Y-BOCS, e.g. Woody *et al.* (1995), and children's version (Scahill *et al.*, 1993)
AO2	Test–retest, e.g. Kim *et al.* (1990) good in short-term but Woody *et al.* (1995) less reliable after 50 days
AO1	Validity, comorbidity, suggests not a 'real' category
AO2	Rosenfeld *et al.* (1992) higher Y-BOCS for OCD patients
AO2	Poor discrimination with depression (Woody *et al.*, 1995)
AO1	Validity – culture-biased, e.g. contamination obsessions
AO2	Diagnostic scales culture-biased, e.g. Williams *et al.* (2005) differences between white and black Americans
AO2	Evidence for universality, e.g. Matsunaga *et al.* (2008)
AO1	Validity – social desirability bias, fear of diagnosis
AO2	Supported by Anthony and Barlow (2004), makes OCD difficult to assess, computerised scales may help
AO2	Improve validity by interviewing friends/family

Answer plan 3

(a) Outline clinical characteristics of obsessive compulsive disorder. (4 marks)

(b) Explain issues associated with the classification **and/or** diagnosis of obsessive compulsive disorder. (10 marks)

(c) Outline and evaluate **one** psychological explanation for obsessive compulsive disorder. (4 marks + 6 marks)

Part (a) Clinical characteristics

AO1	Obsessions, recurrent and intrusive, marked distress and more than everyday worries, e.g. germs
AO1	Compulsions, repetitive, time-consuming and rigid

Part (b) Explain issues

AO1	Validity, comorbidity, suggests not a 'real' category
AO2	Inter-rater reliability high for Y-BOCS, e.g. Woody *et al.* (1995), and children's version (Scahill *et al.*, 1993)
AO2	Test–retest, e.g. Kim *et al.* (1990) good in short-term but Woody *et al.* (1995) less reliable after 50 days
AO2	Validity, comorbidity, e.g. Rosenfeld *et al.* (1992) higher Y-BOCS for OCD patients
AO2	Diagnostic scales culture-biased, e.g. Williams *et al.* (2005) differences between white and black Americans
AO2	Social desirability bias, supported by Anthony and Barlow (2004), makes OCD difficult to assess, computerised scales may help

Part (c) One psychological explanation

AO1	Behaviourist – acquisition of fears, two process theory (Mowrer, 1960)
AO1	Compulsive rituals learned through accidental associations
AO2	Research support behaviourist, e.g. OCD-like people learn more rapidly (Tracy *et al.*, 1999)
AO2	Problems with using non-clinical participants
AO2	Research support, e.g. Rachman and Hodgson (1980) compulsive acts reduce anxiety
AO2	Link with biological explanation, obsessive behaviours inherited by compulsions learned

Model answer

Discuss issues surrounding the classification and diagnosis of obsessive compulsive disorder. (8 marks + 16 marks)

One issue related to diagnosis is reliability. Reliability refers to the consistency of a measuring instrument, such as Y-BOCS (Yale-Brown Obsessive Compulsive Scale), a semi-structured interview used in the diagnosis of OCD. Reliability can be measured in terms of whether two independent clinicians give similar scores (inter-rater reliability). It can also be assessed using test–retest where the same patient is tested twice over a period of time to demonstrate whether the scores remain consistent.

Research has provided evidence of high reliability in the diagnosis of OCD. For example, Woody *et al.* (1995) assessed patients with OCD using Y-BOCS and reported that inter-rater reliability was excellent. The children's version (CY-BOCS) has been shown to have good inter-rater reliability (Scahill *et al.*, 1997).

Research has also found support for good test–retest scores. For example, Kim *et al.* (1990) found good test–retest reliability over the short term (2 weeks). However, Woody *et al.* (1995) found that such scores were poor over the long term. They assessed patients once and assessed them again 50 days later.

A second issue is validity, which concerns both classification and diagnosis. For example, there is the issue of comorbidity, which is the extent that two (or more) conditions co-occur (such as OCD and depression) and therefore the extent to which these conditions are 'real'. If depression and OCD do tend to co-occur this suggests that they are not separate entities.

There is research evidence that does suggest comorbidity is not a problem for OCD. For example, Rosenfeld *et al.* (1992) found that patients diagnosed with OCD had higher Y-BOCS scores than patients with other anxiety disorders and normal controls, i.e. it does distinguish OCD patients from others and therefore OCD is a separate and distinct disorder.

However, there is also research that contradicts this. Woody *et al.* (1995) found poor discrimination with depression, i.e. patients diagnosed with OCD were also often diagnosed with depression. This supports the view that there may be a comorbidity problem with OCD and therefore should not be classified as a separate disorder. You could, for example, just treat depression.

Another aspect of validity is culture bias. If a diagnostic tool or classification system is developed in one culture and used in another culture it may not be applicable because of underlying assumptions based on norms in the country of origin. For example, in the case of OCD, people in the West may fear contamination from germs whereas in India fears might be from being touched by someone from a lower caste.

The consequence of this is that, if a person from India sought treatment in the West saying they feared being touched by people from lower castes, a clinician would not diagnose OCD. This view is supported by Williams *et al.* (2005) who demonstrated that there were significant differences between normal populations of black and white Americans in the scores for contamination obsessions. The researchers suggest that black Americans produce higher scores because of, for example, the fact that they interact less with animals and have a greater concern about the contamination from animals. This would then increase the likelihood of an OCD diagnosis, i.e. would be an example of culture bias.

On the other hand there is evidence that OCD is a universal condition with universal symptoms. For example, Matsunaga *et al.* (2008) studied Japanese OCD patients and found symptoms remarkably similar to those in the West. They concluded that this disorder transcends culture and therefore there would not be issues with culture bias in either classification or diagnosis.

There are other issues related to validity. For example, there is the problem of social desirability bias. People prefer to present themselves in a positive light so, when answering questions in an interview, a patient may give a more socially acceptable answer especially when they don't want to appear odd or mentally ill. There is also the issue that some patients may lack awareness of the severity and frequency of their symptoms.

Anthony and Barlow (2004) support this view and also point out that patients may be fearful of handling questionnaires because they are contaminated. Having such fears means it is difficult to assess OCD. One way to deal with this is to use computerised scales or online versions where people don't have to deal with people or pens/paper.

The other issue relating to a lack of awareness of their own condition may be improved by interviewing close friends/family to get an alternative perspective on the patient's behaviour. This would confirm or otherwise what the patients says, leading to a truer picture of the disorder in that person.

Some exam questions on the topic of 'issues related to classification and diagnosis' are just AO2. Others are AO1 and AO2, as it is here. When both AO1 and AO2 are required it is vital to make the AO1 component clearly separate from the AO2. Many students lose AO1 marks because clear division is missing.

This essay requires that both classification and diagnosis are discussed, whereas some essay titles don't (they say 'and/or').

You can keep track of the relative amounts of AO1 and AO2 by sticking to your plan – have four AO1 paragraphs and eight AO2 paragraphs each about 50–60 words. This ensures that your essay has the right proportions of each.

With this topic there is a fine line between AO1 and AO2 – AO1 is a description of the issue and AO2 is any commentary on the issue, such as research evidence, implications, ways of dealing with the issue and so on. Always try to use AO2 lead-in phrases for the AO2 paragraphs.

The essay totals about 750 words with almost 500 words of AO2.

Division 2 Explanations

Answer plans

Answer plan 1

Discuss biological explanations of obsessive compulsive disorder. (8 marks + 16 marks)

Biological explanations

AO1	Genetic – worry circuit (caudate nucleus, orbitofrontal cortex, thalamus)
AO1	Lower serotonin (effect of antidepressants) and higher dopamine
AO1	Evolutionary (Marks and Nesse, 1994) adaptive behaviours, e.g. grooming, concern for others
AO1	Harm avoidance strategies (Abed and de Pauw, 1998), Involuntary Risk Scenario Generating System, IRSGS
AO2	Family and twin studies, e.g. Nestadt *et al.* (2000) 5× greater risk, Billett *et al.* (1998) MZ 2× more likely than DZ
AO2	COMT gene (Karayiorgou *et al.*, 1997) 50% male OCDs, 10% female OCDs, 16% of general population
AO2	Menzies *et al.* (2007) reduced grey matter in OFC
AO2	SSRIs reduce dopamine in right basal ganglia and OCD symptoms (Kim *et al.*, 2007)
AO2	Worry circuit linked to serotonin and dopamine (Comer, 1998 and Sukel, 2007)
AO2	Universal nature of OCD supports evolutionary approach, e.g. Matsunaga *et al.* (2008) Japanese symptoms
AO2	Osborn (1998) obsessionals less prone to risk taking
AO2	Buttolph *et al.* (1998) increased OCD at critical life stages, e.g. pregnancy

DIY

Work out your own plan for these questions and then write your answers.

(a) Outline at least **one** biological explanation of obsessive compulsive disorder and at least **one** psychological explanation of obsessive compulsive disorder. (8 marks)

(b) Evaluate biological and psychological explanations of obsessive compulsive disorder. (16 marks)

Part (a) Biological and psychological explanations

AO1	
AO1	
AO1	
AO1	

Part (b) Evaluate biological and psychological explanations

AO2	
AO2	
AO2	
AO2	
AO2	
AO2	
AO2	
AO2	

Answer plan 2

Describe **two or more** psychological explanations of obsessive compulsive disorder. (8 marks + 16 marks)

Psychological explanations

AO1	Behaviourist – acquisition of fears, two process theory (Mowrer, 1960)
AO1	Compulsive rituals learned through accidental associations
AO1	Cognitive – intrusive thoughts lead to self blame, exacerbated by associated depression
AO1	Compulsions aim to neutralise intrusive thoughts, act like an addiction
AO2	Research support behaviourist, e.g. OCD-like people learn more rapidly (Tracy *et al.*, 1999)
AO2	Problems with using non-clinical participants
AO2	Research support, e.g. Rachman and Hodgson (1980) compulsive acts reduce anxiety
AO2	Link with biological explanation, obsessive behaviours inherited but compulsions learned
AO2	Cognitive research support, e.g. self blame (Pleva and Wade, 2006)
AO2	Maladaptive thoughts, e.g. Bouchard *et al.* (1999) OCDs believe in control, Clark (1992) intrusive thoughts
AO2	Gender issues, different triggers, e.g. brain injury in men (link with Tourettes), trichotillomania in women
AO2	Reductionist, suggesting too simple solution

Answer plan 3

(a) Outline and evaluate **one or more** biological explanations for obsessive compulsive disorder. (4 marks + 8 marks)

(b) Discuss **one or more** psychological explanations for obsessive compulsive disorder. (4 marks + 8 marks)

Part (a) Biological explanations

AO1	Genetic – worry circuit (caudate nucleus, orbitofrontal cortex, thalamus)
AO1	Lower serotonin (effect of antidepressants) and higher dopamine
AO2	Family and twin studies, e.g. Nestadt *et al.* (2000) 5× greater risk, Billett *et al.*, 1998) MZ 2× more likely than DZ
AO2	COMT gene (Karayiorgou *et al.*, 1997) 50% male OCDs, 10% female OCDs, 16% of general population
AO2	Menzies *et al.* (2007) reduced grey matter in OFC
AO2	SSRIs reduce dopamine in right basal ganglia and OCD symptoms (Kim *et al.*, 2007)

Part (a) Psychological explanations

AO1	Behaviourist – acquisition of fears, two process theory (Mowrer, 1960)
AO1	Compulsive rituals learned through accidental associations
AO2	Research support behaviourist, e.g. OCD-like people learn more rapidly (Tracy *et al.*, 1999)
AO2	Problems with using non-clinical participants
AO2	Research support, e.g. Rachman and Hodgson (1980) compulsive acts reduce anxiety
AO2	Link with biological explanation, obsessive behaviours inherited but compulsions learned

Model answer

Discuss biological explanations of obsessive compulsive disorder. (8 marks + 16 marks)

One biological explanation for OCD is that it is inherited, i.e. it's in your genes. Genetic factors may create an abnormally functioning worry circuit. This circuit consists of the caudate nucleus which normally suppresses signals from the orbitofrontal cortex (OFC). The OFC sends signals to the thalamus about things that are worrying, such as a potential germ hazard. When the caudate nucleus is damaged it fails to suppress 'worry' signals and the thalamus is alerted, which in turn sends signals back to the OFC acting as a worry circuit.

Additional inherited possibilities include lower levels of the neurotransmitter serotonin and higher levels of dopamine. Low levels of serotonin have been suspected because antidepressant drugs that increase serotonin reduce OCD symptoms whereas those drugs that don't affect serotonin don't reduce OCD symptoms. Higher levels of dopamine are suspected because high levels of dopamine in animals lead to the stereotyped movements that resemble the compulsions found in OCD sufferers.

A second biological explanation is that obsessive and compulsive behaviours have an adaptive basis. Marks and Nesse (1994) propose that behaviours, such as grooming are both adaptive and lead to obsessive compulsive behaviours. In mammals, parasitism is reduced by grooming and, in some primate species, grooming smoothes social interaction. Many obsessive compulsives wash and groom endlessly. Another possible adaptive behaviour that may lead to OCD is concern for others – ignoring the needs of other members of the group increases the likelihood of ostracism from the group. Many obsessive compulsives are overly concerned with fear of harming or embarrassing others.

Abed and de Pauw (1998) have proposed a different evolutionary theory for OCD. They suggest that a particular mental module evolved, the Involuntary Risk Scenario Generating System (IRSGS). This allows individuals to imagine certain potential risks before they happen and thus be able to deal more effectively with them when they do happen. An exaggerated IRSGS would lead to OCD.

Genetic explanations are supported by family and twin studies. For example, Nestadt *et al.* (2000) found that people with a first degree relative with OCD (parents or siblings) had a five times greater risk of having OCD at some time in their lives, compared to the general population. Billett *et al.* (1998) found that MZ twins were twice as likely as DZ twins to develop OCD if their co-twin had the disorder. Such studies suggest that inherited factors may underlie OCD.

Another line of evidence for genetic explanations is research studies that have identified particular genes in OCD sufferers. For example, Karayiorgou *et al.* (1997) found that a variation in the COMT gene occurred in 50% of the male OCD sufferers tested, 10% of the females and only 16% of the normal population. This certainly suggests that in males there is a genetic basis.

Further evidence for genetic explanations comes from Menzies *et al.* (2007). They found that OCD patients (as well as their close relatives) have reduced grey matter in key regions of the brain including the OFC. The fact that this difference is present in OCD patients and their relatives suggests a genetic characteristic that is triggered by life events in certain people, an example of the diathesis-stress model.

The role of dopamine is supported by studies of the effect of SSRIs – antidepressant drugs that raise levels of serotonin and also reduce dopamine levels in the right basal ganglia. Reduction in dopamine levels was positively correlated with a reduction of obsessive compulsive symptoms as assessed using Y-BOCS (a scale used to assess OCD symptoms).

Research has also shown that the genetic explanations can be tied together. It has been found that serotonin plays a key role in the OFC and caudate nuclei, therefore low serotonin would cause these areas to function poorly (Comer, 1998). Furthermore, dopamine is the main neurotransmitter of the basal ganglia. High levels of dopamine lead to overactivity of this region (Sukel, 2007). This suggests a link between various genetic explanations.

The evolutionary approach is supported by the fact that OCD rates are fairly similar all over the world (about 2–3% lifetime prevalence). Also Matsunaga *et al.* (2008) studied Japanese OCD patients and found symptoms remarkably similar to those in the West. They concluded that this disorder transcends culture.

The concept of the IRSGS is supported by, for example, Osborn (1998) who found that obsessional patients were less prone to risk taking. It could be argued that overactivity of IRSGS would warn them of the dangers associated with risky activities and thus lead to risk avoidance.

Another line of evidence that supports predictions of the IRSGS is that there should be an increased risk of OCD at biologically critical life stages because that would be the time when the IRSGS would be generating lots of new risks. There is evidence to support this, such as increased risk for OCD during pregnancy (Buttolph *et al.*, 1998).

Candidates often start an essay on explanations of OCD by giving a quick outline of the clinical characteristics. This would gain no credit in any essay unless part of the question specifically asked for clinical characteristics.

Just plunge straight in.

You might be tempted to produce just two paragraphs for the AO1 content (one on genetic explanations and one on evolutionary explanations). Writing four paragraphs, as here, helps you keep your eye on how much you have written because you should know what a 50-word paragraph looks like.

Notice how many of these AO2 points end with a 'so what' statement (e.g. 'This suggests that ...') making the point crystal clear to the examiner (see the three-point rule on page 5).

Always take care to use an AO2 lead-in phrase to make it clear to the examiner that this is evaluation and not description.

You could use an alternative psychological explanation as a form of AO2 but, if you do, make sure you give no more than a brief description of the alternative explanation and mainly focus on the relative strengths/ weaknesses.

A total of about 800 words with a slightly overlengthy AO1 section (about 300 words) but nevertheless sufficient AO2 at approximately 500 words.

Answer plans

Answer plan 1
Discuss biological therapies for obsessive compulsive disorder. (8 marks + 16 marks)

Biological therapies

AO1	Antidepressants, e.g. SSRIs, increase serotonin, normalise worry circuit
AO1	Anti-anxiety, e.g. BZs, enhance GABA by increasing chloride ions and decreasing neuron sensitivity
AO1	D-Cycloserine, antibiotic for TB, enhances GABA
AO1	Psychosurgery, e.g. capsulotomy functionally removes part limbic system (regulates mood), cingulotomy linked to OFC
AO2	SSRI effectiveness, e.g. Soomro *et al.* (2008) meta-analysis of 17 studies, better than placebo
AO2	However, most studies 3–4 months (Koran *et al.*, 2007)
AO2	Appropriateness drugs – limitations, e.g. not a cure, relapse (Maina *et al.*, 2001), side effects SSRIs (nausea)
AO2	Appropriateness drugs – strengths, e.g. no effort, short-term effectiveness
AO2	Psychotherapy (e.g. CT) preferable (Koran *et al.*, 2007), good for compulsions (Schwartz *et al.*, 1996)
AO2	Cingulotomy effectiveness, e.g. Dougherty *et al.* (2002) 45% partly improved
AO2	Research did use double blind so observations may be biased (Koran *et al.*, 2007)
AO2	Appropriateness, e.g. irreversible, side effects

DIY

Work out your own plan for these questions and then write your answers.

(a) Outline and evaluate **one** psychological therapy for obsessive compulsive disorder. (4 marks + 8 marks)

(b) Outline and evaluate **one** biological therapy for obsessive compulsive disorder. (4 marks + 8 marks)

(a) One psychological therapy

AO1	
AO1	
AO2	
AO2	
AO2	
AO2	

Part (b) One biological therapy

AO1	
AO1	
AO2	
AO2	
AO2	
AO2	

Answer plan 2
Outline and evaluate **two or more** psychological therapies for obsessive compulsive disorder. (8 marks + 16 marks)

Psychological therapy 1: Exposure and response prevention (ERP)

AO1	Exposure overcomes negative reinforcement
AO1	Response prevention leads to learning that compulsions aren't needed
AO2	Effectiveness, e.g. Albucher *et al.* (1998) 60–90%
AO2	Best combined with drugs, e.g. antidepressants (Foa *et al.*, 2005), though not always (Foa and Kuzak, 1996)
AO2	Combine with CT (Koran *et al.*, 2007), helps relapse (Huppert and Franklin, 2005)
AO2	Appropriateness – limitations, e.g. not good for depressed (Gershuny *et al.*, 2002), success depends on effort

Psychological therapy 2: Cognitive therapy (CT)

AO1	Challenge and re-interpret obsessions/compulsions
AO2	Thought record of intrusive thoughts and how challenged
AO2	Effectiveness, e.g. Wilhem *et al.* (2005) 15 patients
AO2	Sometimes not effective because not all patients put revised beliefs into action (Ellis, 2001)
AO2	Appropriateness – limitations, e.g. not used on own, cognitive effort
AO2	Ethical problems conducting research, e.g. waiting list or placebo comparison (O'Kearney *et al.*, 2006)

Answer plan 3
(a) Outline at least **one** biological therapy for obsessive compulsive disorder and at least **one** psychological therapy for obsessive compulsive disorder. (8 marks)
(b) Evaluate biological and psychological therapies for obsessive compulsive disorder in terms of appropriateness and effectiveness. (16 marks)

Part (a) Biological and psychological therapies

AO1	Antidepressants, e.g. SSRIs, increase serotonin, normalise worry circuit
AO1	Anti-anxiety, e.g. BZs, enhance GABA by increasing chloride ions and decreasing neuron sensitivity
AO1	Exposure and response prevention (ERP), exposure overcomes negative reinforcement
AO1	Response prevention leads to learning that compulsions aren't needed

Part (b) Evaluate biological and psychological therapies

AO2	SSRI effectiveness, e.g. Soomro *et al.* (2008) meta-analysis of 17 studies, better than placebo
AO2	However, most studies short term, only 3–4 months (Koran *et al.*, 2007)
AO2	Appropriateness drugs – limitations, e.g. not a cure, relapse (Maina *et al.*, 2001), side effects SSRIs (nausea)
AO2	Appropriateness drugs – strengths, e.g. no effort, short term effectiveness
AO2	ERP effective, e.g. Albucher *et al.* (1998) 60–90% get better
AO2	Best combined with drugs, e.g. antidepressants (Foa *et al.*, 2005), though not always (Foa and Kuzak, 1996)
AO2	Combine with CT (Koran *et al.*, 2007), helps relapse (Huppert and Franklin, 2005)
AO2	Appropriateness – limitations, e.g. not good for depressed (Gershuny *et al.*, 2002), success depends on effort

Model answer

(a) Outline at least **one** biological therapy for obsessive compulsive disorder and at least **one** psychological therapy for obsessive compulsive disorder. (8 marks)

One biological therapy is chemotherapy, including antidepressants and antianxiety drugs. Selective serotonin re-uptake inhibitors (SSRIs) are the preferred antidepressant used with OCD. Such drugs increase levels of serotonin, a neurotransmitter in the brain linked to OCD and mood. Serotonin is also part of the 'worry circuit' so SSRIs may normalise this circuit reducing anxiety, obsessions and the need for compulsive behaviours.

Anti-anxiety drugs, such as benzodiazepaines (BZs) are also used with OCD. BZs reduce anxiety levels by slowing down the activity of the central nervous system. BZs do this by enhancing the activity of GABA, a neurotransmitter that has a general quietening effect on many of the neurons in the brain. BZs lock onto GABA receptors on the outside of receiving neurons, which opens a channel to increase the flow of chloride ions into the neuron. Chloride ions make it harder for the neuron to be stimulated by other neurotransmitters.

The way the question is phrased means that one example of each is enough for full marks. The danger in trying to cover more than one is that you end up with more breadth but less depth. Therefore, here we have focused on one example of each approach – although it could be argued that antidepressants and anti-anxiety drugs are actually two different biological therapies!

The most specific psychological treatment for OCD is exposure and response prevention. This is a behavioural therapy which aims to help a patient re-learn conditioned associations. In the first half of the therapy (exposure) patients are presented with their feared object or thought (e.g. a dirty doorknob) and have to continue until their anxiety subsides. Exposures may move gradually from least to most threatening in a manner similar to systematic desensitisation. The underlying principle is that anxieties persist because of negative reinforcement – avoidance of an anxiety-producing stimulus is reinforcing.

Response prevention takes place at the same time. The patient is prohibited from engaging in the usual compulsive response. This is important in order for the patient to recognise that anxiety can be reduced without the compulsive ritual. For example, a woman obsessed about cleanliness might be given a list of therapeutic rules she must accept, such as not cleaning her house for a week and then only spending half an hour vacuuming it.

Part (a) is a lengthy 313 words of AO1. Long AO1 sections leave you less time to produce the all-important AO2, 200–240 words of AO1 is enough for 8 marks.

(b) Evaluate biological and psychological therapies for obsessive compulsive disorder in terms of appropriateness and effectiveness. (16 marks)

Research studies have demonstrated the effectiveness of SSRIs. For example, Soomro *et al.* (2008) reviewed 17 studies of the use of SSRIs with OCD and found these antidepressants to be more effective than placebos in reducing the symptoms of OCD as measured using Y-BOCS to assess how frequent symptoms were.

However, such studies have been criticised because most are only 3-4 months in duration and little long-term data exists (Koran *et al.*, 2007). It is possible that drug therapies are actually not effective in the long term because they only target anxiety and don't deal with, for example, the obsessive thinking.

Many of these AO2 paragraphs begin with 'There is research evidence' – don't feel you have to be creative with your writing, just make the point as clear as possible using AO2 lead-in phrases.

In terms of appropriateness, the limitations of using drugs are that they do not provide a lasting cure, as indicated by the fact that patients relapse within a few weeks if medication is stopped (Maina *et al.*, 2001). In addition there are considerable side effects. For example, nausea, headaches and insomnia are common side effects of SSRIs.

On the positive side drug therapies are always attractive to people because they require little effort and offer a quick fix in the short term at least.

Research evidence also supports the effectiveness of ERP. For example, Albucher *et al.* (1998) report that between 60–90% of adults with OCD have improved considerably using ERP.

The most effective strategy may be to combine ERP with other techniques, such as antidepressants. For example, Foa *et al.* (2005) found that a combination of clomipramine (an antidepressant) and ERP was more effective than either alone. However, Foa and Kuzak (1996) found ERP alone was found to be equally effective to ERP with medication.

Some of these AO2 points are rather long whereas others are short. The average length is 50 words which is just right.

There is other research evidence supporting the effectiveness of ERP combined with cognitive therapy (targeting irrational thoughts and beliefs). Koran *et al.* (2007) concluded, that ERP combined with cognitive therapy probably produces the best results of all. Huppert and Franklin (2005) found that ERP integrated with discussions of feared consequences and dysfunctional beliefs in particular helped prevent relapse.

Not all patients are helped by this therapy. ERP alone is not successful with patients who are too depressed (Gershuny *et al.*, 2002). The success of ERP depends on effort on the part of the patient and a willingness to do their 'homework' – not all patients are willing to commit to this kind of effort. This leads to a substantial refusal rate that may artificially elevate the apparent success of therapy because only those patients who are willing to 'be helped' may agree to participate in research to evaluate the therapy.

Part (b) is longer than part (a) at 417 words – 400–480 words is sufficient for AO2, so there is enough AO2 here but a better AO1/AO2 balance would have been preferable.

Answer for you to mark

See page 174 for examiner's comments.

Question

(a) Outline clinical characteristics of obsessive compulsive disorder. (4 marks)

(b) Briefly describe **one** psychological therapy for obsessive compulsive disorder. (4 marks)

(c) Evaluate psychological therapies for obsessive compulsive disorder. (16 marks)

Student answer

Part (a)

❶ The clinical characteristics for OCD relate to the two characteristic features of the disorder – obsessions and compulsions. Obsessions are more than excessive worries about real-life problems. Such worries cause significant distress and are clearly the product of the patient's own mind rather than being placed there by someone else (as in the case of a schizophrenic patient). An example would be a concern with dirt or germs.

❷ Compulsions aim to neutralise or prevent the obsessions and therefore reduce the anxiety created by the obsessions. They may be mental or behavioural. The compulsions also create distress. They don't have any real effectiveness and are clearly excessive, such as repeatedly washing your hands until they are red raw.

(116 words)

AO1 mark scheme for part (a)

Acceptable clinical characteristics might include: physiological, behavioural, emotional and cognitive signs/symptoms; incidence and prevalence; course and prognosis; and/or diagnostic criteria.

4 marks is about 100–120 words.

Comments and marks for part (a) AO1

Mark	Knowledge and understanding	Accuracy	Organisation and structure
4	Reasonably thorough	Accurate	Coherent
3–2	Limited	Generally accurate	Reasonably coherent
1	Weak and muddled		
0	No creditworthy material		

Tick the terms you think apply to the student's answer.

The **AO1** mark I would give is ☐

Part (b)

❸ The main psychological therapy for OCD is exposure and response prevention (ERP). This is a therapy that is based on behaviourist principles. It basically consists of two parts. One part is exposure and the second part is response prevention. One of the problems with a disorder like OCD is that a person never goes back to behaving normally so they don't know that they will actually feel anxious if they don't do the compulsive behaviours. The behaviours are negatively reinforcing because they make a person escape from an unpleasant situation but if you repeated the unpleasant situation you might find it wasn't so bad afterall. This is what underlies the exposure bit of ERP. The person is exposed to their obsession, such as a dirty cloth and then they try to relax while experiencing that thing. The therapy works a bit like systematic desensitisation where the therapist creates a hierarchy and gradually the patient gets used to each level of the hierarchy.

❹ The patient attends sessions with the therapist about once a week for up to 20 weeks. After that the patient may also have booster sessions to prevent relapse.

(191 words)

AO1 mark scheme for part (b)

If candidates outline more than one therapy, credit should be given to the one that attracts the most marks.

Explanations of a biological therapy would receive no credit.

4 marks is about 100–120 words.

Record mark for part (b) on facing page.

Comments and marks for part (b) AO1

Guidance on marking is given on pages 6–11.

Mark	Knowledge and understanding	Accuracy	Organisation and structure
4	Reasonably thorough	Accurate	Coherent
3–2	Limited	Generally accurate	Reasonably coherent
1	Weak and muddled		
0	No creditworthy material		

The **AO1** mark I would give is ☐

Part (c)

5 *There is evidence that ERP is effective. In one study it was shown that ERP led to fewer OCD symptoms. However, this was a short-term study and we don't know if it is really effective in the long term.*

6 *In terms of appropriateness ERP is good because there are no bad side effects. It is also appropriate because it allows patients to be exposed to the thing that creates anxiety and then they may stop producing the compulsive acts they have got into the habit of doing.*

7 *There are criticisms of the therapy. It doesn't always work for all patients. However this may be because some patients are not really very motivated to follow the therapist's advice. After the therapy they have to keep making themselves experience the thing that makes them anxious and try to make themselves relax. Some people are too lazy so they go back to their old ways. It may be that for people like this drugs are their best option because it is just a matter of taking the drug.*

8 *There are other psychological therapies, such as cognitive therapy. However, research has shown that cognitive therapy has similar problems to OCD because patients have to work hard at it.*

9 *Cognitive therapy involves a therapist challenging the patient's irrational beliefs. The therapist will challenge the obsessions and the compulsions, so they might ask why does the patient think that germs are present and why does the patient think that washing their hands all the time will get rid of the germs. Cognitive therapy may also involve keeping a thought record so the patient can reflect on their irrational thoughts.*

10 *Psychological therapies have been reasonably successful but as we have seen they have their problems. The alternative is to use some kind of biological therapy, such as drugs or even psychosurgery. The best option may be to use some kind of combination, such as ERP with drugs as well to reduce some of the anxiety.*

(226 words)

AO2 mark scheme for part (c)

Credit would be given for the evaluation of any psychological therapy, not just the one described in part (b).

No credit would be given for the description of other therapies.

Evaluation is likely to involve a consideration of effectiveness and appropriateness (strengths and weaknesses) of any psychological therapy.

16 marks is about 400–480 words.

Comments and marks for part (c) AO2

Mark	Analysis and understanding	Focus	Elaboration	Line of argument	Quality of written communication
16–13	Sound	Well focused	Coherent	Clear	Fluent, effective use of terms
12–9	Reasonable	Generally focused	Reasonable	Evident	Clear, appropriate
8–5	Basic, superficial	Sometimes focused	Some evidence		Lacks clarity, limited use of terms
4–1	Rudimentary, limited understanding	Weak, muddled and incomplete	Not effective	May be mainly irrelevant	Often unconnected assertions, errors
0	No creditworthy material				

On Unit 4 there is no requirement for issues, debates and approaches (IDA). If such material is included it would gain AO2 credit – if suitably contextualised.

The **AO2** mark I would give is ☐

Chapter 13 Media psychology

There have been changes to the specification from September 2011 – therefore the updated specification details here are slightly different to those in some editions of the *A2 Complete Companion*.

Section B Psychology in action

Exam questions in Section B of Unit 4 are different to other exam questions. They are usually divided into about four parts and contain stimulus material – see the example on the right.

Therefore, in this chapter, we have focused on part questions rather than whole questions worth 24 marks.

The number of marks available for each part question varies enormously, as you can see from the selection of possible questions on this page. A useful rule is that you should write 25–30 words for every mark.

AQA style question

See student answer on page 140.

(a) Researchers have more and more turned their attention to the effects of video games on behaviour, tending to use correlational studies in their research.

(i) Explain some of the difficulties of conducting research into the effects of video games. (5 marks)

(ii) Discuss research into the effects of video games on behaviour. (4 marks + 5 marks)

(b) Outline explanations of why people are attracted to celebrity. (4 marks)

(c) An advertising company offers a prize to psychology students, asking them to suggest how the advertising company might increase the persuasiveness of their ads for greater appeal to students. The ideas must be based on psychological research.

Suggest at least **two** ways that TV advertisements could be made to be more persuasive. Refer to psychological research in your answer. (6 marks)

Division 1 Media influences on social behaviour

- **Explanations of media influences on pro- and anti-social behaviour**
- **The positive and negative effects of computers and video games on behaviour**

Possible exam questions for this division

Question	Comment
Outline and evaluate **one** psychological explanation of media influence on pro-social behaviour. (4 marks + 4 marks) Discuss psychological explanations of media influence on anti-social behaviour. (4 marks + 8 marks)	This division concerns media influences. First of all you may be asked questions on *explanations* of these influences. When asked about explanations you must not describe research studies. These can be used as part of your evaluation but would not gain description marks. Since the specification separates pro- and anti-social influences it is likely that questions will be concerned with one or the other, so take care to include the right material. For example, if you are outlining the social learning explanation don't just explain social learning theory but make sure you explain how this, in the context of media influences, would account for either pro-social or anti-social behaviour (as appropriate).
People have been arguing for decades about whether all the violence we see in our society is due to what young people witness in films. Discuss what psychological research has told us about some of the media influences on anti-social behaviour. (5 marks + 6 marks)	This question asks about 'psychological research' (rather than explanations) so it would be creditworthy to describe research studies or explanations, or both. If you do describe research studies then you need to be careful about how you provide the AO2 component so you don't simply just describe more research studies (which would be credited as AO1). This is an example of a mini-essay, typical of 'Psychology in action' where you are unlikely to find one blockbuster question. Always pay attention to the mark split in guiding you about how much to write. Here a little bit more AO2 than AO1 is required.
Researchers have more and more turned their attention to the effects of video games on behaviour, tending to use correlational studies in their research. Explain some of the difficulties of conducting research into the effects of video games. (5 marks)	Exam questions in this 'Psychology in action' section often relate the content of the specification to research methods. You are required to combine your knowledge from both areas of the specification when answering the question. Sometimes the beginning, stimulus part of the question, may be slightly misleading – here it suggests that you should focus on correlational research but in fact the question asks about any kind of research.
Discuss what psychological research has told us about the effects of video games on young people. (4 marks + 4 marks)	The specification also includes computers and video games so questions may be set specifically on the effects these have on behaviour.
Tom's mother thinks that playing video games is likely to have negative effects on his behaviour and wants to ban him from playing them. Explain **two or more** arguments that Tom might use to show his mother that video games can have positive effects. Use psychological research to support your arguments. (8 marks)	The specification mentions both positive and negative effects of computers and video games, so questions may focus on one or the other. This is an example of a question where you are required to apply your knowledge – for maximum marks it would not be enough to just outline the relevant research. You must use such knowledge to construct arguments that might be used to show the benefits of playing video games. This makes it an AO2 question.

A psychology class decides to prepare a leaflet for other students about the positive and negative effects of computers and video games on behaviour. Use your knowledge of psychological research in this area to justify your advice. (10 marks)	This final question in this division illustrates how any of these topics might be used in a question where you are required to apply your knowledge to a novel situation. In such cases you must be careful to avoid merely *describing* the relevant research but instead you should list your advice and then link each piece of advice to psychological research.

Division 2 Media and persuasion

- **The application of Hovland-Yale and Elaboration Likelihood models in explaining the persuasive effects of media**
- **Explanations for the persuasiveness of television advertising**

Possible exam questions for this division

Explain how the Hovland-Yale model can be used to account for the persuasive effects of the media. (6 marks)	Questions will be set on the two models named in the specification. However, since the specification says 'The application of ...' it is unlikely that you will just be asked for a straightforward description of the models.
Newspapers have frequently run campaigns to change people's attitudes. For example they have featured articles on recycling. Explain how the Elaboration Likelihood model can be used to account for how the media might persuade people to change their attitudes towards recycling. (10 marks)	The application of the models may be set in the context of a question with stimulus material where you will be asked to apply your knowledge of one (or both) of the named models to a novel situation, as here. Very few marks would be awarded for a description of the model, to gain marks you must interact with the situation described in the stimulus part of the question.
(a) Identify **two** factors that might increase the persuasiveness of television advertisements. (4 marks) (b) Explain how factors such as those you identified in your answer to (a) could be used to persuade young people to purchase sports-related products. (8 marks)	The second part of this division concerns television advertising and again the specification focuses on application – how explanations about persuasiveness can be applied to television advertising. Part (a) involves a straightforward identification of two factors. Part (b) of this question then requires you to apply this understanding to another situation (purchasing sports-related products). Students so often fail to gain marks because they just describe the psychological research they know, rather than using it to answer the question.

Division 3 The psychology of 'celebrity'

- **The attraction of 'celebrity', including social psychological and evolutionary explanations**
- **Research into intense fandom, including celebrity worship and celebrity stalking**

Possible exam questions for this division

Outline and evaluate explanations of why people are attracted to celebrity. (4 marks + 6 marks)	Notice that the mark split is not equal so you should be writing about 100–150 words of AO1 but about 150–200 words of AO2.
Outline **one** social psychological explanation of the attraction of celebrity. (4 marks)	The specification identifies two particular explanations, therefore exam questions may require you to write only about either social psychological or evolutionary explanations.
Evolutionary explanations of human behaviour have become increasingly popular. Use research evidence to consider the value of evolutionary explanations of celebrity. (8 marks)	The form of question here is all AO2, so there would be little or no credit for any description (AO1) of evolutionary explanations. In this question there is no requirement to engage with the stimulus material.
A researcher decided to investigate attraction to celebrity. She designed a questionnaire to collect people's views on celebrity and what they found interesting about them. She also asked participants to fill in a second questionnaire which measured their personality type. Explain **one** methodological and **one** ethical issue that might have arisen in this study. (2 marks + 2 marks)	Occasionally questions are set that are related to research methods. The way the question is phrased means that you need to contextualise your answer so it is specific to the situation described in the stimulus material. Usually when there are separate marks (2 marks + 2 marks) this indicates an AO1 component and an AO2 component – but here it refers to 2 marks for the methodological issue and 2 marks for the ethical issue.
Outline and evaluate findings of research into intense fandom. (4 marks + 6 marks)	Three further topics related to celebrity are listed – intense fandom, celebrity worship and celebrity stalking. Questions could be set on research into any three of these areas.

Division 1 Media influences on social behaviour Answer plans

The questions on this page are derived in part from the examples on page 132. Some further ones have been added.

Answer plan 1 (short question)

Outline **one** psychological explanation of media influence on pro-social behaviour. (4 marks)

Pro-social behaviour

AO1	Social learning theory (Bandura, 1962), observation, vicarious reinforcement, imitation
AO1	Pro-social acts more likely to reinforce social norms and more likely to be rewarded for pro- rather than anti-social

Answer plan 2 (short question)

Outline **one** positive and **one** negative effect of computers on behaviour. (4 marks)

Negative effects of computers

AO1	Facebook increases self-esteem (Gonzales *et al.*, 2011), compared to looking in mirror condition
AO1	Facebook leads to lower grades, Karpinski *et al.* (2009) students underachieved by as much as a grade

Work out your own plan for these questions and then write your answers.

(a) Explain some of the difficulties of conducting research into the effects of playing video games. (4 marks)

(b) Discuss psychological explanations of media influence on pro-social behaviour. (4 marks + 8 marks)

(c) Explain **two or more** arguments that could be used to demonstrate that computers do have positive effects. (8 marks)

Part (a) Video games

AO1	
AO1	

Part (b) Pro-social behaviour

AO1	
AO1	
AO2	
AO2	
AO2	
AO2	

Part (c) Positive effects of computers

AO2	
AO2	
AO2	
AO2	

Answer plan 3 (mini-essay)

Discuss psychological explanations of media influence on anti-social behaviour. (4 marks + 8 marks)

Anti-social behaviour

AO1	Social learning theory (SLT) (Bandura, 1962), observation, vicarious reinforcement, imitation
AO1	Desensitisation – frequent viewing of television violence may cause children to be less anxious about violence
AO2	SLT research support, e.g. Bandura *et al.* (1963) Bobo, learn specific acts and also when violence is rewarded
AO2	However, such imitation is rare outside Bandura-style studies, Cumberbatch (2001) no known link ever found
AO2	Desensitisation research support, e.g. Cumberbatch (2001) violence more likely to make children 'frightened'
AO2	Gender bias in media effects research, because male students used

Answer plan 4 (mini-essay)

Evaluate explanations of media influence on anti-social behaviour. (8 marks)

Anti-social behaviour

AO2	SLT research support, e.g. Bandura *et al.* (1963) Bobo, learn specific acts and also when violence is rewarded
AO2	However, such imitation is rare outside Bandura-style studies, Cumberbatch (2001) no known link ever found
AO2	Desensitisation research support, e.g. Cumberbatch (2001) violence more likely to make children 'frightened'
AO2	Gender bias in media effects research, because male students used

Answer plan 5 (mini-essay)

Outline and evaluate research on the effects of computers on behaviour. (4 marks + 8 marks)

Effect of computers

AO1	Facebook increases self-esteem (Gonzales *et al.*, 2011), compared to looking in mirror condition (or control)
AO2	May be because of positive feedback from friends
AO2	Hyperpersonal Model (Walther, 1996), self-selection of information to represent ourselves
AO1	Facebook leads to lower grades, Karpinski *et al.* (2009) students underachieved by as much as a grade
AO2	Correlation is not cause, other factors, e.g. personality or distractability
AO2	Support for the causal view, e.g. Greenfield (2009) shortens attention span and constant instant gratification

Answer plan 6 (applying your knowledge)

Explain **two or more** arguments that Tom might use to show his mother that video games can have positive effects. Use psychological research to support your arguments. (8 marks)

Video games

AO2	Makes you more helpful, e.g. Greitmeyer and Osswald (2010) *Lemmings* vs *Lamers* or *Tetris*
AO2	Social understanding, e.g. Kahne *et al.* (2008) *The Sims*, explore social issues
AO2	Social commitment, e.g. Lenhart *et al.* (2008) *Halo* (saving humankind), civic and political commitment
AO2	Social learning theory (Bandura 1962), prosocial games – observation, vicarious reinforcement, modelling

Model answer

Parts (a), (b) and (c) would not form an exam question because the various part questions overlap in terms of the content required. The model answer just illustrates part questions for this division.

(a) Outline **one** psychological explanation of media influence on pro-social behaviour. (4 marks)

One explanation for media influence on pro-social behaviour is social learning theory. Bandura (1962) suggested that we learn by observation how to do things. We also learn when it is acceptable to perform them through vicarious reinforcement. So we observe people on TV performing pro-social acts and if they are rewarded, we are likely to imitate this behaviour.

People are likely to imitate pro-social behaviours because, unlike the depiction of anti-social acts on television (e.g. murder and fighting), pro-social acts are more likely to represent established social norms (e.g. helping others). Pro-social acts are likely to reinforce our social norms rather than contrast with them. We are also more likely to be rewarded for imitating pro-social acts than anti-social acts.

This question begins with 'outline' and therefore this is clearly an AO1 question, so evaluation would not be credited.

Part (a) is120 words, which is just perfect for a 4-mark question (100–120 words is our guidance).

(b) Outline and evaluate research on the effects of computers on behaviour. (4 marks + 8 marks)

Gonzales *et al.* (2011) found evidence that Facebook can have a positive influence on self-esteem. They gave students a chance to either interact with their Facebook page or look at themselves in the mirror (or do nothing). Those who had interacted with their Facebook page subsequently gave much more positive feedback about themselves than the other two groups.

One possible explanation for the influence of Facebook on increasing self-esteem is that on Facebook the feedback people leave on your wall is invariably positive, for example lots of birthday greetings or telling you how much they enjoyed seeing you. This increases a person's self-esteem because it makes you feel liked by others and makes you feel popular.

Always elaborate your points of criticism. In this case we have used examples to make the point clear and contextualised.

A second explanation comes from the Hyperpersonal Model (Walther, 1996). This claims that self-selection of the information we choose to represent ourselves (e.g. through photos, personal details and witty comments) can have a positive influence on self-esteem. On Facebook people are selective in the information they choose to make public so this would increase self-esteem.

Another effect of computers is that they may lead to underachievement because of time spent, for example, on Facebook. Karpinski *et al.* (2009) found that the majority of students who use Facebook every day underachieved by as much as an entire grade compared with those who do not use the site.

One criticism of this research is that the evidence is correlational and therefore does not show that Facebook use actually causes the poorer grades. Karpinski suggests that other personality factors are likely to act as an intervening variable. There are other possibilities too, such as it could be that Facebook users are simply prone to distraction which is why they go on Facebook and why they don't do so well at their studies.

There is support for the view that Facebook actually is a causal factor in poor academic performance. Greenfield (2009) has argued that social networks, such as Facebook 'infantilise' the brain by shortening the attention span and providing constant instant gratification. This could explain why people who use Facebook do less well at their studies.

The overall length for a 12-mark answer should be 300–360 words, and this one is about 350 words.

The AO1:AO2 division appropriately reflects the marks available for each skill.

(c) Explain **two or more** arguments that Tom might use to show his mother that video games can have positive effects. Use psychological research to support your arguments. (8 marks)

Video games can encourage you to be more helpful to others. This was demonstrated by Greitmeyer and Osswald (2010) who compared the effects of people who played a pro-social game called Lemmings, (where you have to ensure the safety of the lemmings) with people playing an aggressive game (Lamers), or a neutral game (Tetris). After playing the respective video games for 8 minutes, those who played Lemmings were twice as likely to help the researcher pick up pencils.

The key to gaining marks on this question is to be presenting arguments that Tom might use. Each paragraph must begin with an argument in favour of the positive effects.

Video games may also make you have more understanding for others and for the way that society works. This was demonstrated in a study (Kahne *et al.*, 2008) which found that the majority of those who listed The Sims (a life simulation game) as a favourite game said they learned about problems in society and explored social issues while playing computer games.

Another positive effect that comes from video games is increased civic and political commitment. In games like The Sims people learn about how society functions and Halo where you battle to save humankind. Lenhart *et al.* (2008) found that people who play such games in a multiplayer setting (where they have to negotiate with other players) also were more likely to try to persuade others to vote and were more committed to civic participation than those who played on their own.

Research studies are used to support the arguments.

The underlying argument is related to social learning theory. Bandura (1962) proposed that we learn a lot of our behaviour by observing what others do. We also learn when it is acceptable to learn them through vicarious reinforcement. So when we observe people in video games performing pro-social acts and see them rewarded, then we are likely to model this behaviour.

In part (c) there are about 280 words – slightly more than necessary for a question worth 8 marks.

Division 2 Media and persuasion Answer plans

The questions on this page are derived in part from the examples on page 133. Some further ones have been added.

Answer plan 1 (short question)

Outline **one** application of the Hovland-Yale model. (4 marks)

Hovland-Yale model

AO1	Focus on the message, classroom fear appeals influenced examination performance (Putwain and Symes, 2011)
AO1	Positive effect if mastery approach emphasised, negative if threatening

Answer plan 2 (short question)

Outline **two** factors that might increase the persuasiveness of television advertisements. (4 marks)

Persuasiveness of TV advertisements

AO1	Central route (Elaboration Likelihood), hard sell providing factual information and arguments
AO1	Peripheral route, using celebrity endorsement, familiar face (parasocial relationship) that you trust (Giles, 2003)

Work out your own plan for these questions and then write your answers.

(a) Outline **two** factors that would decrease the persuasiveness of television advertisements. (4 marks)

(b) Outline and evaluate **one** application of the Hovland-Yale model. (4 marks + 8 marks)

(c) Explain how the Elaboration Likelihood model could be used to encourage a person to purchase sports-related products. (6 marks)

Part (a) Factors decreasing persuasiveness

AO1	
AO1	

Part (b) Hovland-Yale model

AO1	
AO1	
AO2	
AO2	
AO2	
AO2	

Part (c) Elaboration Likelihood model

AO2	
AO2	
AO2	
AO2	

Answer plan 3 (mini-essay)

Outline and evaluate **one** application of the Elaboration Likelihood model. (4 marks + 8 marks)

Elaboration Likelihood model

AO1	Understanding online shopping, Lin *et al.* (2011) compared central (quality reviews) and peripheral (quantity) route
AO1	Found both influenced purchasing but high need for cognition participants placed more reliance on quality
AO2	Means quantity of reviews may be good for low need for cognition (NC) audience
AO2	Can guide Internet marketers to design appropriate promotional materials and review formats
AO2	Peripheral route may be temporary, e.g. Penner and Fritzsche (1993) Magic Johnson and AIDS
AO2	Gender bias in media effects research, because male students used

Answer plan 4 (mini-essay)

Outline and evaluate **two** factors that might increase the persuasiveness of television advertisements. (4 marks + 8 marks)

Persuasiveness of TV advertisements

AO1	Central route (Elaboration Likelihood), hard sell providing factual information and arguments
AO1	Peripheral route, using celebrity endorsement, familiar face (parasocial relationship) that you trust (Giles, 2003)
AO2	Individual differences, high need for cognition (NC) more affected by central route (Cacioppo and Petty, 1982)
AO2	Research support e.g. Haugtvedt *et al.* (1992) attitude change when evaluating product attributes
AO2	Peripheral route may be temporary, e.g. Penner and Fritzsche (1993) Magic Johnson and AIDS
AO2	Central route more influential in computer mediated communication (CMC) (Di Blasio and Milani, 2008)

Answer plan 5 (applying your knowledge)

Explain how the Hovland-Yale model could be used to persuade young people to purchase sports-related products. (8 marks)

Hovland-Yale model applied

AO2	Focus on the source e.g. have an sports personality (credible and attractive)
AO2	Focus on the message e.g. moderate level of fear and avoid over zealous sales
AO2	Focus on audience, if high IQ give them both sides of argument, low IQ prefer one-sided
AO2	Age is also important, children have less understanding of persuasive intent

Model answer

Parts (a), (b) and (c) would not form an exam question because the various part questions overlap in terms of the content required. The model answer just illustrates part questions for this division.

(a) Outline **one** application of the Hovland-Yale model. (4 marks)

One application of the Hovland-Yale model is to consider the way that aspects of the message can be used to explain persuasiveness. Putwain and Symes (2011) investigated the effect of fear appeals on examination performance. They wanted to see if teachers' threats about failing exams would improve performance.

They found that when fear appeals emphasised a 'mastery' approach (e.g. they included advice about how to make the most of the time before the exam), their frequency was positively related to examination performance. However, when fear appeals were perceived as threatening (i.e. creating greater test anxiety), they were negatively related to examination performance. This shows that understanding features of the message are important in understanding persuasiveness.

The important thing here is to link your knowledge to the question asked. It would not be sufficient to describe the Hovland-Yale model or to describe a research study. The final sentence of the second paragraph makes the all-important link to the application of the model.

The answer for part (a) is 115 words, just right for a 4-mark question.

(b) Outline and evaluate **two** factors that might increase the persuasiveness of television advertisements. (4 marks + 8 marks)

One factor that might increase the persuasiveness of television advertisements is following the central route, as proposed by the Elaboration Likelihood model. This is the 'hard sell' approach where advertisers focus on the factual content and arguments as a way of increasing the persuasiveness of an advertisement.

A second factor is the peripheral route or more 'soft sell' approach that involves appeals to emotion. The soft sell approach uses celebrity endorsement as a form of emotional appeal. Giles (2003) suggests that celebrities provide a familiar face – a reliable source of information that we feel we can trust because of the parasocial relationship (i.e. not a true relationship where one person is unaware of the other's existence) that we have built up with that celebrity.

You would not receive credit for defining terms that are in the question itself but if you do introduce psychological terms in your answer (such as 'parasocial') you should define them briefly to demonstrate your understanding.

There are individual differences in the effects of these two factors. Some people enjoy analysing arguments and are more likely to focus on the quality of the arguments than their context. They are described as having a high need for cognition (NC). It has been suggested by Cacioppo and Petty (1982) that people who are high NC prefer the central route whereas low NC indiviuals prefer the more emotion-oriented peripheral route.

There is research support for such individual differences. For example, Haugtvedt *et al.* (1992) found that attitude change in high NC individuals was based more on an evaluation of product attributes in advertisements than was the case with low NC individuals. For low NC individuals, simple peripheral cues were more important in shaping attitudes.

Notice how each AO2 point begins with a suitable lead-in phrase to alert the examiner to the fact that this is AO2.

One criticism of the central/peripheral route notion (from the Elaboration Likelihood model) is that the influence of the peripheral route may be temporary, and therefore not a 'real' influence. Penner and Fritzsche (1993) noted that attitudes to AIDS changed dramatically (in a positive direction) after the US basketball played Magic Johnson announced he had the disease. Such a celebrity appeal is an example of the peripheral route. However, after 4 months these attitudes had returned to preannouncement levels.

The central route is more influential in computer mediated communication (CMC). Di Blasio and Milani (2008) arranged for students to have a discussion in a CMC condition or face-to-face. Halfway through the discussion a new, contrasting piece of information from an influential source was introduced. There were fewer opinion changes in the CMC condition (after the introduction of the persuasive message) than in the face-to-face condition, where participants were influenced more by the source rather than the quality of the arguments.

In part (b) the AO1 segment is about 120 words and the AO2 is about 280 words – both are appropriate amounts.

(c) Explain how the Hovland-Yale model could be used to persuade young people to purchase sports-related products. (8 marks)

The Hovland-Yale model identifies three factors. The first is the source of a message. When trying to sell a sports-related product it would be important to use an attractive and credible sports personality, such as Steven Gerrard. Such a source would have greater persuasiveness.

The second factor is the content of the message itself. Research has found that a moderate level of fear is best for persuading someone to buy something. So, if I was selling trainers I might emphasise the damage that can be done to your feet by wearing cheap products. Another aspect of the message that affects success is the pushiness of the salesman – too much is not desirable so I would have my sports personality speaking in a chatty, off-hand manner.

The key thing to note in this answer is the way that the knowledge about the Hovland-Yale model has been used to generate advice that is specifically relevant to selling sports-related products. That is the key to gaining marks on 'applying your knowledge' questions. Your answer must have the psychology but also must have the application.

The third factor is the audience itself. Research has found that a high intelligence audience likes to hear both sides of an argument whereas lower IQ audiences prefer one-sided arguments. Therefore, if I was presenting a TV ad during a darts match, it might be more appropriate to use arguments just giving a simple argument in favour of the product whereas tennis audiences might be better persuaded if you gave some counter evidence (although these assumptions about the audiences would need some market research!).

A further important factor in relation to the audience is age. As we are targeting young people it is important to remember that children have less understanding of the persuasive intent of the message and therefore we might be a little bit more direct in our appeal. For example, if advertising football club replica kit the ad might tell the viewer that wearing one will increase your popularity.

Part (c) is about 275 words, which is plenty for a Grade B.

Division 3 The psychology of 'celebrity' Answer plans

The questions on this page are derived in part from the examples on page 133. Some further ones have been added.

Answer plan 1 (short question)
Outline **one** social psychological explanation of the attraction of celebrity. (4 marks)

Social psychological explanations

AO1	Parasocial, target person unaware of the other's existence, such relationships make few demands, no risk of criticism
AO1	Parasocial relationships with celebrities most attractive, similar and perceived as real (Shiappa *et al.*, 2007)

Answer plan 2 (short question)
Outline the findings of research into celebrity worship. (4 marks)

Celebrity worship

AO1	Frequency, Maltby *et al.* (2003) used CAS, found 5% 'entertainment-social' level, 5% 'intense-personal' level, 2% 'borderline-pathological'
AO1	Maltby *et al.* (2001) lower psychological wellbeing, CAS predicts social dysfunction (e-s), depression, anxiety (i-p)

Work out your own plan for these questions and then write your answer.

(a) Outline **one** evolutionary explanation for the attraction of celebrity. (4 marks)

(b) Outline and evaluate research into celebrity worship. (4 marks + 8 marks)

(c) Identify **two** social psychological explanations for the attraction of celebrity and use these to explain why people have such an interest in celebrities. (8 marks)

Part (a) Evolutionary explanation

AO1	
AO1	

Part (b) Celebrity worship

AO1	
AO1	
AO2	
AO2	
AO2	
AO2	

Part (c) Use social psychological explanations

AO2	
AO2	
AO2	
AO2	

Answer plan 3 (mini-essay)
Outline and evaluate findings of research into celebrity stalking. (4 marks + 6 marks)

Celebrity stalking

AO1	Types of stalker, e.g. love obsession, simple obsession (based on past relationship, not likely with celebrity)
AO1	Cyberstalking of celebrities, emails or spamming
AO2	Stalking may be related to insecure attachment, e.g. Tonin (2004) compared stalkers to other mentally ill and normal
AO2	Cyberstalking may be less reinforcing because can't see impact (Sheridan and Grant, 2007)
AO2	Cyberstalking is not taken seriously, Alexy *et al.* (2005) only 30% judged it to be 'real' stalking

Answer plan 4 (mini-essay)
Use research evidence to consider the value of evolutionary explanations of attraction to celebrity. (8 marks)

Evolutionary explanation

AO2	Evidence for an evolved love of creativity, Shiraishi *et al.* (2006) inherited enzyme linked to novelty-seeking
AO2	Sexual selection, arbitrary because argues that traits preferred just because they're attractive – why adaptive?
AO2	Celebrity gossip, De Backer (2007) gossip monitors social networks, media exposure leads celebrities to seem to be part of social network
AO2	Contrasting social psychological explanations, e.g. parasocial is simpler which may be best (Occam's razor)

Answer plan 5 (applying your knowledge)
Use your knowledge of psychology to explain why some people do not find celebrities attractive. (6 marks)

Attraction to celebrities applied

AO2	Less need for relationships generally, so no need for parasocial relationships
AO2	May be securely attached, parasocial relationships to meet unmet relationship needs (Cole and Leets, 1999)
AO2	Reduced exposure to media therefore less likely to incorporate celebrities in social network (De Backer, 2007)

Answer plan 6 (applying your knowledge)
Maryann's mother is worried about Maryann's obsession with Jennifer Aniston and other celebrities. Use your knowledge of psychology research to suggest what Maryann's mother might do to encourage her daughter to reduce her feelings of attraction to celebrities. (8 marks)

Attraction to celebrities applied

AO2	Discuss relationship issues so she can cope with rejection and criticism, rather than seek parasocial relationships
AO2	Give more unconditional love to meet relationship needs due to insecure attachment (Cole and Leets, 1999)
AO2	Reduced exposure to media therefore less likely to incorporate celebrities in social network (De Backer, 2007)
AO2	Find some other satisfaction for urge for creativity/novelty-seeking (evolutionary explanation)

Model answer

(a) Outline **one** social psychological explanation of the attraction of celebrity. (4 marks)

One social psychological explanation for attraction to celebrity suggests it is due to a need for parasocial relationships. Such relationships are where an individual is attracted to another individual, but the target individual is usually unaware of them. The reason some people have parasocial relationships is because they make few demands and do not involve criticism or rejection, as might be the case in a real relationship.

Parasocial relationships are most likely to form with celebrities who are seen as attractive and similar in some way, and also perceived as real or that they behave in a believable way. Shiappa *et al.* (2007) suggest the reason for this might be because viewers are able to compare how they would behave in similar situations.

Two separate paragraphs may not be strictly necessary but it helps keep you right in terms of knowing how much to write – you should be used to what 50–60 words looks like.

A 4-mark answer should be 100–120 words, and this part (a) is 123 words.

(b) Outline the findings of research into celebrity worship. (4 marks)

Maltby *et al.* (2003) conducted a study to look at the frequency of celebrity worship. They used the Celebrity Atttiude Scale to class people as different types of celebrity worshipper. They found that 15% were at the 'entertainment-social' level of celebrity worship, 5% at the 'intense-personal' level and about 2% would be considered 'borderline-pathological'.

Another study by Maltby *et al.* (2001) found that celebrity worshippers had lower levels of psychological well-being than non-worshippers. They also found scores on the entertainment-social subscale of the CAS predicted patterns of social dysfunction, whereas scores on the intense-personal subscale predicted both depression and anxiety scores.

Note that the question refers to 'findings' and therefore procedural detail would not be creditworthy. There is no plurality in the question so just one study would be enough for full marks, but you'd have to know a lot about one study.

Part (b) is 102 words, just enough.

(c) Use research evidence to consider the value of evolutionary explanations of attraction to celebrity. (8 marks)

One evolutionary explanation is the evolved love of creativity. There is research evidence to support this. Shiraishi *et al.* (2006) discovered an enzyme correlated with novelty-seeking tendencies and a love of creativity. The fact that such tendencies have a genetic basis supports the view that they have been naturally selected.

A second evolutionary explanation is sexual selection. One problem with this explanation is that it suggests traits are preferred simply because they would have been 'attractive'. Such explanations do not provide an adequate adaptive reason to explain why traits, such as creativity in music, art and humour would have been attractive to ancestral members of the opposite sex.

A third explanation is celebrity gossip. There is research support for this. De Backer (2007) surveyed over 800 participants who reported that gossip was seen as a useful way of acquiring information about social group members. Media exposure was also found to be a strong predictor of interest in celebrities. Therefore, media exposure could lead to the misperception that celebrities were actually a part of the social network, thus explaining the interest in celebrity gossip.

There are contrasting social psychological explanations, such as the value of parasocial relationships because they make few demands. Such explanations have the advantage of being simpler and more desirable because of this (as argued by the concept of Occam's razor – the simplest answer is often correct).

Part (c) is all AO2, which can be quite challenging because you have to resist anything but the briefest identification of the explanation and then straight into your evaluation.

Part (c) is 229 words, which is in the right range for an 8-mark question (200–240 words).

(d) Maryann's mother is worried about Maryann's obsession with Jennifer Aniston and other celebrities. Use your knowledge of psychology research to suggest what Maryann's mother might do to encourage her daughter to reduce her feelings of attraction to celebrities. (8 marks)

Maryann's mother might discuss relationship issues with her daughter because one explanation for celebrity worship is that parasocial relationships are appealing, where there are no demands and no experience of rejection or criticism. Perhaps Maryanne needs help in coping with 'real' relationships.

Another feature of people who are attracted to celebrities is that they are more likely to be insecurely attached, as found in a study by Cole and Lewis (2007). Maryann's mother might learn how to give more unconditional love to make her daughter feel more securely attached and to meet her daughter's relationship needs.

It might also be helpful to reduce Mariann's media exposure, e.g. fewer celebrity magazines and less TV and DVDs. This is because research has found (De Backer, 2007) that people who are exposed to a lot of media tend to have a greater interest in celebrities and these celebrities become part of their social network, even substituting for the real thing.

One final possibility relates to novelty seeking. The evolutionary approach suggests that our interest in celebrities is due to the fact that creativity is an adaptive trait and therefore we are attracted to people who are creative, such as celebrities. It might be that people who are high in novelty-seeking are especially attracted to celebrities. So Maryann's mother might try to find other outlets for her daughter's need for novelty.

The key to obtaining marks for this question is to make sure you use the evidence to give advice to Maryann's mother. Both elements are needed for full marks – i.e. psychological evidence and application.

Part (d) is also worth 8 marks and is just right at 227 words.

Answer for you to mark

See page 175 for examiner's comments.

Question

(a) Researchers have more and more turned their attention to the effects of video games on behaviour, tending to use correlational studies in their research.'

(i) Explain some of the difficulties of conducting research into the effects of video games. (5 marks)

(ii) Discuss research into the effects of video games on behaviour. (4 marks + 5 marks)

(b) Outline explanations of why people are attracted to celebrity. (4 marks)

(c) An advertising company offers a prize to psychology students, asking them to suggest how the advertising company might increase the persuasiveness of their ads for greater appeal to students. The ideas must be based on psychological research.

Suggest at least **two** ways that TV advertisements could be made to be more persuasive. Refer to psychological research in your answer. (6 marks)

Student answer

Part (a) (i)

❶ *One difficulty is related to the fact that many studies are correlational. They just look at whether a person who watched violent programmes behaves violently. This kind of research doesn't show a cause and effect but often people assume that it does.*

❷ *Another problem with this kind of research is that some of the participants already have the behaviours so they won't develop them any more because they are already there. Whereas other people may be more impressionable and that is why they are affected more.*

❸ *Another issue is ethics because it is unethical to do experimental studies. Experimental studies would lack ecological validity and cannot be applied to real life.*

❹ *There is also the issue of publication bias where studies are published because they go along with the existing research.*

(129 words)

AO2 mark scheme for part (a) (i)

Ethical and/or methodological difficulties of conducting research in this area would be creditworthy.

A simple list of difficulties would not gain marks above basic (i.e. 2 marks).

5 marks is about 125–150 words.

Comments and marks for part (a) AO2

Guidance on marking is given on pages 6–11.

Mark	Analysis and understanding	Focus	Elaboration	Quality of written communication
5	Sound	Well-focused	Coherent	Fluent, effective use of terms
4–3	Reasonable	Generally focused	Reasonable	Clear, appropriate
2	Basic, superficial	Sometimes focused	Some evidence	Lacks clarity, limited use of terms
1	Rudimentary, limited understanding	Weak, muddled and incomplete	Not effective	Often unconnected assertions, errors
0	No creditworthy material			

Tick the terms you think apply to the student's answer.

The **AO2** mark I would give is ☐

Part (a) (ii)

❺ *Research has shown that playing video games has a negative effect on people. In one study by Gentile and Stone they found increases of levels of hostile feelings and aggression after people had been playing violent games compared to people playing non-violent games. They also found that levels of physiological arousal, such as heart rate and blood pressure increased too.*

❻ *One of the problems with that study was it was only short term. There have been other studies that have looked at the long-term effects of watching/playing video games. A study by Anderson and others studied children over a school year and found that the children exposed to violent video games were more aggressive. Their aggressiveness was determined by peer ratings.*

7 The problem with this research is that it is a correlation and doesn't show that the video games actually caused the aggression. You can't show cause and effect.

8 Gentile and Anderson also backed up this other research and found many studies had found a link between playing violent video games and behaving aggressively. Gentile has also put forward a model called the bi-directional model which says that the process goes two ways. It may be that playing violent games causes aggressive behaviour. But it could also be the other way round. It could be that some people who are more aggressive are more likely to play violent games. Also it could be that if you get involved with playing games you don't have much contact with anyone else and get more isolated and this might make people more aggressive.

9 There are the problems about long-term effects and there are other problems too, such as individual differences because we all react differently. There is also gender bias because more men than women play violent video games and culture bias because only people in some cultures play these games. (307 words)

AO1 mark scheme for part (a) (ii)

Description of relevant research findings – research refers to theories and/or studies.

4 marks is about 100–120 words.

AO2 mark scheme for part (a) (ii)

Methodological criticisms of research studies are likely to be used for evaluation but other issues, such as gender or culture bias could be used.

5 marks is about 125–150 words.

Part (b)

10 One way to explain attraction to celebrity is parasocial relationships. According to Horton and Wohl a parasocial relationship is one where an individual is attracted to someone else (usually a celebrity) who is unaware of their existence. Such relationships are appealing because they make few demands, there isn't the risk of rejection as in a real relationship.

11 One study of parasocial relationships by Schiappa showed that people made parasocial relationships with celebrities on TV who were attractive and also like them. They also had to feel that the character played by the celebrity was real.

12 Derrick found that having parasocial relationships seemed to increase people's levels of self-esteem. (107 words)

AO1 mark scheme for part (b)

Credit would be given here for the psychological factors/explanations rather than the research studies themselves.

4 marks is about 100–120 words.

Part (c)

13 One way would be to use people of the same age because research shows that people are more likely to imitate the behaviour of someone they identify with. It was Bandura who first identified social learning theory and said that we learn by vicarious reinforcement. So ads will be more persuasive if you are vicariously reinforced and it should be someone your own age.

14 A second way would be to try to be less strong in selling the product. One study found that older children trusted ads less if their persuasive intent is obvious. So ads should avoid trying to be too persuasive. (103 words)

AO2 mark scheme for part (c)

This question requires application of knowledge. If only research is described with no application then a maximum of 3 marks. Also if no research evidence is included then the maxium is 3 marks.

6 marks is about 150–180 words.

Comments and marks for part (a) (ii) and part (b) AO1

Mark	Knowledge and understanding	Accuracy	Organisation and structure
4	Reasonably thorough	Accurate	Coherent
3–2	Limited	Generally accurate	Reasonably coherent
1	Weak and muddled		
0	No creditworthy material		

The **AO1** mark I would give part (a) (ii) is ☐ The **AO1** mark I would give part (b) is ☐

Comments and marks for part (a) (ii) and part (c) AO2

Mark Part (a) (ii)	Mark Part (c)	Analysis and understanding	Focus	Elaboration	Quality of written communication	Part (c) only Application of knowledge
5	6	Sound	Well focused	Coherent	Fluent, effective use of terms	Effective
4–3	5–4	Reasonable	Generally focused	Reasonable	Clear, appropriate	Reasonably effective
2	3–2	Basic, superficial	Sometimes focused	Some evidence	Lacks clarity, limited use of terms	Basic
1	1	Rudimentary, limited understanding	Weak, muddled and incomplete	Not effective	Often unconnected assertions, errors	Weak, muddled and mainly irrelevant
0	0	No creditworthy material				

The **AO2** mark I would give part (a) (ii) is ☐ The **AO2** mark I would give part (c) is ☐

Chapter 14 The psychology of addictive behaviour

Section B Psychology in action

Exam questions in Section B of Unit 4 are different to other exam questions. They are usually divided into about four parts and contain stimulus material – see the example on the right. Therefore, in this chapter, we have focused on part questions rather than whole questions worth 24 marks.

The number of marks available for each part question varies enormously, as you can see from the selection of possible questions on this page. A useful rule is that you should write 25–30 words for every mark.

There have been changes to the specification from September 2011 – therefore the updated specification details here are slightly different to those in some editions of the *A2 Complete Companion*.

AQA style question

See student answer on page 150.

(a) Gambling has become an increasing problem in the UK, as well as the rest of the world. It is as much an addiction as hard drugs and can be equally disruptive.

(i) Explain some of the difficulties of gathering data about gambling. (5 marks)

(ii) Outline **one** explanation of gambling addiction. (4 marks)

(b) Discuss reasons why relapse occurs in people with addictive behaviour. (4 marks + 5 marks)

(c) Smoking is becoming a problem in younger children. A headteacher decides to discuss the problem with staff at his school and offers suggestions about how to deal with it.

Using your knowledge of biological and psychological interventions, outline some suggestions the headmaster could make. Refer to psychological research in your answer. (6 marks)

Division 1 Models of addictive behaviour

- **Biological, cognitive and learning approaches to explaining initiation, maintenance and relapse and their applications to smoking and gambling**

Possible exam questions for this division

Outline the learning model of addiction. (4 marks)	This part of the specification concerns three approaches to addiction. Therefore, questions may simply focus on one approach. The trick with answering this question is to reduce what you know about the learning approach to just 4 marks worth (about 100–120 words).
Outline and evaluate the cognitive approach to addiction. (4 marks + 8 marks)	Questions may be description only (as above) or description plus evaluation (as here), a kind of mini-essay. Such questions are typical of 'Psychology in action' where you won't find one blockbuster question. The evaluation may be balanced with the description (4 marks + 4 marks) or, as here, the evaluation may be worth more. You must take care to write the appropriate amount for the question asked; 8 marks is equivalent to about 200–240 words.
Public health campaigns aim to stop people becoming addicted in the first place because once a person starts it is very difficult to stop. Discuss reasons why relapse occurs in people with addictive behaviour. (5 marks + 5 marks)	A further feature of this part of the specification is that different aspects of addiction are identified – initiation, maintenance and relapse. This means that exam questions may be set on any one of these topics individually. The question on the left is also an example of one that has some stimulus material. In this case the question does not require you to engage with the stimulus part of the question.
Outline and evaluate the biological model as an explanation for the maintenance of **one** addictive behaviour. (4 marks + 4 marks)	This question requires you to specifically focus on one model and one aspect of addiction. It also requires AO1 + AO2, so there is a lot to think about in terms of planning exactly what to write.
A group of friends all decide to give up smoking. After 6 months three of them have not had a cigarette but the other two have relapsed. Explain why some of them have been successful whereas others haven't. (8 marks)	Some questions in this part of the specification require you to apply your knowledge, as in this case. Such application makes them an AO2 question (the injunction 'explain' can be AO1 or AO2). Be careful not to just describe the issues around relapse – you must use your knowledge to produce an effective answer.
Outline and evaluate **one** explanation of gambling addiction. (4 marks + 6 marks)	The final component of this part of the specification is the two named addictions. So questions may specifically refer to smoking or gambling. Questions will not require knowledge of any other addiction, although they might just ask about addiction in general – in which case material on either gambling or smoking would be creditworthy (as well as material on any other addiction).

Division 2 Vulnerability to addiction

- **Risk factors in the development of addiction, including stress, peers, age and personality**
- **Media influences on addictive behaviour**

Possible exam questions for this division

Question	Comment
Outline **two or more** risk factors in the development of addiction. (6 marks)	Straightforward questions such as this tend to be rare in this part of the specification, but you must be ready for them.
Discuss the role of stress in the development of addiction. (4 marks + 4 marks)	Four factors are named in the specification (stress, peers, age and personality) so you can expect questions that refer specifically to any one of these factors.
Thomas started smoking cigarettes when he was 16, like many of his friends. He is still at school and gets quite stressed about exams. He is popular with his friends and very outgoing. His hobbies include rock climbing and parachuting. His smoking habit has recently become excessive and he has found it difficult to even cut down on smoking, let alone give up. Using your knowledge of the psychology of addictive behaviour, explain some of the likely reasons why Thomas has become addicted to smoking. (6 marks)	This question requires an application of your knowledge. You will notice that the stimulus material about Thomas refers to the various risk factors you have studied. The question requires you to use your knowledge of these factors to explain Thomas's addiction. Marks are gained both for your psychological knowledge and also for the extent that you can use this effectively to engage with the stimulus part of the question.
Discuss media influences on addictive behaviour. (6 marks + 6 marks)	You know that 1 mark is about 25–30 words, so here you should write about 150–180 words for each assessment objective.
You used to see film stars smoking in movies but this is now considerably reduced, although there are still quite a few films where smoking is glamourised. Use your knowledge of research into media influence on addictive behaviour to explain why films might encourage young people to start smoking. (4 marks)	Questions are likely to be more similar to this rather than the straightforward variety above. Such questions often use a novel situation (such as 'films encouraging young people to smoke') and require you to use your knowledge to explain the novel situation. As the question is worth 4 marks you should write about 100–120 words.

Division 3 Reducing addictive behaviour

- **The theory of planned behaviour as a model for addiction prevention**
- **Types of intervention and their effectiveness, including biological, psychological and public health interventions**

Possible exam questions for this division

Question	Comment
Outline and evaluate the theory of planned behaviour. (4 marks + 4 marks)	It is possible that you will be asked a straightforward question just about the theory of planned behaviour. However, the specification entry says 'as a model for addiction prevention' so it is more likely that you will be asked to use your knowledge in this context, as in the next two questions. The final example also has stimulus material, so you would be required to engage with this when answering the question. The question therefore doesn't just ask you to use your knowledge but specifically requires you to use your knowledge about addiction to smoking.
Explain how the theory of planned behaviour has been used as a model for addiction prevention. (6 marks)	
Smoking is a major problem among young children and there are many campaigns to prevent young people becoming addicted. Outline a strategy, based on the theory of planned behaviour, that could be used to prevent young people becoming addicted to smoking. (6 marks)	
Discuss **one** type of intervention aimed at reducing addictive behaviour. (4 marks + 8 marks)	Questions may ask about types of intervention. You can consider their effectiveness in reducing addictive behaviour as part of the AO2 content.
Outline **one** biological intervention aimed at reducing addiction. (4 marks)	A further possibility is that the specific type of intervention may be identified as the specification names three types of intervention – biological, psychological and public health.
Consider the effectiveness of different types of intervention. Refer to psychological evidence in your answer. (10 marks)	Finally, questions may be set on effectiveness alone. The danger in such a question (which is AO2 with no AO1 element) is that you will waste time *describing* the interventions whereas only considerations of their effectiveness will be creditworthy.

Division 1 Models of addictive behaviour Answer plans

The questions on this page are derived in part from the examples on page 142. Some further ones have been added.

Answer plan 1 (short question)

Outline the cognitive model of addiction. (4 marks)

Cognitive model

AO1	Expectancy theory, expect benefits to outweigh costs, e.g. heavy drinkers have more positive expectations (Southwick *et al.*, 1981)
AO1	Maintenance – unconscious expectancies, primed to stop relapse, e.g. Tate *et al.* (1994) smokers, fewer side effects

Answer plan 2 (short question)

Outline **one** biological explanation for smoking addiction. (4 marks)

Biological model, smoking

AO1	Nicotine affects nAchRs, releases dopamine in nucleus accumbens, pleasure followed by lowered mood
AO1	Relapse – brain continues to receive difficult-to-resist signals of imminent reward

Work out your own plan for these questions and then write your answers.

(a) Using the biological model of addiction, explain why smokers might become addicted. (4 marks)

(b) Outline and evaluate the learning model of addiction. (4 marks + 8 marks)

(c) Use your knowledge of psychology to give advice to smokers about how they might prevent relapse. (8 marks)

Part (a) Biological model, initiation

AO1	
AO1	

Part (b) Learning model

AO1	
AO1	
AO2	
AO2	
AO2	
AO2	

Part (c) Smoking addiction, relapse

AO2	
AO2	
AO2	
AO2	

Answer plan 3 (mini-essay)

Discuss **one** explanation for the initiation of gambling addiction. (4 marks + 6 marks)

Gambling addiction, initiation

AO1	Genetics – Black *et al.* (2006) first degree relatives of pathological gamblers more likely to become gamblers
AO1	What might be inherited? Sensation-seeking (Zuckerman, 1979) or impulsivity (Alessi and Petry, 2003)
AO2	Family similarities may be a product of nurture rather than nature, but Slutske *et al.* (2000) 64% variation genetic
AO2	Lack of research support, e.g. Coventry and Brown (1993) off-track betting lower on sensation-seeking
AO2	Could be explained by learning model, operant conditioning, partial reinforcement, vicarious rewards

Answer plan 4 (mini-essay)

Discuss reasons why relapse occurs in people with addictive behaviour. (4 marks + 6 marks)

Relapse

AO1	Biological explanation – physiological dependence related to dopamine (reward circuit), signals of reward are hard to resist because of ethical issues
AO1	Learning explanation – avoidance of unpleasant withdrawal effects are negatively rewarding
AO2	Biological view based on animal studies, may not apply to humans (Hackam and Redelmeier, 2006); small samples
AO2	Dopamine role has implications for treatment, and such methods preferable to addict-as-delinquent
AO2	Operant conditioning is unconscious and can explain why people consciously wish to quit but relapse

Answer plan 5 (applying your knowledge)

Use your knowledge of psychology to explain why some people become addicted to smoking whereas others don't. (10 marks)

Smoking addiction, initiation

AO2	Inherited predisposition to addiction generally, e.g. Slutske *et al.* (2000) found 64% variation in gambling was genetic
AO2	Rewarding, nicotine leads to release of dopamine, stimulates brain's reward centres
AO2	Seen as more adult/rebellious, leads to peer popularity and willingness to accept unpleasantness (Jarvis, 2004)
AO2	Social learning theory, identification with media figures, vicarious reinforcement leads to outcome expectancies
AO2	Children of mothers who smoke during pregnancy are 2× more likely to become addicted (Buka *et al.*, 2003)

Answer plan 6 (applying your knowledge)

Use your knowledge about the initiation of addiction to suggest how gambling addiction might be avoided. (4 marks)

Gambling addiction, initiation

AO2	Find other outlets for sensation-seeking tendencies, linked to addiction (Zuckerman, 1979)
AO2	Reduce rewards experienced, e.g. make odds on fruit machines lower or restrict positive images on TV

Model answer

(a) Outline the cognitive model of addiction. (4 marks)

According to expectancy theory, which is an example of the cognitive approach, addiction develops because of expectations an individual has, where the benefits outweigh the costs. For example, heavier drinkers have been shown to have more positive expectancies about the effects of alcohol compared to light drinkers (Southwick *et al.*, 1981).

The cognitive model can also explain maintenance and relapse. Brandon (2004) suggests long-term addiction is influenced by unconscious expectancies involving automatic processing. Expectancies can also be manipulated to prevent relapse, e.g. Tate *et al.* (1994) told smokers they should expect no negative experiences when abstaining. This led to fewer reported somatic effects (e.g. the 'shakes') and psychological effects (e.g. mood disturbance) than a control group who were not so primed.

(b) Discuss reasons why relapse occurs in people with addictive behaviour. (4 marks + 6 marks)

According to biological models, relapse occurs because an addict has become physiologically dependent on a drug. This may happen because drugs (including nicotine in smoking) lead to the release of dopamine which stimulates the brain's reward circuit. If an addict tries to give up the brain continues to receive difficult-to-resist signals of imminent reward and this may lead to relapse in order to get the reward.

According to the learning model, after repeated exposure to certain drugs, withdrawal symptoms appear if the drug is discontinued. Because withdrawal effects are unpleasant, any reduction in these effects (from continuing to take the drug) acts as negative reinforcement. Negative reinforcement explains why many addicts relapse after a short period of abstinence.

One of the problems with research conclusions on the effects of dopamine is that they tend to be based on studies with non-human animals, for obvious ethical reasons. Hackam and Redelmeier (2006) argue that even high-quality animal studies of drug addiction rarely replicate in human research. There have, however, been some successes using primates but such research involves small samples because of ethical guidelines for using such animals.

The importance of dopamine in relapse has implications for treatment. It suggests that addiction may be treated by various pharmacological methods. Such an approach is certainly more progressive than those that treat drug addicts as delinquents who must be punished.

One of the strengths with the learning explanation for relapse is that operant conditioning requires no conscious awareness. This can help explain why addicts frequently experience a conflict between the conscious desire to restrain themselves from drinking or taking a drug and the unconscious motivational forces that impel them to continue.

(c) Use your knowledge of psychology to explain why some people become addicted to smoking whereas others don't. (10 marks)

People might become addicted to smoking because they have inherited a predisposition to addiction. Research has shown that many addictions have an underlying genetic component. For example, Slutske *et al.* (2000) found that 64% of the variation in risk for pathological gambling could be accounted for by genetic factors alone.

A second reason why some people become addicted is that they experience some reward from their behaviour, in this case smoking. Smoking may be rewarding because of the nicotine which affects certain receptors in the brain, leading to the release of dopamine which stimulates the brain's reward centres. This creates a short-term sense of pleasure.

Smoking may also be rewarding because the person who is smoking is seen as more grown up and also possibly more rebellious, and this promotes peer popularity. Jarvis (2004) argues that this image is sufficient for the novice smoker to tolerate the unpleasantness of the first few cigarettes, after which the physical effects of nicotine take over.

Social learning theory can be used to explain initiation of smoking. Some people will identify more with individuals they see in films who are smoking and this identification coupled with apparent vicarious reinforcement (it is the cool guys or girls who are smoking) leads to outcome expectancies which influence the individual's behaviour.

There is evidence that, if your mother smoked while she was pregnant with you, it is more likely that you will become addicted. Buka *et al.* (2003) found that, although an expectant mother's smoking during pregnancy did not increase the likelihood that her child will later try smoking or become a regular smoker, women who smoked heavily during pregnancy doubled the risk of their child becoming addicted to tobacco if they did begin smoking.

Parts (a), (b) and (c) would not form an exam question because the various part questions overlap in terms of the content required. The model answer just illustrates part questions for this division.

It probably pays to select a specific cognitive model rather than just generally describing the cognitive approach because this will give you more detail in your answer.

Part (a) is 4 marks and therefore should be 100–120 words. This answer is a perfect 121 words.

The whole point of drawing up the plans on the facing page is to provide a framework for your answer. It is important to follow your plan by writing one paragraph for every 2 marks worth.

Content that is AO2 should as far as possible begin with a clear lead-in phrase to make sure that examiners give you due AO2 credit.

Part (b) contains an appropriate amount of AO1 and AO2 – 118 and 159 words respectively (6 marks = 150–180 words).

Notice how some of the same material is included here as in part (b) above – but the material has been used differently. This is the key to 'applying your knowledge' questions, it is how you use the material that gains credit.

Part (c) is a total of 273 words – 10 marks worth should be about 250–300 words.

Division 2 Vulnerability to addiction Answer plans

The questions on this page are derived in part from the examples on page 143. Some further ones have been added.

Answer plan 1 (short question)

Outline the role of personality in the development of addiction. Refer to research evidence in your answer. (4 marks)

Role of personality

AO1	Sensation-seeking (Zuckerman, 1983), linked to extraversion (Eysenck, 1967), seek cortical arousal
AO1	Addictive personality – Cloniger (1967) novelty-seeking, harm avoidance (pessimism), reward dependence

Answer plan 2 (short question)

Outline **two** risk factors in the development of addiction. (4 marks)

Risk factors

AO1	Stress – daily hassles (NIDA, 1999) or trauma (PTSD in 30% drug addicts, e.g. Driessen *et al.*, (2008)
AO1	Peer pressure – smoking promotes popularity (McAlister *et al.*, 1984), modeling, social norms, social identity theory

Work out your own plan for these questions and then write your answers.

(a) Discuss the role of peers in the development of addiction. (4 marks + 6 marks)

(b) Explain why the media might influence people's attitudes about addictive behaviour. (4 marks)

(c) Outline and evaluate explanations for addiction to gambling. (4 marks + 6 marks)

Part (a) Role of peers

AO1	
AO1	
AO2	
AO2	

Part (b) Media influence

AO2	
AO2	

Part (c) Gambling addiction

AO1	
AO1	
AO2	
AO2	
AO2	

Answer plan 3 (mini-essay)

Discuss media influences on addictive behaviour. (6 marks + 6 marks)

Media influences

AO1	Drug addiction represented as interesting and a way of solving problems, e.g. Sulkunen (2007)
AO1	Negative consequences omitted, e.g. Gunaskera *et al.* (2005) therefore positive model
AO1	Can be used to change behaviour, e.g. antidrug ads on TV with Pablo the dog
AO2	Films do affect behaviour, e.g. Sargent and Hanewinkel (2009) exposure to smoking in films predicted later use
AO2	Contrary evidence, Boyd (2008) claims films do show negative aspects, e.g. prostitution, violence, moral decline
AO2	Drug campaigns may have negative effects (Hornik *et al.*, 2008) because create peer norms (Johnston *et al.*, 2002)

Answer plan 4 (mini-essay)

Discuss the role of stress in the development of addiction. (4 marks + 4 marks)

Role of stress

AO1	Everyday stress – coping with daily hassles contributes to initiation, maintenance and relapse (NIDA, 1999)
AO1	Traumatic stress, especially children (e.g. parental loss, child abuse) and in adults, PTSD linked to addiction
AO2	Research support, e.g. Driessen *et al.* (2008) PTSD in 30% drug addicts, 15% alcoholics
AO2	Individual differences, e.g. Cloniger (1987) Type 1 drink to relieve tension, Type 2 drink to relieve boredom

Answer plan 5 (applying your knowledge)

Using your knowledge of the psychology of addictive behaviour to explain some of the likely reasons why Gareth has become addicted to gambling. (6 marks)

Risk factors applied to gambling

AO2	Stress – coping with daily hassles contributes to initiation, maintenance and relapse (NIDA, 1999)
AO2	Peer influence – modeling, vicarious reinforcement, social norms and social identity (social identity theory)
AO2	Addictive personality, e.g. sensation-seeking to avoid boredom and seek novel experiences (Zuckerman, 1983)

Answer plan 6 (applying your knowledge)

Use your knowledge of research into media influence on addictive behaviour to explain why films might encourage young people to start smoking. (6 marks)

Media influences on smoking

AO2	Role model, social learning theory (Bandura, 1977), vicarious reinforcement
AO2	Peer influence, Johnston *et al.* (2002) antidrug campaigns fail because they create a peer norm
AO2	Glamorised image, Gunasekera *et al.* (2005) tobacco use portrayed without negative consequences

Model answer

(a) Outline the role of personality in the development of addiction. Refer to research evidence in your answer. (4 marks)

One personality trait linked to addiction is sensation-seeking. Zuckerman (1983) suggested individuals high in sensation-seeking have high susceptibility to boredom and seek novel experiences, and this predisposes them to seeking a high from addiction. Sensation-seeking is also linked to extraversion. According to Eysenck (1967) extraverts are chronically under-aroused and bored, seeking external stimulation to increase their cortical (brain) arousal.

Cloniger (1987) suggested that three personality traits predispose individuals to become addicted (the addictive personality). The first is novelty-seeking, which is similar to sensation-seeking. The second is harm avoidance, which includes worrying and being pessimistic. And the third is reward dependence – the extent to which an individual learns quickly from rewarding experiences and repeats behaviours that have been rewarded.

(b) Discuss the role of stress in the development of addiction. (4 marks + 4 marks)

Everyday stress may lead to addiction. People report that they drink, smoke, use drugs, gamble, etc. as a means of coping with daily hassles, such as relationship problems, money worries and workplace stress. Such stressors may contribute to initiation and continuation of addictions, as well as to relapse even after long periods of abstinence (NIDA, 1999).

Traumatic or severe stress may also be a contributory factor. People exposed to severe stress are more vulnerable to addictions, especially children who have experienced, for example, parental loss or child abuse. PTSD (post-traumatic stress disorder) has also been linked to addiction.

There is research support for the role of PTSD in addiction. Driessen *et al.* (2008) found that 30% of drug addicts and 15% of alcoholics also suffered from PTSD. However, the researchers found that exposure to 'mere trauma' (as distinct from PTSD) was not sufficient to lead to an addiction.

There are important individual differences in the role of stress in addiction. Stress creates a vulnerability in some but not all people. For example, Cloniger (1987) suggested that there are two different kinds of alcoholics: type 1 primarily drink to reduce tension and type 2 individuals drink primarily to relieve boredom (and have a tendency towards risk taking). Therefore, stress may explain vulnerability for some (the Type 1s) but not all people.

(c) Using your knowledge of the psychology of addictive behaviour, explain some of the likely reasons why Gareth has become addicted to gambling. (6 marks)

One reason might be that he is stressed. He might have a number of daily hassles, such as relationship problems, money worries and stress at work. Research by NIDA (1999) has found that such stressors may contribute to initiation and continuation of addictions, as well as to relapse even after long periods of abstinence.

A second reason might be that his peer group also gamble a lot. The influence of peers may be because they act as role models. Gareth imitates their behaviour because he sees their enjoyment (vicarious reinforcement). Gareth may also copy the behaviour of the group because, by adopting their social norms, he gains membership to the group and this gives him a social identity (social identity theory).

A third reason may be that he has an addictive personality, i.e. a tendency to become addicted to things, such as gambling, drugs, etc. Zuckerman (1983) suggested that individuals high in sensation-seeking seek novel experiences, and this would predispose them to activities, such as gambling. Once they start playing they would find it hard to give up.

(d) Use your knowledge of research into media influence on addictive behaviour to explain why films might encourage young people to start smoking. (6 marks)

One reason is that films may provide role models. If you see someone you respect and identify with who is smoking, this makes it likely that you will model your behaviour on theirs. This is part of social learning theory (Bandura, 1977). This is why fewer people are seen smoking in the films nowadays because the power of vicarious reinforcement was recognised.

A second reason is that films may enhance existing peer influences. In an interesting twist Johnston *et al.* (2002) suggested that the reason antidrug campaigns sometimes led to an increase (rather than decrease) in drug use was because such campaigns have an implicit message that drug use is commonplace , creating a peer norm. The same could apply to smoking.

A third reason is that films may paint a rather glamourised image. Gunasekera *et al.* (2005) found that films tended to portray addictions including tobacco use positively and omitted the negative consequences, such as the likely consequences of smoking (breathing difficulties, cancer, etc). However, in the US there are now guidelines for the portrayal of illegal drugs.

Parts (a), (b), (c) and (d) would not form an exam question because the various part questions overlap in terms of the content required. The model answer just illustrates part questions for this division.

Students often start their answers with definitions which do not gain marks unless specifically asked for in the question.

The question does not require you to outline more than one way that personality may be linked to addiction, but if you only cover one you may not have enough to write for 4 marks.

An answer for 4 marks should be about 100–120 words; the answer to part (a) is120 words.

AO2 paragraphs should, as far as possible start with a lead-in phrase and end with a conclusion ('so what').

The division between AO1 and AO2 material should reflect the marks available, in this case an equal amount (100–120 words of each). In fact there is slightly more AO2 content in the actual answer (120 words) but still there was time for a reasonable amount of AO1 (100 words).

Notice how some of the same material used above has been adapted slightly to be used effectively in the answer to part (c).

A 6-mark answer should be in the range of 150–180 words, and the answer to part (c) is appropriately 180 words.

The key point is to answer the question – many students just describe relevant research but fail to use it effectively.

Part (d) is an appropriate 179 words.

Division 3 Reducing addictive behaviour   Answer plans

The questions on this page are derived in part from the examples on page 143. Some further ones have been added.

Answer plan 1 (short question)

Outline how the theory of planned behaviour has been used as a model for addiction prevention. (4 marks)

Theory of planned behaviour

AO1	Behavioural attitudes – Slater *et al.* (2011) attitudes about marijuana, e.g. inconsistent with achieving aspirations
AO1	Subjective norms often inaccurate, expose to accurate statistical information (Wilson and Kolander, 2003)

Answer plan 2 (short question)

Outline **one** public health intervention aimed at reducing addiction. (4 marks)

Public health intervention

AO1	Quitline – advice over phone from counselor, may have callbacks to monitor progress
AO1	Stead *et al.* (2006) meta-analysis, 18,000 participants, repeated callbacks increased success by 50%

DIY

Work out your own plan for these questions and then write your answers.

(a) Outline **one** psychological intervention aimed at reducing addiction. (4 marks)

(b) Outline and evaluate **one** biological intervention aimed at reducing addiction. (4 marks + 4 marks)

(c) Evaluate the theory of planned behaviour as a model for addiction prevention. (6 marks)

(d) Consider how the theory of planned behaviour could be used to reduce gambling addiction. (6 marks)

Part (a) Psychological intervention

AO1	
AO1	

Part (b) Biological intervention

AO1	
AO1	
AO2	
AO2	

Part (c) Theory of planned behaviour

AO2	
AO2	
AO2	

Part (d) Applied to gambling

AO2	
AO2	
AO2	

Answer plan 3 (mini-essay)

Outline and evaluate how the theory of planned behaviour has been used as a model for addiction prevention. (4 marks + 4 marks)

Theory of planned behaviour

AO1	Behavioural attitudes – Slater *et al.* (2011) attitudes about marijuana, e.g. inconsistent with achieving aspirations
AO1	Subjective norms often inaccurate, expose to accurate statistical information (Wilson and Kolander, 2003)
AO2	Too rational – emotions or irrational thinking important, effects can't be anticipated (Armitage *et al.*, 1999)
AO2	Predicts intentions rather than behaviour change (Armitage and Conner, 2001)

Answer plan 4 (mini-essay)

Discuss types of intervention aimed at reducing addictive behaviour. (4 marks + 8 marks)

Types of intervention

AO1	Biological, e.g. methadone for heroin, given in increasing amounts to increase tolerance and then decreased
AO1	Quitline – advice over phone from counselor, may have callbacks to monitor progress
AO2	Problems with methadone – addiction, deaths (over 300 in 2007 in UK) and sales on black market for £2
AO2	Psychological methods may be preferable because address original problem, e.g. Sylvain *et al.* (1997)
AO2	Quitline supported by Stead *et al.* (2006) meta-analysis, 18,000 participants, repeated callbacks increased success by 50%
AO2	Beckham *et al.* (2008) combination of Quitline and nicotine replacement therapy effective for US military veterans

Answer plan 5 (evaluation only)

Refer to psychological evidence in your answer. (10 marks)

Types of intervention

AO2	Problems with methadone – addiction, deaths (over 300 in 2007 in UK) and sales on black market for £2
AO2	Psychological methods may be preferable because address original problem, e.g. Sylvain *et al.* (1997)
AO2	Quitline supported by Stead *et al.* (2006) meta-analysis, 18,000 participants, repeated callbacks increased success by 50%
AO2	Beckham *et al.* (2008) combination of Quitline and nicotine replacement therapy effective for US military veterans
AO2	Clinician's illusion (Cohen and Cohen, 1984), treating just severe cases creates the belief that addictions untreatable

Answer plan 6 (applying your knowledge)

Design a campaign to reduce smoking addiction. The campaign should be based on the theory of planned behaviour. (6 marks)

Theory of planned behaviour applied to smoking

AO2	Behavioural attitude – help smokers recognise the dangers of smoking, e.g. visit chronic smokers
AO2	Subjective norms – provide actual data on how many people smoke, and how easy it is to change social norms
AO2	Perceived behavioural control – take small steps to demonstrate self-control and confidence in own will power

Model answer

(a) Outline how the theory of planned behaviour has been used as a model for addiction prevention. (4 marks)

One assumption of the theory of planned behaviour (TPB) is that behavioural attitudes lead to intentions and subsequently to behaviour. Therefore, if such attitudes are changed this should lead to changes in behaviour. A recent campaign to reduce marijuana addiction targeted attitudes (e.g. it is inconsistent with achieving aspirations) and it is suggested that this may be responsible for its success (Slater *et al.*, 2011).

A second assumption of the TPB is that subjective norms underlie intentions and behaviour. Often people have a false idea of how common a particular behaviour is, such as smoking in adolescents. Many adolescents might believe it is relatively common (their subjective norm). Therefore, campaigns should aim to expose people to accurate statistical information (Wilson and Kolander, 2003).

(b) Outline **one** public health intervention aimed at reducing addiction. (4 marks)

One example of a public health intervention is the Quitline service offered over the telephone. People can just ring up once for advice about giving up smoking. The service is confidential and also involves callbacks if desired from trained counselors to monitor your progress.

A meta-analysis by Stead *et al.* (2006) included over 18,000 participants. The study illustrated how the intervention works. People who received repeated telephone calls from a counsellor increased their odds of stopping smoking by 50% compared to smokers who only received self-help materials and/or brief counselling. Stead *et al.* concluded that multiple callback counselling improves the long-term probability of cessation for smokers who contact Quitline services.

(c) Consider the effectiveness of different types of intervention. Refer to psychological evidence in your answer. (10 marks)

One intervention is the use of methadone to treat heroin. There are problems with this approach. Some drug addicts can become as reliant on methadone as they were on heroin, thereby substituting one addiction for another. Methadone is not without dangers, in the UK in 2007 there were 300 methadone-related deaths. A further problem is that addicts sell methadone on the black market for only £2.

Psychological methods may be more effective than biological ones because some of them specifically target underlying problems. Without this the individual may simply return to their addiction (or another addiction). Support for psychological methods comes from Sylvain *et al.* (1997) who studied gamblers given cognitive therapy, social skills training and relapse prevention resulting in improvements after treatment. These gains were maintained at a one-year follow-up.

The use of quitlines for dealing with smoking addiction has proved relatively effective, especially when it involves callbacks from trained counsellors. This was shown in a meta-analysis by Stead *et al.* (2006) with over 18,000 participants. People who received repeated telephone calls from a counsellor increased their odds of stopping smoking by 50% compared to smokers who only received self-help materials and/or brief counselling.

Further support for the Quitline approach comes from Beckham *et al.* (2008) who found that a combination of Quitline counselling and nicotine replacement therapy was highly effective in treating US military veterans.

One issue related to the effectiveness of any intervention is the 'clinician's illusion'. Cohen and Cohen (1984) argue that many clinicians believe that addictions are difficult to treat because they only tend to come across addicts when their condition is well advanced, too severe to effectively respond to treatment. This leads clinicians, and people in general, to believe that addiction can't be treated and undermines the effectiveness of any therapy.

(d) Design a campaign to reduce smoking addiction. The campaign should be based on the theory of planned behaviour. (6 marks)

Since my campaign is based on the theory of planned behaviour I would target the three main assumptions of the theory. First, I would target behavioural attitudes, i.e. people's attitudes towards the consequences of smoking. This would involve helping people to accept the dangers of smoking, perhaps visiting people in hospital who are chronic smokers to see the damage caused.

Second, the campaign should target subjective norms. Individuals may belong to social groups where smoking is an accepted norm but you can show them that many social groups now have no smokers. It just takes one or two people to change the social norms in a group. They should be given actual data.

Third, perceived behavioural control is important to make smokers feel they do have control over their smoking. One way to do this is to give them small tasks, such as not smoking for an hour, to show them that they do have some will power. Extend this a little bit everyday.

Parts (a), (b), (c) and (d) would not form an exam question because the various part questions overlap in terms of the content required. The model answer just illustrates part questions for this division.

Notice how the theory is not simply described. Assumptions of the theory have been applied to addiction prevention, as required in the question.

Part (a) is 123 words, an appropriate length for a 4-mark question.

It is not easy to write 100+ words about one intervention. If you use a research study as a means of supplementing your description make sure it is an illustration rather than supporting research evidence (which would be more AO2 than AO1).

Part (b) is 111 words, again an appropriate length for 4 marks.

Part (c) is all AO2, which can be quite challenging because you have to resist anything but the briefest identification of the intervention and then go straight into your evaluation.

Not all paragraphs have to be 50 words, provided the overall average is about this length.

Part (c) should be between 250 and 300 words because it is worth 10 marks – in fact it is 297 words.

The answer is clearly focused on smoking and a practical application of the theory.

Part (d) is 161 words, well within the range for a 6-mark question.

Answer for you to mark

See page 175 for examiner's comments.

Question

(a) (i) Explain some of the difficulties of gathering data about gambling. (5 marks)

(ii) Outline **one** explanation of gambling addiction. (4 marks)

(b) Discuss reasons why relapse occurs in people with addictive behaviour. (4 marks + 5 marks)

(c) Smoking is becoming a problem in younger children. A headteacher decides to discuss the problem with staff at his school and offer suggestions about how to deal with it.

Using your knowledge of biological and psychological interventions, outline some suggestions the headmaster could make. Refer to psychological research in your answer. (6 marks)

Student answer

Part (a) (i)

❶ One difficulty encountered would be that people are not always truthful about what they actually do when gambling. They might feel ashamed of their behaviour so they underestimate it so they 'look' better.

❷ Another possible problem is that the data changes in every study so you can't tell what the right answer is. Every study produces a different answer so it is difficult to know what is relevant or not.

(70 words)

AO2 mark scheme for part (a) (i)

Ethical and/or methodological difficulties of gathering data are creditworthy.

A simple list of difficulties would not gain marks above basic (i.e. 2 marks).

5 marks is about 125–150 words.

Comments and marks for part (a) AO2

Guidance on marking is given on pages 6–11.

Tick the terms you think apply to the student's answer.

Mark	Analysis and Understanding	Focus	Elaboration	Quality of written communication
5	Sound	Well focused	Coherent	Fluent, effective use of terms
4–3	Reasonable	Generally focused	Reasonable	Clear, appropriate
2	Basic, superficial	Sometimes focused	Some evidence	Lacks clarity, limited use of terms
1	Rudimentary, limited understanding	Weak, muddled and incomplete	Not effective	Often unconnected assertions, errors
0	No creditworthy material			

The **AO2** mark I would give is ☐

Part (a) (ii)

❸ One explanation for gambling addiction is that you inherit it. This is a genetic explanation. It has been found that addiction to gambling does seem to run in families. This is supported by a study by Shah et al. who conducted a twin study and found evidence of genetic factors in men.

❹ People with a gambling addiction have been found to have certain genes related to abnormal production of dopamine. They have a particular D_2 receptor gene which increases the excitement they experience when gambling. Addicts, like addicted gamblers, may have too few dopamine receptors and therefore addiction increases their sense of pleasure.

(103 words)

AO1 mark scheme for part (a) (ii)

The explanation could cover initiation, and/or maintenance and/or relapse.

It would be creditworthy to include several explanations under one umbrella, e.g. discuss the biological explanation and include genetics and the dopamine hypothesis – as long as this is made explicit.

4 marks is about 100–120 words.

Part (b)

❺ Relapse refers to the situation where an addict has given up his addiction for a period of time but restarts the addiction. One of the explanations for relapse is in behaviourist terms. The addiction may begin because of classical conditioning. A drug addict associates the drug with pleasure and therefore repeats it. The addiction is maintained because of the threat of withdrawal. According to West the drug effect is an unconditioned stimulus which challenges the internal regulation of the body. The body produces an unconditioned response to try to restore equilibrium. Any stimulus that precedes the drug becomes a conditioned stimulus leading to a conditioned response in anticipation of the effects of the drug. Conditioned responses in the absence of the drug are experienced as withdrawal and therefore the person is motivated to take the drug again.

6 This approach to relapse is reductionist because it explains a complex human behaviour in simple terms. If conditioning was the explanation for addiction then everyone who enjoyed a drug would become an addict, so it must be more complex.

7 The biological approach to relapse suggests that you are born with certain genes, such as a variant of the D_2 receptor gene, and this makes it more likely that you will become an addict because you need more rewards than people without the variant. So relapse would be predicted because it is harder for such people to stay away from their addiction.

8 The cognitive approach says it is all related to the way you think. People choose to take drugs or smoke and they weigh up the costs and benefits. So it is a rational choice. Such people may decide to give up for rational reasons too, for example they might have become convinced that smoking was bad for you but then they start again because they rationalise it differently. Or it could be that other factors overwhelm them, such as environmental cues, so they aren't so rational after all.

(225 words)

Part (c)

9 One biological intervention would be to deal with the nicotine addiction. The children could be addicted to nicotine and therefore the school could recommend that the children try nicotine patches or nicotine substitutes. This would reduce their craving for cigarettes and they then might be more willing to give up.

10 One psychological intervention is to reduce addiction using rewards. This is based on the fact that smoking addiction may have been acquired because of reinforcement and therefore it can be reduced in the same one. An important reward is the admiration of peers so it may be useful to target the whole peer group so they praise giving up instead of admiring smoking.

11 Rewards could also be given by creating a kind of addicts anonymous where those children committed to giving up meet regularly. The school could even offer some kind of incentive for every week without a cigarette, such as leaving school early. Of course the problem would be that the children might lie about having given up.

(168 words)

AO1 mark scheme for part (b)

At least two explanations of relapse should be covered for full marks.

Even though the question is framed in the context of smoking any addiction is creditworthy.

4 marks is about 100–120 words.

AO2 mark scheme for part (b)

Research studies may be used for evaluation as well as, for example, considerations of individual differences and practical applications.

5 marks is about 125–150 words.

AO2 mark scheme for part (c)

This question requires application of knowledge. If only research is described with no application then the maximum is 3 marks. Also if no research evidence is included then the maxium is 3 marks.

At least one biological and one psychological intervention must be included otherwise the answer constitutes a partial performance and the maximum would be 4 marks.

6 marks is about 150–180 words.

Comments and marks for part (a) (ii) and part (b) AO1

Mark	Knowledge and understanding	Accuracy	Organisation and structure
4	Reasonably thorough	Accurate	Coherent
3–2	Limited	Generally accurate	Reasonably coherent
1	Weak and muddled		
0	No creditworthy material		

The **AO1** mark I would give part (a) (ii) is ☐ The **AO1** mark I would give part (b) is ☐

Comments and marks for part (b) and part (c) AO2

Mark		Analysis and understanding	Focus	Elaboration	Quality of written communication	Part (c) only Application of knowledge
Part (a) (ii)	Part (c)					
5	6	Sound	Well-focused	Coherent	Fluent, effective use of terms	Effective
4–3	5–4	Reasonable	Generally focused	Reasonable	Clear, appropriate	Reasonably effective
2	3–2	Basic, superficial	Sometimes focused	Some evidence	Lacks clarity, limited use of terms	Basic
1	1	Rudimentary, limited understanding	Weak, muddled and incomplete	Not effective	Often unconnected assertions, errors	Weak, muddled and mainly irrelevant
0	0	No creditworthy material				

The **AO2** mark I would give part (b) is ☐ The **AO2** mark I would give part (c) is ☐

Chapter 15 Anomalistic psychology

There have been changes to the specification from September 2011 – therefore the updated specification details here are slightly different to those in some editions of the *A2 Complete Companion*.

Section B Psychology in action

Exam questions in Section B of Unit 4 are different from other exam questions. They are usually divided into about four parts and contain stimulus material – see the example on the right.

Therefore, in this chapter, we have focused on part questions rather than whole questions worth 24 marks.

The number of marks available for each part question varies enormously, as you can see from the selection of possible questions on this page. A useful rule is that you should write 25–30 words for every mark.

AQA style question

See student answer on page 160.

(a) Explain what is meant by pseudoscience. (4 marks)

(b) There are many different kinds os anomalous experience. Probably one of the best known is ESP – the ability of one person to read the thoughts of another.

Explain how a researcher could use the Ganzfeld procedure to investigate ESP. (6 marks)

(c) A psychologist recently presented a TV programme about anomalous experiences, observing that many people report having had them. The psychologist suggested that the key question is not whether or not they did have such experiences but it is about why they believe in them whereas others don't.

Outline **two or more** explanations for anomalous experience. (4 marks)

(d) Consider how explanations can be used to understand belief in psychic mediumship. (10 marks)

Division 1 The study of anomalous experience

- **Pseudoscience and the scientific status of parapsychology**
- **Methodological issues related to the study of paranormal cognition (ESP, including Ganzfeld) and paranormal action (psychokinesis)**

Possible exam questions for this division

Explain what is meant by pseudoscience. (5 marks)	The injunction 'explain' can be AO1 or AO2. You can work out which it is when you see the part question in the context of the whole question (see above) – 'explain' is AO1 in part (a) and AO2 in part (b). However, in the case of these questions the distinction between AO1 or AO2 is often not critical, just answer the question.
Many people claim to have had anomalous experiences. Psychologists have tried to investigate these experiences and provide possible explanations. Discuss the scientific status of parapsychology. (4 marks + 6 marks)	Mini-essays are typical of 'Psychology in action' where you won't find one blockbuster question. Elements of both AO1 and AO2 are required. Often these are balanced (as in the next question) though sometimes the split might be 4 marks + 6 marks. You should reflect this split in the way you answer the question.
Psychologists use the Ganzfeld method to investigate ESP. Outline and evaluate the Ganzfeld method. (5 marks + 5 marks)	You know that 1 mark is about 25–30 words, so here you should write about 125–150 words of AO1 and the same for AO2.
There are many different kinds of anomalous experience. Probably one of the best known is ESP – the ability of one person to read the thoughts of another. Explain how a researcher could use the Ganzfeld procedure to investigate ESP. (6 marks)	Questions often begin with stimulus material. Sometimes the stimulus material is mainly 'scene setting', as in this question. The stimulus part of the question does serve to remind you what the Ganzfeld method is used for (testing psychic powers). Sometimes the stimulus material contains material crucial to answering the question – see examples on the facing page. In such cases you must engage with the stimulus part of the question.
Discuss methodological issues related to paranormal action (psychokinesis). (4 marks + 6 marks)	It is always tempting to take the easiest course of action – in this case writing a *description* of psychokinesis. However, that would gain no marks. The focus on this part of the specification is on how it is *studied* rather than what it is.
Explain how psychologists have investigated paranormal cognition and action. (6 marks)	Always remember that questions can use any phrases from any part of the specification, so make sure you are familiar with the wording of the specification.

Division 2 Explanations for anomalous experience

- **The role of coincidence and probability judgements in anomalous experience**
- **Explanations for superstitious behaviour and magical thinking**
- **Personality factors underlying anomalous experience**

Possible exam questions for this division

What has research shown about personality factors underlying anomalous experience? (5 marks)	Some questions may be relatively straightforward, not requiring application of knowledge but simply description.
A recent television programme showed a large audience watching a psychic healer successfully treating certain members of the audience. Many people were very impressed by this demonstration and expressed their total belief in the healer's powers. Outline **two or more** factors underlying belief in psychic healing. (4 marks)	The topics in division 2 lend themselves to stimulus materials, where a situation is described and you are asked to use your knowledge of anomalous experience to explain the stimulus part of the question. 'Two or more' means that two factors would be sufficient for full marks.
Some of the people watching the television show about psychic healing were not impressed. When interviewed some of the non-believers said they think all anomalous phenomena are not based in fact. Suggest how personality factors might explain why these viewers do not have anomalous beliefs. (5 marks)	Note the slight twist in the question – this time you are asked to explain why some people are *not* believers. Always pay attention to the number of marks available and write sufficient and appropriate material.
Most research on anomalous experience requires a researcher to assess whether participants believe or don't believe. In order to do this the researchers use scales that assess belief in the paranormal. Explain why it is important to use a scale that is valid and reliable when measuring paranormal beliefs. (2 marks + 2 marks)	Questions sometimes make links to the research methods part of the specification. In this case the 2 marks + 2 marks refers to 2 marks for explaining the concepts of reliability and validity, and 2 marks for explaining why they are important.
Lachlan is a keen footballer. In one of the first games he played at primary school he wore socks that didn't match and he scored three goals. Ever since he has always worn odd socks when playing a football game and, in fact, he did the same when taking his exams. How might a psychologist explain Lachlan's superstitious behaviour? (5 marks)	This is a good example of an 'applying your knowledge' question – use what you know about explanations for superstitious behaviour to explain Lachlan's behaviour.
A recent survey showed that children are more likely to believe in anomalous experience than adults. Explain how the role of coincidence **and/or** probability judgements might be used to explain these findings. (6 marks)	Remember that 'and/or' means that you don't have to cover both for full marks. In fact, given that the question is worth just 6 marks you may do better to focus on only one or the other.

Division 3 Research into exceptional experience

- **Psychological research into and explanations for psychic healing, near death and out-of-body experiences, and psychic mediumship**

Possible exam questions for this division

Outline and evaluate psychological research into belief in out-of-body experiences **and/or** near death experiences. (4 marks + 6 marks) Discuss what research into exceptional experience has shown us about out-of-body experiences. (4 marks + 6 marks)	Questions in this division are likely to ask for description and evaluation of research into one of the four named areas. Take care to write sufficient material for the marks available – here you should write about 100–120 words AO1 and 150–180 words AO2.
Consider how explanations for anomalous experience can be used to understand belief in psychic mediumship. (10 marks)	Questions may link divisions, for example asking you to use your knowledge about underlying factors to explain belief in psychic healing.
Outline **one or more** explanations of out-of-body experiences. (4 marks)	Explanations are mentioned in the specification for division 3 and therefore may be required instead of the more general 'research' – the term 'research' means that both explanations and studies would be creditworthy.

Division 1 The study of anomalous experience Answer plans

The questions on this page are derived in part from the examples on page 152. Some further ones have been added.

Answer plan 1 (short question)
Explain what is meant by pseudoscience. (5 marks)

Pseudoscience

AO1	Hypothesis non-falsifiable, e.g. presence of skeptics cause phenomena to disappear
AO1	Lacks carefully controlled, replicable research
AO1	Lacks explanatory framework

Answer plan 2 (short question)
Explain how a psychologist could use the Ganzfeld method to investigate paranormal cognition. (6 marks)

Ganzfeld method

AO1	Receiver – isolated from sensory information (eyes, ears)
AO1	Sender 'sends' an image to receiver
AO1	Independent judge matches receiver's descriptions to images sent

Work out your own plan for these questions and then write your answers.

(a) Explain what is meant by science. (4 marks)
(b) Discuss methodological issues in the study of ESP. (4 marks + 6 marks)
(c) Evaluate research related to psychokinesis. (10 marks)

Part (a) Science

AO1
AO1

Part (b) Methodological issues in ESP research

AO1
AO1
AO2
AO2
AO2

Part (c) Psychokinesis

AO2
AO2
AO2
AO2
AO2

Answer plan 3 (evaluation only)
Evaluate research related to the Ganzfeld studies. (10 marks)

Ganzfeld studies

AO2	Research challenge, e.g. Milton and Wiseman (1999) found no significant Ganzfeld effects
AO2	Carroll (2003) subjective interpretations because receiver's scene involves various images
AO2	Researcher bias, e.g. positive results from believers due to encouraging elaboration (Wooffitt, 2007)
AO2	File drawer effect, removes studies from a meta-analysis with negative findings
AO2	Lacks an explanatory framework (a pseudoscience)

Answer plan 4 (mini-essay)
Outline and evaluate the Ganzfeld method. (4 marks + 5 marks)

Ganzfeld method

AO1	Receiver – isolated from sensory information (eyes, ears)
AO1	Sender 'sends' an image, independent judge matches receiver's descriptions to images sent
AO2	Carroll (2003) subjective interpretations because receiver's scene involves various images
AO2	Researcher bias, e.g. positive results from believers due to encouraging elaboration (Wooffitt, 2007)
AO2	File drawer effect, removes studies from a meta-analysis with negative findings

Answer plan 5 (mini-essay)
Discuss the scientific status of research into anomalous experience. (4 marks + 6 marks)

Scientific status

AO1	Research base, e.g. Honorton (1985) 28 Ganzfeld studies
AO1	Pseudoscience, e.g. lacks explanatory framework
AO2	Research challenge, e.g. Milton and Wiseman (1999) found no significant Ganzfeld effects
AO2	Methodological flaws, e.g. Carroll (2003) subjective interpretations because receiver's scene involves various images
AO2	Other areas of psychology are also accused of being a pseudoscience

Answer plan 6 (mini-essay)
Discuss methodological issues related to paranormal action (psychokinesis). (4 marks + 6 marks)

Psychokinesis

AO1	Researcher bias, participant expectation
AO1	Effect sizes for micro-PK trials
AO2	Research suppor for participant expectation, Wiseman and Greening (2005) some participants told spoon continuing to bend
AO2	Effect sizes should be increasing not decreasing (Bierman, 2000)
AO2	Standards should be high because effects violate physics (Sagan, 1995)

Model answer

(a) Explain what is meant by pseudoscience. (5 marks)

Pseudoscientific studies often have hypotheses that are not falsifiable. For example, a researcher may find no evidence of ESP but then claim that the lack of supporting evidence occurs because the presence of skeptics causes the phenomena to disappear. This means that whatever happens their belief is supported.

Pseudoscience lacks carefully controlled, replicable research. Results may appear impressive but may lack control of, for example, experimenter bias where the experimenter's expectations influence the participant's behaviour. Also replication is important in validating findings. If a study is replicated but the original results are not confirmed this puts the original results in doubt.

Pseudosciences lack a theory to explain the effects. The aim of scientific research is to construct explanations for observations made about the world. Many paranormal phenomena have not, as yet, been given explanations that are likely.

Parts (a), (b) and (c) would not form an exam question because the various part questions overlap in terms of the content required. The model answer just illustrates part questions for this division.

For full marks it is important to explain each point rather than just provide a list.

In part (a) there are about 130 words.

(b) Outline and evaluate the Ganzfeld method. (4 marks + 5 marks)

In a Ganzfeld study the receiver is typically isolated in a red-lit room with half table tennis balls taped over their eyes and earphones playing white noise to cut out sensory information. The receiver is placed in a situation of sensory deprivation so that telepathic messages can be read more clearly.

The sender is in another room or location. He/she may be thinking about a picture randomly selected from four other pictures. Or another method is where the sender goes to a remote location and 'sends' what they are seeing. The receiver describes what he/she is receiving. At the end an independent judge is required to match the receiver's descriptions to the images sent in order to score a hit. If the receiver is really able to read the thoughts of others, he/she should be able, over several trials, to pick the target correctly at a greater than chance level.

An important methodological problem is that the technique involves the receiver describing the scene that is being sent. This description is often quite wordy and may actually involve a number of images. The independent judge then has to match the received description to images that were sent. There is clearly scope for subjective interpretation about what counts as a match (Carroll, 2003). This would explain why there are sometimes better than chance results.

A further problem is researcher bias. For example, Wooffitt (2007) analysed Ganzfeld interviews and found that sceptical researchers didn't encourage the 'receivers' to elaborate their images whereas interviewers who believed in psi often did which led to more positive results. This means that encouragement affected the results, a kind of researcher bias.

Another issue is something called the file drawer effect. Most of the reports of Ganzfeld studies are reviews (or meta-analyses). The outcomes of such reviews change if some studies are removed (the 'file drawer effect', referring to researchers filing away studies with negative outcomes). The views of a researcher may influence which studies are left in or out and thus bias results.

Always try to use separate paragraphs so the examiner can see you have identified and explained various distinct aspects of the topic.

As always you should use lead-in phrases to flag up AO2 paragraphs, and try to finish the paragraph off with a 'so what' comment.

In part (b) there are about 150 words of AO1 and 180 of AO2 – slightly more than necessary for a question worth 5 marks + 5 marks.

Essentially you should write 25–30 words per mark.

(c) Discuss methodological issues in the study of psychokinesis. (4 marks + 6 marks)

One methodological issue is researcher bias. A research's expectations may influence the way that participants behave. Equally there is a problem with participants' expectations. This means that if either a researcher or a participant believes in psychokinessis, such a belief is likely to lead to changes in the results.

A second methodological issue is the effect size. Research on micro-PK (predicting the outcome of a random number generator) has produced small effect sizes for individual trials but when added across trials these can appear quite large and impress people.

There is research support for the problems with researcher bias and participant expectation. Wiseman and Greening (2005) showed participants a video where a fake psychic placed a bent key on a table. In once condition the participants heard him say that the key was continuing to bend – these participants later were more likely to report further bending than participants in a no-expectation condition. This shows that expectations did influence results.

In terms of effect sizes one way to evaluate this is to consider the fact that there has actually been a steady decline in the effect size (Bierman, 2000). Usually, if there is a real effect, the size of the effect becomes greater over time because scientists are progressively better able to identify and control extraneous variables. By contrast, increasing control has had the opposite effect in psychokinesis research – leading to smaller effect sizes which suggests that the phenomena are not real.

The issue of sound methodologies is especially important in this area of research. Sagan (1995) argued that a higher standard of proof is required when investigating claims that violate the laws of physics, such as research on psychokinesis.

It would be easier to describe studies of psychokinesis here – but not creditworthy. The question requires a description of the methodological issues, and then an evaluation of these.

It always helps to use the question wording in your first sentence to keep you straight.

Part (c) – the overall length for a 10-mark answer should be 250–300 words, and this one is 279 words.

The AO1:AO2 division appropriately reflects the marks available for each assessment objective.

Division 2 Explanations for anomalous experience Answer plans

The questions on this page are derived in part from the examples on page 153. Some further ones have been added.

Answer plan 1 (short question)
Outline **two or more** factors underlying belief in anomalous experience. (4 marks)

Factors underlying belief

AO1	Coincidence, seeing patterns where none exist
AO1	Personality, e.g. fantasy proneness

Answer plan 2 (short question)
What has research shown about personality factors underlying anomalous experience? (5 marks)

Personality factors

AO1	Neuroticism, e.g. Williams *et al.* (2007) tested 300 children, + .32 correlation
AO1	Fantasy proneness, e.g. Wiseman *et al.* (2003) deep absorption
AO1	Locus of control, e.g. Allen and Lester (1994)

Work out your own plan for these questions and then write your answer.

(a) What has research shown about the role of coincidence in anomalous behaviour? (4 marks)

(b) Ted wears odd socks when taking exams because he believes this will guarantee success. Suggest how both superstition and magical thinking can explain Ted's behaviour. (8 marks)

(c) Outline and evaluate explanations for the role of personality factors in anomalous experience. (4 marks + 8 marks)

Part (a) Coincidence

AO1	
AO1	

Part (b) Superstition and magical thinking

AO2	
AO2	
AO2	
AO2	

Part (c) Personality factors

AO1	
AO1	
AO2	
AO2	
AO2	

Answer plan 3 (applying your knowledge)
'Sally takes her childhood teddy bear into all her exams for good luck.'
Suggest how magical thinking might explain Sally's behaviour. (5 marks)

Magical thinking

AO2	Sally might need defense mechanism to cope with anxiety (Freud, 1913)
AO2	Animism, pre-operational thinking (Piaget, 1954), teddy bear knows what Sally is feeling
AO2	Law of contagion, Sally may make link to past good events

Answer plan 4 (mini-essay)
Lachlan is a keen footballer. In one of the first games he played at primary school he wore socks that didn't match and he scored three goals. Ever since he has always worn odd socks when playing a football game and, in fact, he did the same when taking his exams.
How might a psychologist explain Lachlan's superstitious behaviour? (5 marks)

Superstitious behaviour

AO2	Evolutionary – Type 1 error is adaptive
AO2	Behaviourist – operant conditioning (Skinner, 1947), maintained through negative reinforcement (Mowrer, 1947)
AO2	Illusion of control, e.g. Witson and Galinsky (2008)

Answer plan 5 (applying your knowledge)
Abbie, Lachlan's friend, cannot understand why he is so upset. She has worked hard and revised thoroughly and does not feel that she needs a T-shirt or anything else to get her through the exam.
Suggest how personality factors might explain why Abbie does not have anomalous beliefs. (5 marks)

Personality factors

AO2	Abbie might not be neurotic, tending towards more positive thinking
AO2	Abbie might not be fantasy prone, less suggestible and more focused
AO2	Abbie might have an internal locus of control, therefore no need for external token of luck

Answer plan 6 (mini-essay)
Discuss the role of probability judgements in anomalous experience. (4 marks + 6 marks)

Probability judgements

AO1	Underestimate probability of repetitions for dice throwing (Brugger *et al.*, 1990)
AO1	Conjunction fallacy, more common in 'sheep' (Rogers *et al.*, 2008)
AO2	Contrasting evidence, e.g. Blackmore (1997) no difference between believers and non-believers
AO2	Depends what measurement used for paranormal belief, e.g. Blackmore just asked about ESP
AO2	Correlation isn't a cause, might be cognitive ability

Model answer

(a) Outline **two or more** factors underlying belief in anomalous experience. (4 marks)

One factor is coincidence, when two events happen at about the same time people may believe that one causes the other. It might be that people who believe anomalous experiences exist are less likely to assess coincidences appropriately because they tend to see patterns where none exist.

A second factor is personality, for example fantasy proneness has been linked to anomalous experiences. Fantasy proneness refers to the tendency to become so deeply absorbed in a fantasy that it feels as if it is actually happening. Evidence suggests that believers are more fantasy prone, for example, research has found a link between belief in the paranormal and mental imagination.

(b) How might a psychologist explain Lachlan's superstitious behaviour? (5 marks)

Lachlan's superstitious behaviour might be explained in terms of the evolutionary concept of adaptiveness. A preference for making a causal link between two unrelated events is adaptive because it is better to assume causality between unrelated events that co-occur (make a Type 1 error) than occasionally miss a genuine one that might be fatal (a Type 2 error where you believe there is no causal link when there is one). Thus Lachlan is erring on the side of a Type 1 error.

A behaviourist explanation for Lachlan's behaviour would be that an accidental stimulus-response link is learned (operant conditioning). Skinner (1947) demonstrated this with pigeons where the pigeons learned that turning around 'caused' food to appear and therefore they repeated the behaviour. Lachlan has done the same with his green T-shirt. Mowrer (1947) realised that there is a second component – negative reinforcement. Lachlan always wears his green T-shirt and avoids failed exams so this causes him to repeat the behaviour. If he took the exam without his green top and passed he would 'unlearn' his superstition but he avoids this and therefore the superstition is maintained.

A further explanation is illusion of control. Thinking that his choice of clothing affects his success gives Lachlan a sense of control. Whitson and Galinsky (2008) found people were more likely to believe in superstitions when they felt out of control. Lachlan might be particularly worried about his exams because he didn't revise enough and therefore feels out of control.

(c) Abbie, Lachlan's friend, cannot understand why he is so upset. She has worked hard and revised thoroughly and does not feel that she needs a T-shirt or anything else to get her through the exam.

Suggest how personality factors might explain why Abbie does not have anomalous beliefs. (5 marks)

Abbie might have a personality that tends to more positive thinking. Research has shown that neurotic personalities are more likely to have paranormal beliefs possibly because they view the world more negatively and use this kind of thinking to deal with their anxiety. Abbie therefore doesn't need such a defense mechanism.

Abbie might also lack fantasy proneness or suggestibility, both linked to paranormal beliefs. She might be more focused in her thinking (convergent rather than divergent and creative) and less easily influenced by suggestions.

Abbie might have an internal locus of control where she always feels very much in control and responsible. Research has found that people who believe in paranormal experiences tend to have an external locus of control where they believe that factors outside of their control explain their life experiences.

(d) Discuss the role probability judgements in anomalous experience. (4 marks + 6 marks)

Probability judgements may be linked to anomalous experiences because if people underestimate probability they attribute causality when in fact the events are simply random. For example, people who believe in the paranormal have been found to underestimate the probability of events being repeated – when asked to describe random dice throws they don't give any repeats (Brugger *et al.*, 1990).

Another example is the conjunction fallacy, occasions where two events co-occur and causality is assumed, such as reading your horoscope and something similar happening to you. Rogers *et al.* (2008) found that sheep (believers in the paranormal) made more conjunction errors than goats.

There is contrasting evidence, for example Blackmore (1997) tested people on the likelihood of certain events happening and found that both believers and non-believers are equally accurate in judgements of probability. This suggests that probability misjudgement does not explain paranormal belief.

One reason for the difference between studies may lie in the way that belief in anomalous experiences is measured. In many studies a general belief scale is used which includes a wide variety of different anomalous phenomenon (such as ghosts and the Loch Ness monster). Whereas in Blackmore's study there was simply one question about whether the participant believed in ESP.

Another issue is the assumption that a correlation between belief and probability misjudgement doesn't mean that the misjudgement is the cause of the belief. There may be other intervening factors, such as cognitive ability – poor probability judgements may be due to low cognitive ability.

Parts (a), (b), (c) and (d) would not form an exam question because the various part questions overlap in terms of the content required. The model answer just illustrates part questions for this division.

It is nice to use references but not essential here as long as your point is clear.

In part (a) the most important thing is that you cover at least two factors and that you have written enough – you could select more factors and write less about each or cover just two and provide elaboration.

Your answer should be about 100–120 words – this answer is 108 words.

There is a key difference between part (a) and parts (b) and (c) where you are required to apply your knowledge. Notice how each point in parts (b) and (c) is linked to Leon/Abbie rather than just described. Applying your knowledge is an AO2 skill and therefore should be practised.

Parts (b) and (c) are both worth 5 marks, about 125–150 words each is required. Our answers are 246 and 132 words respectively. The problem with overlong answers is they reduce the time available for answering other parts of an exam question, which may ultimately lose you marks.

Don't forget to use AO2 lead-in phrases when writing evaluation in an essay, and also end paragraphs with 'so what?' Remember the three-point rule described on page 5.

Part (d) – for a 10-mark question we would expect about 250 words minimum which is what we have presented here.

Division 3 Research into exceptional experience Answer plans

The questions on this page are derived in part from the examples on page 153. Some further ones have been added.

Answer plan 1 (short question)

Outline **one or more** explanations of out-of-body experiences. (4 marks)

Out-of-body experiences (OBEs)

AO1	Electrical stimulation of temporal-parietal junction (TPJ) (Blanke *et al.*, 2002)
AO1	Sensory disturbance (Blackmore, 1982), brain reconstructs visual field using memory and imagination

Answer plan 2 (short question)

Outline **one** study of psychic healing. (4 marks)

Psychic healing

AO1	Rosa *et al.* (1998) 21 therapeutic touch, placed hands through hole. Experimenter's hand 4 inches above.
AO1	Findings – correct 44%, not even as good as chance

DIY

Work out your own plan for these questions and then write your answers.

(a) Outline **one** explanation of near-death experiences. (4 marks)

(b) Discuss what research into exceptional experience has shown us about our psychic mediumship. (4 marks + 8 marks)

(c) Consider how factors underling anomalous experience can be used to understand belief in psychic healing. (8 marks)

Part (a) Near-death experience

AO1	
AO1	

Part (b) Psychic mediumship

AO1	
AO1	
AO2	
AO2	
AO2	
AO2	

Part (c) Psychic healing

AO2	
AO2	
AO2	
AO2	

Answer plan 3 (mini-essay)

Discuss what research has shown us about psychic healing. (4 marks + 6 marks)

Psychic healing

AO1	Cha *et al.* (2001) effect of prayer on infertile women, twice as many became preganent than those with no prayer
AO2	Not replicated, one author withdrew, results questionable (Flamm, 2005)
AO1	Rosa *et al.* (1998) hands through hole, 4 inches from experimenter's hand, 44% success, worse than chance.
AO2	TT supporters say experimenter not ill therefore not surprising, and designed by young girl
AO2	Long *et al.* (1999) repeated with ordinary people and 3-inch gap, results better than chance

Answer plan 4 (mini-essay)

Outline and evaluate psychological research into belief in near-death experiences. (4 marks + 6 marks)

Near-death experiences (NDEs)

AO1	Ring (1980) 100 people, 60% sense of peace, 33% OBEs, 25% experience a tunnel
AO1	Nelson *et al.* (2006) people who had NDEs also more likely to experience REM intrusions
AO2	Cultural differences, e.g. Augustine (2008) similarities e.g. tunnel, but in Japan no lights appearing
AO2	Difficult to study NDEs, can artificially induce using ketamine
AO2	Artificially induced NDEs suggest a physiological explanation, hypoxia triggers glutamate which causes neuronal death (Janson, 2009)

Answer plan 5 (applying your knowledge)

Consider how factors underlying anomalous experience can be used to understand belief in psychic mediumship. (10 marks)

Factors underling belief, applied to psychic mediumship

AO2	Belief in the paranormal (sheep) leads to having more anomalous experiences
AO2	Fantasy proneness and suggestibility lead to easier deception
AO2	Personality, tendency towards neurosis, psychic may reduce negative emotional state
AO2	Poor probabilistic reasoning leads to belief in things psychic might say
AO2	External locus of control, more accepting of other's interpretations of events

Model answer

Parts (a), (b) and (c) would not form an exam question because the various part questions overlap in terms of the content required. The model answer just illustrates part questions for this division.

(a) Outline **one or more** explanations of out-of-body experiences. (4 marks)

One explanation is that out-of-body experience (OBEs) are created by stimulation of the temporal-parietal junction. Blanke *et al.* (2002) induced OBEs accidentally by electrically stimulating this area of the brain in a woman who suffered epilepsy in that region. This led them to study neurologically normal subjects as well. They found that stimulation of the TPJ resulted in OBEs whereas stimulation of other areas did not.

A second explanation is that OBEs are caused by sensory disturbance. Blackmore (1982) suggests that normally we view the world as if we were behind our eyes. In situations where sensory input breaks down the brain attempts to reconstruct the visual field using memory and imagination. Memory images are often birds' eye views so that is what is constructed. Any further sensory input re-establishes normal sensory interpretation and ends the OBE.

There is no credit for defining an OBE. Just plunge straight in.

Part (a) – 4 marks should be about 100–120 words, and this is about 130 words. The only problem with writing too much is you leave yourself less time for the rest of the question.

(b) Outline and evaluate psychological research into belief in near-death experiences. (4 marks + 6 marks)

In one research study Ring (1980) interviewed 100 people who reported having had near death experiences (NDEs). He found that about 60% of survivors reported a sense of peace, 33% reported having had out-of-body experiences where they had an experience of seeing their own body from a location outside their physical body, and 25% said they entered a tunnel.

Nelson *et al.* (2006) studied 55 people with NDEs and 55 controls. He found that the NDE group were more likely to also experience 'REM intrusions'. REM sleep is associated with dreaming during which people sometimes experience sensations of falling or floating – an experience common in an NDE. An REM intrusion occurs when the brain is awake but flips into an REM state.

Cultural similarities and differences have been reported. For example, Augustine (2008) presented a review of NDEs in different cultures and reported a number of consistent features, such going through a tunnel, feelings of peace and OBEs. There were also differences, such as in Japan there were no instances of any light appearing. Such differences and similarities suggest that both psychological and physiological factors are involved.

One problem with studying NDEs is that they can only be studied after a person has had such an experience. This makes any findings biased because the experience may have changed a person not just because of the NDE but other associated factors, such as being in hospital. There have been attempts to artificially induce NDEs but that may produce quite a different experience.

Research on artificially induced NDEs supports a physiological explanation. Janson (2009) has found that hypoxia (a lack of oxygen caused by, for example, a heart attack or fainting) creates a flood of the neurotransmitter glutamate which in turn causes neuronal death. At the same time the brain creates a protective blockade and this might be the basis of an NDE.

It is critical to recognise that this question has both AO1 and AO2 in it, and it may help you to clearly separate them, as we have done here, to ensure the right amount of each in your answer.

The total for part (b) should be around 250–300 words, with 2:3 AO1:AO2. The total is actually 310 words of which 40% is AO1 – exactly right, demonstrating the value of using our paragraph technique.

(c) Consider how factors underlying anomalous experience can be used to understand belief in psychic mediumship. (10 marks)

One factor in anomalous experience is being a believer (called a 'sheep'). Research shows that people who are 'sheep' are more likely to have anomalous experiences, such as finding that what a psychic medium says is true. Of course it is difficult to determine the direction of causality – it could be that a positive experience with a psychic led to belief in the first place,

Fantasy proneness and suggestibility are two further factors linked to anomalous experience. A person with such characteristics would be more likely to have their imagination activated and would be more willing to be swayed by a psychics' deceptions.

Another aspect of personality that might be important is neuroticism which has been linked to anomalous beliefs. People who are neurotic have a tendency towards negative thinking which creates anxiety. Therefore, they may particularly seek positive news which a psychic medium tries to suppy.

Poor probabilistic reasoning might also explain belief in psychic mediumship. If the psychic asked if you knew someone called Dave you might be impressed because you have an uncle called Dave. However, in fact it is likely that everyone actually knows someone called Dave. Therefore, poor understanding of probabilistic reasoning may underlie belief in what the psychic says.

External locus of control is a characteristic of people who have anomalous experiences. They believe that life circumstances are controlled more by factors outside themselves (e.g. luck) rather than internal control (e.g. personal ability). This may make them more willing to accept the suggestions of a psychic medium rather than rely on their own experiences.

In part (c) any factor would be creditworthy – as long as you can then make the link from your named factor to belief in psychic mediumship. That is the AO2 skill to answering part (c).

You've got the points in the plan but your task in an exam is to elaborate these clearly to communicate your understanding and your ability to analyse the question being asked.

Part (c) is about 250 words, an adequate length.

Answer for you to mark

See page 176 for examiner's comments.

Question

(a) Explain what is meant by pseudoscience. (4 marks)

(b) There are many different kinds of anomalous experience. Probably one of the best known is ESP – the ability of one person to read the thoughts of another.

Explain how a researcher could use the Ganzfeld procedure to investigate ESP. (6 marks)

(c) A psychologist recently presented a TV programme about anomalous experiences, observing that many people report having had them. The psychologist suggested that the key question is not whether or not they did have such experiences but it is about why they believe in them whereas others don't.

Outline **two or more** explanations for anomalous experience. (4 marks)

(d) Consider how explanations can be used to understand belief in psychic mediumship. (10 marks)

Student answer

Part (a)

❶ *Pseudoscience is the opposite of someone doing science. It isn't real science which is why it is called pseudoscience, as it is like fake science which is what pseudo means. Pseudoscience can create problems because people might believe it and think it is like science, but it isn't because there are flaws in it.*

❷ *Pseudoscience lacks reliability because the results don't need to be repeated in order for people to take them as facts.*

❸ *There may be methodological problems with pseudoscience.*

(81 words)

AO1 mark scheme for part (a)

There are many features of pseudoscience that could be used in this part. Both breadth and depth are important, so a list of various characteristics would not lead to full marks because such answers lack 'coherence'. Each point needs to have some elaboration.

4 marks is about 100–120 words.

Comments and marks for part (b) (i) AO1

Guidance on marking is given on pages 6–11.

Tick the terms you think apply to the student's answer.

Mark	Knowledge and understanding	Accuracy	Organisation and structure
4	Reasonably thorough	Accurate	Coherent
3–2	Limited	Generally accurate	Reasonably coherent
1	Weak and muddled		
0	No creditworthy material		

The **AO1** mark I would give is ☐

Part (b)

❹ *The Ganzfeld procedure was invented as a way to test a person's ESP abilities, that is their abilitiy to read the thoughts of someone else.*

❺ *The procedure involves selecting one person who is going to act as the receiver and another person who is going to act as the sender. The receiver may well be someone who has shown the ability to read minds. This receiver is placed in a sound-proof room and is on their own. The room has nothing in it so that there are no stimuli to affect their thoughts. The receiver has to try to think what image the other person is sending.*

❻ *The image that is described is compared to the actual image and if the results are greater than chance then you can conclude the person has some mind reading ability. If the results are at the chance level then you should conclude that there isn't any ESP.*

(157 words)

AO2 mark scheme for part (b)

A clear explanation should include key details of what the sender and receiver are both doing, what controls are necessary and how performance is assessed.

6 marks is about 150–180 words.

Record your mark on the grid at the top of the facing page.

Comments and marks for part (b) AO2

Mark	Analysis and understanding	Focus	Elaboration	Quality of written communication
6	Sound	Well-focused	Coherent	Fluent, effective use of terms
5–4	Reasonable	Generally focused	Reasonable	Clear, appropriate
3–2	Basic, superficial	Sometimes focused	Some evidence	Lacks clarity, limited use of terms
1	Rudimentary, limited understanding	Weak, muddled and incomplete	Not effective	Often unconnected assertions, errors
0	No creditworthy material			

The **AO2** mark I would give is ☐

Part (c)

❼ *One explanation is belief in coincidence. This is when two events happen at the same time, such as a close friend dying and a little bird appearing on your windowsill. You think that the two are related in some way. Believing that the two are linked might explain why some people believe in anomalous events.*

❽ *Another example could be the illusion of control. Believing in coincidences and superstition gives you the feeling you are in control of things that are outside your control.*

(83 words)

AO1 mark scheme for part (c)

Any appropriate factors would be creditworthy. A candidate who only describes one would receive a maximum of 2 marks.

4 marks is about 100–120 words.

Comments and marks for part (c) AO1

Mark	Knowledge and understanding	Accuracy	Organisation and structure
4	Reasonably thorough	Accurate	Coherent
3–2	Limited	Generally accurate	Reasonably coherent
1	Weak and muddled		
0	No creditworthy material		

The **AO1** mark I would give is ☐

Part (d)

❾ *Psychic mediumship refers to situations where one individual attempts to contact the dead.*

❿ *The idea of probability misjudgment could be used to explain why some people do believe in psychic mediums. They are not able to recognise the likelihood that a person could actually contact someone who is dead and so, rather than think this is extremely unlikely, they think it is likely and therefore believe in the medium.*

⓫ *Of course people may believe because it is true and there is research evidence to back this up. One study found that five mediums were very accurate in their readings of two women. However, a further analysis of this study found that the reason the mediums were so accurate was because both the women were over 40 so it was easy to say things that would probably fit. Research by Wiseman has found that mediums only provide information at the level of chance.*

⓬ *The personality of a person may be another factor. People who are more extravert might be more likely to believe. This was shown in a research study which found a positive correlation between extraversion and paranormal beliefs. It might be that people who are extravert are more open to new experiences and this would explain the correlation.*

(208 words)

AO2 mark scheme for part (d)

In this part candidates should apply the knowledge identified in part (c) to the specific case of psychic mediumship.

For top marks candidates should refer to research evidence that supports or challenges any explanation.

There is a depth/breadth trade off.

10 marks is about 250–300 words.

Comments and marks for part (d) AO2

Mark	Analysis and understanding	Application of knowledge	Elaboration	Quality of written communication
10–9	Sound	Effective	Coherent	Fluent, effective use of terms
8–6	Reasonable	Reasonably effective	Some elaboration	Clear, appropriate
5–3	Basic, superficial	Basic		Lacks clarity, limited use of terms
2–1	Rudimentary, limited understanding	Weak, muddled and incomplete		Often unconnected assertions, errors
0	No creditworthy material			

The **AO2** mark I would give is ☐

Chapter 16 Psychological research and scientific method

Exam questions on psychological research contain stimulus material, for example describing a study. On this page we have included the stimulus material for January 2010 (see right). On the following pages you will find the stimulus material for the other questions. The questions on this spread give you a flavour of the exam questions that have been asked in the past few years.

AQA A exam question, January 2010

Stimulus material

A psychologist was interested in testing a new treatment for people with eating disorders. She put up adverts in several London clinics to recruit participants. Thirty people came forward and they were all given a structured interview by a trained therapist. The therapist then calculated a numerical score for each participant as a measure of their current functioning, where 50 indicates excellent, healthy functioning and zero indicates failure to function adequately. The psychologist then randomly allocated half the participants to a treatment group and half to a no-treatment group. After eight weeks, each participant was re-assessed using a structured interview conducted by the same trained therapist, and given a new numerical score. The trained therapist did not know which participants had been in either group.

For each participant, the psychologist calculated an improvement score by subtracting the score at the start of the study from the score after eight weeks. The greater the number, the better the improvement.

Table 1: Median and range of improvement scores for the treatment group and for the no-treatment group

	Treatment group	No-treatment group
Median	10.9	2.7
Range	2.1	0.8

In this left-hand column we have listed the contents of the specification. On the right there are examples of questions related to each specification entry.

Preamble to the specification

Candidates will be expected to:	What were the researchers' aims in this study? (2 marks) AQA, June 2011
Build on their knowledge and skills developed at AS level	Write a non-directional hypothesis for this study. (2 marks) AQA, June 2011
	Explain why it is important to operationalise the independent variable and the dependent variable in this study and suggest how the psychologist might do this. (5 marks) AQA, January 2011
Design investigations	The psychologist could have used a matched pairs design. Explain why this design would have been more difficult to use in this study. (2 marks) AQA, January 2011
	The psychologist asks some of his students to conduct a separate observational study at the same time on the same group of children. The aim of this observational study is to test the idea that eating a healthy breakfast affects playground behaviour. Design an observational study to investigate the effects of a healthy breakfast on playground behaviour. Include in your answer sufficient detail to allow for reasonable replication of the study. You should state the hypothesis you are setting out to test. In your answer, refer to: • An appropriate method of investigation • materials/apparatus and procedure. Justify your design decisions. (12 marks) AQA, January 2011
Understand how to analyse and interpret data arising from such investigations	With reference to the data in **Table 1**, outline what the findings of this investigation seem to show about the effectiveness of the treatment. (2 marks) AQA, January 2010
	The psychologist assumed that improvements in the treatment group were a direct result of the new type of treatment. Suggest **two** other reasons why people in the treatment group might have improved. (4 marks) AQA, January 2010
	In the discussion section, researchers are also expected to consider any possible applications of their research. Suggest **one** practical application that might arise from these findings. (2 marks) AQA, June 2010
Report on practical investigations	The psychologist noticed that female and male participants seemed to have responded rather differently to a treatment. She decided to test the following hypothesis: Female patients with an eating disorder will show greater improvement in their symptoms after treatment with the new therapy than male patients. She used a new set of participants and, this time, used self-report questionnaires instead of interviews with a therapist. Imagine that you are the psychologist and are writing up the report of the study. Write an appropriate methods section which includes reasonable detail of design, participants, materials and procedure. Make sure that there is enough detail to allow another researcher to carry out this study in the future. (10 marks) AQA, January 2010

Division 1	The application of scientific method in psychology
The major features of science, including replicability, objectivity, theory construction, hypothesis testing, the use of empirical methods	Explain why the teacher's personal opinion cannot be accepted as scientific evidence. Refer to some of the major features of science in your answer. (6 marks) AQA, January 2011
	Explain what is meant by 'replication' in the context of research investigations. (2 marks)
	Explain why objectivity and hypothesis testing are important features of science. (4 marks)
	Discuss the application of the scientific method in psychology. (4 marks + 4 marks)
	Consider the application of the scientific method in psychology. Use examples of psychological research in your answer. (6 marks)
Validating new knowledge and the role of peer review	Outline what is meant by the term *peer review* in psychological research. (2 marks) AQA, June 2010
	Explain why peer review is important in psychological research. (5 marks) AQA, June 2010

Division 2	The application of scientific method in psychology
Selection and application of appropriate research methods	The psychologist could have used self-report questionnaires to assess the participants instead of using interviews with the therapist. Explain **one** advantage and **one** disadvantage of using self-report questionnaires in this study rather than interviews. (4 marks) AQA, January 2010
	What is meant by the term *content analysis*? (1 mark) AQA, June 2010
	Explain how the psychologist might have carried out content analysis to analyse these drawings. (3 marks) AQA, June 2010
Implications of sampling strategies, for example bias and generalising	The psychologist used a random sampling method. Explain how he could have obtained his sample using this method. (3 marks) AQA, January 2011
	Explain limitations of using random sampling in this study. (3 marks) AQA, January 2011 I
	Identify an appropriate sampling method for this study and explain how the psychologist might have obtained such a sample. (3 marks) AQA, June 2011
Issues of reliability, including types of reliability, assessment of reliability, improving reliability	What is meant by reliability? Explain how the reliability of the scores in this study could be checked. (4 marks) AQA, January 2010
	If the psychologist does find low reliability, what could she do to improve inter-rater reliability before proceeding with the observational research? (4 marks) AQA, June 2010
	Describe **two** different types of reliability. (4 marks)
Assessing and improving validity, including internal and external	What is meant by validity? (1 mark) AQA, June 2011
	Explain how **one** factor in this study might affect its internal validity and how **one** factor might affect its external validity. (2 marks + 2 marks)AQA, June 2011
	A researcher criticised a previous observational study, claiming the study lacked validity. Give **one** example of how an observational study might lack validity and suggest how this could be dealt with. (3 marks)
Ethical considerations in design and conduct of psychological research	The psychologist needed to obtain informed consent from her participants. Write a brief consent form which would be suitable for this study. You should include some details of what participants could expect to happen in the study and how they would be protected. (5 marks) AQA, January 2010
	Other than parental consent, identify **one** ethical issue raised in this study and explain how the psychologist might address it. (2 marks) AQA, January 2011

Division 3	Data analysis and reporting on investigations
Appropriate selection of graphical representations	Use the data in *Table 2* to sketch a scattergram. Label the axes and give the scattergram a title. (4 marks)
Probability and significance, including the interpretation of significance and Type 1/ Type 2 errors	What is the likelihood of the psychologist having made a Type 1 error in this study? Explain your answer. (2 marks) AQA, January 2010
	Explain what is meant by '$p \leq 0.05$'. (2 marks) Sample paper
	Identify an appropriate level of significance to use in this study and explain why you have selected that level. (3 marks)
Factors affecting choice of statistical test, including levels of measurement **The use of inferential analysis, including Spearman's Rho, Mann–Whitney, Wilcoxon, Chi-Square**	The psychologist used a statistical test to find out whether there was a significant difference in improvement between the 'treatment' and 'no-treatment' groups. She found a significant difference at the 5% level for a one-tailed test ($p \leq 0.05$). Identify an appropriate statistical test for analysing the participants' scores. Explain why it would be a suitable test to use in this study. (4 marks) AQA, January 2010
	The psychologist used a Mann–Whitney test to analyse the data. Give **two** reasons why he chose this test. (2 marks) AQA, January 2011
	Identify an appropriate statistical test to check the inter-rater reliability of these two observers. Explain why this is an appropriate test. (3 marks) AQA, June 2010
Analysis and interpretation of qualitative data	Explain the difference between quantitative and qualitative data. (3 marks)
	A psychologist was interested in the emotional development of adolescents. He asked two students to produce diaries of their feelings over the period of one year. Outline how he might produce a qualitative analysis of the students' diaries. (5 marks)
Conventions of reporting on psychological investigations	What is the purpose of the introduction section of a report? (2 marks) AQA, June 2011
	Outline the key features of a discussion section in a report of a psychological investigation. (3 marks)

Exam question

Question

AQA, January 2011

A teacher has worked in the same primary school for two years. While chatting to the children, she is concerned to find that the majority of them come to school without having eaten a healthy breakfast. In her opinion, children who eat 'a decent breakfast' learn to read more quickly and are better behaved than children who do not. She now wants to set up a pre-school breakfast club for the children so that they can all have this beneficial start to the day. The local authority is not willing to spend money on this project purely on the basis of the teacher's opinion and insists on having scientific evidence for the claimed benefits of eating a healthy breakfast.

(a) Explain why the teacher's personal opinion cannot be accepted as scientific evidence. Refer to some of the major features of science in your answer. (6 marks)

A psychologist at the local university agrees to carry out a study to investigate the claim that eating a healthy breakfast improves reading skills. He has access to 400 five-year-old children from 10 local schools, and decides to use 100 children (50 in the experimental group and 50 in the control group). Since the children are so young, he needs to obtain parental consent for them to take part in his study.

(b) The psychologist used a random sampling method. Explain how he could have obtained his sample using this method. (3 marks)

(c) Explain limitations of using random sampling in this study. (3 marks)

(d) Explain why it is important to operationalise the independent variable and the dependent variable in this study and suggest how the psychologist might do this. (5 marks)

(e) The psychologist used a Mann–Whitney test to analyse the data. Give **two** reasons why he chose this test. (2 marks)

(f) He could have used a matched pairs design. Explain why this design would have been more difficult to use in this study. (2 marks)

(g) Other than parental consent, identify **one** ethical issue raised in this study and explain how the psychologist might address it. (2 marks)

The psychologist asks some of his students to conduct a separate observational study at the same time on the same group of children. The aim of this observational study is to test the idea that eating a healthy breakfast affects playground behaviour.

(h) Design an observational study to investigate the effects of a healthy breakfast on playground behaviour. Include in your answer sufficient detail to allow for reasonable replication of the study. You should state the hypothesis you are setting out to test.

In your answer, refer to:

- An appropriate method of investigation
- Materials/apparatus and procedure.

Justify your design decisions. (12 marks)

Questions often have stimulus material throughout – you must read this carefully.

DIY

Work out your own answer to the question below.

Research has found that attractive defendants in court cases tend to be given shorter sentences than less attractive defendants. A group of psychology students decide to test this by visiting their local court and assessing each defendant as well as recording the length of the sentence they were given.

Describe how you would conduct such a study. Your answer should include information about the hypothesis, the variables to be measured and any ethical issues. The procedures should be clearly outlined in sufficient detail for replication to be possible. (10 marks)

Use the separate lines to help you plan an answer of the right length.

Model answer

(a) Personal opinion cannot be relied on as scientific evidence because it lacks key features of scientific evidence:

- Replication – research is repeated to check if the same results occur. The teacher is alone in her observations, they have not been confirmed elsewhere.
- Objectivity – scientific research aims to be objective by recognising bias and conducting carefully controlled studies. The teacher is likely to be unaware of her possible biases, e.g. she might always have had good breakfasts herself and this leads her to think they are important.
- Theory construction – scientists develop an explanatory framework. The teacher has no explanation underlying her belief, therefore it's just a belief.
- Hypothesis testing – scientists design studies to test their hypotheses. The teacher needs to provide actual evidence to support her belief. This could be done by operationalising the variables and conducting an experiment.

(b) The psychologist might give each child in all 10 schools a number – 400 children in total. A random number table can then be used to select numbers. The researcher can start anywhere in the table and then the first 50 numbers will be placed in the experimental group and the next 50 in the control group.

(c) One limitation is that the final sample may not be truly representative because some parents may refuse to let their children take part, so this biases the sample. Another issue is the time and effort to draw a random sample. You could just use a systematic sample.

(d) Operationalisation is important because the researcher has to be clear about what exactly is being measured. The IV (healthy breakfast) could be operationalised by specifying what a healthy breakfast would consist of (e.g. a piece of fruit or an egg). The DV can be operationalised by using a reading test to assess reading ability, so the operationalised DV is the score on the reading test.

(e) One reason is because the study is an independent groups design, the second reason is that the researcher needs a test of difference.

(f) Matched pairs design would be more difficult because it is quite time-consuming to match participants on the characteristics you identify. In this case there are so many potential characteristics, such as IQ (which could explain differences in reading ability), their normal diet, parental income and gender so matching would take a long time and be difficult with 400 children.

(g) One other ethical issue is confidentiality. This could be dealt with by referring to all children by number and not recording their names.

(h) In order to conduct an observational study I would:

- Have a hypothesis – There is difference between the behaviours of children in the playground who eat healthy breakfasts and those who don't.
- Use three observers (to establish the reliability of observations).
- Prior to the study I would conduct a pilot study to create a behaviour checklist.
- The behaviour checklist would have categories representing all the behaviours typical of children in the playground, such as playing with others, rough and tumble play.
- The observers would then be trained to use this behaviour checklist.
- We would select a subsample from the original 400 children to observe, because it is not possible to observe that many children. One child could be selected from each of the 10 schools.
- We would interview the children about their typical breakfasts and use a point system to score their breakfast in terms of healthiness.
- Parents might be interviewed as well to establish the validity of the children's answers about their breakfasts.
- At playtime a video would be recorded of the child at play and then the observers could watch.
- The videos would be taken over the period of two weeks.
- I would decide on a sampling method – every 30 seconds the observers would record what the target child was doing using the behaviour checklist.
- The children and parents should be debriefed afterwards.

Part (a) – candidates need to show that they understand what differentiates opinion from scientific evidence. The answer here has been organised around some of the things identified in the specification as features of science.

An effective answer will relate these features to the teacher's personal opinion.

Part (b) – sufficient elaboration is needed for the full 3 marks.

Part (c) must be contextualised. For 3 marks one or more limitations must be explained in reasonable detail.

Part (d) requires both why and how. There is a maximum of 3 marks if only one or the other is addressed.

Part (e) – there is a third possible reason – because the data is ordinal or better. Only two reasons are needed.

Part (f) – 1 mark for a basic explanation (matching is difficult), 1 mark for elaboration/contextualisation.

Part (g) – some issues would be difficult to deal with (e.g. giving some children a poor diet). These are best avoided.

Part (h) – no credit is given for details already provided in the stimulus material, such as gaining parental consent.

Any other relevant details are creditworthy. The main criterion is whether there is enough detail for replication.

Since the question is worth 12 marks it would be sensible to have 12 points to make.

Exam question

Question

AQA, June 2011

It is thought that colours might affect our performance when carrying out certain tasks. Research in this area has been inconclusive. Some studies have shown that red improves performance but others have found the opposite. It could be that these contradictory results have arisen because red is beneficial only for certain kinds of mental processing. Some psychologists tested this hypothesis in a series of independent groups design experiments using students at a Canadian university.

The experiments involved computer tasks, with either a red, blue or neutral background appearing on the monitor. The researchers found that participants were better at a word-recall task and a spell-checking task when the screen background was red rather than blue or neutral. However, participants thought of more creative ideas when the screen was blue rather than red or neutral.

The researchers concluded that red is beneficial for tasks that require attention to detail whereas blue aids creativity.

(a) What were the researchers' aims in this study? (2 marks)

Imagine that you are writing up the report for this series of experiments.

(b) What is the purpose of the introduction section of a report? (2 marks)

A psychological report also contains a discussion section. Researchers are expected to consider their findings critically and discuss issues, such as validity.

(c) What is meant by validity? (1 mark)

(d) Explain how **one** factor in this study might affect its internal validity and how **one** factor might affect its external validity. (2 marks + 2 marks)

(e) In the discussion section, researchers are also expected to consider any possible applications of their research. Suggest **one** practical application that might arise from these findings. (2 marks)

In a further experiment, participants were given 20 blue shapes or 20 red shapes. They were then asked to pick five shapes and use them to make a toy suitable for a child aged between five and 11 years. They were given a limited time to carry out this task. Participants given red shapes made toys that independent judges rated to be more practical but less original, whereas participants given blue shapes made more creative toys.

(f) Explain why the researchers asked independent judges to rate the toys. (2 marks)

(g) Write a set of standardised instructions that would be suitable to read out to participants in this experiment. (5 marks)

Psychological research suggests an association between birth order and certain abilities. For example, first-born children are often logical in their thinking whereas later-born children tend to be more creative. A psychologist wonders whether this might mean that birth order is associated with different career choices. She decides to investigate and asks 50 artists and 65 lawyers whether they were the first-born child in the family or not.

(h) Write a non-directional hypothesis for this study. (2 marks)

(i) Identify an appropriate sampling method for this study and explain how the psychologist might have obtained such a sample. (3 marks)

The psychologist found the following results:

- 20 of the 50 artists were first-born children
- 35 of the 65 lawyers were first-born children.

She analysed her data using a statistical test and calculated a value of $\chi^2 = 2.27$. She then looked at the relevant table to see whether this value was statistically significant. An extract from the table is provided below.

(j) Imagine that you are writing the results section of the report on this investigation. Using information from the description of the study above and the relevant information from the statistical table, provide contents suitable for the results section.

Table 1: Critical values of χ^2

	Level of significance for a one-tailed test			
	0.10	0.05	0.025	0.01
	Level of significance for a two-tailed test			
	0.20	0.10	0.05	0.02
df				
1	1.64	2.71	3.84	5.41

Calculated value of χ^2 must be equal to or exceed the table (critical) values for significance at the level shown.

You must provide all of the following:

- an appropriately labelled 2 × 2 contingency table
- a sketch of an appropriately labelled bar chart
- identification of the appropriate statistical test with justification for its use
- identification of an appropriate significance level
- a statement of the results of the statistical test in relation to the hypothesis.

(12 marks)

Use the separate lines to help you plan an answer of the right length.

Work out your own answer to this question.

In the study described above there were three independent judges. Explain why having three judges might improve reliability and how this could be assessed. (4 marks)

Model answer

(a) The aim of the study was to see if colours affect performance of particular tasks. Specifically whether the colour red improves performance.

(b) The purpose of the introduction section of a report is to review past research, providing the background to this particular study. This review should lead logically to the aims of the study and also to the hypothesis/hypotheses.

(c) Validity refers to the legitimacy of a study and concerns control of variables and generalisability.

(d) Internal validity might be affected by a confounding variable, such as whether one group contained more people who liked the colour red which might bias their responses to red.

External validity might be affected by the fact that university students were used who would be above average in intelligence and therefore the results might not generalise the whole population.

(e) One practical application would be to situations where people are engaged in tasks where creativity is important, such as in an art class or working in an advertising company. If the surroundings had a blue bias this would improve creativity.

(f) Independent judges were asked to rate the toys so they wouldn't be biased. If they knew that the hypothesis was that the colour red improves attention to detail (i.e. they were not independent of the study), this might have affected their ratings.

(g) The standardised instructions might be

1. You will be required to make a toy suitable for a child aged between 5 and 11 years.
2. You will be given 40 shapes of different colours to use in making this toy.
3. You are only permitted to use five of these shapes in making your toy.
4. You have 10 minutes for the task so don't take too long in choosing your shapes.
5. At the end of the task you will be debriefed.

(h) There is an association between birth order and career choice.

(i) One suitable sampling method would be volunteer sampling. The psychologist would put an ad in an art college and a law college in order to get suitable participants. The ad would give details of what would be involved and ask students to get in touch.

(j) 1. Contingency table

	Treatment group	Lawyers	No-treatment group
First born	20	35	55
Later born	30	30	60
Total	50	65	115

2. Bar chart showing birth order of artists and lawyers

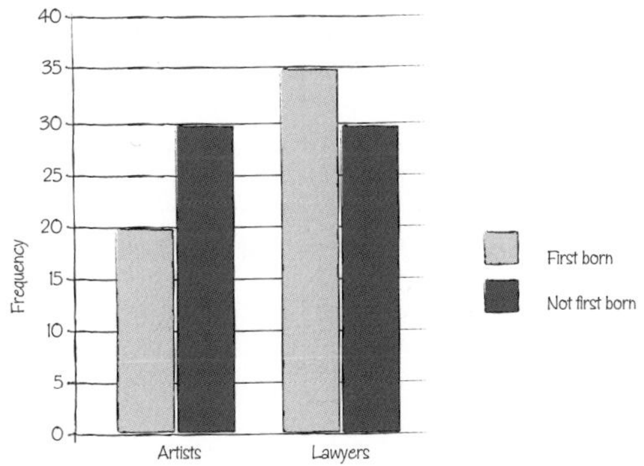

3. Appropriate test would be chi-squared because the data is frequency data and each cell has a frequency greater than five, we are looking for a difference/association.
4. Appropriate significance level would be 5%.
5. The observed value of χ^2 is 2.27. There is one degree of freedom for a 2 x 2 contingency table. The critical value of χ^2 for a two-tailed test (non-directional hypothesis) is 3.84 ($p \leq 0.05$). As the observed value is less than the critical value the results are not significant. We therefore must accept the null hypothesis and conclude there is no association between birth order and career choice.

Part (a) must be an aim and not be a hypothesis.

Part (b) is only worth 2 marks so you are not required to write much. The two key points are literature review and hypothesis.

Part (c) requires just a brief answer for 1 mark and can define internal or external validity or both.

Part (d) requires contextualisation for full marks. There are 2 marks for an explanation of internal validity and some contextualised elaboration, and the same for external validity.

Parts (e) and (f) – any plausible explanation is creditworthy but they must be elaborated/contextualised for 2 marks.

Part (g) – since this question is worth 5 marks it helps to ensure you have said five things by numbering the instructions. For full marks you need to provide accurate detail of the procedure and go beyond the information given in the question, e.g. provide details of time allowed for completing the task.

Part (h) – a directional hypothesis or a correlation would not be creditworthy. The hypothesis may express an association or a non-directional difference (e.g. 'There is an association between birth order and choice of career' or 'There is a difference in career choice depending on birth order').

Part (i) – any appropriate sampling method is creditworthy but must take into account that only particular kinds of participants are required.

Part (j) – it is crucial to address each element of this question – that's why the list of things to be included has been provided.

Answer for you to mark

See page 176 for examiner's comments.

Question

AQA, June 2010

(a) Outline what is meant by the term 'peer review' in psychological research. (2 marks)

Peer review is the process whereby one scientist reviews the work of another scientist.

(b) Explain why peer review is important in psychological research. (5 marks)

Peer review is important because it is the only way we can be sure that a study is true, or can be believed in. It aims to prevent studies being published that are not very good, for example it might be biased or flawed in some way. If it was published people might believe it.

Read the text below and answer parts (c) and (d).

A psychologist was interested in looking at the effects of a restricted diet on psychological functioning. A group of 20 healthy, young adult volunteers agreed to spend four weeks in a research unit. They were kept warm and comfortable but given only water and small amounts of plain food. They were able to socialise with one another and watch television, but they had to keep to strict, set meal times and were not allowed to eat anything between meals. The psychologist carried out various tests of emotional and cognitive functioning during this four-week period. One area of interest for the psychologist was the effect of the dietary restriction on the perception of food. He tested this by asking the volunteers to draw pictures of food at the end of each week. When all the drawings had been completed, the psychologist used content analysis to analyse them.

(c) What is meant by the term 'content analysis'? (1 mark)

Content analysis is a method whereby you can analyse the content of something. You analyse qualitative data.

(d) Explain how the psychologist might have carried out content analysis to analyse these drawings. (3 marks)

In order to analyse the drawings the psychologist might have looked at the different kinds of foods that people drew and separated them into groups, such as fatty foods or healthy foods. Then the psychologist could count how many of each type of food there were.

(e) The psychologist needed to be sure that his participants understood the nature of the study so that they were able to give informed consent.

Write a consent form which would be suitable for this study. Make sure there is sufficient information about the study for the participants to make an informed decision. (5 marks)

This study is looking at the effects of dieting on psychological functioning. As a participant you should be aware that you have the right to fully informed consent and the right to withdraw.

Taking part in the study will involve eating small amounts of food at strict meal times and you will not be allowed to eat between meals.

You will be tested during the study on tests of cognitive and emaotional functioning.

(f) The psychologist was also interested in the effects of a restricted diet on memory functioning and he expected memory to become impaired. The psychologist's hypothesis was that participants' scores on a memory test are lower after a restricted diet than before a restricted diet. He gave the volunteers a memory test when they first arrived in the research unit and a similar test at the end of the four-week period. He recorded the memory scores on both tests and analysed them using the Wilcoxon signed ranks test. He set his significance level at 5%.

His calculated value was T = 53.

State whether the hypothesis for this study is directional or non-directional. (1 mark)

It was directional.

Mark scheme for part (a)

No marks for simply saying 'other psychologists look at the research'.

Mark scheme for part (b)

5 marks for effective analysis and understanding, 4–3 marks for reasonable, 2 marks for basic and 1 mark for rudimentary.

Mark scheme for part (c)

E.g. a technique for analysing data according to themes or categories.

Mark scheme for part (d)

There are three points to cover: identify categories, count examples, compare before and after. The answer must be contextualised, i.e. it is not enough to explain how a content analysis is carried out – you must describe how you would do this using the data from this study (different kinds of food).

Mark scheme for part (e)

Both methodological and ethical issues should be included, and the content of the consent form should be contextualised so it relates specifically to this study.

Mark scheme for part (f)

The answer is 'directional'.

(g) **Table 1:** Extract from table of critical values from the Wilcoxon signed ranks test

Level of significance for a one-tailed test	0.05	0.025
Level of significance for a two-tailed test	0.1	0.05
N	$T \leq$	
19	53	46
20	60	52
21	67	58
22	75	65

Calculated T must be equal to or less than the critical value (table value) for significance at the level shown.

Using **Table 1**, state whether or not the psychologist's result was significant. Explain your answer. (3 marks)

The result is not significant because there were 20 people in the study and a two-tailed test is required which means that T must be equal to or less than 52 to be significant.

Mark scheme for part (g)

1 mark for saying 'significant' and a further 2 marks for saying why this is correct. N = 20, one-tailed test, therefore T should be less than or equal to 60 to be significant at the 5% level.

Read the text below and answer questions (h) and (i).

A psychologist is using the observational method to look at verbal aggression in a group of children with behavioural difficulties. Pairs of observers watch a single child in the class for a period of one hour and note the number of verbally aggressive acts within 10-minute time intervals. After seeing the first set of ratings, the psychologist becomes concerned about the quality of inter-rater reliability. The tally chart for the two observers is shown in **Table 2.**

Table 2: Observation of one child – number of verbally aggressive acts in 10-minute time intervals

Time slots	0–10	11–20	21–30	31–40	41–50	51–60
Observer A	2	5	0	6	4	3
Observer B	4	3	2	1	6	5

(h) Use the data in **Table 2** to sketch a scattergram. Label the axes and give the scattergram a title. (4 marks)

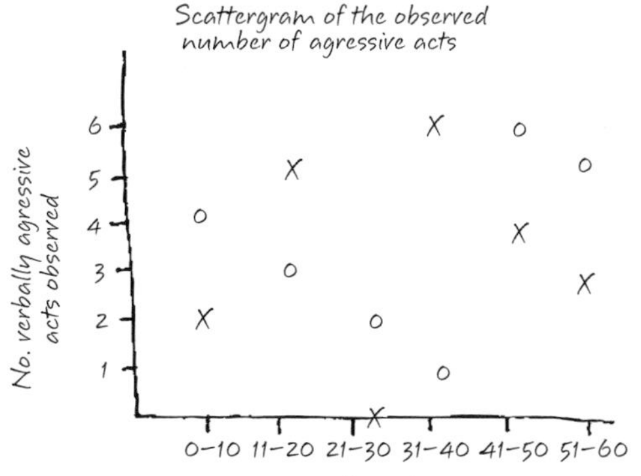

Mark scheme for part (h)

For full marks there should be a title and both axes should be labeled appropriately (one axis is Observer A and the other is Observer B). Points should be plotted accurately.

No marks if something other than a scattergram is sketched.

(i) Using the data in **Table 2**, explain why the psychologist is concerned about inter-rater reliability. (4 marks)

The data isn't consistent. You can see that sometimes the numbers are bigger for observer A than B and sometimes they are smaller. They don't agree at all.

Mark scheme for part (i)

1 mark for saying 'the observers don't agree with each other', 3 marks for further elaboration.

(j) Identify an appropriate statistical test to check the inter-rater reliability of these two observers. Explain why this is an appropriate test. (3 marks)

The appropriate test would be Spearman's Rho because it is a correlation.

Mark scheme for part (j)

1 mark for Spearman's Rho or Pearson's, 2 marks for justification (looking for a correlation and data can be treated as ordinal).

(k) If the psychologist does find low reliability, what could she do to improve inter-rater reliability before proceeding with the observational research? (4 marks)

The psychologist might improve inter-rater reliability by providing more training for the observers so that the observers can understand more clearly what the categories they are using are. It might be that they are a bit confused at the moment and therefore they put the behaviours in the wrong category. Another thing the psychologist could do would be to ask the observers to be more careful with their observations.

Mark scheme for part (k)

Answers may deal with one improvement (and provide elaboration) or several improvements (with less elaboration).

Examiner's marks and comments

See pages 6–11 for guidance on marking.

Prelims (see pages 6–11)

Pages 6–7	**Part (a) AO1 = 8 out of 8 marks**. The answer is generally well-detailed especially in the time available. The material is all relevant. There is a substantial evidence of both depth and breadth. The structure is reasonable. **Part (b) AO2 = 7 out of 16 marks**. Some of the points belong to the 12–9 band and some to the 8–5 band. However, more probably belong to the lower band. A little bit more elaboration or IDA would have gained an extra few marks and turned this into a Grade A answer.
	Total = 15 out of 24 marks, likely to be a Grade B.
Pages 8–9	**Part (a) AO1** This answer is clearly in the 3–2 band. We are not tempted by 'reasonably thorough' (the band above) nor 'weak and muddled' (the band below). A generous **3 out of 4 marks**. **Part (b) AO1** is reasonably thorough in terms of breadth and coherence = **4 out of 4 marks**. **Part (b) AO2** is basic. The lack of elaboration and IDA pull this down towards the bottom band but the line of argument compensates slightly, **6 out of 16 marks**.
	Total = 13 out of 24 marks, likely to be a Grade C.
Pages 10–11	**Question (a)** The lack of effective application of knowledge (almost no reference to the leaflet) means the answer must score in the 5–3 band 'basic and superficial' but is at the top of this band, **5 out of 10 marks** (50%, performing at the level of Grade C). **Question (b)** The first paragraph is sound and effective but overall there is insufficient material for 4 marks, so **3 out of 4 marks** (75%, performing at the level of Grade A*). **Question (c)** The answer is better than basic because there is a reasonable attempt to apply knowledge but this is not fully effective and lacks firm basis in psychological research, so **5 out of 8 marks** (62.5%, performing at the level of a Grade B).

Chapter 1 Biological rhythms and sleep (see answer on page 20)

Paragraph	Examiner comments	Mark
1	Appropriate references have been cited, and a concise outline of the sleep–wake cycle is presented.	**Part (a) AO1** Outline is limited, but accurate and coherent = 3–2 mark band. Since the answer is closer to the top band. **= 3 out of 4 marks**
2	The **AO2** material (including **IDA**) is not creditworthy in an **AO1** part of the question.	
3	Not really an explanation	**Part (b) AO1** Outline is limited, reasonably coherent, closer to the bottom band. **= 2 out of 4 marks**
4	Brief explanation (**AO1**).	
5	Brief explanation (**AO1**).	
6	Gender differences are considered, though this is not effective **AO2**.	**Part (c) AO2** Analysis is basic and superficial. It is better than rudimentary because a breadth of points has been considered. Some attempts at elaboration, but often not effective. Superficial reference to **IDA**. Expression of ideas lacks clarity. Closer to 'rudimentary' than to 'reasonable'. **= 6 out of 16 marks**
7	Reductionism (**IDA**) is mentioned and there is some attempt to contextualise it.	
8	A methodological point is made about reliability, but it is not very clear (lacks elaboration).	
9	Age differences are considered, again not very effective as **AO2**. An additional methodological point is reasonably made.	
10	A further, brief methodological point with some brief elaboration.	
11	Genetic predisposition is mentioned but the point is rudimentary.	
12	A couple of rudimentary points are presented in the conclusion.	
	Total	11 out of 24 marks, likely to be a Grade D.

Chapter 2 Perception (see answer on page 30)

Paragraph	Examiner comments	Mark
1	An introduction, which does not attract any credit.	**AO1** The descriptions are accurate and reasonable. There is evidence of both breadth (six studies covered) and depth (reasonable detail). Because of this balance the mark is pushed up to the top band. **= 7 out of 8 marks**
2	A reasonably detailed description of an infant study (**AO1**). The final sentence offers some superficial analysis (**AO2**).	
3	A second infant study is described in reasonable detail (**AO1**). The final sentence offers a comment on ethical issues (**AO2**) but this is not elaborated.	
4	A third infant study again in reasonable detail, this time looking at visual constancy (**AO1**). The studies in paragraphs 2 and 3 were all concerned with depth/distance perception.	

5	A fourth infant study again on visual constancy, reasonably detailed **AO1**. The findings/conclusion ('This suggests that infants could tell the difference between cubes of different sizes') is not related to depth perception – what the study shows is that the infants had developed size constancy. Thus these comments provide only restricted **AO2** credit.	**AO2** There are a range of **AO2** points though they tend to be fairly restricted and many opportunities are lost for interpretation. For example, paragraphs 3 and 4 might have included a comment on whether these studies support nature or nurture. However, the attempts at explanation in paragraphs 6 and 7 lift the **AO2** mark out of the bottom band. The mention of ethical issues means some reference has been made to **IDA**. **= 5 out of 16 marks**
6	The fifth study concerns cross-cultural research (so avoiding the partial performance penalty). The study is described in slightly less detail than above but still reasonable. Two findings are mentioned (related to the trapezoid and Müller-Lyer illusion). The final part of this paragraph offers some explanation of the studies and so gains **AO2** credit.	
7	And finally a sixth cross-cultural study in reasonable detail (**AO1**) with a little explanation of why the results may have occurred (less experience of buildings and the use of depth cues). This counts towards **AO2**.	
	Total	12 out of 24 marks, likely to be a Grade C.

Chapter 3 Relationships (see answer on page 40)

Paragraph	Examiner comments	Mark
1	Fairly basic introduction which relies on a weak example that fails to really add much to the description of this theory (**AO1**).	**AO1** The descriptive content is generally accurate, although relies too much on examples rather than meaningful detail. Overall there is probably too much description (although a good deal of this is examples) to the detriment of the more important **AO2** content. The **AO1** is closer to 'basic' than it is to 'accurate and well-detailed'. **= 5 out of 8 marks**
2	Accurate, but brief and fairly limited in its scope (**AO1**).	
3	Generally accurate. The example does add some relevant detail (**AO1**).	
4	Basic understanding of the CLA, but description is fairly vague. Again there is over-reliance on an example, which is relevant, but doesn't really support the description given (**AO1**).	
5	This may well be true, but no evidence is offered to support the claim. Worth some basic credit, but the lack of elaboration through evidence restricts its impact (**AO2**).	**AO2** There really isn't enough **AO2** here, and the student has made the classic error of not planning their answer to fit the vastly different proportions of **AO1** and **AO2** marks. Although relevant and focused on the two theories, the evaluation constantly lacks elaboration, and therefore is not as effective as it otherwise might be. So, more **AO2** is needed and more elaboration to give it impact. As it is, this **AO2** content would be at the bottom of the basic and superficial band. **= 5 out of 16 marks**
6	Again, evidence would have helped here, but this is a fair point, and it is expressed in a suitably evaluative way (**AO2**).	
7	Moghaddam's claim is accurate, although it is expressed in a fairly vague manner (**AO2**). Brief reference to cultural bias (**IDA**).	
8	An accurate but rather basic outline of the theory (**AO1**).	
9	This is not the most effective way of providing detail for a description. It does get some credit, but an explanation of the main characteristics of each phase would be more useful (**AO1**).	
10	Deals with ethical issues (**IDA**) clearly placed in the context of relationship breakdown, something that is vital for **IDA** (**AO2**).	
	Total	10 out of 24 marks, likely to be a Grade D.

Chapter 4 Aggression (see answer on page 50)

Paragraph	Examiner comments	Mark
1	Reasonable introduction describing (**AO1**) genetic influences. Does not explain why twin similarity would show a strong genetic influence.	**AO1** The descriptive content contained in the first four paragraphs is generally accurate and reasonably detailed. There is evidence of breadth (four areas covered) more than depth. The lack of detail and a poor clarity in this description would probably push the mark toward the lower end of the 6–5 mark band for **AO1**. **= 5 out of 8 marks**
2	Accurate description (**AO1**) but limited, fails to mention that it is the contrast with adoptive children and their adoptive parents that demonstrates the importance of genetics.	
3	There is a little confusion here as MAOA is an enzyme, not a gene. However, the description is reasonably accurate (**AO1**).	
4	Mostly speculative and lacking in detail (**AO1**).	
5	Two appropriate studies described here, but both rather superficial **AO2**.	**AO2** There is a decent range of **AO2** points made although at times they can be a little superficial. Overall this would fit the description of the 12–9 band for **AO2** (i.e. the analysis and understanding is reasonable and the use of **IDA** points is reasonably effective at best). There is some evidence of elaboration, but this is not always the case. It is closer to the bottom of this band than the top. **= 10 out of 16 marks**
6	There is some basic relevance here, but real life anecdotal examples do not count as scientific evidence (**AO2**).	
7	There are two evaluations, but neither is sufficiently elaborated to have any sort of impact (**AO2**).	
8	This is effective evaluation (**AO2**). First the critical point is identified (there is a sampling problem), then this point is elaborated and explained.	
9	An appropriate **IDA** point (**AO2**) with some elaboration.	
10	An appropriate **IDA** point (ethical issues) is made here, although it lacks development and elaboration (**AO2**).	
11	This final paragraph is also an **IDA** point. As with the previous point, it lacks development and therefore is only reasonably effective (**AO2**).	
	Total	15 out of 24 marks, likely to be a Grade B.

Chapter 5 Eating behaviour (see answer on page 60)

Paragraph	Examiner comments	Mark
1	Quite superficial as an explanation of media influences on eating behaviour although does have two main points (**AO1**).	**Part (a) AO1** The descriptive content is generally accurate, but lacks detail and with some reliance on content that doesn't contribute to the explanation being outlined. = **2 out of 4 marks**
2	This is interesting, but adds very little to the media influences explanation (**AO1**).	
3	A fairly general paragraph about the EEA, which doesn't explain why this would impact on food preferences (**AO1**).	**Part (b) AO1 + AO2** Although the first of the three explanations wasn't sufficiently detailed, the other two were. Two focused and accurate explanations are enough for full marks. = **4 out of 4 marks** for **AO1** There really isn't enough **AO2** here. Although relevant and focused on the explanations, the evaluation lacks elaboration. This **AO2** content would be towards the bottom rather than the top of the 'basic and superficial' band. = **6 out of 16 marks** for **AO2**
4	A relevant point, although should have mentioned the adaptive differences rather than just lifestyle differences (**AO2**).	
5	Fairly superficial point, which fails to stress *why* these food were so important (**AO1**).	
6	Makes a similar point to previous paragraph, but slightly more convincing (**AO1**).	
7	A good point, appropriately elaborated (**AO2**).	
8	Another descriptive explanation, clearly too much description for the 4 marks available (**AO1**).	
9	This counts as **IDA**. The real-world application is embedded solidly within the context of taste aversion, which counts as contextualised elaboration, something that is vital for **IDA** (**AO2**).	
10	A continuation of paragraph 9.	
	Total	12 out of 24 marks, likely to be a Grade C.

Chapter 6 Gender (see answer on page 70)

Paragraph	Examiner comments	Mark
1	An accurate and reasonably detailed account (**AO1**) of Kohlberg's theory, going beyond a list of the stages. The ages have not been mentioned. There is a brief point of evaluation at the end that is not creditworthy in part (a).	**Part (a) AO1** Three approaches are covered with a reasonable balance between psychological and biological approaches. The answer has a good range and the organisation is coherent, however depth (detail) has been sacrificed for breadth in covering all three. = **6 out of 8 marks** (lack of detail)
2	A much briefer outline (**AO1**) of gender schema theory, relatively superficial but adding breadth to the answer.	
3	An accurate and reasonably detailed summary (**AO1**) of the biological approach covering genes, external genitalia and brain development (which could have been related to hormones).	
4	Appropriate research evidence with clear linking sentences at the beginning and end (**AO2**). The end sentence is crucial in gaining credit here because it ensures the point is effective. The paragraph is perhaps overly descriptive.	**Part (b) AO2** The evaluation is well focused and the line of argument is clear. The **IDA** points range from effective to superficial so, on average, are reasonable. Research evidence also varies between reasonable and weak but a lot more of it is 'reasonable'. This clearly places the answer is the second band (12–9 marks) and tending towards the top of that band (we are more tempted by the band above than 'basic, superficial'). = **11 out of 16 marks**
5	Again a clear lead-in sentence and final linking sentence (so what) making the point effective (**AO2**). Reasonable elaboration.	
6	Research evidence for the psychological approach, effective and with reasonable elaboration (**AO2**).	
7	This second psychological study is less effective because there is only some evidence of elaboration (**AO2**).	
8	An **IDA** point, looking at different approaches. Contextualised and effective.	
9	A brief **IDA** point, contextualised but superficial.	
10	An attempt to make research (**AO2**) on gender dysphoria relevant to this answer but not effective, weak focus.	
11	Conclusion satisfies the requirement in mark scheme to address the question of whether psychological or biological is best but rather basic.	
	Total	17 out of 24 marks, likely to be a Grade A.

Chapter 7 Intelligence and learning (see answer on page 80)

Paragraph	Examiner comments	Mark
1	Given that there are only 4 marks available for **AO1**, this material is somewhat of a luxury, with only some relevance to the question (**AO1**).	**Part (a) AO1 + AO2** The descriptive (**AO1**) content is accurate, coherent and reasonably thorough. There is a lot here, more than needed. **= 4 out of 4 marks** There are three good **AO2** points made (200 words) demonstrating sound analysis and understanding. The lack of **IDA** pulls the mark down to reasonable. **= 6 out of 8 marks**
2	Detailed description (**AO1**) of the results of twin studies in this area.	
3	A competent and detailed description (**AO1**) of adoption studies and what they show about the development of intelligence.	
4	A good critical point (**AO2**), well elaborated.	
5	Again a very good **AO2** point that is appropriately elaborated.	
6	This is an effective **AO2** point as it includes a 'This would suggest…' conclusion at the end of the point, a good way of elaborating the point.	
7	This is both accurate and detailed description (**AO1**).	**Part (b) AO1 + AO2** This starts well, but the points become less detailed. **= 3 out of 4 marks** There really isn't enough **AO2** in part (b) (only 115 words). The **AO2** content is basic and superficial with some evidence of **IDA**. However, we are more tempted by the band above rather than below. **= 4 out of 8 marks**
8	Although accurate, this point lacks detail, and there appears to be a realisation that too long has been spent on part (a) (**AO1**).	
9	A further **AO1** paragraph, with limited detail.	
10	An appropriate critical point (**AO2**), lacking elaboration.	
11	Another basic **AO2** point, lacking elaboration.	
12	As with the other **AO2** points in part (b), this lacks elaboration, but does qualify as an **IDA** point.	
	Total	17 out of 24 marks, likely to be a Grade A.

Chapter 8 Cognition and development (see answer on page 90)

Paragraph	Examiner comments	Mark
1	This paragraph is largely descriptive (**AO1**), with much detail of how the Sally-Anne task is performed and only minimal information about development.	**AO1** The descriptions are generally accurate and reasonably structured. However, the range is restricted and, perhaps most importantly, the developmental aspect of Theory of Mind has taken a back seat. **= 4 out of 8 marks** **AO2** The **AO2** material is just better than rudimentary. There is some understanding of potential critical issues and some evidence of elaboration. **IDA** is present. **= 5 out of 16 marks**
2	Baron-Cohen's work is again presented descriptively rather than as support for any particular point (**AO1**). Development is implied insofar as autistic children fail to develop Theory of Mind.	
3	A rather weakly developed **IDA** point. The point about social factors is a bit muddled though is explained more in the next paragraph.	
4	The **IDA** point is expanded looking at the role of experience. This can be taken as **AO2** though it could be more effectively presented as evaluation.	
5	Smarties tube test is described with a final comment on the age this appears, basic **AO1**.	
6	A brief **AO2** point about language.	
	Total	9 out of 24 marks, likely to be a Grade E.

Chapter 9 Schizophrenia (see answer on page 100)

Paragraph	Examiner comments	Mark
1	No credit for repeating the quotation or stating what you will be covering.	**AO1** The descriptions of three explanations are covered, each relatively basic though the genetic explanation was better than this. However, the lack of depth is compensated for by the breadth. There is not substantial evidence of both but the answer is coherent. **= 6 out of 8 marks** **AO2** The evaluation tends more towards 'basic' than 'reasonable' but we should also take into account that the answer is well focused and the line of argument is clear. There is appropriate use of terms. **= 10 out of 16 marks** NB no requirement for IDA on Unit 4 exam questions.
2	Basic description of genetic explanation (**AO1**), brief evaluation (**AO2**).	
3	Study by Joseph credited as expansion of genetic explanation (**AO1**), reasonably detailed. Followed by evaluation of this kind of research study (**AO2**), reasonable evaluation.	
4	Commentary (**AO2**) on relative strengths of different kinds of study.	
5	First half is basic evaluation (**AO2**) with some evidence of elaboration. Second half is a description of a study (**AO1**).	
6	Conclusion of the study, basic **AO2**.	
7	Basic explanation (**AO1**).	
8	Reasonable evaluation (**AO2**).	
9	Third explanation described, basic **AO1**.	
10	Evaluation (**AO2**), some evidence of elaboration but fails to link the point back to the explanation – basic.	
11	Basic **AO2**, similar to previous paragraph.	
12	Improved evaluation because makes the link in the final sentence, reasonable **AO2**.	
	Total	16 out of 24 marks, likely to be a Grade A.

Chapter 10 Depression (see answer on page 110)

Paragraph	Examiner comments	Mark
1	First biological explanation, basic outline (**AO1**), no mechanism mentioned by which genes exert an influence.	**Part (a) AO1** A range of material covered providing breadth but lacking depth – in some cases the detail is rudimentary. The structure is coherent. = **5 out of 8 marks**
2	Rudimentary account of neurotransmitters (**AO1**).	
3	First psychological explanation (**AO1**), reasonably detailed account of Beck's theory, tending towards basic.	
4	Basic/rudimentary explanation (**AO1**), brief.	
5	Sound evaluation (**AO2**) with coherent elaboration, covering two research studies.	**Part (b) AO2** The answer is well-focused and the line of argument is clear. Fluent communication but limited use of terms. Overall the analysis and understanding is reasonable, a mixture of 'sound' and 'basic' with more of the former. = **11 out of 16 marks**
6	A useful **AO2** point, evaluating the research discussed in paragraph 5 with reasonable elaboration.	
7	A further **AO2** point considering issues with twin studies, some evidence of elaboration.	
8	Rudimentary **AO2**.	
9	Two points made, both basic – some evidence of elaboration (**AO2**).	
10	Slightly better evaluative (**AO2**) point, edging on reasonable.	
11	A sound piece of analysis (**AO2**) but should really have mentioned diathesis-stress.	
12	A rudimentary point, adds little to the essay.	
	Total	16 out of 24 marks, possibly a Grade A.

Chapter 11 Phobic disorders (see answer on page 120)

Paragraph	Examiner comments	Mark
1	This outline is reasonably thorough, a good spread of information about phobic disorders is present and the account has been coherently structured (**AO1**).	**Part (a) AO1** Clearly **4 out of 4 marks**.
2	An accurate explanation (**AO1**) of counterconditioning and the basis of Wolpe's theory.	**Part (b) AO1** Sufficient detail. = **4 out of 4 marks**
3	The background information about cats is largely irrelevant as the concept of counterconditioning has already been well explained.	
4	Reasonably thorough outline (**AO1**) of the concept of a hierarchy with some reference to different types of systematic desensitisation.	
5	Somewhat superficial reference to research evidence (**AO2**) with no specific information provided. A clear point about *in vivo* methods.	**Part (c) AO2** The comments on this answer place it firmly in the 8–5 mark band – largely superficial. However, in addition, the answer is generally focused and the line of argument reasonable, giving some draw to the band above. On the other hand the answer is on the short side and not all of it is creditworthy. = **6 out of 8 marks**
6	Further superficial research evidence (**AO2**) – source not identified but detailed information about ancient fears.	
7	A more reasonable **AO2** point – identified and then reference to Freud providing some evidence of elaboration.	
8	Very rudimentary point (**AO2**).	
9	This paragraph is descriptive and therefore not creditworthy.	
10	Superficial but relevant criticisms (**AO2**) of REBT.	
11	There is no need for **IDA** in psychopathology answers and this muddled point gains no credit.	
	Total	14 out of 24 marks, likely to be a Grade B.

Chapter 12 Obsessive compulsive disorder (see answer on page 130)

Paragraph	Examiner comments	Mark
1	Accurate and reasonably thorough account of one characteristic of OCD (**AO1**).	**Part (a) AO1** Perhaps a little on the short side for 4 marks but an outline of clinical characteristics often requires less content. Sufficient detail. = **4 out of 4 marks**
2	Also reasonably thorough, perhaps could have included some further information, e.g. about childhood OCD (**AO1**).	
3	The description (**AO1**) is reasonably thorough and accurate, focusing on only one aspect of the therapy – exposure.	**Part (b) AO1** Overall the account is limited because there is no explanation of the response prevention component though it is implied. = **3 out of 4 marks**
4	Brief additional material (**AO1**) on the mode of action contributing rather little.	

Paragraph	Examiner comments	Mark
5	Rudimentary point of evaluation (**AO2**), made slightly more effective with reference to duration of study.	**Part (c) AO2** The content is mainly relevant, though some description is included which is not relevant – so best described as 'sometimes focused'. Some rudimentary points but also one section that was reasonable, so on balance in the 8–5 mark band but tempted by the band below. **= 5 out of 16 marks**
6	Rudimentary evaluation (**AO2**). Simple comment about lack of side effects but little else that is creditworthy.	
7	Reasonable critical point with some evidence of elaboration (**AO2**).	
8	Rudimentary comment (**AO2**) about cognitive therapy.	
9	Uncreditworthy description of cognitive therapy.	
10	First sentence is just a summary but last two points offer some analysis (**AO2**) and elaboration.	
	Total	12 out of 24 marks, likely to be a Grade C.

Chapter 13 Media psychology (see answer on page 140)

Paragraph	Examiner comments	Mark
1	Reasonable elaboration, focused (**AO2**). The actual difficulty with correlational research is not spelled out.	**Part (a) (i) AO2** This is better than a list of difficulties, so must get more than 2 marks. Since the answer is generally focused there is a draw towards the 'reasonable' band but we are not tempted further by the band above. **= 3 out of 5 marks**
2	Reasonable elaboration (**AO2**).	
3	Weak, neither point is explained (**AO2**). The second one is too general and may not apply any way. Not effective.	
4	Basic explanation (**AO2**).	
5	Description of several effects, reasonably thorough **AO1**.	**Part (a) (ii) AO1 + AO2** For the **AO1** we are not tempted by 'weak and muddled'. There is some evidence of reasonably thorough but not enough. **= 3 out of 4 marks** Some of the evaluation (**AO2**) is basic but the amount lifts it to the reasonable band. It is generally focused and fluent. **= 3 out of 5 marks**
6	Very brief **AO2** comment, followed by a slightly more limited description (**AO1**) of a second study.	
7	Basic **AO2**, with some evidence of elaboration.	
8	First sentence is evaluation (**AO2**) because supportive research. Bi-directional model could be seen as evaluation (**AO2**) considering the way the findings can be interpreted. The point is reasonably elaborated.	
9	Basic list of possible critical points (**AO2**) with some elaboration.	
10	Definition is uncreditworthy. Description of several factors (**AO1**).	**Part (b) AO1** The description is limited but we are not tempted to the band below. **= 3 out of 4 marks**
11	Two further factors are identified (**AO1**).	
12	Weak **AO1** but relevant and based on research.	
13	One way is identified and this has been linked to research, more effectiveness than persuasiveness but creditworthy **AO2** rather than just description.	**Part (c) AO2** The requirement for application and research evidence is fulfilled. Two ways could be sufficient for full marks but would require more detail related to persuasiveness. A basic answer with some evidence of elaboration and reasonable effective application. **= 3 out of 6 marks**
14	A second way is identified and again linked briefly to research (**AO2**).	
	Total	15 out of 24 marks, likely to be a Grade B.

Chapter 14 The psychology of addictive behaviour (see answer on page 150)

Paragraph	Examiner comments	Mark
1	Appropriate outline of one difficulty, with some elaboration (**AO2**).	**Part (a) (i) AO2** Overall the answer is rudimentary. **= 1 out of 5 marks**
2	Not creditworthy because not an issue related to data gathering.	
3	Brief explanation (**AO1**), study used as part of description.	**Part (a) (ii) AO1** The genetic explanation (**AO1**) is weak but dopamine explanation reasonable. **= 3 out of 4 marks**
4	Link to dopamine hypothesis, reasonable attempt to explain this (**AO1**).	
5	The definition is not creditworthy, and the same applies to much of the paragraph which is focused on initiation and maintenance. Some of the material is peripherally relevant to relapse (**AO1**).	**Part (b) AO1 + AO2** Most of this answer is descriptive (**AO1**) but much of the descriptive material is not creditworthy so, overall a limited answer closer to the band below. **= 2 out of 4 marks** Rudimentary **AO2**. **= 1 out of 6 marks**
6	**IDA** points are credited as **AO2**, the attempt to contextualise this is peripherally relevant to relapse.	
7	Limited description (**AO1**) of how the biological approach might explain relapse.	
8	Weak attempt to explain relapse in terms of the cognitive approach (**AO1**), with a tiny bit of **AO2** at the end.	

9	A reasonable suggestion (**AO2**) but little link to psychological evidence.	**Part (c) AO2** The answer avoids partial performance but lacks psychological research, so 'basic' and drawn towards band below. **= 2 out of 6 marks**
10	A second reasonable suggestion (**AO2**) with some psychological support.	
11	Commonsense advice with little psychology.	
	Total	9 out of 24 marks, likely to be a Grade E.

Chapter 15 Anomalistic psychology (see answer on page 160)

Paragraph	Examiner comments	Mark
1	The basic point is repeated several times. It is creditworthy (**AO1**) but only a small point.	**Part (a) AO1** The information is generally accurate but not well explained. Calling it 'limited' is generous! **= 2 out of 4 marks**
2	Another weak point (**AO1**) with a little explanation.	
3	Weak point (**AO1**), no elaboration.	
4	Irrelevant introduction.	**Part (b) AO2** There is enough information to lift this to 'basic' rather than being 'rudimentary' but a lot of information has been omitted. **= 3 out of 6 marks**
5	Basic explanation (**AO2**) of what the sender and receiver are doing. Key information omitted, such as how the sender's eyes are covered.	
6	The issue of chance is mentioned but the method of establishing this is not explained (**AO2**).	
7	An appropriate explanation (**AO1**), understanding is a bit limited.	**Part (c) AO1** A limited answer, tempted by band below. **= 2 out of 4 marks**
8	A second explanation (**AO1**), weak outline.	
9	No credit for explaining the key term.	**Part (d) AO2** Overall the length of the answer indicates that the content is 'basic' (should be 300 words for 10 marks, whereas it is only 206 words). The answer is generally focused and there is some evidence of elaboration and application of knowledge. **= 5 out of 10 marks**
10	A reasonable attempt to apply knowledge (**AO2**) to mediumship.	
11	Relevant research evidence (**AO2**) used to argue both sides of the issue though details are a little sketchy.	
12	Second explanation used (**AO2**) and explained, with rudimentary reference to research.	
	Total	12 out of 24 marks, likely to be a Grade C.

Chapter 16 Psychological research and scientific method (see answer on page 168)

Paragraph	Examiner comments	Mark
(a)	Accurate but insufficient information even for 1 mark, should add 'before it is published' or 'to check validity'.	**0 out of 2 marks**
(b)	Answer shows *basic* understanding, with some elaboration. Some actual examples would help the clarity of the answer.	**2 out of 5 marks**
(c)	A definition using the same words is uncreditworthy. The same is true for just referring to qualitative data.	**0 out of 1 mark**
(d)	The answer does engage with the stimulus material by mentioning food types, and also provides some information about how the analysis would be conducted but further detail is missing (e.g. making before and after comparison).	**2 out of 3 marks**
(e)	Both ethical and methodological issues are covered, though the ethical issues are rather brief. There is no mention of, for example, protection from harm nor debriefing.	**3 out of 5 marks**
(f)	Correct answer.	**1 out of 1 mark**
(g)	Answer is incorrect. Even though some of the justifcation is correct (N = 20) this gains no credit.	**0 out of 3 marks**
(h)	Unfortunately this is not a scattergram as the two items (score from Observer A and score from Observer B) have not been plotted against each other.	**0 out of 4 marks**
(i)	A correct answer with some elaboration.	**2 out of 4 marks**
(j)	Correct answer and some justification.	**2 out of 3 marks**
(k)	One reasonable improvement with some elaboration. The second improvement ('be more careful') is not creditworthy.	**2 out of 4 marks**
	Total	14 out of 35 marks, likely to be a Grade E.